Female Spectacle

SUSAN A. GLENN

Female Spectacle

THE THEATRICAL ROOTS OF MODERN FEMINISM

Harvard University Press

Cambridge, Massachusetts, and London, England · 2000

Library of Congress Cataloging-in-Publication Data

Glenn, Susan A. (Susan Anita)
  Female spectacle : the theatrical roots of modern feminism / Susan A. Glenn.
    p. cm.
  Includes bibliographical references and index.
  ISBN 0-674-00333-0
    1. Women in the theater—United States—History—20th century. 2. Women in the
  theater—United States—History—19th century. 3. Feminism and theater—United States.
  4. Actresses—United States—Biography. I. Title.

PN1590.W64 G59 2000
792′.082′00973—dc21   00-040683

To Rachel and Jim

Contents

Illustrations

20. Ziegfeld *Follies* ensemble (WWI era). Photo by White Studio, courtesy of the Harry Ransom Center.
21. Chorus, Ziegfeld *Follies of 1916*. Courtesy of the Harry Ransom Center.
22. Ned Wayburn and the *Follies* chorus (c. 1917), courtesy of the Harry Ransom Center.
23. Fanny Brice in the *Follies of 1910*. Courtesy of the Harry Ransom Center.
24. Olive Thomas in the *Midnight Frolic of 1916*. Photo by Campbell Studio, courtesy of the Harry Ransom Center.
25. "Rotisserie" scene from *Artists and Models* (1925). Courtesy of Culver Pictures.
26. Ina Claire in *The Gold Diggers* (1919). Photo by White Studio, courtesy of the Billy Rose Theatre Collection, New York Public Library, Astor, Lenox and Tilden Foundations.
27. Mae West in *Diamond Lil* (1928). Photo by White Studio, courtesy of the Billy Rose Theatre Collection, New York Public Libary, Astor, Lenox and Tilden Foundations.

Female Spectacle

Introduction

I am part of a cohort of women who grew up haunted by the ghost of actress Sarah Bernhardt. Among the memories of my adolescence in the early 1960s, few are more vivid than the familial response to my emotional outbursts. At those moments when both my mother and grandmother happened to be present, they would eye each other knowingly and utter in unison: "Oh, Sarah Bernhardt! There she goes again." Today, when I ask women of a certain age what the name means to them, they often tell similar stories. Typically, they recall their youthful emotional excesses would lead at least one parent to remark "Don't be such a Sarah Bernhardt!" or "Don't pull a Sarah Bernhardt." As one woman put it, "it never occurred to us that Sarah Bernhardt had long been dead. We were under the impression that she was very [much] alive, inhabiting our homes, always behind the scenes of any emotional outburst." In the folklore of her family, Bernhardt was "somewhat of a dybbuk, inhabiting our souls, controlling our behavior . . . all we had to do was rid ourselves of her."[1]

Sarah Bernhardt came to America to perform her plays for the first time in 1880 and completed her last American tour in 1918. She was seventy-eight years old when she died in Paris in 1923. These dates are significant, for it is unlikely that many of those who admonished their daughters not to be Sarah Bernhardt had themselves ever actually seen the actress perform or read the voluminous newspaper accounts of her American tours. And yet, for half a century after her death, the name and the concept "Sarah Bernhardt" remained an important form of cultural shorthand for volatile displays of female emotion.

Today these collective memories have faded. Once a household word in the United States, the actress no longer occupies a vaunted place in our cultural imagination.[2] It may be that at the turn of the twenty-first century, when women take up a relatively large amount of social and cultural space, it is no longer appropriate to ask them to make their personal dramas less conspicuous. Then too the older generation, those who remembered Bernhardt and kept her image alive, no longer exercises the same degree of influence. "Oh, yes, Sandra Bernhard," younger women will say when I ask them what Sarah Bernhardt's name means to them. They think I am referring to today's stand-up comic and singer. Yet this is not just a case of cultural confusion. Beyond the similarity of their names and their ethnic identities (both Jewish), Sarah Bernhardt and Sandra Bernhard are associated with the idea of women provoking controversy by making spectacles of themselves. The sharp-tongued comic, like the outspoken and flamboyant tragedienne before her, has built a public persona by deliberately acting out of the bounds of traditional female behavior, in part by calling attention to her own self-importance. Watching Sandra Bernhard's 1990 film, *Without You I'm Nothing* (based on her popular off-Broadway play by the same title), we see that she has deliberately sought to identify herself with the legendary French actress—as when the announcer in a Los Angeles nightclub where Bernhard is performing makes the deliberate "mistake" of twice introducing her as "Sarah Bernhardt."[3] More recently Bernhard's 1998 show, suggestively titled "I'm Still Here . . . Damn It!" simultaneously pushes the audience to confirm her own staying power as a celebrity (à la Sarah Bernhardt) while viciously mocking the vanities of other stars.[4]

This is not a biography of Sarah or Sandra, but the issues raised by the unorthodox public careers of both women are central to the intellectual project of this book. My interest is in how and why performers like Sarah Bernhardt and some of Sandra Bernhard's cultural predecessors in the American popular theater exercised such a powerful sway upon late nineteenth- and early twentieth-century public consciousness, and how their work on the stage contributed to changes in women's social roles and cultural representations.

In the years between the late 1880s and the end of the 1920s, theater was America's foremost entertainment industry. Popular entertainments like vaudeville, musical revue, and musical comedy as well as so-called legitimate drama were central institutions of commercial leisure, critical arenas for cultural exploration, and powerful agents of cultural transformation. *Female Spectacle* is a study of some of the ways that popular theater helped to define the modern sexual and social terrain. It argues that in a crucial epoch of historical upheaval, female performers became agents and metaphors of changing gender relations, and it shows the importance of the popular theater as a venue for acting out and staging the cultural, social, and political assertions as well as the anxieties associated with the era of the New Woman.

The phenomenon of spectacle was at the heart of that era's public culture. It is also the central concern of this book. On stage and off, turn-of-the-century women were increasingly drawing attention to themselves, asserting their rights to education, to political participation, to employment, to sexual expressiveness, to a voice as cultural critics. The New Women of the American popular theater—Gertrude Hoffmann, Fanny Brice, Nora Bayes, Marie Dressler, Cissie Loftus, Trixie Friganza, Aida Walker, Eva Tanguay, Elsie Janis, and scores of others, including Sarah Bernhardt (the spectacle of spectacles)—occupied a rather unique place in their own cultural moment. As performers, they exercised a degree of freedom that was rarely available to women in public. Nevertheless they were also influenced and constrained by the conventions of the theater as an institution, and by the culture in which they were situated. This book examines popular theater's expressive possibilities for women performers and its effect on audiences. It points to the pivotal importance of theater for women's changing public images and self-definitions. And it illuminates the ways in which widely divergent forms of female spectacle resonated with and helped shape larger off-stage social and cultural developments.

Assertive self-spectacle *by* theater women was of crucial importance for changing concepts of womanhood at the turn of the century. Equally significant was the way theatrical producers made a spectacle *of* women, positioning them as passive objects for audience consumption. The result was a dynamic tension between women's desire (on as well as off the stage) to use theatrical spectacle as a vehicle for achieving greater voice in culture and politics, and theater's countervailing urge to turn female spectacle into a symbolic expression of male mastery. It is in the interplay between active and passive female spectacle that we see most vividly how the theater became an important progenitor of two very different, but nevertheless equally modern, concepts of femininity.

The various kinds of female spectacle played out on the popular stage cannot be understood outside of several overlapping historical contexts:

the history of American theatrical practices, the history of gender relations, and the wider social, cultural, and intellectual ferment of which they were a part.

Although historians have acknowledged the significance of popular entertainments for our understanding of the re-negotiation of gender roles and relations in the twentieth century, they have devoted relatively little attention to the specific contributions of theater to the emergence of a modern feminist perspective.[5] Looking at women's history through the lens of the popular theater forces us to complicate our way of thinking about the past. It is customary to talk about the period from the 1880s to 1910 as the time that preceded the birth of modern feminism in the United States. Women were active in various kinds of civic and political reform movements in the 1880s and 1890s, the argument goes, but it was not until about 1910, with the emergence of a reinvigorated suffrage movement and the entrance of a younger, more diverse, and ultimately more radical generation of women activists, that we witness what historian Nancy Cott has called the "grounding of modern feminism."[6]

When we turn to the theater, however, it becomes clear that the grounding of modern feminism began as early as the 1880s and 1890s. By 1910, when off-stage feminists were first beginning to see themselves as a social and ideological formation, the feminist moment within the theater was already well underway. What made the period from 1880 to 1910 a feminist moment in the popular theater was neither a widely shared set of ideological principles, nor a specific political agenda or movement among female performers. For that matter, "feminist" was not a term that most of these performers would have used to describe themselves. Rather, the feminism of women on stage was a form of cultural and professional practice. Theater women articulated—through their performances and their professional careers—some of the themes that later became central to the projects of off-stage women who called themselves feminists.

The feminism that emerged off stage in the 1910s was less a coherent movement than a set of principles and goals. These included the belief in the social, political, and economic equality of the sexes, and the idea that although men and women were biologically different, gender roles and identities were not "predestined by God or nature" but shaped by socialization. Unlike their predecessors of the suffrage and reform movements in the nineteenth century, these more modern feminists did not believe that all women shared a common set of concerns. They acknowledged that women differed from each other across class lines and other points of social location, but they believed that it was necessary for women to organize together in order to attain equality with men.[7] After 1910 two other themes became increasingly important to the emerging feminist agenda. One was the demand that women be given greater freedom to express their sexuality. Feminists called for more honest acknowledgment that women had sex drives and insisted on an end to the double standard of morality.[8] The other was a growing emphasis on the theme of "individualism—in the sense of self-development," in Nancy Cott's words. Feminists labeled this the right to "realize personality," by which they meant the right of a woman to claim her independent identity, a selfhood independent not only of what men would impose upon her but also separate from other women. Feminist anthropologist Elsie Clews Parsons put the matter somewhat differently when she wrote in 1916 that "the *new woman* means the woman not yet classified, perhaps not classifiable, the woman *new* not only to men, but to herself." Feminist demands for a greater sexual freedom for women and for their right to an independent "personality," were, as Cott suggests, crucial "forms of cultural blasphemy." Because they amounted to a rejection of more traditional belief in femininity as sexual purity and self-sacrifice, these were the values that made modern feminists "modern."[9]

But modern feminism did not come about all at once in the 1910s. Other historians have shown that in the late 1860s and 1870s and early 1880s, a small but highly visible band of women's rights radicals, among them Elizabeth Cady Stanton, Susan B. Anthony, Anna Dickinson, and Victoria Woodhull demanded economic and political equality for women and their freedom to function as private individuals in the public sphere. Some, like Woodhull, were "sex" radicals who condemned conventional marriage for stifling female passion. Others saw suffrage as the key to female emancipation. The most radical argued that "woman was made for herself" and deserved a full and complete life.[10] For all of their boldness, however, these nineteenth-century rebels did not have a wide popular appeal.

In the 1880s and 1890s, however, another highly visible group of unorthodox females—well-paid and independent women who made their living in the theater—were beginning to carry some of those radical notions into the cultural mainstream. They helped make unorthodox female behavior more attractive and enjoyable than the nineteenth-century political radicals had been able to do and, as a consequence, helped give new views of women wider acceptance. Aided by commercially minded producers who understood that male and female audiences would pay to watch bold New Women, these self-conscious performers demonstrated and encouraged new ways of acting female.

Not all of the tenets of early twentieth-century feminist ideology were put into practice by the New Women in the popular theater either before or after 1910. Yet on the critical demand for women's right to sexual expressiveness and personality or self-development, female performers clearly constituted a kind of proto-feminist vanguard. The creativity with which female performers put these cultural blasphemies into practice in the years between 1880 and 1910 laid some of the groundwork for feminism even before the term was coined. Precisely for that reason, both the theater and the proto-feminist figure of the actress became important symbols and resources for female activists who engaged in various forms of political agitation in the first decade of the twentieth century.

Rather than call women who performed in the popular theater feminists or even proto-feminists, however, I refer to them as New Women. The New Woman was a social reality and a cultural concept. Coined at the end of the nineteenth century, the term was used from the 1890s to the end of the 1920s to describe women who experimented with new forms of public behavior and new gender roles. The usage was inconsistent and was applied to and appropriated by several generations of assertive women who defied traditional expectations. At the turn of the century, ambitious, educated middle-class women, many of whom eschewed marriage and dedicated their lives to the cause of social reform and political agitation (including women's rights), were labeled New Women. By the time of World War I, the term described a younger generation of independent women who demanded not only economic, political, and intellectual opportunity, but also sexual fulfillment. It included, but was not limited to, those who thought of themselves as feminists.

The New Women of the popular theater overlapped chronologically with several generations of so-called emancipated women. But they also differed from them in crucial ways. First, as women of the stage they occupied a unique cultural and social zone where females were not only permitted but expected to live unconventional lives and play unorthodox parts. Indeed, in the period from the late 1870s up to the time of World War I, the stage was practically the only place where a woman could be rewarded in spite of, or even because of, her transgressiveness. Second, and even more significant, the stage encouraged women to cultivate their individuality and their uniqueness, the very qualities that came to be seen as the building blocks of human personality. Stage women of all kinds demonstrated the distinctive force of their personalities. But nowhere was this more apparent than in vaudeville. There, Caroline Caffin observed in her 1914 study, the approach of these performers was "personal and unashamed." Vaudeville women greeted the spectators "straight in the face" and said in effect, "Look at ME! I am going to astonish you!"[11]

By opening a space for female performers to become *both* spectacles *and* personalities, the popular theater promoted the development of the first self-consciously "modern" expression of new womanhood. Henry James marks its appearance in his 1890 novel, *The Tragic Muse:* the central character is an actress whose "greatest idea must always be to show herself." Miriam was a "strange girl," who "exhibit[ed]" her "body" and "soul" before crowds of onlookers for money. But her strange self-spectacle, which obliterated the ideological dividing line between the private sphere (associated with femininity) and the wider public sphere (associated with masculinity), had more than commercial value. Rather, James writes, she was "a real producer . . . whose production is her own person."[12] James was not the only novelist who turned the figure of the actress or female performer into a symbol of women's longing for personhood. In different but related ways Theodore Dreiser's *Sister Carrie* (1900), Mary Austin's *A Woman of Genius* (1912), and Willa Cather's *The Song of the Lark* (1915) also used the performing woman to explore this theme of female self-production through stage spectacle.[13]

These characters, the stuff of literary fantasy, had their real-world counterparts. While theater's capacity to create new images and representations of women made it an important incubator for modern ideas about femininity, equally important was the crucial role that female performers played in the process of representing themselves. The extraordinary self-consciousness with which they positioned themselves in relationship to modern social, intellectual, and aesthetic practices and debates made them more than symbols of cultural change. They were also active participants in and critical observers of their own cultural moment.

Their participation was complicated by the diverse positions of women within the theatrical hierarchy, by the racial tensions of the time, and by the gender politics of the popular stage. The fierce political agitation around women's rights and suffrage that occurred in the pre- and post-Civil War eras, the hardening of the color line at the turn of the century, and the growing immigrant presence shaped the broader social context in which the popular theater developed, the issues addressed on stage, and the ways they were handled.

Theater mattered to women. But the role it played in the emergence of modern feminist consciousness was hardly without ambiguities or contradictions. Although the stage did not so much resolve as register debates about changing gender roles and other modern anxieties, there were nevertheless clearly identifiable moments when women's voices were either amplified or suppressed by stage spectacle. And the balance between those moments would shift with the times. In the late nineteenth and early twentieth century, popular theater gave women important new sources of cultural authority and visibility. Ironically, however, theater reworked older stereotypes of the so-called emancipated female and spawned its own particular set of New Woman typologies. Thus the stage contributed to changing ideas about female identity in paradoxical ways, criticizing even while promoting the notion of female emancipation. For just as the institution of the theater welcomed and profited from the unorthodox behavior of women on stage, it was frequently hostile to women's growing assertiveness off stage. This hostility was the source of new visual and rhetorical representations that challenged the very idea of an independent female personality. By the time of World War I, and increasingly in the 1920s, competition between the spectacle of female self-assertion and theatrical spectacles that worked to obliterate the notion of female autonomy and personality turned the stage into a battleground of ideas and images.

The Bernhardt Effect

SELF-ADVERTISING AND THE AGE
OF SPECTACLE

1
"In Paris and in all fashionable circles," wrote a French journalist in *Le Figaro* in August of 1878, "there is talk only of the actions and gestures of Mademoiselle Sarah Bernhardt. Even the question of Bosnia has receded into the background. The chief editors of the Paris papers forget everything, in order to concentrate on Mademoiselle Sarah Bernhardt."[1] He was not alone in observing the Bernhardt effect. The following year, Henry James reported on "the extraordinary vogue of Mademoiselle Sarah Bernhardt." Covering the London performances of the Comédie Française for the American journal *The Nation,* James confessed that "it would require some ingenuity to give an idea of the intensity, the ecstasy, the insanity as some people would say, of curiosity and enthusiasm provoked by Mlle. Bernhardt."[2] Then he went on to diagnose the causes of the insanity. Although James believed that as an actress Bernhardt possessed "remarkable gifts," he was certain that the ecstasy over Bernhardt existed quite apart from "the proper lines" of the theater. As James saw it, her vogue reflected "the success of a celebrity, pure and simple." Not only did Bernhardt crave celebrity with "an intensity that has rarely been equaled," but she employed all means to achieve this end. This "fantastically impertinent victrix," as he labeled her, "has in a supreme degree what the French call the génie de la réclame—the advertising genius; she may, indeed, be called the muse of the newspaper." As "a child of her age—of her moment," she "has known how to profit by the idiosyncrasies of the time." If "the trade of celebrity" had not been invented before her visit to London, James surmised, "it is certain she would have discovered it."[3] With biting irony he predicted that the French actress, who performed entirely in her native tongue, would triumph in the United States: "She is

too American not to succeed in America. The people who have brought to the highest development the arts and graces of publicity will recognize a kindred spirit in a figure so admirably adapted for conspicuity."[4]

James predicted correctly. The American press did find Bernhardt irresistible. Four months later, at the end of October 1880, the New York City press reported that even during the last week of a heated presidential campaign, Bernhardt's upcoming American tour was beginning to cause "a sensation."[5] "No matter how crowded the daily papers were with political appeals, predictions, reports, speeches, letters, telegrams, facsimiles, advertisements, and warnings," a journalist observed, "room was always made for paragraphs about Bernhardt." Even if the celebrated French actress turned out to be "a humbug," she would "certainly be the greatest humbug in the world."[6] By the time Bernhardt made her New York City debut in early November of 1880, the extraordinary publicity mania that had preceded her visit had itself become ripe enough for satire. One Manhattan variety theater featured a humorous parody called: "The Arrival of Bernhardt," while another offered a comedic send-up of the great "Sarah Heart-Burn."[7]

Whether Bernhardt's success in the United States had more to do with her celebrity than with her ability as dramatic artist would become a matter of fierce debate on both sides of the Atlantic. One thing was clear, however: Americans did come to have their own particular set of investments in the image and idea of Sarah Bernhardt. Bernhardt cast a long shadow upon the American scene. All told she made nine different tours of the United States between 1880 and 1918, giving an estimated 1,500 performances and playing 50 different dramatic roles.[8] Bernhardt made her first American tour in 1880–81, her second in 1887, and seven additional American tours in 1891–92, 1896, 1900–01, 1905–06, 1910–11, 1912–13, and 1916–1918.[9] But her effect echoed well beyond the theater.

Bernhardt exercised a formative impact on the cultural imagination of turn-of-the-century Americans. For those who came of age before 1900, she was not just a revered French actress. More than any other figure of the late nineteenth-century stage, Bernhardt symbolized the radical new possibilities that theater presented for elaborating new forms of female identity.

To understand the nature and significance of the effect she had in America, we need to appreciate Sarah's power to energize and exploit the cultural tensions of her age. As a performer and as a woman

Bernhardt was a transitional figure. A highly self-conscious and influential cultural provocateur, she bridged the boundary between traditional bourgeois or Victorian sensibilities and modern attitudes and perspectives. Indeed, the fascination she held for modernists like James and Freud can be attributed to her ability to integrate the symbols, practices, and images that many regarded as incompatible.[10]

A capacious figure, Bernhardt was both a symbol and practitioner of the high art of serious drama, and a performer who aggressively exploited the techniques and institutions of mass culture. She was among the last of the great nineteenth-century romantic tragediennes, but her approach to acting also had much in common with the performance modes of the early twentieth-century theater. Daughter of France, she was also Sarah "Barnum"—cultural descendant of the founding father of modern American popular culture. She represented the transgressiveness of the sexual libertine and the audaciousness of the outspoken social critic. Yet she evinced the "civilized" femininity expected of respectable or "womanly" women. Known for her uncanny modern youthfulness, she made a career of playing tearful dying women. Praised for her femininity, she brazenly usurped dramatic roles intended for men. Feminine and masculine, sinful and civilized, high and low, exotically foreign and symbolically American, a modern New Woman who was capable of acting like a traditional "true" woman, Bernhardt synthesized the cultural dichotomies of her age.[11] Her power as a cultural provocateur stemmed from her capacity to defy all efforts to categorize her. Chicago critic Amy Leslie spoke for many of her contemporaries when she called Bernhardt "a perplexing dramatic outlaw, amenable to no government but the irresistible whirlwind of her own intensity."[12]

As a figure of transition between traditional and modern values, Bernhardt thus constitutes a perfect starting point for understanding how the theater helped Americans explore and redefine femininity in the years between 1880 and 1910. At a time when actresses and female performers exhibited the unorthodox and increasingly fashionable qualities that would come to be associated with women's revolt against tradition, Bernhardt proved to be a highly elastic symbol of feminine irreverence. Because of that, she became a touchstone for a number of ambitious American women in as well as outside the theater: from female comics in vaudeville to activists in the woman suffrage movement.

Bernhardt's provocative methods of self-display set the standard to which others, especially other female performers, would aspire and against which they would be measured. Although she was not the only actress or performer of her time to provoke new conversations about the role and image of women, "the most famous actress in the world" did it with greater fanfare and certainly with more deliberateness than most of her contemporaries.

Bernhardt was a progenitor of two related cultural shifts: the birth of female self-promotion, and the birth of a modern culture of spectacle. In the late nineteenth century, when womanliness was still defined as selfless devotion to others, whether husband and children or a society in need of uplift and reform, Bernhardt eschewed female traditions of self-renunciation and pioneered the radical new practice of female self-advertisement. The self-dramatizing nature of her stage work and the self-magnifying project of her off-stage performances together consti-tuted the foundation for the coming of a new kind of female subjectivity.

The Culture of Spectacle

The enabling condition for Bernhardt's radical rewriting of the female social script was the felicitous alliance of her own egotism and the rebel-lious bohemianism of her artistic milieu together with the emergence of a modern urban transatlantic culture of spectacle that she helped usher in. When Henry James called Bernhardt "a child of her age," he meant the age of late nineteenth-century metropolitan mass culture, a culture devoted to the individual pleasures and commercial profits derived from seeing and being seen. Bernhardt's tours coincided with and contributed to what James had labeled a peculiarly American fondness for "conspic-uity." New York City was renowned for its eagerness for spectacle, as one reporter put it in 1904, but it was an eagerness long shared by the residents of London, Paris, and other metropolitan centers.[13] The insti-tutional basis for this transatlantic culture of spectacle came from the-aters, metropolitan newspapers, print and billboard advertising, World Fairs and exhibitions, amusement parks, plush restaurants, huge new department stores, traveling circuses and musical shows, and eventually from dance halls, cabarets, nickelodeons and movie houses—all of which catered to the public's desire for stimulation, pleasure, and the vi-carious experience of moral danger.

In part, as historian John Kasson has written, this public commercial culture of amusement and spectacle represented the earliest stages of a growing rebellion against "genteel standards of taste and conduct." But it was a rebellion at least in part sanctioned by a larger liberalizing tendency in which leisure activities, including theater, were recognized as an essential aspect of modern existence.[14]

Women played a central part in this cultural transformation, and nowhere was their contribution as producers and consumers of urban spectacle as important as in the theater. Between the time of Bernhardt's first American tour in 1880 and the start of her sixth tour in 1905, the institution of the theater had grown by leaps and bounds. In the United States the number of stage performers of all kinds jumped from just over 2,000 in 1870 to nearly 10,000 by 1890.[15] From large metropolitan centers to small towns across America, theater-going was an important form of recreation among all classes of society. Local theaters and touring companies (the later mainly headquartered in New York) proliferated, providing a vast array of entertainments including so-called legitimate (spoken) drama, musical comedy, opera, and the fast-paced type of variety theater known as vaudeville.[16]

A new generation of female performers fed public taste for sensation as they acted out and stimulated modern desires and fantasies. By 1900 the census showed that "actresses and professional show-women" (among them chorus girls, dancers, and circus performers) comprised 43 percent of the theatrical profession.[17] Year by year the numbers of female performers grew. Between 1870 and 1880 women working in the acting profession rose from 780 to 4,652. By 1910 the numbers of theater women more than tripled to reach 15,436. By 1920 the figure stood at 19,905.[18]

Equally (if not more) important, women achieved the status of theatrical stars. As such they were not only expected to be the center of public attention, but they were exceedingly well paid. We can get some idea of what these salaries meant when we consider that the average female wage earner in American industry in the 1910s made between $5 and $15 dollars a week, depending upon her occupation. In the theater, on the other hand, star salaries allowed women to earn as much as the best paid men of any occupation. Female stars commanded not only handsome but sometimes astronomical salaries. Vaudeville was an especially lucrative venue for female stars. Female "headliners" (as vaudeville stars were called) earned between $1,000 and $4,000 per week in the first-class theaters. Bernhardt commanded an astonishing $7,000 a week during her first vaudeville run in 1912–13. But even standard acts earned from $200 to $500 a week. Stars of the dramatic stage, on the other hand, typically drew between $300 and $500 a week, which helps explain why, although vaudeville had less cultural prestige, many actresses, Bernhardt among them, willingly performed pieces drawn from their dramatic repertoires for vaudeville audiences.[19] Besides being among the highest-paid stars of the legitimate stage, Bernhardt was among a tiny but highly visible minority of women on both sides of the Atlantic who distinguished themselves by their ability to attain almost complete artistic independence. She ran her own production company from 1880 on, and in 1898 she opened a theater in Paris named after herself.[20]

The growing phenomenon of the female star went hand in hand with the rise in female spectatorship. Whereas in the earlier part of the nineteenth century men had dominated both the audience and the stage, by mid-century theaters catering to so-called respectable middle-class audiences were attracting more female spectators, and by the 1890s it was not uncommon to find women occupying the majority of seats at certain plays. This, however, was not the case for Bernhardt's performances, which consistently drew mixed-sex audiences. At other kinds of theatrical entertainments such as vaudeville, which attracted a cross-class audience, and musical comedy and revue, which catered mainly to the upper end of the social scale, audiences tended toward a mixture of both sexes, though matinee performances at vaudeville theaters were often heavily attended by women.[21] By the beginning of the twentieth century concepts like "the Matinee Girl" and "the Stage-Struck Girl" had entered the American vocabulary to describe what one observer, clearly no fan of this trend, saw as the "omnivorous theatergoing" of "indolent young women."[22]

Women's increased attendance at the theater, especially vaudeville, has been explained as a response to the effort of some theater managers to eliminate morally repugnant material from their shows. But this effort to sanitize the content and image of popular theater always remained more of an ideal than a cultural reality.[23] What may better explain the rising level of women's theater attendance in the years after 1880 was the increasing visibility of members of their own sex in the theatrical profession. At a time when so-called New Women sought personal fulfillment through college education and the pursuit of professional careers, theater did more than offer the promise of employment: it provided an influential public space for experimenting with new, and sometimes controversial forms of female self-expression. With more and more women making a living on the boards, their range of roles and types expanded. In turn, women in the audience could vicariously experience themselves in the same enlarged capacities. They could enjoy the pleasures and dangers of these often daring female performances from a safe distance across the footlights, and still maintain their own pretenses to respectability. Though fixed in their seats, they could nevertheless emotionally partake in the action taking place on stage, either through identification or revulsion or both.[24]

Outside of the theater, women also played an increasingly prominent role in the urban culture of spectacle. At the turn of the century, women at both ends of the class spectrum in the large metropolitan centers engaged in the practice of conspicuous self-display. To be sure, personal display itself was not especially new. For centuries social elites had been putting wealth and status on public view; what was new at the turn of the century was the democratization of stylish self-presentation. At one end of the spectrum, a leisure class of old and new monied society women, the subject of Edith Wharton's *The House of Mirth* (1905), paraded their gowns, jewels, and extravagant style of living. This wealthy Gilded Age elite, a writer for the gossip magazine *Town Topics* observed in 1896, "do not spare pains, expense, or advertising for the sake of maintaining a brilliant and refined series of continuous social performances." They were actors who put on their show for "the rest of us spectators."[25] But new opportunities for social performance also came to young working-class women. Though they could scarcely afford to squander their meager resources, they similarly delighted in putting on style with cheap but fashionable hats and clothing, thus signaling not only their desire for respectability but also their longing for self-expression.[26] By the end of World War I, all classes of women were beginning to use make-up as well. The newly glamorized "paint," formerly used almost exclusively by actresses and prostitutes, eventually became a fashionable option for female self-display.[27]

Legendary Beginnings

By 1880 Bernhardt had become an international symbol of the new culture of spectacle. When she first toured the United States that year, she was already thirty-six years old. Born in Paris in 1844 to a young Dutch-Jewish woman named Julie (or Youle) Bernardt (Sarah later changed the spelling to Bernhardt) and a father whose identity remains shrouded in mystery, Sarah was educated and later baptized at a convent school near Versailles. At age sixteen she was admitted to the Conservatoire—the prestigious Paris Conservatory of Music and Drama. This historic institution supplied leading players to the most revered institution of the French classical theater, the Comédie Française. The story is that Sarah's mother, a beautiful courtesan whose lovers included the Duc de Morny and other men with friends in high places, used her connections to open the door of the Comédie Française to her daughter.

However she gained entry, Sarah began her first career at the Comédie Française in 1862. But the next year, after a quarrel with another actress, she was forced to resign. After several years of playing minor parts at a fashionable Paris theater called the Gymnase, and the birth of her illegitimate son, Maurice, in 1864, Sarah re-established her professional credentials as an actress. From 1868 until 1872 she was a featured player at the other national theater of France, the Odéon, where she established a following among the professors, students, and artists of the Left Bank. During the siege of Paris in the Franco-Prussian War, she set up a makeshift hospital there. In 1872, after a highly successful run as the Queen of Spain in Victor Hugo's *Ruy Blas* at the Odéon, the director of Comédie Française persuaded her to return to the company. In 1875, after she proved her power as a leading lady in plays by the giants of French literary and dramatic tradition, Hugo, Racine, and Molière, the Comédie Française promoted Sarah Bernhardt to its highest salaried rank of *sociétaire*.[28]

Acting was not Bernhardt's only claim to fame. In the 1870s she took up painting and also had a remarkably successful career as a sculptor. At the same time she cultivated a flamboyant circle of artists, actors, and writers, had a number of notorious romantic liaisons amongst them, and became what her biographers called the well-publicized queen of "an extravagant bohemia."[29]

Bernhardt was a magnet for publicity, attracting attention wherever she went. During the 1878 Paris Exposition, she became front-page news when she ascended in a spectacular free-flight balloon ride over the city of Paris and later published a widely read fantasy of her adventure, *Dans les nuages* (In the Clouds).

The year before Bernhardt's American debut marked a critical turning point in her career. In 1879, in the aftermath of her highly successful London appearances with the Comédie Française, during which the Gaiety Theatre had billed her as a star, the Prince of Wales had feted her, and members of society had invited her to give private performances, the actress had a stormy and much-publicized second fall-out with M. Perrin, the director of the Comédie Française, who objected to the excessive amount of publicity that Bernhardt's off-stage exploits had created. Seduced by a lucrative offer to tour as an independent star, Bernhardt signed a contract with American impresario Henry Abbey, resigned from the Comédie Française, formed her own theater company, and now, as actress-manager, entered a new phase of her career—international touring.[30]

From her first American tour in 1880 until her sixth in 1905, the classically trained actress played exclusively on the legitimate American dramatic stage, a venue which, along with opera, attracted audiences that wanted to demonstrate their cultivated dramatic tastes. These first tours were largely highbrow affairs, played before the relatively well-to-do who willingly paid the (then) exorbitant price of $3 a ticket to view the reigning queen of French drama. But during her sixth tour (1905–06) Bernhardt also began to test her appeal to American mass audiences, performing her French language plays in a series of "tent" shows throughout the South, West, and Midwest. One took place in Kansas City where she and her company performed in a specially designed round-top tent (called "The Sarah Bernhardt") that accommodated 6,000 eager spectators. *Theatre Magazine* estimated that her Kansas City tent show grossed the "largest single night's receipts from a dramatic entertainment ever known in the history of the stage."[31] These tent shows, where tickets could be obtained for as little as $1, as well as performances that took place in other popular venues such as skating rinks, began as a publicity stunt after the theatrical Syndicate, which held the monopoly over legitimate theater bookings, refused to allow their business rivals Sam and Lee Shubert and their associate, William F. Connor, to book Bernhardt's performances in their theaters.[32]

Bernhardt's tent shows increased her already formidable celebrity. The popular success of a classically trained actress who performed only in French, New York theater critic Louis De Foe explained, was a consequence of her capacity to convey "the universal language of the human emotions"—which she did through a combination of spoken lines and pantomimic gesture.[33] But just as important was the phenomenon of the actress herself. It was not what Bernhardt said but how she said it that engaged audiences; not who she played on stage but who she was that they cared about. They came to see a woman who had attained the status of a cultural phenomenon. To some she was "Madame Bernhardt," to others she was "Sarah," to still others she was simply "The Bernhardt."[34]

The star's 1905–06 tour marked a crucial turning point in her relationship to the American public for another reason as well. By that time she was already 61 years old, and old age itself had become an important aspect of the Bernhardt spectacle. Certainly it was a major theme of her last two American tours (1912–13 and 1917–18), during which she performed abbreviated versions of her plays for popular audiences in packed vaudeville houses across the country.[35] While tickets for her earlier full length performances on the legitimate stage had cost at least $1, in 1912 vaudeville patrons could watch her grand spectacle of lust and death for a mere 25 cents.[36] The vaudeville tour included one well-publicized performance before 2,000 prisoners housed at the maximum security prison in San Quentin.[37] That same year Bernhardt sought to secure her cultural legacy and to improve her financial situation by making two silent films: a version of her new play *Queen Elizabeth (Elisabeth, Reine d'Angleterre)*, and an adaptation of *La Dame aux Camélias.*[38] On the final American tour in 1917, the aged envoy of war-torn France was supported by an artificial leg (the result of an earlier amputation) and carried about in a folding chair.[39] As theater critic Charles Darnton had put it, these last tours attracted audiences not because of what Bernhardt could still do on stage, but rather because of "what she has been and what she has done."[40]

Sinful and Saved, Feminine and Masculine

What had Bernhardt "been" and "done" for Americans? For one thing, she had challenged some of the established categories of thinking about the female sex. On Bernhardt's first tour in 1880, she played the classics of mid-nineteenth-century French drama in her native tongue: works by Hugo, Dumas *fils*, Scribe, and Racine. American and British audiences especially loved her controversial Marguerite Gautier, the tragic tubercular courtesan in Dumas *fils'* *La Dame aux Camélias,* which she performed on all nine American tours. Bernhardt recalled that on her 1880 tour the public rushed to see this play about a "modern Magdalene," a play that often shocked "the over-strained Puritanism of the small American towns."[41] But even in New York City she created a frenzy. At her December 4, 1880 performance of the play, police had to be called in to control the mob that had gathered at the door of the theater. Eager onlookers handed her armfuls of bouquets, young men begged her to autograph their shirtsleeves, and one woman attempted to cut off locks of Sarah's hair to take home as a souvenir. The play itself lasted an hour longer than usual because of the seventeen curtain calls that followed the third act, and the twenty-nine more that followed Bernhardt's spectacular death scene.[42]

Subsequent American tours also featured sensationalist melodramas written for Bernhardt by Victorien Sardou: *Fédora, Théodora, Cléopâtre, Gismonda,* and *La Tosca,* among others. With Sardou's plays as her vehicle, Bernhardt turned herself into a series of emotionally volatile *femmes fatales* who, as theater historian John Stokes puts it, were "torn between uncontrollable impulses of power-hungry aggression and passive subservience." Invariably, the heroines fell in love with men whom they must "either sacrifice or destroy" before they themselves died a repentant death—or rather, not simply death but a long, drawn-out, stylized form of dying at once flamboyant and glamorous.[43]

Before Bernhardt's arrival, Americans had already seen decades of "Camilles" and other fallen-women melodramas, but most of them had been staged to imply rather than graphically reveal the sexual elements of the story. The one exception had been Irish American actress Matilda Heron, who in her signature role as "Camille" in the late 1850s eschewed the romantic and poetic elements in the play to deliver what was considered an astonishingly frank portrayal of a fallen woman's earthy and unrefined sexuality. One critic even complained that Heron's Camille was so devoid of Parisian charm that it had all the allure of an Irish washerwoman. Heron gave Camille the sexual honesty of the prostitute, but none of the graceful affectations of the upper-class courtesan. By contrast, Bernhardt's Camille and her other fallen heroines combined romantic grandeur with overt and unapologetic sexuality. This was an actress who aimed not only to attract but also to seduce her audiences. Body language and gesture contributed to that effect. Her smoldering gazes, her "serpentine" undulations, her ability to arrange her slim figure into a curving "spiral," even her unusual habit of smiling on stage, made a Bernhardt performance into an erotically charged event.[44] Writing in 1892, a New York critic captured this aspect of her stage persona when he claimed that "Bernhardt's skill lies in portraying the abandonment of animal passion—the idiosyncrasies, the hysteria, the caprices, and the tragic denouements of illicit love."[45]

But the repertoire of classical and melodramatic fallen-women plays that Bernhardt brought to the United States in the late nineteenth century blurred the lines between good and bad women. The deaths of her redeemed courtesans signified spiritual purification.[46] Thus for many American (and British) critics, there were two Sarah Bernhardts on stage. One was the indecent libertine who imparted to her characters the kind of sensual passion and emotional abandon that made them seem dangerously and irredeemably sexualized. The "fearful immorality" of Bernhardt's characters, recalled one writer, who later characterized the play *Adrienne Lecouvreur* as the story of "the mistress of a married man who is also the lover of a married woman whose husband appears in the play," only served to underscore her reputation as a "perverted Parisienne."[47]

But the other Sarah Bernhardt was a womanly woman, capable of projecting virtues associated with true or traditional femininity. Theater critic Richard Grant White's 1881 review of Bernhardt's New York performances captured this duality.[48] Despite the sinfulness of her characters, and what he believed was the "thin" moral nature of a "French-Hebrew" actress, White insisted that Bernhardt radiated the feminine virtues of "purity and tenderness" in ways that were rarely equaled either in "real life" or "on the stage."[49] Her acting style demonstrated what "we Anglo-Saxon folk" call "womanliness pure and simple." That, he noted with irony, was "Bernhardt's forte."[50] Thus while exhibiting all of the tearful passions and foibles of a sexual outlaw (her own as well as those of the characters played) Bernhardt could, through the dramatic resolution of her performances, still claim to be on the side of the angels. Having it both ways, she appealed to men as well as women, and particularly to women who had one foot in the camp of moral rectitude and another in the world of experimentation. Indeed, it was the moral equivocation of her stage characters and her person that for many people constituted the hallmark of Bernhardt's modernity.

Even Bernhardt's copious stage tears contained that dual potential for her audiences. The "sacred" tears valued by nineteenth-century Victorian sentimentalists were most often expressed as private or individual emotions and best reserved for domestic settings.[51] For women tears symbolized "deep femininity." Thus when the redeemed courtesans of nineteenth-century French drama wept, the tears signified a ritual cleansing that led to the rediscovery of their true womanliness.[52]

On the other hand, women's tears could not always be trusted for they also counted as weapons of the manipulative strategies of feminine coquetry. Or they were interpreted as signs of women's erotic volatility and their supposedly innate tendency toward nervous disorder, such as the "fits" of the crying female hysteric discharging her sexual urges.[53] Freud, the foremost expert on the subject of female hysteria and an early advocate of the "repeal" of sexual "reticence," had found Bernhardt's acting completely believable. He became an instant admirer of her creative self-transformations after he saw her perform in Paris in 1885 and would later keep a photograph of her prominently displayed in his Vienna consulting office.[54]

In the era of the New Woman, overwrought emotionalism had political connotations as well. In 1883, for example, the conservative British novelist Eliza Lynn Linton derided the emotional volatility of the "shrieking sisterhood" of "Advanced Women" who made a "hysterical parade" of their social and political wants and intentions. Two decades later American journalist Margaret Deland railed against the "excited" and "conceited" New Woman who allowed her uncontrolled "passions" for power and authority to dictate a hasty and misguided quest to "make the world over."[55]

Such opinions did nothing, however, to lessen the appeal of watching a woman like Bernhardt work herself into an emotional frenzy on stage. "Sarah's name and fame rest upon one specialty—the power to electrify any crowded house of foreigners [i.e. Americans] by the simulations of a terrific cyclone of rage, agony and horror," wrote theater critic Alan Dale in 1904. "That is the specialty in which she is expected to indulge. People wait until 11 p.m. if necessary and sit through hours of her tedious 'liquid gold,' [a reference to the quality of her speaking voice] but they must be treated to it. It is their only use for Sarah Bernhardt."[56]

The very fact that some critics considered it unladylike for an actress to make a scene with emotional pyrotechnics may have added to its guilty pleasures. Female audiences in particular strongly identified with and wanted to see actresses giving free reign to their passions, whether they be grief or love. Along with Bernhardt, popular turn-of-the-century American actresses like Clara Morris (the "Queen of the Streaming Eye"), Fanny Davenport ("the American Bernhardt") and Mrs. Leslie Carter (Caroline Louise Dudley), all had legions of female fans who found in their spectacles of hysteria an outlet for their own pent-up feelings and desires. For some members of the female audience, however, Sarah was in a class by herself. "Bernhardt interests the matinee girls more than any other actress," wrote Cady Whaley in 1906. "We girls are strung up and tuned in key with sympathy and grief. We fairly revel and delight in the spasms of pain we feel for her." Constance Skinner also confessed that she found Bernhardt's tears a delicious "luxury" and, in a sexually charged passage, described those powerful scenes when the actress "rises to climax after climax . . . and bears down all before her in her gorgeous rages."[57]

At the same time that she was confounding traditional notions of femininity, Bernhardt was also playing with masculinity. She counterpoised the erotically charged womanliness of her tearful heroines by claiming the right to play roles written for men. She also played male roles written expressly for her, such as the Duc de Reichstadt (or "Eaglet")—the doomed son of Napoleon—in Edmund Rostand's popular 1901 play *L'Aiglon*.[58] While this role generated relatively little controversy (no doubt because it was intended for her), Bernhardt's doubly scandalous French-language version of *Hamlet* was another story.

Audiences and critics believed that when a woman usurped a male part in a serious dramatic production (as opposed to a humorous burlesque), it undermined the masculinity of the character.[59] Bernhardt was not the first dramatic actress to play Hamlet, but she was certainly among the most provocative. Her well-established association with womanly femme fatale parts added a critical edge to her Hamlet, as did her highly publicized penchant for off-stage cross-dressing. Moreover, she actively defended her right to play a male part by publicly denouncing traditional stereotypes of masculinity and femininity, a move that later made her something of a cult figure among homosexuals in Europe and America.[60] In a 1900 article, she insisted that actresses were actually more adaptable than actors to complex roles like Hamlet because they possessed both the "light carriage" of youthfulness and the "mature thought" of the male mind required to convincingly play the part.[61]

Many critics were not convinced, however, and took to calling Bernhardt's character "Hamletina," or "Hamlet, Princess of Denmark."[62] Others were willing to concede that her "rough and violent" rendition seemed "as masculine as a woman could make it."[63] Still others applauded the ease with which she moved back and forth between masculine and feminine roles. As journalist Carolyn Cross put it in her 1906 review of Bernhardt's performances in *Hamlet* and *La Dame Aux Camélias*: "few would attempt to jump across the fearful gulf between this dismal masculine role of tragedy, as felt by man, to the passionate, loveable, wholly womanly character of Camille, but nothing daunts Sarah."[64]

"The Most Self-Advertised Woman in the World"

Bernhardt's capacity to "jump across the fearful gulf" between masculinity and femininity and to blur the line between good and bad women constituted crucial aspects of her power to provoke audiences. Yet these provocative and sometimes controversial aspects of her stage work need to be situated within the broader cultural transformation that she participated in. Bernhardt demonstrated that theater could provide a unique site of female self-expression and self-invention. To be sure, women did not suddenly come to appreciate or advocate female individuality just when Bernhardt burst on the American scene. There are many examples of nineteenth-century writers and activists who insisted upon woman's right to define and be herself. But Bernhardt came along at a moment when this idea was beginning to gain a wider cultural currency in the United States, and her radical self-exhibitionism on as well as off the stage made her the high priestess of its most recent incarnation.

Bernhardt's biographers have labeled her acting style, with its melodramatic crying and dying and its stylized gestures and pantomimes, as the last of the old. But it was equally the first of the new. Henry James noted that while he admired the "delicacy and grace" of some of Bernhardt's "plaintive passages," he recoiled at the "violent scenes" in which she "forces her note beyond all reason," calling her acting style, "painfully shrill and modern."[65] But it was not just violent female emotionalism that made Bernhardt's style seem painfully modern to some critics. Bernhardt took what was then the revolutionary step of encouraging audiences to believe that what they saw on stage was not an actress playing a character, but a woman using that character to reveal her self to the spectators. Anton Chekhov, clearly no fan of Bernhardt's immodest acting style, reviewed her Moscow performances in 1881, complaining that Bernhardt "remakes her heroine into exactly the same sort of unusual woman she is herself. . . . You watch *Adrienne Lecouvreur* and you see not Adrienne Lecouvreur in her but the ultra-clever, ultra-sensational Sarah Bernhardt." Describing her performance style as if it were no different from her off-stage publicity methods, he noted that Bernhardt "goes in pursuit not of the natural but of the extraordinary. Her goal is to startle, to amaze, to dazzle.. . . Every step she takes is profoundly thought out, a stunt."[66]

British drama critic William Archer also registered disapproval: "She does not dream of taking a great piece of literature and bending her genius to its interpretation." Rather, Bernhardt overturned the rules of drama. "It is the playwright's business to interpret *her*—to provide her with a new name and new costumes in which to go through the old round of poses and paroxysms."[67] But it was playwright and social critic George Bernard Shaw who in 1895 offered the most scathing criticism of her self-promoting dramatic style. Unlike his favorite player, the Italian actress Eleanora Duse, Bernhardt "does not enter the leading character" but "substitutes herself for it." The "dress, the title of the play, the order of the words may vary," wrote Shaw, "but the woman [on stage] is always the same."[68] Sarah defended herself by criticizing Duse, whom she labeled a "very great" actress but "not a great artist." Unlike the "artist" who "creates" a stage "personage" that "can be identified by her name," wrote Bernhardt in her 1907 memoir, Duse "has not created a being or a vision which reminds one of herself."[69]

Shaw considered Bernhardt's style antiquated because it resembled the learned, unchanging, and often grandiose poses, pantomimes, and gestures of the traditional dramatic stage.[70] Yet in turning her characters into so many versions of herself, Shaw conceded, Bernhardt was not merely antiquated. Paradoxically she also exemplified what he referred to as the "high modern development of the circus and the waxworks"—mass cultural forms dependent upon the principle of "personal fascination" rather than artistic subtlety.[71] It was precisely that high modern emphasis upon personal fascination that enabled Bernhardt to move from legitimate drama to the popular stage. For as journalist Hutchins Hapgood put it, in terms that also described the aesthetic practices of vaudeville, the immodesty of Sarah's "shattering" personality and "attitudinizing" fit well with "the prevailing bad taste of the Broadway idea"—an idea which permitted "some central figure" who demanded "recognition of her or his charming personality" to overshadow the whole dramatic production.[72]

Ironically, even the stage deaths for which Bernhardt was so famous provided a vehicle for the showcasing of her shattering personality. Bernhardt's self-magnifying use of the stage yielded not moments of self-negation but captivating scenes of self-aggrandizement.[73] Audiences were astounded by the "pantomimic choreography" of her famous death scene in *La Dame aux Camélias*. It was Bernhardt's practice, a French critic noted in 1881, to murmur her last words to her lover Armand not from the traditional position expected in a death scene (lying or sitting), but on her feet, "defying death and breathing life with all the strength of her being." Then, "using herself as a pivot, she suddenly reels and makes a half-turn, and, as if finally vanquished, she falls from her height in the most elegant and poetic pose imaginable."[74] Not everyone greeted her death-defying innovations with such enthusiasm, however. "To stand erect, stiffen herself, and flop—downward in Adrienne, sideways in Camille, forward in Frou Frou, backward in The Sphinx—is Bernhardt's method of dying," complained a New York critic in 1880. He wanted more "nature" and less Bernhardtian "art." But naturalism was never Bernhardt's concern. Her claims to fame were the signature gestures and grand bodily attitudes she transported from one play to the next. In doing so she virtually guaranteed that the dominating aspect of the mise-en-scene was the spectacle of Sarah herself.[75]

The self-dramatizing aims of Bernhardt's stage work had their counterpart in the self-magnifying tactics of her off-stage spectacle. On the eve of her first American tour, as Henry James had observed in London, Bernhardt had already learned how to engineer her own celebrity. Her first two American tours only served to confirm her reputation for publicity seeking, a reputation that grew more exaggerated over time. Indeed, no woman in the United States or elsewhere was as closely associated with self-promotion as Bernhardt. A Philadelphia journalist noted in 1887 that while most actresses spare no effort to "keep their names in the papers, and keep themselves talked about," Bernhardt "has probably done more for this sort of notoriety than any other actress of her time."[76] In 1902 another American journalist was ready to call Bernhardt "the greatest self-advertiser in the world."[77] A 1913 article in the *Cleveland Leader* by William Sage put it more boldly still. "Pear, the soap man, is 'some advertiser'," wrote Sage, "so is our own Post, who nonchalantly spends a million or so to put a new breakfast food on your table and mine. Epps, Gillette, Mennen, any of the big auto companies, have lavish hands in getting their wares before the public." But "they are all merely pikers besides Bernhardt." While other advertisers were "limited geographically by the nature of their allowances for advertising," he observed, "the Gallic Barnum" had made herself "universal and cosmopolitan . . . There isn't a land where she is not more or less a household word."[78]

The association of Bernhardt with Barnum is significant here. Bernhardt's artistic roots were in the high domain of the French national theater, but her cultural effect as a woman lay in her ability to seize the possibilities for self-construction and self-exposure afforded by the modern mass culture of spectacle. Other nineteenth-century actresses, including the British-born Charlotte Cushman, the Italian Adelaide Ristori, and especially the flamboyant American Jewish poet and musical comedy star Adah Isaacs Menken, had proven the commercial value not only of publicity but of "manufactured controversy."[79] But in the relentless pursuit of publicity, "The Menken," as the self-promoting performer was called, never matched "The Bernhardt," who was the only woman of her time ever to be directly compared to America's most revered showman, P. T. Barnum.

Perhaps no commentator had done more to link the name of Bernhardt with that of Barnum—the most formidable and famous emblem of American popular culture—than had rival French actress Marie Colombier, author of the widely read 1883 pseudo-biography, *The Life and Memoirs of Sarah Barnum*. In this influential book, Colombier, a disaffected and vindictive member of the ensemble of actors who had accompanied Bernhardt on her 1880 American tour, painted a viciously anti-Semitic portrait of "La Barnum," as a "self-willed," "egotistical," "capricious" woman who would stop at nothing in the pursuit of lovers, money, publicity, and fame.[80] Colombier was not the only French observer to criticize Bernhardt's devolution into Barnumism. The former manager of the Comédie Française accused her of debasing her own talent as well as the cultural heritage of her nation by agreeing to play before American audiences, which had more appreciation for "an elephant walking on bottles" than for true artistic "genius."[81]

It was not just the defenders of French culture or even Bernhardt's jealous detractors who made the Barnum analogy. When American journalists equated Bernhardt with Barnum they usually meant it as a compliment. For the legendary P. T. Barnum was not only America's most revered showman, he was also one of the nineteenth century's most aggressive, ingenious, and wealthy self-made men. Audiences flocked to see "wonders," "freaks," and "humbugs" at Barnum's museum, most of them elaborate hoaxes like the infamous "Fejee Mermaid." Yet as cultural historian Neil Harris has shown, these humbugs were only part of what attracted audiences. The other attraction was Barnum himself. Spectators longed to know how the ingenious Barnum had engineered these spectacular deceptions. His own power to entice and deceive was a crucial aspect of the exhibit and the most important ingredient in his self-cultivated reputation as the "presiding genius" of American showmanship.[82] Still, neither Barnum himself nor the human and artificial curiosities, wonders, and freaks that he featured in his exhibits would have become public successes if they had not been extensively, hyperbolically, and fallaciously advertised. Barnum, the master of humbug, pioneered the modern publicity stunt.[83]

Bernhardt was one of its shrewdest practitioners. Of all her publicity stunts, few proved as valuable as the so-called Farewell Tour. Beginning in 1887, each of Bernhardt's American tours was billed as positively the last one she would ever make.[84] And each was arranged to include delegations of enthusiastic admirers who arrived at the New York dock to welcome her with bouquets of flowers and to bid her a last emotional farewell when she departed again for Paris, supposedly never to return again. The American farewell tour was hardly a new publicity stunt: the promoters of other European performers, such as Ristori, had used it as a form of advertising in the 1860s.[85] Yet Bernhardt emerged as the undisputed queen of the farewell tour. A 1910 article in the upscale humor magazine *Judge* dubbed her "the international heavyweight for final tours," adding that Bernhardt "has told this country good-bye so many times that she can now go through the ordeal without rehearsal."[86] Bernhardt's not-so-last farewells actually inspired a new expression in American theatrical slang. When a performer announced that he or she would no longer appear on stage and then made a surprise comeback (as George M. Cohan did in 1914), they were said to have "Sarahbernhardted" themselves.[87]

The comparison of Bernhardt to Barnum did not stand on humbuggery alone. Just as important was Bernhardt's determination to turn herself into a female "curiosity." When Sarah was still a child in France, Barnum had fastened onto what would eventually become the formula for the making of a modern celebrity: the creation of a distinctive public persona that would make the performer appear to be an exemplary or unusual representative of her or his gender. Barnum had done that to fashion his own celebrity. And Americans who were alive before the Civil War had vivid memories of how he had done the same to make a celebrity phenomenon out of the womanly attributes of Swedish opera singer Jenny Lind. She was the object of Barnum's most famous and most highly orchestrated advertising campaign. In 1850, before Jenny Lind had "sung a note in America," writes Neil Harris, Barnum had embarked upon an unprecedented publicity blitz to acquaint Americans with Lind's extraordinary capacity for "charity," "simplicity," and "goodness." Whether Lind actually possessed all of the lofty virtues Barnum advertised was hardly the point. As one opera impresario put it, Barnum manufactured the singer's American reputation not "by the inch" but "by the cart-load," and audiences were as much interested in Lind's qualities as a super-virtuous female curiosity as in her talents as a singer.[88]

Bernhardt and her promoters adopted similar strategies, but with different implications for female identity. Every form of advance publicity for her American tours stressed two themes: her reputation as a dramatic artist and the unusual personal qualities that made her a female curiosity. Yet the difference between her promotion and that of Lind was crucial. While Lind was hardly a passive beneficiary of Barnum's advertising campaigns, it was Barnum and not Lind who fabricated the singer's reputation. Bernhardt, on the other hand, played a central role in the manufacture of her own public image, becoming an outspoken and prolific contributor to the making and marketing of her own cultural myth. Put another way, Sarah played the role of Barnum in order to promote the idea of Bernhardt. Like Barnum, Bernhardt had seized upon a form of public self-fashioning that historically had been the province of social and political elites. The public self that Bernhardt invented and promoted was the very opposite of the womanly simplicity, charity, and self-effacing goodness that Barnum claimed for Jenny Lind. Bernhardt presented herself as a high-strung, egotistical, and individualistic female rebel, ready to flout convention at every turn.

In doing so, Bernhardt helped usher in an important shift in women's relationship to publicity. Her exhibitionism was overt rather than covert, self-magnifying rather than self-denying. As a New York City reporter put it in 1880 after the actress had announced her resignation from the Comédie Française, Bernhardt was a "self-made woman" who "exaggerates her own merits and the importance of her conquests." Here was an individual woman who was "ambitious of shining before mankind as a universal genius." She "pants" not only for fame but for domination.[89]

This new style of female self-promotion did not win universal approval. Few observers probed the gender anxieties provoked by women's appropriation of Barnumism as deeply as Henry James. Two of his novels—*The Bostonians* (1886) and *The Tragic Muse* (1890)— explored the ways that women were learning to seize upon the stage and the press to create grotesque public selves free from "the box" of domestic captivity.[90] In contrast to the self-effacing angel Verena Tarrant in his

earlier novel *The Bostonians,* who gives up the lecture circuit and re-
treats to "the box," James figured his Bernhardt-like character, the actress Miriam Rooth in *The Tragic Muse,* as "a kind of monster" who refuses to display the meekness and decency expected even from a woman
artist. Like Bernhardt, Miriam lives life "in a high wind of [public] exhibition"; no man can possess her because she gives him "nothing to take
hold of."[91] For just as James had labeled Bernhardt the "muse of the
newspaper," he calls Miriam Rooth the "predestined mistress" of the
"roaring deafening newspaperism of the period." The "machinery [of
publicity] was ready, the platform laid; the facilities, the wires and bells
and trumpets," were all in place and "waiting for her" to "press her foot
on the spring and set them all in motion." Miriam's "spectacle would be
. . . thrilling, the drama . . . more bustling than any she would put on the
stage . . . It would be splendid dreadful grotesque."[92]

By adopting Barnumism Bernhardt ushered in a new cultural phenomenon: the egotistical female artist who not only promotes her plays
but actively constructs, exhibits, and advertises her own curious and
flamboyant personality. In staking out this ground, Bernhardt did more
than contribute to women's enlarged visibility in the public culture of
the late nineteenth century; she demonstrated how women might
change the terms of their engagement with public culture. It was not
just the fact of female spectacle that distinguished a Sarah Bernhardt
from her cultural predecessors. What was important was the new meaning she gave it. Bernhardt demonstrated women's willingness to reject a
posture of self-effacement and embrace the possibilities for self-
magnification.

This new Bernhardtian model of femininity anticipated by two decades a central tenet of modern feminism: what one 1914 writer would
call the demand for the freedom of "the individual woman" not only to
realize a distinctive personality but to "eliminate . . . martyrdom and
self-abnegations."[93] That same year another writer would describe feminism as a woman's right not only to "be a self," but also "to be for herself." Simply put, this amounted to a belief in the primary right to bring
"feminine individuality to supreme and perfect unfolding."[94] This was
not a new idea. But it was not until the 1910s that women's rights activists who called themselves feminists successfully turned the concept of
self-realization into the theoretical foundation of a broader political
project. For Bernhardt, however, the right to be herself was not a politi-

cal project but a highly romantic individual one. Enacting Oscar Wilde's dictum that truth was "a matter of style," she invented an egotistical and individualistic public self and promoted it with consummate skill.[95]

Many of the images that would become a permanent part of the Bernhardt legend were contained in a promotional biography published in New York on the eve of her arrival in 1880, *The Life of Sarah Bernhardt*. The booklet, typical of the publicity materials churned out by Bernhardt and her agent, Edward Jarrett, contained her photograph, autograph, and "anecdotes of her, on and off the stage." Even as it claimed to correct the many exaggerations and misrepresentations that obscured the "true colors" of Sarah Bernhardt, its mission was actually to reiterate the bizarre lies that were making the name of Bernhardt a "household word in America." Painting a portrait of an individual of extraordinary self-determination, it described her as a Jewess by birth who was "brought up as a Christian" in a Catholic convent outside of Paris. Vowing to become a nun if she could not fulfill her ambition to become an actress, Bernhardt "won distinction in all the paths that she has chosen to trod," overcame "all obstacles," and "has proven herself a woman of remarkable genius." Her ambition was fulfilled because on stage the electrical "effect of her outbursts of passion" had commanded the sympathy of her audiences. It went on to praise the actress's other talents as a sculptor and a painter, and contained elaborate detail on the extravagant and costly dresses she designed for her performances as well as stories about her "luxurious manner of living in Europe." But it was the list of disclaimers—that she did not, as had often been reported, "sleep in a coffin"; that her "favorite dishes" were not "burnt cats, lizard's tails, and peacock's brains *sautées au beurre de singe*"; that she did not make it a habit of playing croquet with human skulls, even though she kept "the skeleton of a man who is said to have destroyed himself on account of disappointment in love"—that fed her reputation for exoticism and eccentricity.[96]

Painting a portrait of herself as an eccentric and rebellious female genius, Sarah used the machinery of publicity to play the role of the outspoken social critic. Positioning herself as the sophisticated Parisian doyenne, she became the authority not only on the subject of her own life but on the world at large. "Bernhardt," wrote a reporter in 1895, "can talk on any subject, from theosophy and politics to . . . the best breed of dogs."[97] Among her favorite topics was the rising demand for female emancipation, an issue she milked both for the controversy provoked (which was always good for box office receipts), as a form of self-promotion, and for its genuine appeal to her female audience. "I adore your country," she announced in an article published in the *New York World* on the eve of her fourth American tour in 1896. "Woman reigns and reigns so absolutely. She comes and goes. She orders, wills, exacts, instructs, spends money recklessly, and gives no thanks. This shocks some people, but it only charms me."[98]

Yes, she admired American women for their achievements in higher education, athletic development, and their independence, she told reporter Fanny Fair in 1906. But in a typically self-referential ploy she insisted it was French women who understood the sine qua non of feminine power: personality. "They do not wish to grow like other persons. They wish to grow more and more like themselves . . . they keep their individuality and make it felt."[99]

Sarah's construction of her rebellious individuality was inseparable from the idea of her "Hebrew" blood. While suffering the personal wounds inflicted by fin-de-siecle anti-Semitism, she nevertheless recognized that her status as a Jew only increased her power to provoke and captivate. She had come of age at a moment when exotic foreigners from (or pretending to be from) Africa and the Middle East were a mainstay of European and American scientific and commercial spectacles, including Barnum's American Museum. Unable to escape the taint of her Jewish ancestry, Bernhardt learned how to manipulate it. While playing up her Frenchness at every opportunity, she managed the question of her Jewish background from a defensive posture that swung between denial and confession. Either way, she emphasized her status as an outsider, or what her 1907 autobiography calls an unruly "little Bohemian."[100] "I am a Jewess, but not a German," Bernhardt wrote to a Paris newspaper editor in 1873, after she had received an "avalanche of insulting and threatening letters" alleging her German ancestry. Insisting "I am French, absolutely French," while adding that her family had come from Holland, she insisted that "if I have a foreign accent . . . it is cosmopolitan, but not Teutonic. I am a daughter of the great Jewish race, and my somewhat uncultivated language is the outcome of our enforced wanderings."[101] But during one of her North American tours, when the French Canadian clergy denounced her immorality during a visit to Montreal in 1898, she loudly proclaimed: "I am not a Jewess, but a Christian and a French Woman . . . the early portion of my youth was passed in the convent of Grandchamps in Versailles."[102]

In France Bernhardt had faced the growing outbursts of anti-Semitism that climaxed with the Dreyfus Affair. Numerous cartoons and caricatures that appeared in the press beginning in the late 1870s pictured her as a hook-nosed, frizzy-haired, money-grubbing, perverse, and disease-ridden "daughter of Israel." Bernhardt's peculiarly Jewish "lust for profit" was a central theme in Marie Colombier's vitriolic biography .[103]

Americans also viewed Bernhardt's Jewish ancestry as a defining element in her on and off-stage personality. The mystery of Bernhardt's parentage and her ethnic origins was the subject of intensive speculation in the American press in the 1880s and 1890s, as reporters offered conflicting stories about whether it was Bernhardt's father, mother, or both who were Jews, what occupations they practiced, and whether they were of Dutch, French, or German ancestry.[104]

But in contrast to the virulent anti-Semitism of Bernhardt's French critics, American commentary on her ethnic traits, though sometimes pointed, was rarely vicious. In 1902, for example, the writer William Dean Howells reported that while watching Bernhardt perform her "She Hamlet," he never forgot for a moment "that it was a woman who was doing that melancholy Dane, and that the woman was a Jewess, and the Jewess was a French Jewess."[105] Occasionally there were subtle intimations in the American press that Bernhardt's personal habits and artistic temperament were peculiarly Jewish. "This amazing Jewish woman," wrote Frank Lloyd, "now has a new folly! This time it is jewels." Her passion for jewels, the writer claimed, was yet more evidence of "that tremendous energy, that fierce vitality, that ungoverned and untrained impetuosity that her fifty-six years of hysterically strenuous life has not dulled."[106]

Despite rising racial animosity, xenophobia, and social exclusion generated by the migration of millions of Jewish newcomers from Eastern Europe to the United States, Bernhardt herself was rarely the target of the kind of crude anti-Semitic diatribes and caricatures that were common in France and Germany. More commonly, American critics attributed her eccentricity and self-indulgences to her "Frenchness" rather than her Jewish parentage. Her Jewish background, or what some called her "oriental" disposition, merely heightened the exoticism of what Americans considered her unruly and inscrutable Gallic temperament.

If any group seemed particularly eager to make Bernhardt's ethnic background an explanation for her behavior, it was American Jewish writers. Just after Bernhardt's death in 1923, for example, an editorial in a St. Louis Jewish paper asking "Was Sara [sic] Bernhardt Jewish?" insisted that although Bernhardt did not practice the Jewish religion, her "histrionic art" was an inescapable "product of her Jewish blood." Bernhardt, claimed the writer, was a "superb delineator of woe, sufferings, passionate desire, disappointment, desolation, and self-sacrifice." She had "inherited" a "Jewish emotional nature" that was "born of the centuries of ancestral affliction, sorrow and endurance." Behind the "rare intensity, vitality and fervor" of her stage portrayals, rang the "anguished moans and sobs" of "her persecuted people,. . . all the way from Egyptian slavery," to the pogroms of "bloody Kishineff."[107]

In her own way Bernhardt herself had actually encouraged such a view. While for the most part she treated her Jewish background as something of a political liability, especially in the context of the growing threat of French anti-Semitism in the years of the Dreyfus Affair, she also made the image of the victimized outsider a prominent part of her public persona. She even went so far as to insert herself into the literary and dramatic tradition of the noble *belle juive*—the beautiful Jewess who, like Walter Scott's heroine in *Ivanhoe,* is a source of both erotic attraction and danger to Christian manhood. On her 1891–92 American tour, for example, she played her own version of the martyred *belle juive* in the popular American drama, *Leah the Forsaken.* She further broadcast this image of herself as a victimized heroine by having the famous New York photographer Napoleon Sarony create a full-length publicity shot of her as Leah standing before a huge crucifix—a reference to the moment in the play when a mob of villagers, unconvinced of Leah's goodness, are about to stone her to death.[108]

Later she found new uses for ethnic difference, incorporating it into her already legendary reputation for eccentricity and exoticism. In her widely read 1907 memoir, *My Double Life,* for instance, she discusses the "disordered," "rebellious," and "horrible" state of her naturally curly hair, which she likened to that of a "white negress."[109] While never mentioning the word Jew, she racialized her identity, playing off Europeans' tendency to associate both Jewish and black females with sexual exotica, as well as traditions of European anti-Semitism that associated Jews with blackness.[110] In later years, the French "white negress" became an outspoken critic of American racial bigotry. While touring the United States in 1913, for example, she came to the defense of black women whom a St. Louis hotel refused to admit by publishing a scathing editorial protesting the odious "racial hatred" practiced by Americans. Railing against the "ostracism" of "blacks by whites" (and, by inference, of Jews by anti-Semites), she maintained that it was extraordinary that in a "new republic of a quite young nation one should wish to exclude an entire race."[111] Bernhardt's strategic manipulations of her outsider status and the gentle but persistent reminders of her Jewish forebears in the American press only served to establish and underscore her distance from mainstream middle-class Protestant American culture. Sarah was an eccentric, temperamental artiste—Parisian, Jewish, and quintessentially rebellious. As an actress and as a woman she could be adored or hated, but she could never be ignored.

The Bernhardt Industry

Bernhardt's self-promotions and those of her contemporaries on the stage would not have been nearly as effective in shaping new views of women had it not been for the birth of the New Journalism. Outside of the theater, no institution of the late nineteenth and early twentieth century was as crucial to the promotion of Bernhardtian-style female self-advertisement. The urban culture of spectacle was in large measure constituted by the sensationalist press and the brazen journalistic practices of the 1880s and 1890s. For newspapers and magazines did more than report on female spectacle in and outside of the theater: they also helped manufacture it. Before that the nineteenth-century "penny press" had also puffed and manufactured the reputations of players. But at century's end these practices took on a whole new meaning when newspapers became big business and theatrical producers, managers, and performers developed a mutually enhancing relationship with the press.[112] The new style of metropolitan journalism of the 1880s and 1890s, epitomized in America by the Austrian Jewish immigrant Joseph Pulitzer and his *New York World*, blurred the lines between news and entertainment. Practitioners of so-called action, detective, and stunt journalism drew upon various forms of urban spectacle (especially crime and scandal, both real and invented) for their stories, yet they were as much involved in making spectacle as in reporting it.[113]

A new generation of male and female reporters made their own exploits as hunters and gatherers of urban stories into a form of self-mythologizing news.[114] In many cases they became the story. Journalist Nelly Bly, who wrote for Pulitzer's *New York World* in the late 1880s, led the ambitious band of Pulitzer's "nervy young women" or "stunt-girls."

Her dare-devil theatrics, which included feigning insanity so that she could be committed to the Women's Lunatic Asylum on Blackwell's Island long enough to gather material for an exposé on the shocking abuse of inmates ("Inside The Madhouse"), and arranging for her own arrest on grand larceny to report on the poor treatment of women prisoners, put *her* on the front page. In 1889 she accepted a challenge posed by a theatrical promoter who dared Bly to try to beat the current record for traveling around the world. By speeding around the globe in 72 days (beating the hero of Jules Verne's novel), she not only boosted circulation for the *World* but also succeeded in turning her name, like Bernhardt's, into a household word.[115]

In the era of Nelly Bly and Sarah Bernhardt, the press and the stage actually developed a symbiotic relationship. The increasingly elaborate use of illustrations and, in the 1890s, of half-tone photography, along with larger and more pungent headlines, were among the many forms of journalistic spectacle that served the theater and the press.[116]

The very same strategies that sold newspapers also promoted the careers of performers. Conversely, the flamboyant styles of actresses like Sarah Bernhardt also helped make the careers of journalists. That was especially true of the professional drama critics, who wrote not only for metropolitan dailies and mass circulation magazines but also for high-toned journals like *The Nation*. From the late 1870s to the end of the first decade of the twentieth century, Sarah Bernhardt offered real and imaginary excesses out of which drama critics could fashion their own literary performances. These critics could be roughly divided into two schools—those who maintained the pretense of highbrow gentility and refinement, and those who deliberately catered to popular appetites for sensationalism. Devotees of the genteel school of dramatic criticism included Richard Grant White, Walter Prichard Eaton, Amy Leslie, and the moralistic William Winter, better known as "Weeping Willie" because of his penchant for Victorian-style sentimentalizing. At the other end of the spectrum was the Hearst Syndicate's drama critic Alan Dale, a writer whose playfully sensationalistic style of theater criticism helped him achieve the status of celebrity-journalist.[117]

If the drama critic occupied one position within the spectacle-making apparatus of press and stage, another was filled by a new breed of professional journalist called the theatrical press agent. Press agents, many of them former newspaper reporters, worked directly for performers and theatrical producers.[118] In the language of the day, the press agent's job was to "plant" outlandish stories—most of them fake—about a performer, thereby ensuring her visibility. This "essentially American product, this manufacturer of reputations," as drama critic Walter Prichard Eaton labeled the press agent, was in his opinion the real source of "theatrical greatness." As Eaton put it, the stories planted by an inventive press agent could make an actress famous even among those who had "never seen her act."[119]

Press agents also helped promote performers' reputations by setting up what came to be known in journalistic slang as "canned" interviews. Bernhardt became an early and astute practitioner of this publicity strategy, and like many other actresses, she learned by heart predigested scripts of her life story in order to narrate them to reporters who would in turn present them as an intimate behind-the-scenes glimpse of her private life and truthful facts about her career.[120]

Yet not even Sarah "Barnum" could completely control the terms of her own cultural representation. A powerful medium for the reinvention of female identity, the New Journalism was driven by purposes and agendas all its own. Bernhardt herself claimed to have been as much a victim as a beneficiary of "that monster advertisement." Throughout her career she protested "the bad things written against me," complaining that she had scarcely made her theatrical debut before "epigrams, puns, jokes, and caricatures concerning me were indulged in by every one to their heart's content."[121]

Building on the steady stream of Bernhardt's own autobiographical materials, and abetted by the earlier development of the transatlantic cable network which allowed newspaper stories to criss-cross the ocean and circulate among international news agencies, a steady traffic in journalistic Bernhardtiana—all weighing in to delineate the qualities that made Bernhardt "Bernhardt"—became a thriving industry at the end of the nineteenth century.[122] The lady herself had licensed and encouraged this project, and in many respects it was indistinguishable from her own efforts at self-invention and self-publicity. But it also had a life of its own.

An iterative process, which tended to feed on itself, the Bernhardt industry thrived on journalists' desire to exploit the celebrity and exoticism of the eccentric French actress for their own literary theatricals. Drama critics and press agents reaped rich rewards from what might be called the enterprise of describing Bernhardt. It was an enterprise driven by imitation and performance. By paralleling and parodying Bernhardt's pyrotechnics and trading on her legend, journalists created dazzling, spectacular, playful, excessive, and self-reflexive articles designed to secure their own fame and celebrity. Take New York drama critic Alan Dale. In a whimsical article of 1906, he plotted "The Logical Death of Sarah Bernhardt." Dale joked that "Sarah . . . has died in all styles. She has jumped into a river and ended; she has been extinguished by poisons; she has succumbed to tuberculosis; she has been shot to kingdom come. . . . The idea of living happily ever after has invariably been repulsive to her." How would Sarah Bernhardt's own life end, he asked, before he went on to concoct an elaborate fantasy about her "last sensational feat" on stage, a dramatic moment when she would ingest real poison in the last act of a new Sardou play, expiring before her audience.[123] A 1912 satire in the New York *Globe* used her trademark tears as another occasion for journalistic performance. It featured a drawing of Bernhardt with an unruly mass of frizzy hair and huge tear drops streaming from her eyes. Accompanying it was a poem called "Hoo's Hoo":

> Who's done Camille in ev'ry clime from here to Zanzibar, and trickled briny tears enough to float a man o-war? Who did it when our grandma was a lassie blithe and gay? Who'll still be doing it, no doubt, when Baby Doll is gray?. . . . Who slips it o'er in perfect French, assures us that it's art, and hauls our Yankee shekels from the show shop in a cart? Who makes us say, "How wonderful!" and "Mabel, ain't it fine!"—and wonder what it's all about? Why, Bernhardt, the Divine.[124]

If Sarah had encouraged the public to believe that she was an unrepresentative example of her sex, journalists fashioned an entire subindustry dedicated to the whys and wherefores of her bizarre femininity. No topic provided as much mileage as the myth of Bernhardt's eternal youth. The older Bernhardt got, the more journalists would spin out tales of her invincible youthfulness. Increasingly, articles echoed the hyperbolic tone of the 1898 piece in the *New York World* which played upon the 54-year-old actress's "insistent juvenescence" "grewsome [sic]," "eerie," "incomprehensible," and "defiant indifference to time."[125] Like other actresses, Sarah encouraged these stories by giving frequent press interviews about her personal secrets for staying young, and journalists eagerly mined the sensationalist possibilities. Typical was a 1905 article for the *New York Telegram* by reporter Fanny Fair, who claimed that Bernhardt (then in her early sixties) "might be any age or no age at all." This "strange being," whose "entire physical make-up" had "ceased to be governed by the hampering laws of the flesh," seemed like "something super-natural."[126]

Just when it seemed that the mystery of the actress's ageless counte-nance had been thoroughly exploited, journalists invented a dazzling new concept to describe the Divine Sarah: the "Superwoman." Here, re-porters claimed, was the female counterpart to philosopher Friedrich Nietzsche's self-realized individual, the Overman, or Superman. This superwoman, a 1908 article announced, had let neither time nor any man "master her."[127] The "imperishable Sarah" was "never natural," an-other writer maintained. She had "never been just a woman," and could never "be judged as a person or individual by any of the standards to which others are obliged to submit." If any woman "now living" had transcended "the limitations of her sex," it was Bernhardt. The proof was her "uncanny" agelessness, which seemed "a defiance of all laws of nature."[128]

These overwrought articles themselves became the basis for still other kinds of journalistic spectacles. As the actress approached the age of seventy, for example, theater critic George Jean Nathan penned a scath-ing satire of this "frenzied" journalistic "gush" over Bernhardt's ageless-ness. The gush Nathan insisted, had turned the once Divine Sarah into "the Infernal Sally." In his parody of "Sally No. 1" he mimicked the arti-cles that portrayed Bernhardt as an elusive figure with "inexhaustible physical and spiritual resources," a "creature of febrile genius," a "fan-tastical atmospheric individuality," both "overhuman and unreal." In "Sally No. 2" he parodied articles that described a "slender figure, alert . . . dominant, vigorous, full of sap, and verdant . . . Of age—not a ves-tige, not a symptom, not a suspicion. The horror of senility has passed her by." He stopped there, noting only that "Sallies from No. 3 to 297 in-clusive" were constructed by journalists "parading far more colossally riotous adjectives than ever were advocated by Barnum's Circus." While acknowledging that audiences were probably justified in calling her "the most proficient actress of her time," Nathan blasted what he called "this hellish seeking to proclaim youth" in a woman who no longer possessed it. Rejecting the "fanatic idolatry" and "histrionic" tone of mass journal-ism, Nathan the modernist urged his readers to face the facts: Bernhardt was not "divine," as she and the press would have the public believe, but "human." Admittedly, the actress "is still working hard at an age when most women are rheumatic grandmothers, grumbling at their sons-in-law between the slobbers of toothless gums," but it was time to recognize that this "wonderful woman" was nevertheless a "changed woman." If Bernhardt was "a true artist," asked Nathan, why was it still necessary to "parade" her as "a curiosity, as a freak. . .?"[129] Yet as Nathan himself was well aware, that was precisely the point. Bernhardt's vast celebrity and cultural effect was in large measure predicated on her value as a female curiosity, a freak who appeared to defy both the laws of nature and the traditions of culture.

Looking back over her long career as a public figure, Bernhardt recalled in her 1907 memoir that recrimination over her "fits of ill-temper," her caprices, and her eccentricities, and "general freedom in all respects" had contributed to her fame but also created enemies. Her contemporaries complained that "I had caused too much fuss to be made about me." But, she asked rhetorically, "is it my fault if I am too thin? Is it my fault, too, if my hair is too curly, and if I don't think just as other people do?" And then she conceded, in self-analysis, that "there was no happy medium about me; I was 'too much' and 'too little,' and I felt that there was nothing to be done for this."[130]

Yet for all of her protests, Bernhardt was well aware that being both "too much" and "too little"—exceeding and falling short of the expectations placed upon women in her time—were the very qualities that proved to be the source of her cultural power. Her entire career had been devoted to crafting and then magnifying a defiant self who refused to smooth all the edges in order to fit in. Her candor and her unwillingness to play by the rules of feminine comportment provided American women with a compelling example of how a female rebel might successfully invent (and play a starring role in) a new public drama of personal freedom. Other turn-of-the-century women including suffragists and those who would later claim the identity of feminists lived with the stigma of being both too much and too little. It was Bernhardt's genius and those of her contemporaries on the popular stage to turn female eccentricities into commercially viable virtues. It is not surprising to discover, therefore, that "too much/too little" were the critical categories through which the first generation of female comics on the American stage enacted the desires and exposed the dilemmas of modern womanhood.

Mirth and Girth

2   It was almost axiomatic to turn-of-the-century cultural commentators that if women had "a sense of humor," it was qualitatively different from men's. While many were prepared to acknowledge, with French actor Constant Coquelin, that "the sense of humor is universal," they shared his view that the sexes did not find the same things funny, nor could they produce laughter on the same terms. Men liked "jokes" that were "boisterous and broad and rough," Coquelin maintained in a 1901 article; women's more "subtle" sense of humor was "too delicate for the rude touch." Using Sarah Bernhardt as an example (a woman "full" of humor, whose "sense of the ridiculous is most keen," for whom there was "no bit too subtle"), Coquelin brushed aside other aspects of her persona when he argued that "the lighter," the "daintier," and more "gentle" the humor, the more likely it was that it would appeal to a woman. As Coquelin summed up the gendered division of comedy, while females did evince "humor" and "gentle wit," in general "woman does not try to be funny. She leaves that to man."[1] Robert Burdette further analyzed the distinctions. "The masculine perception of humor is largely the enjoyment of buffoonery," he wrote. What made men laugh was "horse-play," "grotesque" spectacle, and "a shade of brutality." Women's "appreciation of humor," on the other hand, "is far more refined." If brutality "shocks her," Burdette reasoned, it is because she delights in "true humor"—"delicate, sympathetic, refined to the highest culture."[2]

Turn-of-the-century commentators like Coquelin and Burdette had complicated reasons for believing that humor was part of the masculine sphere. Although women had long contributed to various forms of literary humor and had acted comic roles in melodramas and plays on the

40

nineteenth-century stage, females were still viewed largely as the targets rather than the creators of comedy.[3]

In the 1890s, however, that was beginning to change. As an influential group of women in musical comedy and vaudeville challenged the assumption that comedy was a male domain, the right to be funny gained increasing cultural legitimacy and eventually became an item on the emerging feminist agenda. As female performers became active participants in framing and performing comic materials on stage, they found new ways to call attention to themselves and to comment on the world around them. Yet even as comedy provided women with new forms of cultural authority, females as such remained an important source of comic grist. Moreover, while humor enlarged women's cultural sphere, female performers did not necessarily use it to further other kinds of change. On the contrary, while the forms of women's comedic expression on stage were radical, the politics of the comedians could just as often be conservative.

The movement of female performers into the comic sphere needs to be understood in the context of a general shift in comic practices in the years after 1890, a period when observers began to distinguish between new and traditional forms of stage comedy. At the turn of the century audiences for popular theater came to watch the so-called New Humor, a visceral, fast-paced, direct, physically demonstrative and sometimes violent style of comedy. In contrast to more cerebral, thoughtful, and didactic forms of narrative humor, the new humor created joking and laughter for its own sake. Most important, unlike some older forms of comedy, the jokes, gags, bits, and routines of the new humor exposed social and cultural anxieties and incongruities without necessarily offering any moral resolution.[4]

What contemporary observers singled out as particularly representative and alarming about popular stage comedy was its appeal to the senses over the intellect, an appeal that relied upon emotional release through physical violence and sexual innuendo. Violence in particular became a hallmark of vaudeville comedy. In 1912, for example, the Jewish immigrant comedy team of Joe Weber and Lew Fields provided an analysis of what they called "stage business," meaning the physical gestures and simulations of popular comedy. Weber and Fields echoed the common belief that "the greatest laughter, the greatest comedy, is divided by a hair from the greatest tragedy." The popularity of rough physical comedy or "slapstick" derived from what they called "spectacles" of physical pain (for example, "when a man sticks one finger into another man's eye"), minus the actual injury. So long as people could be assured that the "object of the attacks" was not really hurt, they would "scream with mirth" to watch someone who "might have been hurt badly, but wasn't." Similarly, comedian George M. Cohan argued in an article for *McClure's Magazine* in 1913 that "the most successful tricks or jokes are all based on the *idea* [as opposed to the reality] of pain or embarrassment."[5]

Yet the newness of the new humor was relative. Studies of the carnival tradition in European comedy, the American minstrel stage, and more general patterns of nineteenth-century humor suggest that the themes of violence and sexuality had long been a staple of popular comedy.[6] The slapstick "business," a central element of low comedy in this period, was part of a hybrid mixture of comic practices on the popular stage. This entertainment blended "knockabout" humor with romantic plots, parody, satire, minstrelsy, ethnic caricature, and topical jokes, which themselves relied upon the use of excess, exaggeration, and comic incongruity. By the beginning of the new century, Broadway musical comedies and revues produced by George M. Cohan, Florenz Ziegfeld Jr., and the Shubert brothers combined slapstick with topical humor that lampooned the fads, foibles, and social questions of the day and created hilarious parodies of contemporary plays and operas. Vaudeville comedy ran the gamut from slapstick to topical humor that reflected on contemporary social issues. When Brett Page published his 1915 instruction book entitled *Writing for Vaudeville,* he listed as topics of "universal interest": politics, love, marriage, women's dress, woman suffrage, drink, baseball, and money.[7] These themes were explored in songs, jokes, conversations, and narrative "sketches" performed as comic monologues, and as "two-acts" between two men, a man and a woman, or two women. Even more than skits and joke-telling, song was considered a particularly effective mode of communicating topical humor on the popular stage. As Jean Havez and Leo Donnelly put it in their 1912 article on the craft of vaudeville comedy writing, the American "public will laugh heartily at a joke . . . when used in a song, when they would sit in stony silence if the same bit of fun were told them in the form of dialogue narrative,"[8] a fact that women comics were quick to exploit.

Although popular comedy at the turn of the century was but a hybrid mixture of old and new forms, several things had changed by then. First, as film historian Henry Jenkins points out, it was not so much the form that changed as the availability and popularity of comic materials that lay outside older traditions of morally refined and uplifting humor. A "massive proliferation of comic materials" threatened to undermine traditional standards of self-restrained bourgeois decorum.[9] Second, the shifting landscape of humor was closely intertwined with other kinds of changes that stirred up cultural and social anxieties. While older forms of cerebral, moralistic, and thoughtful humor were associated with the supposedly more refined and edifying sensibilities of Protestant middle-class values and the so-called genteel traditions of literary comedy, the new emotional styles of low or broad and unrestrained comedy were viewed as products of the working classes, the new immigrant masses, and African Americans, all of whom, it was believed, laughed mainly at what shocked and surprised their nervous systems.[10]

Women tended to fall between the cracks of this alleged divide between old and new humor. On the one hand, the supposedly well-developed moral, spiritual, and sympathetic capacities of women seemed to make them unfit for the sometimes crude physicality and raucous sexual innuendoes of modern joking. "Measured by the ordinary standards of humor," Boston critic Charles Young insisted in 1909, woman "is about as comical as a crutch." As Young saw it, "real comedy" was a "masculine trait."[11] From the perspective of some middle-class moralizers this was just as well, since a woman's status as a respectable female or lady was jeopardized by her participation in the unsubtle and excessive joking that increasingly dominated the popular stage. Moreover, as men's alleged intellectual inferiors, women supposedly lacked the capacity to cast a critical eye on their own cultural moment, which was the traditional province of humorists. The female comic who uses satire, irony, and other forms of social criticism to poke fun at contemporary values and mores has historically been seen as a transgressor of women's traditional stance of social and intellectual subordination.[12] Dorothy Parker pointed out that for the humorist "there must be courage, . . . a disciplined eye and a wild mind." And there must be "no awe," for humor is "encapsulated in criticism."[13]

Well before Parker joined the ranks of female humorists in the 1920s, some of these ideas had already occurred to members of the burgeoning feminist movement, who began to see in the production of comedy an important basis for women's social equality. "Woman," feminist literary humorist Helen Rowland asserted, had been man's "Great Original Joke." And women's shortcomings, including their allegedly inferior sense of humor, were ever the target of men's jests. In a 1911 article called "The Emancipation of 'The Rib'," she set out to show that "woman now shares equal honors with man in seeing a joke and sometimes sees it first," and this, she insisted, "has done more to bring about the equality of the sexes and their mutual understanding than any thing else, from coeducation to the suffrage movement." Women came into their own as humorists, Rowland declared, when they discovered that "Man" could be a source of laughter too. Yet she also felt compelled to issue some words of caution: "the wise woman laughs with a man just a little oftener than she laughs at him." For "the girl who tries to be brilliant and 'funny' at all costs . . . is apt to be even more unpopular than the woman who is never witty." Though Rowland echoed the contemporary belief that the "quality" of women's humor differed from men's in its tendency to be "more delicate, keen edged, and finely pointed than that of the lord of creation," she nevertheless stressed the growing social acceptance of the funny woman. "Woman" was "no longer Man's plaything, but his playmate," and, she concluded, with premature optimism, "now that they can *laugh together,* the great 'War of the Sexes' is at an end."[14]

In point of fact women's appreciation of jokes and their production of humor was part and parcel of the gender tensions of the era. And what Rowland called the War of the Sexes was itself a major focus of early twentieth century humor—from the anti-suffrage cartoons that issued forth in the daily press, to the monologues and skits of the popular theater—where women, New and Old, were the butts of comedy. Rather than resolving the growing tensions surrounding women's roles outside the theater, women's entrance into the ranks of professional stage humorists only served to magnify them. Even the most successful and best-paid female comics understood that their own ability to break into a world dominated by men did not necessarily reflect or guarantee a widespread acceptance of female equality as a social principle. In a 1912 article in *Green Book Magazine,* for example, the popular stage comic May Irwin still felt compelled to assert that "woman's sphere is the same as man's." "Woman," Irwin admonished, "need not be confined to a little piece of it called home"; "woman isn't trying to be a man . . . she's trying to get herself and man to stop thinking she's just a piece of household machinery."[15]

Yet Irwin's own career testified that Rowland was correct in other respects. Not only did increasing numbers of women display their desire and capacity to produce laughter, but, as Rowland put it, "Woman's wit is selling at par" with men's. This "emancipation of the rib" had permitted female comics to move beyond mouthing "witty or stupid lines, just as they are written," and opened up the possibilities for "original interpolations and interpretations." America, she observed, "is full of professional woman 'wits' and humorists; woman cynics, woman satirists, woman pessimists, and woman optimists, all of them wide awake . . . and most convincing, *well paid*." Among them she cited newspaper and magazine journalists, like columnist Dorothy Dix, successful playwrights like Margaret Mayo, and "modern" stage "comediennes" like Marie Dressler and May Irwin.[16]

"A New Sphere for Stage Women"

On the turn-of-the-century stage, women, though still the targets of comedy, were increasingly becoming the active agents of laughter, and categories like the "girl comedian" and the "funny lady" were entering the American cultural vocabulary. By the summer of 1902 the shift was clearly visible. As one writer summed it up, "The day of the comic actress has dawned. She is now the essential thing." The development had important implications for concepts of gender, since, as this writer put it, "'comedian' girls" had "jump[ed] to the front," thereby demonstrating that the business of comedy had become what he called "a New Sphere for Stage Women."[17] While there was no shortage of "male funmakers," women's comedic status had altered dramatically.

Claiming that "the male comedian's day is over" and "Broadway is under the spell of the girl comedian," another observer insisted that "while heretofore the women in the casts of farcical productions have had to look prim and pretty and be satisfied with that, . . . nowadays they . . . furnish food for risibility." In the past "we said to ourself [sic] that women seldom have a sense of humor. And we looked over our list of comediennes and counted them on the fingers of one hand easily. There were May Irwin, Marie Dressler and Marie Cahill . . . But with the demand came the supply. The funny girl has arrived."[18]

The funny girl was most often seen in two theatrical venues: vaudeville and musical comedy. Typically, a turn-of-the-century vaudeville show had at least nine different and unrelated acts or "turns," each from fifteen to thirty minutes in length. A standard vaudeville bill usually featured at least one woman in a solo comedy act. Often she was a singing comedian, who also may have performed dance numbers, comic imper-sonations, or parodies. In between her singing and dancing numbers the solo female comic would sometimes address the audience directly, giv-ing brief "impromptu" monologues which extended the topical materi-als from her songs. In addition to the solo acts, there were male-female comedy teams, "sister" acts, or female duos. Many of these teams per-formed both song-and-dance numbers and topical joke routines. Some of the same funny women who did solo routines in vaudeville also played in full-length musical comedies, where they typically took the role of the "soubrette." The soubrette, in contrast to the more staid ro-mantic heroine, was often a saucy maid-servant who sometimes ca-vorted about the stage in revealing tights.[19]

Whether they performed before the large urban cross-section that at-tended vaudeville shows or the middle- and upper-class audiences for musical comedy, these "newcomers in grotesquerie," as the rising gener-ation of funny women was labeled, adopted the posture of the female ec-centric. Like the serious dramatic actress Sarah Bernhardt, these adven-turous women won their claims to fame by going overboard, violating gender norms through their excessiveness. As one theater critic put it, with the "flurry of their dances," the "strenuousness of their music," their tremendous displays of physical energy, and their "insinuating appeals to the senses," these "clever women do not hesitate to sacrifice all of the vanities of their sex—looks and grace—to evoke laughter from their audience."[20] Musical comedy star Marie Dressler, another critic observed, "frankly abandons any ambition to be pretty or even attrac-tive. The ludicrous is her aim, and in that object there is no sacrifice too great for her."[21] A reviewer for *Variety* who described the "character songs" of vaudeville singer Nellie Wallace, a British comic appearing in New York in 1908, made a similar point about the "grotesque" comic ef-fects in which "she sacrifices all attractiveness of appearance." Wallace's comic "business," he wrote, "is to make her audiences laugh at any cost."[22]

Exactly how Wallace went about enduring such a sacrifice is not alto-gether clear. Yet the descriptions of the stage work of many other female comics of this era suggests how concepts of attractiveness and notions of the grotesque together defined what was funny about the funny woman.

Excess has historically been an important element in popular comedy. Too-muchness—too much fat, too much noise, too much physicality, too much political or worldly ambition, too much of whatever exceeds the normative standards of femininity—has provided the comic grist in many different societies.[23] It is not surprising therefore to find that what might be called "cultural girth" was a central element in the popular theater. Yet if grotesque too-muchness has long been and remains to this day an important tool of the comedian's craft, helping to create comic tension by transgressing the standards of acceptable behavior and comportment, the specifics vary with the times and the historical context. In turn-of-the-century American stage comedy, girth encompassed various kinds of physical and verbal excess: boisterousness, physical violence, ethnic and racial caricatures, and especially, though by no means exclusively for women, excess body weight. The use of terms like "grotesque," "uncouth," and "strenuous" to describe female comic girth in this period, and the accompanying claims that such behavior constituted a sacrifice of beauty, looks, and grace, signaled an acute awareness of the ways funny women on stage, like New Women off-stage, disturbed cultural expectations about the feminine.

At the same time, however, the so-called pretty woman remained a central fixture of the modern stage. If anything, the funny girl arrived on the scene at precisely the moment when beauty was becoming something of a cult in the world of popular entertainment.[24] As an article in *Cosmopolitan* declared in 1893, "ours is the country of the Stage Beauty." The "might of a fair face" was "so great that the happy owner conquers managers, triumphs over critics and wins the golden favor of the public, even though her histrionic abilities are of the slenderest."[25] A melodious singing voice, a fine sense of rhythm, a talent for dance and movement, a strong dramatic presence were requisites for stage work, but by the turn of the century something called "beauty" was practically a form of talent, an aspect of feminine presence as highly prized as any other quality a woman might bring to the stage. Or as historian Faye Dudden puts it, "physical appearance, with or without a modicum of talent, became a kind of capital." Those who did not measure up to prevailing standards of looks could only hope to compensate by donning the latest in fashionable clothing.[26]

At this time both the stage and press were filled with images of beautiful women—young and Anglo-Saxon (or appearing to be). The spread of photography made this the era of the "camera celebrity," as *Broadway Magazine* called her in 1902—the pretty woman whose face was more "widely photographed than anyone else."[27] Illustrators produced

(Charles Dana) "Gibson girls," (Howard Chandler) "Christy girls," (Nell) "Brinkley girls," (James Montgomery) "Flagg beauties." Sunday newspaper supplements and glossy theater magazines featured artists' models, chorus girls with bare shoulders, and richly attired leading ladies. These beauties greeted the spectator with inviting smiles or demure glances, self-confident stateliness or haughty splendor. And actresses, only too happy to reap the publicity benefits, freely dispensed advice on beauty secrets, dress, and diet, or lent their names to perfume and cosmetics lines.[28]

As a form of aesthetic spectacle, female beauty took many forms in turn-of-the-century commercial culture, but nowhere was it more lavishly displayed than in Broadway musical comedies and revues. Musical comedies always featured one or more beautiful romantic heroines as well as comely chorus girls. It was also the period when vaudeville, with its emphasis on family-style performances suitable for women and children, began to feature "girl" acts with ensembles of chorus performers. At the same time rival vaudeville houses held contests to decide which had "secured the most beautiful woman for next week's bill."[29] But the apotheosis came in musical revues where beautiful girls collectively danced, paraded, posed, and sang in the elaborately engineered beauty pageant known as the Broadway chorus number, a form of female spectacle most closely associated with the Ziegfeld *Follies*.

Yet even in Broadway girl spectacles, beauty and comedy together defined and structured the evening's entertainment. As Florenz Ziegfeld, Jr. himself put it in 1911, audiences expected "girls and laughter." Whatever else it provided, a good show has "got to amuse. It simply has to make you laugh."[30] The exact proportion of comedy to beautiful girls varied from show to show and shifted with the times. Before about 1914 comedy kept pace with girls in the Broadway musical revue. After that, the growing emphasis on the display of female beauty tended to overshadow the laughter in spectacular Broadway revues like the *Follies,* and theater critics complained in almost ritualistic fashion about the absence of good comedy. As one writer for the *New York Times* remarked in 1922, "it is customary when the '*Follies*' comes to town to utter loud rejoicing over its beauties, which nearly always manage to be more striking than ever before, and to lament just a little the paucity of the extremely humorous."[31]

In the two decades before the First World War, however, "the extremely humorous" was as much a part of Broadway musical entertainments as was female beauty. And it was the growing visibility of both funny women and stage beauties in vaudeville and musical theater that contemporary critics found especially significant and worthy of extended comment. Far from spelling the demise of what one theater critic in 1902 called "the eternal feminine," the rise of the female comedian expanded the spectrum of possibilities for stage women. "The girl shows are more so than ever," said the writer, "but to the singing girls, the dancing girls, the posing girls, the revealing girls, the alluring girls, there has been added the comedian girl."[32] Significantly, the writer used a double noun, pairing the masculine "comedian" and feminine "girl" to emphasize the gender transgressions implied in this addition. In many respects, then, the very presence of stage beauties—whether chorus girls or romantic heroines—shaped the frames of funny women's comic personae. Though nobody denied that a beautiful woman might perform humorous material, to be truly funny a woman would have to be either unattractive (excessive) to begin with or be willing to sacrifice her beauty and other feminine attributes in the service of laughter.[33] Between these two poles—the idealization of the beautiful (read young and white) woman on the one hand, and the performance of what contemporaries called grotesquerie (comedic excess) on the other—funny women made their way into contemporary stage humor, and by extension probed the relationship between comedy and femininity in their own time. Not just gender roles but sexuality itself was at the nexus of that relationship. Playing with the grotesque and the beautiful, funny women articulated their period's cultural nervousness about the lines between permissible and forbidden desire.

The Color of Humor

Ethnicity and race were critical elements in female comedic "sacrifice." In an era when the color line became firmly established not only as a Southern but an American cultural divide, and a massive influx of immigrants flooded the cities, a whole generation of comics in vaudeville and musical theater relied upon racial and ethnic stereotypes.[34] But the material was not evenly divided among men and women. Ethnic humor, which caricatured working class and upwardly mobile Jewish, Irish, and German (called "Dutch") immigrants, provided what was arguably the most important element in the vaudeville routines of male comics. Women comics most commonly used black/white racial references or more generalized images of exotic foreignness rather than group-specific caricatures of immigrant ethnicity to express cultural excess— the few exceptions being the Irish immigrant sketches of the Elinore Sisters (Kate and May) and the Jewish caricatures of Fanny Brice and Sophie Tucker.

The singing and "shouting" of so-called coon songs performed with ragtime piano accompaniments pervaded vaudeville and musical theater. The term "coon" was a racial slur referring to African Americans. And after the turn of the century, as an editor for the *Indianapolis Freeman* complained in 1909, "the air was rank with 'coon' songs. Every song of Southern melody or ragtime was titled a 'coon song.'" Though by this time, noted the writer, the trend was gradually dying out because "the words 'coon,' 'nigger' and 'darkey' are now being omitted by song writers," the "great damage" done by the insulting language of these songs—songs written by both white and black composers—persisted well into the twentieth century.[35]

Given the proliferation and popularity of racial and ethnic humor, it was no accident that funny women participated in it. Not only was it the sine qua non of the Tin Pan Alley lyrics mass-produced by black, immigrant, and native white tunesmiths, but it practically defined the nature of vaudeville stage comedy. In many respects this reflected the process by which the commercial music industry and the popular theater absorbed and reconstituted nineteenth-century minstrel stage stereotypes and traditions. As the performers and music migrated to vaudeville and musical theater in the years after 1890, and as increasing numbers of African American songwriters and performers contributed to the creation of mainstream American popular culture, the racial idioms of the minstrel stage were appropriated for new purposes by the New Women of the popular theater.[36]

Theater management was also defined and guided by considerations of race. Theaters that catered to mixed race audiences restricted black patrons to the cheap and less desirable seats up in the gallery. Performance conventions were also governed by racial criteria. While African American performers were not permitted to look white and were discouraged from presenting themselves as racially ambiguous, white women and men freely participated in a variety of racial disguises. Moreover, while the vaudeville stage made room for a seemingly unlimited range of white performers, white vaudeville audiences and theater managers usually insisted that black performers limit themselves to comedy and to so-called plantation-style dancing.[37] As one reviewer for *Variety* put it with uncharacteristic empathy in 1907: "the American public refuses to take the colored race seriously as entertainers. It wants them with a dash of comedy and consistently refuses to accept them in any guise than the jester's motley."[38] That did not mean, however, that African American performers always adhered to the formula. On the contrary, singers, dancers, and actors of both sexes struggled to transcend the discriminatory line of proscribed racial roles in the theater, taking advantage of the very limited opportunities available to them in the world of serious culture, including realistic drama.[39]

Within popular theater's racial parameters at the turn of the century, white women freely reworked conventions of American minstrelsy. Black female images could be used to summon a range of comedic intentions. In a nation that still lived with the legacies of slavery's combination of economic and sexual exploitation, black women remained symbols of illicit white sexual desire. African Americans as a group (like Eastern and Southern European immigrants, allegedly over-fecund because they could not sublimate their sexual urges) were stereotyped as sexual suspects—libidinous, carnal, and generally disrespectful of the bodily controls that were supposed to (but did not always) govern bourgeois white society. The sexual was only one aspect of racial and ethnic humor. In a more general sense, many white people assumed that African Americans were by definition unacceptable and therefore funny. Hence laughter and its underlying pathos could be mobilized by the performance of racial stereotypes—ranging from the vicious to the lascivious to the sentimental—and by the use of syntax and idioms that came to stand for African American cultural roots.

With and without blackface makeup, white female comics performed songs or dances that caricatured African Americans. Perhaps no other turn-of-the-century female comic was as closely associated with the coon song idiom as May Irwin. A "brighter, wittier, and noisier entertainer could hardly be asked by even longshoremen, politicians, and schoolboys," wrote Chicago critic Amy Leslie in 1899 of Irwin's "darky music and rough colloquial comedy." Irwin perfected what Leslie called "conversational entertainment." She "comes out and takes her audience into her confidence, tips a daring wink to the knowing, and 'plays horse' with the ingenuous. . . . She has reduced the art of intimacy with an audience to so exact a science," Leslie observed, that "every point" in her plays seemed to be "an impromptu." Because of Irwin's success, "darkies grew to be the rage, and imitative white soubrettes copied Irwin's [black] wench walk awkwardly" until the "entire army of song-and-dance women was limping bowlegged about the stage in something bordering on locomotor ataxia, producing the effect of an epidemic hip disease."[40]

Irwin was perfectly at home singing songs like Ernest Hogan's controversial "All Coons Look Alike to Me," which she featured in her 1896 musical comedy, *Courted into Court*.[41] But by 1904 Irwin had fully adapted to what one article called the changing fashions in this genre. Her "neat coon song[s]" created a "certain restrained atmosphere" that appealed to the supposedly refined sensibilities of musical comedy audiences. But she also played to patrons who appreciated the rougher verses of her old-time hits—"strenuous" and "loudmouthed" songs like "Dat Bully," and "Crappy Dan," with their topical focus on gambling and violence.[42] The combination of violent masculine imagery of some of her songs ("Dat Bully") and the feigned sentimentality of others ("Ma Sweetest Girl") allowed her to play the bulky aggressiveness of her physique against good-natured mammy-like friendliness; this androgynous mix, as historian Alison Kibler describes it, defined Irwin's comic persona.[43]

Although most white female comics performed racially inflected material without the use of blackface makeup, a minority assumed the entire costume of racial caricature. By the late 1880s at least sixteen white male-female comedy teams appeared in blackface routines in New York City vaudeville theaters, where they presented "grotesque" dances and "eccentric" caricatures.[44] Women occasionally performed solo comedy acts in blackface as well. Among the most famous was the Jewish immigrant who came to be known variously as the "World-renowned Coon Shouter," "Manipulator of Coon Melodies," or "Refined Coon Shouter"—Sophie Tucker. Many years later, in an effort to justify what had by then become an embarrassment to her, Tucker claimed she had been compelled to take up that role. In what is by now a legendary bit of American theater history, Tucker reported in her 1946 autobiography that Chris Brown, manager of the 125th Street Theatre in Harlem where she got her start at an amateur night audition, forced her to use blackface: he told her she was "too big and ugly" to perform without a racial mask. With face and neck blackened, and wearing white gloves, a red bandanna, and lipstick that outlined what she called "a grotesque grinning mouth," Tucker made her mark in small-time vaudeville. Later her look evolved from "high yellow" to what she called "perfect black" makeup and a black wig. Audiences, Tucker recalled, would "gasp" and then "howl" with laughter when, at the end of each performance, she peeled off one of her gloves and waved her hand in the air, "to show I was a white girl."[45]

Several issues are of interest here. The first is Tucker's claim that managers and agents insisted she needed to disguise her allegedly "too big" body and "too ugly" face behind the mask of minstrelsy. Rather than liabilities, however, such forms of girth were considered assets for the funny woman. The rotund female body had a venerable place in American comedic tradition. Voluptuous bulk was *de rigueur* for the scores of female minstrel and burlesque troupes that reached the height of their popularity at the end of the nineteenth century, among them the two-hundred pound women who performed in W. B. (Billy) Watson's legendary all-female troupe, the "Beef Trust."[46] The second issue is that even after Tucker abandoned her burnt-cork disguise and reappeared as the hypersexual "red hot mama" of the New York nightclub scene, she continued to sing in what one historian calls "blackvoice," performing in the same Southern accent she learned for her blackface act, and adding an occasional Yiddish word or phrase to provide an extra "kick."[47] All of Tucker's physical and vocal props—her ample size, her fake Southern black accent, the Yiddishisms that marked her as an immigrant outsider, her blatant use of sexual innuendoes, and in the earlier part of her career, the minstrel-style make-up—were forms of female excess or girth that functioned like a set of cultural codes on the popular stage. Any one of these symbols could be mobilized for laughing purposes, packaged together, they were an especially potent mix.

Tucker's "fat" and "ugly" presence aside, it was not only overweight and unlovely female comics who incorporated racist materials. So did stage beauties like Lillian Russell and Anna Held, whose efforts at humor relied in some measure on racial and ethnic material.[48] Examining the ways in which attractive white women used race shows even more clearly how female comedy played in the interstices between the beautiful and the grotesque and suggests that in the late nineteenth and early twentieth centuries both racialized and lower-class figures remained powerful symbols in what one historian describes as the "thrilling and repellent sexuality" of middle-class fantasy.[49] White fantasies and fears about the sexual excesses of African Americans (and other ethnic groups) did make these figures subversively erotic, at least in the safe space of the theater.

Lillian Russell and Anna Held are good examples of how glamorous white women increased their sexual naughtiness and their comedic breadth by performing racial material. Russell, the graceful and elegant ideal of "Anglo-Saxon" female perfection and American artistry, was called "a self-evident example of American loveliness in its most beautiful form." Her starring role in Gustave Kerker's 1896 comic opera, *An American Beauty,* only confirmed her public image as the representative of true American womanliness.[50] However, Russell's theatrical persona as stage beauty and emancipated woman-about-town took on another dimension in 1899, when at age 38 the shapely, now somewhat overweight star joined the popular "Dutch" (German) dialect team of Weber & Fields and the famous "Hebrew" comedian David Warfield in a musical comedy burlesque called *Whirl-i-Gig.*[51] Using low comedy slapstick techniques and incorporating minstrel-style melodies and songs, this and other Weber & Fields shows parodied and satirized the dramas and operettas that were currently playing at Broadway theaters, adding contemporary topical humor to create hilarious send-ups of upper-class taste and pretension.[52]

To the surprise of the critics, Russell the diva demonstrated a previously untapped talent for low comedy, making what one reviewer called the "descent" from art into "grotesquerie."[53] A crucial aspect of the American beauty's comedic descent was her willingness to play with blackness.[54] A publicity story by Nora Donley entitled "Lillian Russell Sings Coon Songs in New Burlesque" suggests how much the element of comic surprise or shock of her role in *Whirl-i-Gig* derived from the idea of a lovely (and beloved) white beauty singing in a low comedy black idiom. "Will May Irwin Be Jealous of the Golden American Beauty?" asked the writer, who quoted Russell's claim that she would learn coon singing not from Irwin but by visiting Thompson Street "to see just how the darkies act." But then, as if to reassure readers that this was still the same old Lillian Russell, Donley discussed the singer's intention to return to operas and described the hyper-femininity of her dressing room, where the walls "hung with much pink silk lingerie," as "pink is the pretty woman's favorite color."[55]

The juxtaposition of white beauty and racial excess also gave a comedic edge to the song and dance routines of Florenz Ziegfeld's prototypical stage beauty, the pert Parisian music hall performer Anna Held.[56] In 1896, the year that Held arrived from Europe to star in one of Ziegfeld's musical shows, a writer in *Vogue* described her as "a petite, winsome, girlish figure, a charming fairy-like creature" with "all the artlessness of a child combined with great cleverness."[57] Held, the daughter of Polish Jews who had emigrated to Paris, had a voluptuous figure, sultry eyes, and a heavy French accent that created an illusion of Parisian naughtiness. Her singing voice was unremarkable, and her acting talents unproven. But she reaped the benefits of Ziegfeld's talented press agents who, capitalizing on the public's thirst for sensation, manufactured titillating stories about Held's extravagant lifestyle, including her taste for bathing in milk.[58]

Held knew how to appeal to the tastes of people who thought it was humorous to watch and listen to a French woman with a poor command of English perform in what was arguably the most American of all cultural forms, coon songs and cakewalks.[59] She sang "I Want Dem Presents Back" in a heavy Gallic accent against the backdrop of what was called an "animated song sheet." This prop, which would become increasingly popular among female and male coon singers, was described as a "huge reproduction of the vocal score of the chorus, with both words and music, but where each note should have been there protruded the woolly head of a negro chorister—thirty-three in all—who at a signal from Miss Held, burst into the chorus of the song."[60] This kind of racist humor was hardly immune from the critical commentary of African American musical theater. Held herself was lampooned in Bob Cole and Billy Johnson's turn-of-the-century musical comedy, *A Trip to Coontown*, whose satirical song "In Dahomey" ("the only place on earth where all coons look alike") contained references to the saucy French "coon singer" taking photographs of "amusing natives."[61]

But Held was not dissuaded. On the contrary, her subsequent stage work in Broadway musical comedy increasingly stressed race-inflected comic songs and dances, none perhaps as crude as a number called "The Charcoal Seller," a routine she performed in the 1904 Weber and Ziegfeld production, *Higgledy-Piggledy*. A publicity photograph shows the winsome figure with her upper body encased in a wicker basket. Suspended from the front of the basket was a grotesque life-sized mannequin of a black man's upper body: head, torso, and arms. The visual effect made it seem as if two bodies, joined at the waist, were supported by one set of legs. The two merged figures require the viewer to consider the sexual implications of such a union of opposites.[62]

Whether combined with beauty, fat, sexual suggestiveness, or Jewishness, blackface and, more commonly, blackvoice defined the terms of American popular comedy well into the twentieth century. Yet the three themes of excess—sexual innuendo, blackness, and fat—could also stand separately as comedic agents. And in the first decade of the twentieth century, fat in particular took on a life of its own among women's comic strategies.

The Size and Aggressiveness of Humor

Of all the female problems, none was more readily embraced as comic material than the overweight woman's body. The overweight woman was a sight gag: her portly figure the topic of her own self-referential jokes and songs and the explanation for her comic instincts and abilities. After the turn of the century the cult of slenderness replaced voluptuousness as the mark of fashionable beauty. Slim was now the most desirable body type, whether for a chorus girl in the musical theater or the beautiful leading lady on the dramatic stage. Popular wisdom admonished that the beautiful woman was never fat. The rage for dieting and reducing of the female population at large was reflected in the pages of the popular magazines and journals of the day.[63]

Fat provided both the costume and the comic persona of a number of funny women. By the opening years of the twentieth century the most important comic headliners, among them May Irwin (b. 1862), Fay Templeton (b. 1866), Marie Dressler (b. 1869), and Trixie Friganza (b. 1870), all of them in their late thirties and early forties and all of them living through the historical transition to a new standard of female beauty, used their excess weight as visual and verbal sources of comedy.[64] Although "it is not requisite to an expression of humor," one critic observed in 1902, Trixie Friganza "thinks she must allow herself to become stout to be a genuine comedienne."[65] Her signature tune, "Nobody Loves a Fat Girl," and Marie Dressler's theme song, "A Great Big Girl Like Me," deliberately drew attention to their unfashionable girth.

Marie Dressler's comic identity rested in part upon her ample figure and in part upon her self-advertised ugliness. A large woman prone to heaviness (her five foot seven inch frame sometimes carried as much as

220 pounds), Dressler deliberately cultivated the appearance of awkwardness and unattractiveness.[66] Acknowledging in her autobiography that "the first requisite for a woman's success" on the stage "is supposed to be a face that's easy on the eyes," she announced that her own career as a stage comic prospered by virtue of the fact that "I was born homely" and "serious."[67] In a 1910 interview, Dressler argued that women were "natural comediennes," but were so vain that their talent was never allowed to develop. Several women currently performing in New York "could get right to the top in the comedy line if they would only stop trying to look pretty and to act funny at the same time," she claimed, but "dignity and comedy cannot go hand in hand."[68]

Dressler is best remembered for her comic tour de force as the fat and pathetic "boarding house drudge" Tillie Blobbs in the 1910 musical comedy, *Tillie's Nightmare*. Subtitled "A Melange of Mirth and Melody in Three Acts," it was also the basis for Dressler's popular "Tillie" films released between 1914 and 1917.[69] Slaving away in the kitchen to help support her tyrannical mother and beautiful sister, the homely and downtrodden Tillie falls asleep and dreams she marries a millionaire with a yacht. In the dream the seasick bride is thrown overboard as excess ballast. Throughout the production Dressler showed her talent for what one reviewer called "lumbering around like a battery of elephant-drawn artillery."[70] At one point she performs burlesque imitations of Sarah Bernhardt, opera singer Luisa Tetrazzini, and the "poetry dances" of Maud Allan; eventually she herself becomes the prima donna of a comic opera troupe.[71]

Dressler's Tillie grew out of her earlier career in turn-of-the-century Broadway musical comedies, where she honed her signature character—the clumsy, boisterous, oversized woman whose proportions and powerful physicality were magnified by the beautiful and slender young women who sang and danced in the chorus numbers. In the role of Dottie Dimple in an 1898 San Francisco run of a musical comedy called *Courted into Court,* she made a spectacle of her homeliness, "contort[ing] her face until it looks like the wattles of a turkey gobbler in a rage and . . . sway[ing] her huge frame about until she falls into all sorts of awkwardness."[72] In 1904 she joined the cast of *Higgledy-Piggledy,* a musical comedy about nouveau-riche immigrants. Dressler played Phillopena Schnitz, a "big, awkward, bashful, but muscular girl"[73] whose father (played by the short and rotund Joe Weber) was a social-climbing millionaire.[74] Though the show featured a chorus of "the handsomest, most stunning and statuesque set of girls that ever swarmed . . . this little stage," it was Dressler who stole the show with self-deprecating songs sung in a voice that sounded, as one reviewer put it, "like an ocean-going freighter in distress."[75]

What distinguished Dressler from other "fat" women comics was her tough physicality and athleticism, qualities which many observers associated with masculinity. Dressler used her whole body—arms, legs, face, and voice—to create her rough-and-tumble scenes.[76] Sizing up the "virility" and "masculine" strength of Dressler's comedic style, an admiring reviewer wrote that while she was "feminine enough by the natural limitations, her grip of the comic is masculine in its strength.. . .She will fall over a small man and utterly crush him. She can do it. Both vociferous and muscular, she goes through contortions of the most violent kind."[77] Chicago critic Amy Leslie, who found Dressler's aggressive physicality "irresistible" and "amazing," claimed that this "rowdy" comic "knows nothing of delicacy or taste; she calls a spade a spade with the courage of a bad boy."[78]

The "bad boy" physicality of Dressler's stage work was especially evident in the 1906 Weber & Fields show *Twiddle-Twaddle*. There, as one critic put it, an "athletic and ebullient" Dressler used sheer physical prowess to command center stage, plunging through her scenes "like a wild-cat locomotive or a star full-back."[79] In one scene, Dressler—playing the daughter of a millionaire sausage manufacturer whose father was trying to marry her off to a European nobleman—picked up her father (Weber) by the nape of his neck, tucked him under her arm, threw him over her shoulder, and finally laid him over her lap for a spanking. The hilarity of this scene was matched only by Dressler's travesty of a Spanish Fandango dance, in which she swung her ample hips from side to side, hitting Weber and comedian Charley Bigelow in a way that made them look "like rubber balls batted with a sledgehammer."[80]

By the outbreak of World War I, audiences were willing to see the funny woman's willingness to sacrifice her femininity as a form of artistic virtue. Watching the 1914 Broadway comedy called *A Mix-Up*, a New York critic found it "astonishing" how much physical activity Dressler could produce in a single evening: "Here is a big woman who is not afraid to tumble over sofas, crawl along the floor on her hands and knees, dash around in a manner that would tire a trained athlete, sing, dance, create roars of laughter by her facial expressions and then, now and again, strike a note of pathos that is worthy of a great actress."[81]

Still, a degree of uneasiness persisted about the facility with which women played within the conventions of the male comic sphere. Two years earlier, "travesty queen" Trixie Friganza had felt compelled to defend the "big fat black and blue marks" she suffered on account of being "mauled and hauled and bumped all over on stage," as "evidence of devotion to my art."[82] Yet something more complicated was also at work here. To sacrifice femininity, even in the name of artistic devotion, was really to emphasize it by calling attention to the difference between sanctioned and unsanctioned female behavior and looks. By playing with and against the grain of contemporary culture, female comics allowed their audiences to experience both the pleasures and pains of social transgression. That kind of ambiguity permitted female comics to appeal implicitly and explicitly to the point of view of women. Specifically, it allowed funny women like Dressler and Friganza, both of them budding feminists and suffrage sympathizers, to make common cause with the funny (excessive) women in the audience, women who were unable or unwilling to fit within the established beauty and behavior standards of their time.

This was not a completely new aspect of American women's relationship to the comic. As Nancy Walker and others have demonstrated, a number of nineteenth-century women writers specialized in satires on gender roles and domestic humor that appealed to other women.[83] And in our own time, when female stand-up comics routinely joke about their problems—dating, dieting, and overcritical relatives—audiences have long been accustomed to the self-reflexive, self-deprecating woman willing to make a spectacle of her own problems in order to poke fun at the state of modern gender relations.[84] Although historians have largely ignored the connection between the comedic practices of women in vaudeville and those of late twentieth-century stand-up comics, a closer look at performers like Trixie Friganza suggests some important analogies and antecedents.

Trixie Friganza was one of the earliest predecessors of the modern stand-up comedians. Violating the normative standards of femininity, she turned "grotesquerie" into commentary that spoke specifically to the pressures of modern femininity from a female point of view. It was female rather than feminist in the sense that it did not directly challenge the status quo of gender ordination or imply the need for political participation. But her art had in common with early twentieth-century feminism the assumption that for all of their differences, women had a commonality of preoccupations. In the routines of vaudeville's funny women, these included weight control, personal attractiveness, fashion, and marriage.

Friganza entered the world of musical comedy when the touring company of *The Pearl of Pekin* came to town in 1889.[85] Changing her name from Delia O'Callaghan to Trixie Friganza and moving between musical comedy and vaudeville, she discovered that she could make a good living in the theater by making fun of what a 1907 article called her "rapidly increasing portliness."[86]

Friganza's self-styled occupational narrative typified the too much/not enough dilemma of a number of female comics. Like other funny women (among them Marie Dressler, Fanny Brice, and Josephine Baker) who entered the world of the theater as chorus girls or singing soubrettes, Friganza began her career with other ambitions. In each case however, some marker of excess suggested another path. Too much weight, too much awkwardness, not enough beauty, and in Baker's case too much color pointed all these women in the direction of comedy. A 1912 press release issued for a Shubert production quotes Friganza claiming that "There was a time when I was slender and lissome. . . . So I applied for apprenticeship to a chorus." As "a chorus girl," she confessed, "I was distinctly not much of a success. I couldn't keep time with the rest or jig the right jiggle, or kick the right kick."[87]

Trixie Friganza's fat humor exemplified the vaudeville lineage of contemporary female stand-up comics. When she moved from musical comedy to a solo act in vaudeville, one of her most popular routines involved accentuating her already ample body by padding herself with innumerable costumes and discarding them one at a time.[88] Her vaudeville acts also included a collection of songs and monologues about "the troubles of a fat girl," and "a great deal of kidding" with the audience.[89] The humor of her size was also showcased in a number of musical comedies and revues, such as the Shuberts' *Passing Show of 1912,* which featured a "tank number" staged by the famous dance director Ned Wayburn in which groups of scantily clad "chorus girls illustrated the classic dances" of nineteenth-century ballet, while Friganza comically "travestied" their movements. The finale, staged with a beautiful "bevy of diving girls" performing stunts in a tank of water, reached its humorous climax when the hefty Friganza "flopped over into the tank . . . as though stumbling into the water."[90]

The press covered the ups and downs of Friganza's weight, publishing copies of her latest diet strategies and her advice on how to "assail the excess tissue" by consuming a steady stream of buttermilk.[91] Friganza claimed that while she "didn't get fat purposely," it was "a pretty good stock in trade for a comedienne." For as she told a Cleveland reporter in 1907, "nobody laughs at a skinny woman." Thus, for example, if "some little demure creature" fell down in the street, "all the gentlemen in Cleveland would be there to pick her up." By contrast, "let me tumble down the street . . . and everyone who saw me would laugh with diabolical glee."[92]

But Friganza hinted at another, less acknowledged aspect of the "fat" woman's comic appeal—the ways she embodied the sensuality of unrestrained appetites for certain kinds of enjoyments. As Friganza joked in a 1907 newspaper article about overweight comediennes, while leading lady parts required a "willowy" and even a "famine-stricken" appearance, fat had a no less important exchange value. She predicted the day when stage managers would "select their comediennes, not by reputation, but by weight." Female comics "will be placed on the scales and paid for, like confectionery, by the pound." Discussing the theatrical capital in female fat, Friganza noted that "superfluous flesh, which is supposed to put a quietus on an actress' chances on the stage, is really a very valuable asset. This is, of course, providing that the one having it doesn't take herself seriously, and is willing to point with pride, like a Democratic orator, to its possession."[93]

Friganza understood that fat was not just a problem of looks. It was also a moral issue in a society in which both sexes were struggling with questions of personal control and discipline.[94] Excess fat connoted the failure of self-control and unruly habits. A 1908 newspaper story on Friganza even suggested that her fatness provided a source of pleasure and identification to the audience, which rewarded a fat woman's indulgence and allowed her to break the rules of self-control in their behalf. "Fat" worked "in her favor" because "her fatness is satisfying, gratifying," the writer observed. "She [Friganza] appears well fed and nourished. She makes the general public feel that . . . it is responsible for her happy condition."[95] Comic singer May Irwin also explained her fear of getting thin on similar grounds. Explaining why she took "every precaution" to "keep fat," Irwin noted that "theatre-goers know me as stout May Irwin" and might not think she was funny if she were "lean." "You can always depend on a fat person as being jolly and looking at the bright side of life. Most lean persons . . . look sorrowful, starved, stingy, as if they didn't treat themselves well."[96]

Trixie Friganza deliberately cultivated female audience identification, both by direct address to women during the performance and through the kind of off-stage commentary she planted in a 1909 article in the *Chicago Tribune* entitled "Six Trixie Friganza Tricks Which Make Women Laugh," in which she declared her practice of playing to the feminine half of the audience. "Eminently," she told the reporter, "I am a woman's woman . . . because I understand them"; "I make it my business . . . to compel women to laugh."[97] Friganza's tricks for evoking women's laughter are worth quoting at length, for they reveal several important presumptions about comedy as a social force. Significantly, they demonstrate that performers at the time presumed a community of feminine sensibilities that could be mobilized around a particular set of issues. And, most importantly, they show one of the mechanisms of women's humor, namely, that it worked simultaneously to create a female ideal type and then to deflate and critique it by self-deprecating ridicule.[98]

"In the first place," noted Friganza, "you must present an appearance of humility." To get a woman to laugh the female comic "must not let her for a moment get it into her head that because you are an actress you know it all. Quite the reverse. You must have her think that your position is not a happy one, that you wish you were in her boots and had her husband. Then you have her." The second "trick" was actually the means to the first: "you must make fun of yourself." As Friganza put it: "I enlarge on the fact that I am pretty gross and I bring in as often as I can the fact that most men, large and small, prefer the sylphlike things in the audience." The third was to make the routine seem unpracticed and believable. The fourth and related trick was to create a sense of intimate identification between performer and audience. The comic "must always act as though she is a woman herself," explained Friganza, "her attitude must be 'My dear, I know just what a time you have with your husband.'" She must communicate the idea that "oh it's fierce to be a woman, but we're all women together—leagued against a common enemy." Friganza's fifth trick was to convince the audience that she was both older and less attractive off stage than she appeared on, and that whatever attractiveness she achieved was largely though "pencil," "dye," and "false hair." Her last tactic was always to "select one woman well down front to whom you play." Preferably she should be "neither rich nor poor, and one who has apparently never been soured by the lack of masculine attention." "Talk to her, laugh with, not at her. Get a woman like this in sympathy with you and chances are you will have no trouble with the rest."[99]

As her advice and such songs as her 1915 lament "Won't Someone Kindly Stake Me to A Man"[100] suggest, Friganza's particular brand of self-deprecating humor—her method of comic sacrifice—spoke especially to the concerns of modern middle-class women caught up in the cult of physical attractiveness that defined the attainment of beauty as a kind of cultural duty. By speaking for the disgruntled women who were either too unattractive to lure a husband or had trouble with ones they married, Friganza offered her alleged inadequacies as a salve for the travails of her sex.[101]

Friganza's self reflexive—if-you-think-you-have-problems-you-should-look-at-mine—kind of comedy worked on the principle of making herself low so that others could feel high. Eva Tanguay's self-deprecating rituals operated on a somewhat different principle. Unlike Friganza, who bemoaned her fat and blamed it for her problems, Tanguay made a virtue of her negative qualities, "flaunting her mediocrity," as theater critic Rennold Wolf put it, and reveling in references to her unfitness for the stage. Her humor played on the idea that audiences applauded her in spite of and also because of her inadequacies.[102]

Wolf, who described Tanguay as "a voiceless soubrette, possessed of a brazen personality, an irrepressible energy," echoed a common refrain: "Eva Tanguay is not beautiful, Eva Tanguay is not talented, Eva Tanguay is not clever, and Eva Tanguay is not artistic." She was, however, "the highest salaried actress in America," or at least one of them. And her $3,500 a week pay check could only be explained by "her willingness to poke fun at herself and to rebuke an audience for liking her." What they liked, he observed, was that Tanguay "possesses in an unlimited degree the quality of making people on the other side of the footlights interested in her," a "talent" that "few statesmen" could claim.[103]

Eva Tanguay appealed to both sexes. Women and men alike came to marvel at her verbal unruliness and her physical abandon. Women, including members of the suffrage movement (they were among her biggest fans), saw her as a liberated "hoyden" with an exaggerated ego. Others admired her ability to express the physical abandon that was still considered taboo off stage, and they loved the antics of a bombastic

fashion plate whose acts featured rapid-fire costume changes into outlandish and elaborate gowns, sequins, feathers, and hats.[104]

Aside from the "divine" Sarah Bernhardt, no other woman on the
early twentieth-century stage was as adept at self-advertising as Eva
Tanguay. Likewise, her self-advertisements were not confined to the
work of press agents or published autobiographical sketches; rather,
they comprised the centerpiece of her vaudeville routines. For, as more
than one observer noted, Tanguay's "whole performance is of herself, for
herself, by herself. She is motive, cue, subject and sub-subject."[105]

A description of one her 1913 vaudeville performances by a writer for
the *New York Tribune* is worth quoting at length, for it demonstrates
Tanguay's mastery of what might be termed the autobiographical grotesque:

> When she bounded into view dressed in grotesque richness there was the
> satisfied feeling that an audience indicates when its favorite is there be-
> fore it. In a rather shrill voice but with distinctiveness of enunciation she
> began a ditty wholly devoted to her own personal peculiarities. Moving
> incessantly in one direction and then in another she recounted the im-
> pression she made on all who saw her in public. She sang about the re-
> marks made concerning her in restaurants, in sleeping cars and other
> public places. Such wholly autobiographical material offered for the en-
> tertainment of others has seldom been heard of.[106]

These "self-centered chantings," as Caroline Caffin described them,
amounted to "a mere recitation of her own eccentricities, her extrava-
gances, her defiance of all conventions." Tanguay "keeps on telling us
how extraordinary she is, how successful, how unassailable by criticism
and how popular." Caffin likened Tanguay's thoroughly "modern" style
of self-presentation to "the perfect sky-scraper of illusion" resting on a
"flimsy edifice."[107]

Tanguay honed an image of gleeful eccentricity. "Winsome eccentric
Eva Tanguay, with her falling waves of hair and happy, abandoned air of
joviality," aimed to give credence to the idea of her own lunacy. "The
first impression she gives is that she is crazy and as the conviction grows
upon one, she becomes glad of it," wrote one critic who saw her perform
in Rochester in 1907.[108] Neither a trained singer—one reviewer described her voice as "a hairshirt to the nerves"—nor a skilled dancer,
Tanguay was known for her ear-piercing enthusiasm and her wildly energetic physicality.[109]

She "frankly admits in her songs that she cannot sing and similarly passes other criticisms on herself, but the fact remains that she is one of the strongest cards in vaudeville," wrote a Cleveland critic in 1907.[110] Her irreverent theme song "I Don't Care" (1902) said it all:

They say I'm crazy, got no sense,
    But I don't care . . .
You see I'm sort of independent,
Of a clever race descendant,
My star is on the ascendant,
    That's why I don't care.

The chorus followed with:

I don't care! I don't care!
What they may think of me.
I'm happy-go-lucky
Men say I'm plucky,
So jolly and carefree . . .[111]

As another verse put it, "My voice may be funny, but it's getting me the money, So I don't care."[112]

Born in Quebec in 1878 and reared in Holyoke, Massachusetts, Eva Tanguay had built a career out of the persona of the "cyclonic" wild woman. With her tousled "wild mop" of curly blond hair, her "large, smiling mouth" and "loud, chattering voice," Tanguay seemed "strident" and "voluble" to reporter Ada Patterson. "Every inch of her is alive, nervous, vital," her "dynamic personality" was "all nerves and excitement."[113] "She makes no claim to beauty, her shapeliness being her chief claim to attention, and her hair falls over her eyes like the mane of a badly trimmed French poodle," wrote a critic in 1912.[114] Her "wild mop of stiff, tousled blonde hair," observed Caroline Caffin, "seems so charged with electric vigor that no amount of combing or brushing could alter its assertive unruliness."[115] Audiences flocked to hear her deliver the audacious and sometimes crude lyrics of songs like "That Wouldn't Make a Hit with Me," which Tanguay performed on an "all comedy bill" at Hammerstein's Victoria Theater in New York in 1908:

When you marry some old guy
Who hasn't the decency to die,
Or you marry some old pill

Who you can neither cure nor kill,
That wouldn't make a hit with me.[116]

Yet to many people it mattered less what she sang than the style in which she sang it. When she made her vaudeville debut in 1904, "Tanguay put so much business and ginger into her work that the audience did not get a chance to find out what the song was about," said a critic for the *New York Dramatic Mirror*.[117] One reviewer described her as "that strange creature who lacks a voice but possesses an aggressive individuality that captures her audience."[118]

Like Marie Dressler, Eva Tanguay cultivated the image of a stage athlete. Her "physical strength and endurance" were "abnormal," offered Rennold Wolf. "She is a tornado, a whirlwind, . . . a whirling dervish of grotesquerie."[119] Yet Tanguay's athleticism appeared playfully feminine and sensual, not clumsy and masculine like Dressler's. Her early repertoire, for example, included a "drinking song" in which Tanguay soaked her hair with a bottle of champagne and dashed from one side of the stage to the other, shaking her hips and breasts, kicking her legs, and cavorting with sensual abandon.[120] Advertised by her press agents and celebrated by theater critics as the "Madcap Genius," "The World's Greatest Eccentric Comedienne," "The Electrifying Hoyden," and "The Evangelist of Joy," Tanguay was said to have a "temperament" that was "so volatile that no photographer has dared, but once, to ask her to remain quiet the length of time necessary to produce a really classic picture."[121] Miss Tanguay "can never keep still. She is going all the time she is on stage or off of it, constantly moving about."[122]

Tanguay's defiantly eccentric comedic style, with its powerful and incongruous combination of self-deprecating and self-advertising humor and its incorporation of sartorial spectacle, looked backward to the grotesquerie of turn-of-the-century musical comedy and forward to a new era of jokes about women told from a female point of view. Neither comic stance, however, transcended the cultural paradigm which situated female humor in the framework of comedic sacrifice of normative femininity and beauty.

"Something of a Rarity with Comediennes"

In the first decade of the new century, however, the rising popularity of two "singing comediennes," Nora Bayes and Irene Franklin, both of whom challenged the propositions that a funny woman could not be attractive and an attractive woman could not be funny, pointed to the emergence of a new relationship between femininity and comedy. In a revealing comment on Nora Bayes, one critic noted that she was "very good to look at, which is something of a rarity with comediennes."[123] Others noted her "slim, graceful" figure and "slight, almost fragile" "curves" that showed off her "exquisite" and "attractive" gowns to the best advantage.[124] Likewise, a critic hailed singer Irene Franklin as "the daintiest and cleverest bit of femininity" he had seen in some time, remarking that each time she appeared on stage she looked "more lovely than the last."[125]

Bayes and Franklin did not abandon all forms of cultural girth associated with low comedy, but neither did they rely upon them exclusively. Rather, they turned the critical instrument of comedy into a something that acceptably feminine women could use. They proved, in other words, that one did not have to be grotesque or fat in order to wield the comedian's sword. This was not a completely new development, as the careers of Anna Held and Lillian Russell suggest. Yet Bayes and Franklin represent an important shift in cultural direction. Held and Russell had largely been known as singing beauties who descended into low comedy. By contrast, Bayes and Franklin were first and foremost comediennes in their own right, who also happened to be attractive.

Bayes and Franklin helped pioneer this renegotiation of female identities and gender categories on the popular stage. First, their stage work blurred the line between rough or low comedy and the more refined style of humor that women were supposedly drawn to. Second, and related, they used the outward symbols of their femininity and attractiveness to comment upon more complicated and controversial gender identities, especially with regard to the questions of marriage and career. Taken together, their comedic strategies represented not the end of traditional gender concepts but rather a more fluid and experimental handling of them. Significantly, they showcased a new female image—the respectable, middle-class married woman who was at once fashionable, attractive, aggressive, humorously irreverent, and a little bit naughty.

With Bayes's "effervescent" comedy, her "intelligent" way of creating "nonsense," and her "handsome, rakish" style, a review of the Ziegfeld *Follies of 1907* enthused, her work was more "brilliant . . ." than that of "the rowdy actresses of the day."[126] It was a style, said another reviewer, that made Bayes "irresistibly potent."[127] Chicago theater critic Amy

Leslie, who saw Bayes perform in the Ziegfeld *Follies of 1908,* observed that in this show Bayes had "recovered from that brilliant kind of ruffianism in which she romped when she first went on stage." Her new approach "is quiet, effective, delightful and decidedly more amusing for her piquant quelling of her own obstreperous low comedy."[128] In 1914 Caroline Caffin added to this chorus of praise, noting the "delicacy" and "gentleness" of Bayes's comic manner on the vaudeville stage. "She needs no boisterous energy; you do not wish that she should have to work too hard for you." Bayes "can emphasize a point by a sly glance . . . far better than by loudness or force."[129]

"Potent" and "delicate," "rakish" and "gentle," "quiet" and "brilliant," "sarcastic" and "effervescent"—this mixture of contradictory adjectives situated Bayes at a kind of cultural crossroads where the attractive womanly woman could occupy the (formerly masculine) subject position of the joker. In a 1909 interview with journalist Charles N. Young, Bayes coyly explained that she became a comedienne "by accident." "When I first sang Wurzburger [a reference to her 1904 hit "Down Where the Wurzburger Flows"], I had planned to sing [it] straight—without the [comic] interpolations that I later added to it." But one night, Bayes insisted, she forgot the verses, and began to improvise.[130] Whether she actually forgot the lines to this German-style Tin Pan Alley drinking song about "flowing rivers of beer" is less important than what she remembered to replace them with.[131] "It was delirious," claimed a reviewer who praised Bayes's "own original assassination" of "Wurzburger's" lyrics. "First she sang it passionately; then she sang it Germanly; then she made an oration of it, and ultimately she told the story of her life with it."[132]

Bayes's recovery from obstreperousness and her ascent to the realm of quiet comic brilliance was, however, only a partial one. Her partner and husband, Jack Norworth, had been known in his pre-Ziegfeld *Follies* days primarily as a "black-face monologist." And coon songs along with Irish and Italian ethnic dialect songs remained a staple of the Bayes-Norworth repertoire on the Progressive era vaudeville stage, as did Bayes's use of low-comedy sexual innuendo.[133] "Bayes must shake off all reminders of her burlesque days and overcome entirely any proneness to the clownish," the critic Montgomery Phister complained in 1911. Despite "all of the delicacy of her best comedy moments," he protested, Bayes projected a "rough edge" which "grates harshly upon the finer sensibilities."[134] But interpolating occasional bits of "clownish" or "rough" comedy into her "intelligent" act allowed Bayes and her audience to have it both ways—giving them the playful naughtiness of low humor and the delicacy many thought more befitting of the female sex.

Like Bayes, Irene Franklin deliberately exploited the tensions between rough and refined comedy. Franklin's vaudeville song repertoire also included typical Tin Pan Alley fare, consisting of ethnic and racial dialect songs ("Dutch," "Hebrew," Irish, and coon melodies) as well as catchy ragtime piano tunes played by her husband, Bert Green.[135] But her youthful good looks and fashionable attire contributed to the public's perception of her as a rare example of really funny but attractively feminine women.[136] She wore a different outfit for each song, making female fashion, or her version of it, a centerpiece of her act.[137] One critic estimated it took an average of 24 seconds to change costumes for each of her songs.[138] "I can't sing another song as I have not another dress," Franklin told a vaudeville house audience at a performance she gave in 1907.[139] At least one observer was convinced that "the feminine portion of the audience" was "especially interested in Miss Franklin's extensive wardrobe."[140]

But fashion was not Franklin's sole claim to fame. In 1908 she had won the title of the Queen of Vaudeville in a popularity contest held among the patrons of the Colonial, Alhambra, and Orpheum theaters, three large New York vaudeville houses operated by impresario Percy G. Williams. With more than 7,000 votes in her favor, Franklin beat out a stiff competition among fellow performers, including Eva Tanguay (who received over 6,000 votes), British music hall singers Alice Lloyd (sister of Marie) and Vesta Victoria (more than 2,000 votes apiece), dancer and mimic Gertrude Hoffmann, and Marie Dressler, each of whom received more than 1,700 votes.[141]

Franklin's popularity derived from the success with which she, like Nora Bayes, managed to combine respectable and fashionable femininity with the sexual suggestiveness of low comedy. In her public relations statements Franklin honed the persona of female goodness by claiming to sing clean songs aimed at a female audience. "We all know," she told a reporter in 1913, "that . . . the easiest way to get a man's laugh" is "with a smutty song. But I would rather have the man go home and tell his wife to go to the matinee and hear my songs than have him come again and hear the risqué."[142]

But Franklin's songs and her commentary on performance also reveal the disjuncture between the advertised moral codes of vaudeville and the more broad-minded tastes of big city audiences. Although vaudeville managers, especially on the powerful Keith circuit, had long claimed a policy of moral censorship, different sectors of the audience (both male and female) exhibited profoundly diverse concepts of entertainment, and standards of decency varied from locale to locale, with New Yorkers permitting the greatest latitude and small towns tending toward stricter regulations.[143] Franklin disliked "playing in little towns" because her characters might be misconstrued there. "Out of town they have an idea that a woman trying to be funny is simply trying to be fresh [naughty]," said Franklin. "One can do things in New York and feel sure one's efforts will be rightly interpreted."[144]

Franklin's popularity was also a measure of her engagement with the changing ethos of urban life. After the turn of the century, but especially in the prewar era, young urban women of all classes demonstrated their yearning for personal freedom and self-expression by listening and dancing to ragtime music in dance halls and late-night cabarets, and by patronizing vaudeville shows and musical theater, where their favorites included sensual but girlish dancers like Irene Castle (and her dashing husband/partner Vernon)[145] and attractive and racy singing comediennes like Bayes and Franklin.

Franklin's tunes, which she embellished with numerous bodily contortions and facial grimaces, caricatured the styles, foibles, and tragedies of modern-day working-class urban female types—worldly-wise children, waitresses, shop clerks, and frustrated chorus girls.[146] Her 1908 hit, "The Talkative Waitress" (also called "The Waitress from Childs"), was a slangy number about a bold young waitress at a quick-lunch New York City restaurant, "who will stand no impertinence from her [male] customers."[147] "Never Trust a Traveling Man" (later retitled as "Experience") told of the plight of a hotel chambermaid who had her "trusting heart" "busted" by a sweet-talking traveling salesman. "Waiting at the Church" was a humorous look at the woes of a deserted bride. "All Wrong" portrayed an attractive, slightly overdressed, "broadly slangy" young woman known as a "salamander," "smart sponger," or gold-digger, who, as Franklin put it, "can be found in every cafe and restaurant in New York."[148]

Going beyond the well-worn female caricatures of low comedy, Franklin, a self-described Brooklyn girl, sought to portray what she called "characters among the average walks of life." "I try to make my characters use the words they would actually speak in real life. The phrasing must be absolutely human."[149] While "you may caricature and you may exaggerate, . . . you must not depart very far from the fact" because audiences "like to laugh about the things they know."[150]

The true-to-life relevance of Franklin's comedy endowed the singer with the cultural authority of the modern social observer. Yet her comedic stance was hardly one of personal detachment. In addition to her satiric portraits of urban working women, this dainty, gorgeously dressed, and highly successful performer offered herself as a subject for comedic scrutiny. Of her character songs, none was as closely identified with Franklin as the autobiographical "kid" song, "Redhead." First introduced in 1908, the "killingly funny" song[151] told the tale of "a rough and ready little red-headed girl who tells the names other children call her."[152] Dressed in short plaid rompers, bare legs and bobby sox, Franklin reeled off the epithets—"Redhead! Redhead! Gingerbreadhead! Carrots, Bricktop, Golden Rusthead! . . . Freckleface! Strawberry Blond Head!"—and the laments: "Gee! I'd like to throw him in the pond! Why wasn't I born a blond!"[153] In what became a legendary publicity stunt, Franklin held vaudeville matinee performances at the Orpheum and Colonial theaters in the winter of 1908, at which "all the small 'redheads' . . . from kindergarten to high school" were admitted for free.[154]

For Franklin, a genuine redhead born in New York in 1876, this was more than a song; it was the voice of her professional persona and a way to establish her claim to understand the misfortunes of others. According to Franklin, "Redhead" communicated the injuries—both psychological and professional—that having a "gingerbread" head had caused her personally.[155] Red hair had also kept her from achieving her "own ambition" to play dramatic "character" roles on the legitimate stage, she told a reporter, when she was rebuffed with the reply: "What, with that hair?"[156]

Franklin's problematic hair was the means by which she made common cause with the pathos of her urban female types, with their slangy sexuality and assertive working-class demeanor. It was how she revised and updated the definition of clean comedy. So too did the unconventional gender symbolism in her stage/marital partnership with pianist and songwriter, Bert Green, which worked both to bolster and undercut Franklin's image as a dainty and respectably feminine comedienne.

Unlike hundreds of other male-female comedy teams in American vaudeville with routines that dealt predominantly with the battle of the sexes, both the Franklin-Greens and the Bayes-Norworths fashioned their stage personae on the claims of happy, modern companionate-style marriages and professional partnerships. Indeed, the topic of marital and professional compatibility comprised a crucial aspect of the stage repartees of both couples.[157]

On stage Nora Bayes and Jack Norworth posed as lovebirds in song duets like "Shine on, Harvest Moon," and gave the press fairy-tale versions of their off-stage marital bliss.[158] Bragging to a reporter that the two were as happy in "private life" as on stage, Nora claimed that "Jack and I haven't been separated six hours since we were married."[159] It "isn't make-believe either," one reviewer insisted, "for everyone who knows them will tell you they are 'awfully in love.'"[160]

But in the happy partnerships of "Mr. and Mrs. Jack Norworth" and "Mr. and Mrs. Bert Green" it was the women who dominated. This deliberately reversed the gender ordination of most male-female comedy teams, in which the man played the comic role and the woman served as the "straight" or "feeder."[161]

The expected conflict in the "unorthodox arrangement" between the dominant figure of Irene Franklin and her more retiring husband was "mitigated by their bonds of their affection," a Milwaukee journalist reported in 1915. "He is willing to remain in the background" because "mutual appreciation" and "absolute harmony" and "devotion" in the "Franklin-Green alliance" precluded any sort of professional jealousy on the man's part.[162] A parallel theme emerged in the marital performances of Bayes and Norworth, especially in Nora's most famous publicity ploy, the billing of herself as "Assisted and Admired by Jack Norworth."[163] The image was further magnified in publicity stories that emphasized Jack Norworth's "quiet and undemonstrative style," which "never obtrudes in any action or scene," as contrasted with the "high strung" and "exceedingly nervous disposition" of his wife, who reportedly earned almost twice his salary.[164]

But there were important differences in the marital performances of the Franklin-Green/Bayes-Norworth teams. Franklin and Green showcased their marital stability. Bayes and Norworth, despite their claims of wedded bliss, made the social tensions in their marital-professional arrangement part of their act. The unorthodox modernity of the Bayes-Norworth partnership was further amplified by strategically timed press agent's rumors of their marital discord, rumors that provided some of the subtext for their comic duets.[165]

Known as "an expert in SONGS and MATRIMONY," Bayes eventually

played the happy divorcee nearly as well as the contented wife.[166] Not
only did her marriage to Jack Norworth occur on the heels of her much
publicized divorce from a previous husband; it too eventually exploded
in another well-publicized divorce in 1913, only to be followed by a
third marriage to her newest stage partner, Harry Clarke.[167] After that, as
theater critic Archie Bell put it, the lore of Bayes's "thrice wedded-
career," along with public disclosure of her Jewish identity (including
the fact that the former Miss Goldberg signed her first theatrical contract in Yiddish), circulated in the press as "The Confessions of Nora."[168]

Like Franklin's "Redhead" song, Tanguay's "I Don't Care," and Friganza and Dressler's self-deprecating fat comedy, Nora's confessions
played with normative social expectations, only to debunk them. Although in this case too girth or excess—here in the forms of Jewishness
and the scandal of divorce—continued to be an integral part of the
funny woman's stock in trade (as they do to this day), her career helped
establish new frames for looking at women and humor. Bayes and
Franklin had demonstrated that being attractive did not preclude being
smart, ambitious, and irreverent. And both had shown that pretty and
fashionable wives could also be aggressive take-charge comedians of the
first rank. By challenging the traditional distinctions between passive
feminine beauty and active (masculine) worldliness, they helped move
comedy and women into the modern century. Ironically, though neither
Bayes nor Franklin joined the feminists' ranks, this challenge was
closely related to the very issue that preoccupied American and English
suffragists in the 1910s, when they attempted to present a more fashionably feminine image of the activist woman, a figure long caricatured as
masculinized and funny.

The Strong Personality

3   In the winter of 1907, theatrical producer Joe Weber tried to stop comedienne Marie Dressler from singing her theme song, "A Great Big Girl Like Me," at the Colonial Theater in New York. Weber claimed that she had first sung that song at Weber & Fields Music Hall, which gave the Music Hall exclusive performance rights to it. The singer defended herself by claiming that in her performances at the Colonial she was only "giving an imitation of someone giving an imitation of her" singing that song.[1]

Dressler's claim was hardly as idiosyncratic as it seems. For it was the case that while women's stage humor took many forms in the early years of the twentieth century, nearly all funny women used some kind of imitative comedy—and quite a few depended upon it almost exclusively. That was true of what one observer called the "epidemic" and another referred to as "the great army" of mimics who descended upon the vaudeville stage beginning in the early 1900s.[2] So popular was mimicry that one musical revue playing in Chicago in 1908 featured several numbers mocking the trend, including a song called "The Imitation Craze."[3]

Though male performers had also caught the fever, imitations, especially imitations of well-known performers, were largely the province of female comics.[4] Among them were the great headliners Cecilia (Cissie) Loftus, Gertrude Hoffmann, Elsie Janis, and Juliet Delf (who, dispensing with her surname and adding a question mark, went by just "Juliet?").[5] These women personified the mimetic moment in American comedy in the years between 1890 and the end of the 1920s. On the popular stage of vaudeville and musical revue every conceivable kind of comic imita-

74

tion was in full flower: blackface minstrelsy, gender impersonation, burlesque, parody, and ethnic caricature.[6]

But something new was taking place as well. While the women mimics did sometimes perform gender impersonation and racial/ethnic imitations, their stage work also represented a significant break from this genre. Unlike those who devoted themselves exclusively to the comedy of blackface caricature and gender impersonation, these vaudeville mimics moved beyond generic and stereotyped images of race and gender to what could best be described as the comedy of personality. This was the imitation, sometimes in a satiric vein, of the particular style and repertoire of *specific individuals*—mainly well-known female and male performers. Much of the time they were impersonating white female performers—women they envied or admired. From the perspective of the mimics and their audiences, it was the focus on the individual rather than on a generic type that distinguished the comedy of personality from other forms of mimetic humor. As Cissie Loftus put it in a 1907 article, rather than copying a type, where only "general accuracy" was needed, her imitations required her to "get inside . . . and reveal the real personality" of the "particular person."[7] In a single evening during her winter show of 1909–10, for example, another popular mimic, Gertrude Hoffmann, gave the audience fourteen imitations of fellow performers, including Ethel Barrymore, Eva Tanguay, Eddie Foy, George M. Cohan, Ruth St. Denis, Anna Held, Isadora Duncan, Valeska Suratt, Harry Lauder, Eddie Leonard (in blackface), Nora Bayes and her partner Jack Norworth, and Annette Kellerman.[8]

To a far greater extent than other forms of popular comedy, the comedy of personality provoked a critical dialogue about its cultural significance. Female mimics themselves took an active part in this dialogue. Their attempts to situate their comic practices within the cultural discourses of their day reveal an extraordinary degree of self-consciousness about their craft. It was also a consequence of the broader cultural changes that made "imitation" a highly charged and widely discussed concept in both aesthetic and social theory.

The mimetic moment in American comedy coincided with the mimetic moment in American social thought. As social scientists, psychiatrists, and cultural critics pondered the psychological, social, and aesthetic meanings of imitation, including its implications for understandings of gender, vaudeville mimics themselves sought to explain the inner workings and the meanings of their art. The dynamic interplay between theatrical and nontheatrical concepts of imitation in this period was fueled by contemporary fascination with mass production, the role of the artist as critical observer, and debates about the significance of imitation for the constitution of the self. The questions that mimicry opened—about the relationship between self and other, individuality and reproducibility—made it a provocative and historically significant mode of cultural enactment.

The Comedy of Personality

"Watch the nervous rigidity of her figure, the angle of the knee as she [Loftus] impersonates [the actress] Mrs. Fiske," wrote Caroline Caffin in 1914. "Listen to the metallic tensity of the voice. Then see her melt into the soft, diaphanous personality of Maude Allan, all lissomeness and pliability. Hear the sobbing monotone of her voice and note the nervous languor of her movements, as she portrays Jane Cowl, and contrast them with the clean-cut rhythmic movement of her Sarah Bernhardt."[9]

Such rapid-fire switching from one personality to the next was also a trademark of Elsie Janis's mimetic comedy. Eddie Foy, who shared a vaudeville bill with her in 1904, described the "Jekyll and Hyde" effect of her imitations. How "uncanny," the way in which this "sweet, simple, magnetic" girl appeared on stage, looked at the audience, brushed her hair back from her forehead, lowered her jaw, and in the next instant reproduced his own mannerisms with astounding accuracy.[10]

It was even more striking that, unlike the male and female impersonators of the day, neither Janis nor Loftus used make-up or cross-dressing to disguise their own identities. Usually they wore simple feminine dresses or gowns, perhaps adding a hat, umbrella, or shawl. That was true whether they were imitating male stars like Foy, the African American comic Bert Williams, or female performers like Dressler or Bernhardt.[11] Elsie Janis's most important prop—beside the rubber-like twists and grimaces of her face and her fabulous vocal range—was her long hair, which she twisted, tucked, and pinned in different ways to gain a new visual effect before each imitation.[12] An exception to this spare style was Gertrude Hoffmann, who did use make-up, costume changes, and elaborate sets.[13] Yet even Hoffmann deliberately established her own presence within each imitation. She first appeared on stage as "herself" and sang a song about the theme of impersonation. Then she entered a special dressing room arranged at the rear of the stage but in full view of the audience. Assisted by two maids, Hoffmann would strip down to her undergarments and change costume and make-up, thereby exposing the mechanics of the transformations that were part of her stage act.[14]

For audiences the pleasures of this kind of transformative comedy were many. The fantasy of the fluid self was one appeal. In a review of the double booking of Cissie Loftus and Gertrude Hoffmann at Keith and Proctor's 125th Street Theater in Harlem in the spring of 1908, theater critic Alan Dale explained that mimicry appealed to those who felt "chained" to their own "individuality." "Isn't it exquisite," he asked rhetorically, "to be occasionally somebody else?"[15] Vicarious freedom from the "fettered" self was one source of pleasure. Another was the fun of recognizing the original figure and appreciating its exaggeration.[16] The mimics performed two kinds of imitations: "sympathetic" or "purely descriptive" characterizations, and satiric portraits with a mocking and sometimes "murderous" comic edge. Especially in satiric studies the strategy of the vaudeville mimics was to draw out and exaggerate a prominent characteristic or idiosyncrasy of the subject.[17]

To heighten the comic effects, vaudeville shows often featured at least one mimic whose routines included imitations of someone else performing on the same bill, sometimes directly following the person they were imitating.[18] A number of theaters also followed the practice of booking two headline mimics together on the same bill to create a sense of competition.[19] A 1902 Louisville show that brought together vaudeville singer Josephine Sabel and teenage mimic Elsie Janis gives us a sense of the performance range. For a number of years Janis, who had compared herself to a newspaper cartoonist "who purposely exaggerates certain characteristics in order to give a more striking air of reality to the finished picture," had delighted audiences with her Josephine Sabel imitations.[20] But Sabel's own repertoire also included a number of imitations of other performers, including one of Cissie Loftus doing an imitation of Sabel.[21] According to reviewers, the highlight of the evening came when Janis, who followed Sabel on the bill, gave "an imitation of Josephine Sabel in her imitation of Cissy Loftus giving an imitation of her." At the conclusion, Janis dragged Sabel back on stage and together they gave "the Loftus imitation."[22]

Known as the "queen of mimics," Cecilia Loftus was born in Glasgow in 1876. Her mother, Marie Loftus, was a famous music hall singer, and it wasn't long before Cissie began performing her imitations of stage personalities at London music halls, where she billed herself as "the mimetic marvel."[23] In 1895 Cissie Loftus made her New York debut at Koster and Bial's Music Hall, with imitations of Letty Lind, Sarah Bernhardt, and Yvette Guilbert. She remained on the American popular stage until the 1930s, moving back and forth between vaudeville, legitimate drama, and musical theater.[24] It was Loftus who inspired Elsie Janis's work as an imitator. Born Elsie Jane Bierbower in 1889 in Ohio, teenage Elsie Janis began her vaudeville career in 1900, with her mother Jennie as her stage manager. Billed variously as "The American Cissie Loftus," "The Miniature Cissie Loftus," "The Pocket Edition of Cissie Loftus," and "Cissie Loftus' Only Rival," by 1905, at the age of sixteen, Janis was also a rising star in Broadway musical comedy. That year Henry Tyrrell, a critic for *Theater Magazine,* gave her the ironic title of "the inimitable child" and noted that her repertoire included at least 80 "living portraits." Her earliest routines on the vaudeville stage consisted of impersonations of Cissie Loftus's imitations of other performers. Janis would first perform her own imitation of a celebrity, followed by an imitation of Loftus's original imitation of the same performer.[25] It was a strategy that Loftus herself had perfected on the London music hall stage during the "Cissie Loftus-Letty Lind dancing war," when Loftus's burlesque of Lind's dancing led to a series of counterimitations and ended with Loftus giving an "imitation of Miss Lind's imitation of my imitation of her." A similar round of imitative countering took place between Loftus and Lillian Russell.[26]

What are we to make of women's deep involvement with mimetic comedy? And how are we to understand the larger cultural meanings of this fascination with imitations, imitations of imitations, and originals imitating their imitators? To begin to answer these questions we first have to consider how the theater as a cultural institution facilitated new forms of female behavior. Vaudeville was a highly competitive industry, and female stage personalities vied with one another to get and keep the spotlight. As Caroline Caffin observed, only "the strong personality" and "the ability to get it across the footlight and impress it upon the audience" could assure a performer's popularity.[27] The new style of mimicry enhanced the personalities, and hence the celebrity, of both the imitator and the imitated. Even the ritualized competition between female mimics expanded the cultural capital of each party. It was well known, for example, that an imitation by Hoffmann, Janis, or Loftus was to vaudeville performers what a Weber & Fields Music Hall parody was to a legitimate Broadway play: both a symbol of and a boon to one's popularity.[28] Not only did Ethel Barrymore, Sarah Bernhardt, Marie Dressler, and other famous actresses condone this practice; they regularly attended vaudeville shows to see how the mimics portrayed them.[29]

The famous 1908 "feud" between Gertrude Hoffmann and Eva Tanguay shows how such cultural capital was exchanged when women played off each other's personalities and careers. Eva Tanguay was one of the most imitated comics of her time, as well as one of the most self-referential and self-parodic. She frequently performed imitations of other imitations of her and advertised her iconic status in the song "Give an Imitation of Me."[30] In it Tanguay invites some aspiring performer with no special talents of her own to "watch me while I'm on the bill and then jump into vaudeville" and "give an imitation of me."[31] Thus she encouraged her imitators to engage in bouts of ritual combat not unlike the competition that ensued when two mimics shared the bill.

During the winter of 1908 Tanguay attempted to generate publicity by issuing a warning to the mimics that no further imitations of her singing "I Don't Care" would be tolerated. Tanguay's warning was as fake as the feud that then ensued when Gertrude Hoffmann, then appearing on the same bill with Tanguay, would not stop her Tanguay imitations.[32] Tanguay apparently staged one of her legendary tantrums to have Hoffmann removed from the bill, but kept the feud going by taking out a full-page advertisement in the press addressed to "the public" and "especially to Miss Hoffmann." "I do original work," Tanguay's ad proclaimed, "and have always held my place on the bill. . . . Miss Hoffmann left the theater not because I wouldn't play with her, but because she COULDN'T have my place on the bill. The FACT was the ORIGINATOR remained, and the IMITATOR quit."[33] To which Hoffman replied in the press: "EVA TANGUAY! STOP Four-Flushing and Make Good! If you think you are so extremely clever, appear on any bill with me. I will follow you and wager any amount . . . that I will receive as much genuine applause as you do. You might bluff foreign artists [a reference to Tanguay's earlier contest with English comic singer Vesta Victoria], but your hand is called now."[34] Keith and Proctor's vaudeville shows continued to stoke the fires by scheduling Hoffmann (and her Tanguay imitations) on a tour that followed Tanguay to each theater one week later.[35]

Though there is not much record of what audiences thought about these performances, we can imagine that the spectators found at least some pleasure in watching women symbolically slug it out. When highly paid female celebrities imitated other highly paid female celebrities, they were engaging in aggressive rituals of competition—sometimes respectful, other times less so—but in any case rituals that, outside of competitive sports, were rare among women in public life in this period.[36]

Like modern mud-wrestling, this ritual competition may have simply created new opportunities for males to take pleasure in female strife. But females comprised half to three-quarters of the audience, and the most popular and successful vaudeville mimics were women who made most of the decisions about what material they would perform.[37] In that sense, the aggressive, competitive nature of early twentieth-century stage mimicry was an instance of female celebrities using the celebrity of other performers to enhance their own. Paying tribute to others was ultimately a way to draw attention to oneself.

Nevertheless, even as these rituals increased the visibility of the performers, they also posed a symbolic threat. Eva Tanguay's warning to her competitors to cease their imitations was more than a publicity stunt. The Tanguay-Hoffmann feud also suggests something of the nervousness in this period about the relationship between individual autonomy and cultural reproduction. For if mimicry was flattery and advertisement, it was also a form of appropriation that threatened to violate the very notion of the unique individual. As Eva Tanguay hyperbolically stated the case, Gertrude Hoffmann's imitations called into question just who was the originator and who was the imitator, or, as she also put it, which of the two could occupy Tanguay's place on the vaudeville bill. The comedy of personality not only posed the question of what happened to the individual personality when someone else "became" you. It also raised issues about what happened to the mimic's individuality when she became someone else.

These questions were not confined to the stage. This form of comedy, coming as it did at that particular historical juncture, did more than merely facilitate and legitimate new forms of female aggression and competitiveness, which in any case constituted only one element in the mimics' vaudeville repertoire. More significant was the way mimicry engaged both its practitioners and its audiences in a wider conversation about questions of selfhood, individuality, and creativity in the urban industrial age.

The Mimetic Art

Mimetic comedy—the comedy of imitation and parody—thrived upon the tension between nineteenth-century bourgeois fascination with imitation and the early twentieth-century modernist intellectual glorification of authenticity. With late nineteenth-century manufacturing able to offer consumers imitations of every kind, affordable reproductions became as desirable as the real thing. By the early decades of the twentieth century, Miles Orvell argues, though imitation remained an integral part of popular culture, a reaction was taking place amongst a new generation of artists and intellectuals who breathed new life into the concept of authenticity.[38] Cultural critic Andreas Huyssen has explored the gendering of modernist reactions against mass culture, noting that in the intellectual history of the West, authentic culture or art came to be associated with the masculine realm, while mass or inauthentic culture was labeled as feminine. "Fear of mass culture," he argues, would increasingly be articulated as fear of women and the masses.[39]

Perhaps no other creation of early twentieth-century culture personified the female as a symbol of inauthenticity better than Theodore Dreiser's New Woman of 1900, Sister Carrie. She is, Dreiser tells us, "the victim" of urban mass culture's "hypnotic" displays. Lacking a core identity of her own, and driven by a craving for fine clothing, material comforts, and pleasure, Carrie learns the ways of the world and builds a number of selves by mimicking the styles, expressions, and gestures of the upwardly mobile women around her. Carrie, writes Dreiser, was "naturally imitative." Her "passivity of soul" mirrored "the active world"; her "innate taste for imitation," her "sympathetic and impressionable nature," gave her the ability to "restore dramatic situations she had witnessed by re-creating, before her mirror, the expressions of the various faces taking part in the scene."[40] Like Carrie, the mimics on the vaudeville stage could be understood as a threat to both old and new notions of authenticity. They could be seen as personifications of a feminized urban consumer culture where being and imitating were one and the same.

But the female mimics proved especially shrewd at defining and defending the integrity of their craft. At the very moment that the epidemic of mimicry hit the popular theater, concepts of "true acting" were undergoing a profound shift, as were the concepts of art and authenticity. Actors on the legitimate stage moved away from classic or heroic styles and the performance of ideal character types, toward a new aesthetic of realism.[41] New methods of realistic acting emphasized natural speech, subtle physical gestures, and the psychology of the character being played. Equally important, actors were urged to allow their own feelings and personality to shape the interpretation of the role.[42] Bernhardt, who rejected more subtle forms of realism in favor of a heroic style, also had a reputation for taking her personal interpretation to an extreme point, and, as we have seen, was repeatedly accused by critics of substituting her own personality for that of the character.

The debate over realistic or personality acting extended to discussions of comic imitation on the popular stage. As one theater critic put it in 1907, stressing the mimic's intellectual gifts, Cissie Loftus is able "to interpret in the most delicate of satire, the inner selves, as above the mere outer mannerisms, of her subjects."[43] The mimics, eager to defend their work against charges that only those performers who lacked real or authentic dramatic sensibilities turned to imitation, argued that comic imitation was the same as, and even superior to, the art of true acting. Elsie Janis claimed that just as well-known actors and actresses "have made a specialty of imitating the personal traits and individual characteristics of people of everyday life," so "I and Miss Loftus have made a specialty of imitating the mannerisms and marked personalities of well-known actors and actresses." She maintained that while the audience was in no position to judge how well the actor or actress playing a "straight part" deviated from "the models of everyday life," the audience could determine how well "the imitator . . . takes off a stage character whose work is known to them." And then boldly added: "Miss Loftus and I might be forgiven for contending that our imitations constitute the greater achievement."[44] J. Arthur Bleackley, a British mimic who argued in his 1911 book that "the art of mimicry, and the art of acting are almost identical," even claimed that the mimic "has gone a step further than the actor in executing his powers of observation."[45] Theater critic Walter Prichard Eaton made a similar point: "Cissie Loftus imitating Bernhardt, Sarah herself imitating her imaginative idea of how Phedre behaved—at the bottom the two processes are the same. We merely call Sarah the greater artist because she imitated not a known model, but a creation of the imagination," and added that acting was "only mimicry raised to the nth power."[46]

The mimic Juliet offered perhaps the most acute deconstruction of the perceived boundaries between mimicry and the high-culture notion of true acting. Taking aim at the pretensions of the legitimate stage while defending her own line of work, in her 1912 article for *Green Book Magazine* she insisted that "all actors are counterfeits" to the extent that they make "simulations" of life "appear to be the reality." Because all actors were in some respects "imitators," she argued, vaudeville mimics like herself were actually "counterfeiting the counterfeits."[47]

The most radical challenge came from those who claimed that to mimic was not just to copy—it was also to originate. In an article for *Broadway Magazine* in 1899, Cissie Loftus had stressed the difference between the "art of imitation" and "imitation pure and simple." Like that of dramatic actors, she declared, her comic art involved a process of "interpretation."[48] Mimic J. Arthur Bleackley echoed her view when, in an attempt to place popular comedy on the same plane as serious culture, he urged his fellow mimics to "strive to be an original thinker, a creative artiste, and not just a mere imitator."[49] But it was one of Cissie Loftus's admirers who staked the new cultural claim squarely when he wrote that "her imitations are—though it may sound paradoxical—original artistic creations"—so much so, that a Loftus "copy" "is in itself an original."[50]

This paradox—the idea that imitations could also be original creations—was central to early twentieth-century intellectual reformations. Imitative comedy tweaked the sacred notion of authenticity upon which bourgeois concepts of culture and individuality rested, a notion which, some writers have claimed, was the crucial foundation of modernist thought.[51] But modernist culture was composed of a number of diverse perspectives, some of which interpreted imitation as the sign of a pernicious machine-age mass culture which threatened individuality and autonomy, while others presented it as the enabling condition of human development and creativity.

In the first decade of the twentieth century, a time of shifting cultural sensibilities and ambivalences about the meaning of imitation, comic mimicry had the power to entertain as well as provoke. It provoked some observers because it suggested that human beings might take on the machine-like qualities of the emerging industrial culture with its standardized products. Perhaps no critic was more sure of the implications of mimetic comedy than French philosopher Henri Bergson. In his essay *Laughter*, which was published in 1900, Bergson argued that the comical resided in the character's ability to expose the repetitious, machine-like behaviors of human beings. He called this "the illusion of a machine working in the inside of the person."

Imitation and mimicry brought laughter, according to Bergson, because "our gestures can only be imitated in their mechanical uniformity." And the modern tendency to behave mechanically was precisely what threatened "our living personality." Human beings "become imitable only when we cease to be ourselves." Laughter came when we perceived "something mechanical encrusted on something living." The comic talent of the imitator, Bergson argued, resided in the ability to expose and make "ludicrous" the "element of automatism" of the person being imitated.[52] What enabled others to imitate us, he insisted, was the appearance of a "ready made element in our personality, which resembles a piece of clockwork wound up once and for all and capable of working automatically." Bergson argued that it was "comic to wander out of one's own self," just as it was comic to become "a category" or mechanical self into which others might "wander."[53]

Writing in 1905 about the comic pleasures of imitation, Sigmund Freud quoted Bergson in support of the notion that "attitudes, gestures, and movements of the human body are laughable in exact proportion as that body reminds us of a mere machine." Comic imitation produced its humor by suggesting a "deflection" or "degradation" of life "towards the mechanical."[54] Anxieties raised by imitation in the machine age surfaced among American commentators as well. One turn-of-the-century theater critic took offense at a newspaper story which suggested that Cissie Loftus "reproduced the tones of those she sought to mimic with the fidelity of a phonograph." The critic considered this comparison "unkind and needlessly cruel." Loftus, he argued, was "better than a Phonograph"; her work was "finished and artistic."[55]

Others were more inclined to emphasize their appreciation of the ability of human beings to emulate mimetic technology. Reviewing a 1908 performance by two rival headline mimics at Keith and Proctor's 125th vaudeville house, theater critic Alan Dale spoke enthusiastically about the technological wonders of "The Cissie Loftus Talking Machine," the "Gertrude Hoffmann-ograph," and the "likeness" to machines that duplicated human voices.[56] In Loftus's case the metaphor was actually quite appropriate, since she sometimes made "graphophone" (the prototype for the phonograph) sound recordings of her subjects' voices before working on her copies.[57] Not only that, in her imitations of opera singer Enrico Caruso, Loftus actually played a phonograph recording of his performances and then followed it with an imitation of his voice on the "talking machine."[58]

Loftus's routine bore a striking resemblance to the advertisements then appearing for the Victor Talking Machine. These ads showed photographs of famous opera singers such as Caruso or Luisa Tetrazzini opposite a photograph of a talking machine and asked: "Which is which?" The copy below read: "You think you can tell the difference between hearing grand-opera artists sing and hearing their beautiful words on the *Victor*. But can you?" Then the ad declared: "Even in the *Victor* laboratory, employees often imagine they are listening to a singer making a record while they really hear a *Victor*." [59]

The mimics also considered the relationship between comic art and technological reproduction. Yet it was the camera rather than the phonograph that provided their symbol. In their attempts to create a metaphorical language to describe the mechanics of imitation, mimics (and those who observed them) invoked the notion of the performer as a camera and the imitation as a photograph. As Juliet explained in a 1912 article, "the imitator makes of herself a camera to photograph the imitated." Like "the development and toning of a role of film or a set of plates," the imitator must perfect the "psychological chemistry" necessary for making her imprint.[60] George M. Cohan, a frequent subject of vaudeville imitations, once described Elsie Janis as "the best photographer I ever had."[61]

The idea of mimicry as camera work brings up a number of important issues. The first returns us to Freud and Bergson's discussion of imitation as an articulation of machine-age fascinations and anxieties. Key technologies and symbols of mass culture, both the camera and the phonograph have been described as "mimetically capacious machines"—machines capable of turning nature (the natural voice and the natural subject) into cultural reproduction.[62] Like the vaudeville mimics, cameras and their photographs had the capacity to detach an image "from a unique existence" and substitute a "plurality of copies," as philosopher Walter Benjamin later put it.[63] "Analyse the impression you get from two faces that are too much alike," wrote Henri Bergson in his study of laughter. "You will find that you are thinking of . . . two reproductions of the same negative—in a word, of some manufacturing process or another."[64]

Of all the mimetic technologies of the late nineteenth century, the visual reproduction of the camera had the most far-reaching impact on cultural consciousness. With the mid-century invention of new techniques for mass production of photographic portraiture, the human subject could be endlessly reproduced, purchased, and circulated in the form of small postcard-like portraits called *cartes de visite*. Among the most popular subjects of this "cardomania" were actresses, who used these photographs as a means for enhancing celebrity.[65]

The cultural meaning of photography itself, however, was undergoing something of a shift at the end of the nineteenth century. In the 1890s photography still connoted a literal copy, and investigators of various kinds—ethnologists, psychiatrists, criminologists, and journalists—used the photograph to describe, catalogue, and diagnose diverse specimens of human nature. Along with its uses as a tool of social and political surveillance and control, photography also became a tool for documenting and exposing urban and industrial conditions and social "facts."[66] But older notions of photography as "a seemingly literal imitation of reality" soon competed and even combined with the idea of the photograph as a medium for delivering more fantastic and illusory images of the world.[67] Finally, the photograph began to emerge as artistic interpretation. This concept, promoted by Alfred Stieglitz and the journal *Camera Work*, proposed that the photograph did not reproduce "normal vision"; rather, it was a conspicuous medium of human control and revelation. As a modernist art critic wrote in 1901, the photographer "does not attempt to depict the actual thing, but the impression which it makes upon him."[68]

The photograph as an artistic, human interpretation of nature rather than a literal copy was exactly what a number of observers had in mind when they described the vaudeville mimics of their time. As one writer put it, "it is Miss Loftus' mental brilliancy that lifts her studies from mere photographic perfection to true greatness. She is a remarkable analyst."[69] Caroline Caffin, author of the 1914 study *Vaudeville*, expressed a similar opinion, one that was no doubt influenced by the aesthetic philosophy of modernist photographers like Stieglitz, with whom her husband, art critic Charles Caffin, was closely associated.[70] "Just as the photographer, by focus and arrangement of light . . . can influence the result of his photograph," argued Caroline Caffin, so too the vaudeville "imitator" may "give us the result in differing ways, each way being none the less a true imitation."[71] As the mimic Juliet put it, just as in the photographer's development of films or plates, so in the imitation of stage personalities "there must be the same consideration of light and shade, the same retouching, the same toning up or toning down, the same care in printing."[72]

The gender issues surrounding the idea of mimicry as camera work are by no means clear cut. When the simplified technology of the Kodak camera democratized photography at the turn of the century, women joined the ranks of "amateur" photographers, dozens also entered the professional world of studio portraiture, and still others moved into art photography, where they experienced what one practitioner called a "new power of observation."[73]

What is most striking, however, is the way the metaphor of the camera was used to describe and legitimate the role of the female comic as critical cultural observer and commentator. Discussions by mimics and commentators anticipate the ideas of later cultural critics, who have called the camera a tool of "surveillance" which enables the photographer to create "a second figure who can be examined more closely than the original."[74] This was very close to how one theater critic described the work of Gertrude Hoffmann in 1907: her "amazing art . . . enables you to see Anna Held, Elfie Fay, George Cohan, Eddie Foy, and Vesta Victoria better than they are themselves."[75] Similarly, critic Amy Leslie observed that in each of her imitations Cissie Loftus used her elaborate powers of photographic observation to create "a brilliant work of art" based on "her own opinion of the amusing and impressive characteristics of her model."[76] In being likened and in likening themselves to photographers, the mimics and their audiences not only asserted the right of women to look powerfully at others, but their ability to creatively elaborate what they observed.

The Mimetic Self

If the camera was a tool of observation, it was also an instrument for self-reflection. To look powerfully at others is also to acquire new knowledge of oneself.[77] In their metaphorical roles as photographers, the mimics played the part of what the French called the *flâneur*. At the end of the nineteenth century, claims art historian Judith Wechsler, the urban photographer became the "portent" and the "emblem" of the male *flâneur* as self-conscious spectator. A figure closely associated with the birth of modernist sensibilities, the *flâneur* was the artist who began "to shift his preoccupation from the city scene to his own relation to the scene."[78]

In this new sense of imitation as creative and self-reflective activity, the vaudeville mimics contributed to a modern dialogue about identity.

For it was the "play of the self," as much as the imitation of the other, that the mimics' work articulated.[79] Self-knowledge figured prominently in the mimics' discussions of comedy, as female performers pondered in very serious and deliberate ways the relationship between their art and wider questions of human psychology.

The female mimics went to remarkable lengths in interpreting their own cultural position. Their effort reveals an extraordinary self-consciousness about how their humor touched on the weightier questions of human development and how the theater resonated with changes in the wider culture.

The comic practices described here were part of a larger cultural reorientation toward new concepts of selfhood, concepts that used theater and theatricality as central metaphors. Crucial to this reorientation was a performative model of personality. By the beginning of the twentieth century, traditional notions of a fixed, immutable, and intrinsic human character were giving way to the more fluid concept of personality as something to be learned or performed.[80] Unlike the concept of "character," which some identified as intrinsic to the masculine self, "personality," as it was articulated in popular and psychiatric literature, was not a gender-specific concept. As historian Elizabeth Lunbeck has argued, personality was perceived as malleable, understood as "a strategy of self-presentation," an outward effect displayed by everyone, regardless of sex.[81] Yet the very notion of personality as performative or theatrical was itself partly a product of a theoretical turn in psychology that relied on a new notion of the imitative self.

The vaudeville mimics contributed to these discussions both materially and theoretically. First and most obvious, their comedy helped build the early twentieth-century "cult" of personality and celebrity. Second, and more important for our purposes, it helped shape the dialogue about the connections between imitation, personality, and subjectivity. Though the theater is a particular cultural zone where acting is understood to be the staging rather than the documenting of social truths, it is nevertheless clear that the explosion of mimicry in vaudeville coincided with and contributed to complex theorizing about the psychological meanings and implications of imitation.

From 1890 on, two prominent theories of imitation competed among both Continental and American psychologists, psychiatrists, and social scientists. The older paradigm related human imitation to abnormal psychology, especially to the female malady of hysteria, and portrayed it as an involuntary and potentially dysfunctional phenomenon. At the turn of the century many psychiatrists still shared the views of French clinicians Jean-Martin Charcot and Pierre Janet, who associated hysteria with "an enormous development of the tendency to imitation," "the growth of mental suggestibility," and the tendency to develop dissociated (multiple) personality states.[82] When American psychiatrist Morton Prince published his study of the multiple personalities of "Miss Beauchamp" in 1905, his book was an instant success, widely reviewed and sensationalized in popular periodicals, later turned into a Broadway play and a silent film. Prince hypothesized that Miss Beauchamp's alternating personalities resulted from the hysteria or "traumatic neurosis" produced by "nervous shocks" to her system. It was especially striking that one of her personalities—the boisterous "Sally"—tended to "impersonate" Miss Beauchamp herself and "play her part" by "copying as far as she was able her mannerisms and tone."[83]

The case of Miss Beauchamp underscored the links between hysteria and the perceived capacity of women to stage multiple personalities. As the primary candidates for hysterical disorders, historian Ruth Leys has written, "women were seen as diffuse, changeable, lacking any core of individuality and permanent identity"; they could be said to signify "mimeticism itself."[84] This view was consistent with more general associations between mimicry and what one turn-of-the-century psychologist called "the lower, less volitional types of mind." In addition to the hysteric, these included "the undeveloped child, the parrot, the idiot . . ."[85] As anthropologist Michael Taussig has shown, it was no accident that technologies of mimesis (such as the phonograph) were advertised and marketed with images of dogs, birds, and women.[86]

The issue of mimetic capacity becomes all the more interesting if we consider the feminist theorists' argument that Western culture has trouble acknowledging female individuality. Not only have women been characterized as instinctively imitative, but, as reproducers of other bodies, they were ipso facto less capable than men of maintaining the boundaries between self and other.[87] Suspected of lacking a stable self, they fell into the category of beings perceived to be lower on the scale of intellectual development than men of European ancestry.[88]

At the same time that mimicry was taking on epidemic proportions on the American vaudeville stage, a new and powerful model of imitative behavior was changing the direction of American psychology and social science.[89] Over and against traditional understandings of the primitive and pathological locations of mimetic behavior, this newer and eventually predominant model in American social science viewed imitation as a universal human faculty, key not only to the development of a healthy or normal selfhood but also to a harmonious, well-functioning social order. In the new social theory both the outward play of personality and the inner psychology of the human being were constituted through a process of imitation.

French sociologist Gabriel Tarde's *The Laws of Imitation* (1890), a treatise on the social origins of the self which was to exercise a major impact on Progressive-era social scientists in the United States (an English translation was published by Elsie Clews Parsons in 1903), argued that imitation was the key to understanding the general process of social development and the formation of the individual self.[90] Using the metaphor of the camera much the same way as did the female comics, Tarde argued that social imitation consisted of "the action at a distance of one mind upon another" and of "the quasi-photographic reproduction of a cerebral image upon the sensitive plate of another brain." He defined imitation as "every impression of an inter-psychical photography, . . . willed or not willed, passive or active."[91]

Though Tarde's book emphasized the importance of both conscious and unconscious imitation, his theories drew in part upon new work in hypnotism, especially the notion of hypnotic suggestion. Many students of hypnotism believed that during a hypnotic trance the psychological boundaries between the self and other dissolved, leading the patient to unconsciously identify with and imitate the hypnotist. This theory posed a significant challenge to the idea of the autonomous self.[92]

Popular interest in the concept of hypnotic imitation-suggestion spawned numerous turn-of-the-century literary fantasies, including tales about criminals hypnotizing innocents and causing them to commit crimes. The most influential treatment of the theme, one that also became a runaway sensation on the American stage, was George du Maurier's best seller of 1894, *Trilby*. Daughter of an English lord, Trilby came of age in Paris, where she worked as a seamstress and an artist's model. Tone-deaf and with no musical talent whatsoever, Trilby comes under the hypnotic spell of a music teacher, the sinister Jew called Svengali. Under his hypnotic trance, Trilby becomes the brilliant concert singer "Svengala" and eventually agrees to become the hypnotist's wife. Without the power of Svengali's hypnotic suggestion, Trilby cannot sing. Under hypnosis, however, her vocal capacities (like Miss Beauchamp's multiple personalities) are seemingly endless in their variety.[93] In 1895 "Trilbymania" swept the United States as Paul M. Potter adapted the novel to the stage. One year later 24 productions of the play ran simultaneously in American theaters, including several parodies. A fashion spin-off quickly followed.[94]

The popularity of this play was a testimony to the cultural centrality of questions of selfhood: not only the vulnerability and mutability of the female self, but also the larger question that faced both sexes confronting an emerging industrial society where hypnotic suggestibility might be induced by the lure of material goods, by the manipulations of advertising, or, as some social theorists worried, by the psychological sway of the crowd or the mob.[95]

If Trilby sensationalized the darker side of imitation-suggestion theory, emergent theories in social science as they were formulated by Gabriel Tarde and his intellectual followers stressed its functional capacities, arguing for the importance of both conscious and unconscious imitation as basis for a stable social order. In Tarde's model, imitation begins with social "inferiors" imitating "superiors" and proceeds to the development of social grouping held together by "imitative assimilation" and "incessant accumulation of similarities," especially as they are regulated by custom and law.[96] Even before the 1903 English translation of Tarde's book, his theories exerted a profound impact on James Mark Baldwin, one of the most influential American social psychologists of this era. Baldwin's pathbreaking study of child psychology, *Mental Development: The Child and the Race* (1894), followed Tarde in rejecting the notion that imitation was largely the consequence of nonvolitional behaviors such as those associated with highly suggestible hysterics. Rather, he argued that "imitation represents the general fact that normal *suggestibility* . . . is . . . the very soul of our social relationships with one another," and, following the ideas of Josiah Royce, that "rational ideas" in mankind were "products" of imitation. "The self," Baldwin insisted, "is realized in taking in 'copies' from the world."[97]

Building upon the work of Tarde, Baldwin, and William James's writings on the "many social selves" that make up the individual, American social scientists like George Herbert Mead, Jessie Taft, Charles Horton Cooley, and Elsie Clews Parsons theorized the self as a social phenomenon constituted through a process of individuals and groups imitating one another.[98] In this way imitative theories of personality presented a significant challenge to traditional nineteenth-century concepts of selfhood founded on Emersonian individualism and self-reliance. Mimetic or changeable identity came to be valued for its intensification of sensibility and a greater responsiveness to all of life's possibilities.[99]

In contrast to traditional notions that imitation was the province of the primitive and disordered mind, the new school of social psychology sought to locate imitation in the realm of what George Herbert Mead called "creative imagination." Mead argued that there were important distinctions between the "sympathetic" and "self-conscious" capacities of human imitation and the purely instinctual imitation of the animal world. Significantly, his descriptions drew upon the metaphors of the theater: "sympathy and imitation are both due to taking the role of another, reconstructing the individual—not simply accepting him as real, but actually constructing him, standing in his . . . shoes and speaking with his intonation. It is that sort of imitation which is impossible for the lower animal to be subject to, because he has no self-consciousness."[100] When we play "the part" of another, Mead argued, we not only "take on another's intonation and attitude but tend to take them into ourselves."[101] Role playing was not only an external but an internal process, by which the mimic played the behavior of the other on the "inner stage" of the imagination.[102] Mead believed it was the healthy individual who could merge the various selves acquired by imitation into "a single personality." Conversely, the unhealthy person evidences "a dissociation of selves," which can only be cured by bringing together the multiple selves into a functional unity.[103]

Like Mead, the mimic Cissie Loftus viewed imitation as a psychological process of standing in the shoes of the other person and even taking him into the self. But whereas Mead rejected the idea that in imitation the individual effected the "merging of his personality in the other," Loftus was less consistent.[104] On the one hand, she explained that "I absorb my subject so thoroughly that when I show Rose Stahl for instance, in my own mind I am Rose Stahl. I sink my personality completely and substitute Miss Stahl's."[105] As she put it on another occasion, "when I throw myself into the personality of one of these stage people I lose my own; forget that I am Cecilia Loftus, cease to have any personal emotions."[106] Yet she also insisted on the centrality of the mimic's own personality, arguing that she could absorb the "temperament of another person into my own without losing my own individuality."[107] Indeed, both the mimics and their admirers believed that the imitator's personality and individuality (Mead's "core" self) were crucial to the success of the mimetic art.[108] As one theater critic remarked, "that the imitator's . . . own individuality should infuse the imitation is to a certain extent inevitable and necessary," and went so far as to argue that "to the extent that the imitator has a distinctive personality, the imitation will have a greater value."[109]

The resonances between the stage and social theory did not stop there. In terms that were strikingly similar to those the vaudeville mimics used to defend imitation as creative art, the social theorists boldly proclaimed that true genius and inventiveness lay in the imitative capacity. In 1902 Charles Horton Cooley argued that Baldwin was correct in asserting there is "no radical separation" between invention and imitation. "There is no imitation that is absolutely mechanical and uninventive,. . .a man cannot act without putting something of his idiosyncrasy into it—neither is there any invention that is not imitative in the sense that it is made up of elements suggested by observation and experience."[110] That same year psychologist Mary Whiton Calkins (a former student of William James's) made an even more pointed declaration about the relationship between invention and imitation, arguing that "the usual road to inventiveness is through imitation." In some cases, "inventiveness consists solely in the selection of unusual persons or ideas for imitation." Like Mead, Calkins used theatrical metaphors to argue that imitation was a mode of self-invention whereby one's "act" follows the path of other actors. Fundamentally, she asserted, "imitation of other selves" is "a richly personal experience . . . a conscious attempt to make oneself into this fascinating personality."[111]

These imitative concepts of selfhood posited a radical new environmentalist model in which social experience rather than fixed or innate qualities explained human development. It was a model of crucial significance for the evolving feminist project, for an interactive model of the self located in imitative relations with others challenged the proposition that biology was destiny.[112] As Mead's student Jessie Taft argued in her study of *The Woman's Movement from the Point of View of Social Consciousness* (1916), girls had "no attitude" toward themselves at birth. Rather, their development depended upon the nature of their opportunities for mimetic social observation and interaction. For Taft female emancipation went beyond problems of politics and economics to issues of psychology.[113]

Ironically, imitation, which had traditionally been linked to the primitive, the hysteric, and the overly labile female mind, had now become an important concept for Progressive era feminist social scientists. Indeed, many Progressive thinkers, male and female, were elevating a pattern formerly associated with the highly suggestible and allegedly inferior woman's mind to the status of a normal human trait. A previously feminine and now increasingly feminist concept, imitation as a theory of psychological and social development threatened traditional gender categories.

The gender anxieties unleashed by the hypothesis of the imitative self apparently proved too unsettling for some social theorists, including Mead. For as Ruth Leys suggests, the idea that individuals were always in flux and always susceptible "to the influence of others" undermined any claims for a stable, autonomous self. And, in the era of the New Woman, even a notion as previously unassailable as sexual difference might be threatened by concepts of the imitative self. Mead and some of his colleagues moved to suppress the radical implications of their own theories in favor of ideas that posited the existence of an originary self which "precedes" the imitative socialization process, thereby reinforcing foundational notions of sex difference and identity. Without rejecting the concept of imitation as a theory of human and social development, Mead et al. sought to retain within it the idea of the differentiated subject who, even while imitating, remains conscious of the lines between other and self.[114]

Yet the backlash in formal theory could not suppress what popular culture had already absorbed. The theater had a life of its own, and the female mimics and their audiences traded on widely available concepts of personality to fashion their own ideas on the psychological and cultural implications of mimetic comedy. Caroline Caffin's *Vaudeville* echoed the "imitative school" of social psychology with the assertion that mimicry was central to the process of human development. As she put it, "the imitative faculty is so inherent in the human race that the limits of its influence are difficult to appreciate." Caffin noted that while the vaudeville mimics consciously and deliberately performed their imitations, the audiences at vaudeville shows unconsciously mirrored the expressions of the actors on stage.[115] As a modernist critic and a feminist writing about the popular theater, Caffin articulated the conceptual bridges between the world of the stage and the world of off-stage ideas.[116]

Although it would be tempting to suggest that the discourses of popular theater and social theory were mutually constitutive, it is difficult to determine exactly how much the new school of social psychology directly shaped intra-theatrical discourse and how much the theater itself was a model for the mimetic turn in social theory.[117] There is at least circumstantial evidence that performers like Cissie Loftus were aware of some of the key psychological concepts of their time. Conversely, we have every reason to believe that psychological theorists were familiar with the comic practices of the popular theater of their time.

If we can never know exactly how the ideas of the stage and those of social theory influenced each other, neither is it possible to determine with any precision which of the two had a greater impact on the broader society. Though its concepts were not as sharply defined as those of formal theory, the popular theater reached a far broader audience and was potentially a more powerful force in shaping the public's cultural perspectives. Whatever the points of origin and interaction, there is little doubt that both the comics and the social theorists spread and popularized complementary notions of the social self. Both groups challenged the idea that imitation was a primitive or inferior animal reflex with the assertion that mimicry was a self-conscious interpretive act. To imitate was not only to copy; it was also to invent something new.

The vaudeville mimics brought an additional dimension to the growing assertiveness of women in public life. As performers like Cecilia Loftus acted out the routines and articulated the concerns that made imitation a much-debated topic, they took on a new female role: that of the artist-intellectual who both participated in and critically evaluated the cultural practices of the day. The self-consciousness with which the mimics discussed the psychological dynamics and the aesthetic meanings of their comic art exemplified how female performers, and the institution of the theater more generally, were helping to chart the direction of modern thought.

The Americanization
of Salome

4 "The country is Salome mad," announced a reporter in July of 1908, when vaudeville mimic Gertrude Hoffmann took her "Vision of Salome" on a cross-country tour. "Every community has its delegation at the railway station breathlessly awaiting her advent."[1] Between 1907 and 1910, "Salomania"—as the public's thirst for Salome dancers was labeled—criss-crossed Europe and America, enticing many different kinds of performers and audiences.[2] Observers at the time had little doubt about the reason for Salome's national popularity. "She is bad," wrote one New York critic in 1908, "and that is a great element in her attraction."[3]

Well before bad Salome had created a national sensation in the popular theaters of the United States, she was already an old story in European high culture. Well-established in late nineteenth-century painting, poetry, theater, and dance, Salome was a powerfully transgressive symbol of women's desires, passions, and powers. This figure entered the world of live theater via Oscar Wilde's scandalous play of 1892. Banned by censors in England when it was first written, Wilde's *Salome* was published in French the next year; an English edition, accompanied by Aubrey Beardsley's notoriously bizarre and erotically charged illustrations, appeared in 1894. Wilde's play was loosely based on a Biblical tale. It is a story about the sexual vengeance of a voracious but thwarted woman. Salome, the virgin princess of Judaea, is the daughter of Queen Herodias and the stepdaughter of King Herod. Attracted by Salome's mysterious beauty, King Herod begs her to dance for him. Salome at first refuses, but later accedes to his request when Herod promises to reward her with anything she desires. At the close of her erotic dance, Salome asks the king for the head of Jokannan (John the Baptist), the impris-

96

oned prophet who had rejected both Salome's declarations of love and her physical overtures and had insulted her mother by imputing that Herodias was an adulterous whore. At Salome's bidding Herod chops off Jokannan's head and delivers it to the dancing princess on a silver platter. Salome then takes the bloody head and symbolically acts out a sexual encounter with it, kissing it and declaring her love to it. The play ends when a horrified King Herod orders Salome's execution.[4]

An entire sub-industry of literary criticism has been devoted to analyzing Wilde's *Salome* and the faithful adaptation of the text in Richard Strauss's 1905 opera. Most literary critics stress that *Salome,* like Flaubert's *Salammbô* (1862) and related *femmes fatales* of fin-de-siècle literature and painting expressed the period's fears of women out of control. Salome and her counterparts were misogynist and anti-Semitic fantasies and projections of feminine sexual excesses and moral degeneracy. While the Salome of the Bible was a girl who obeyed her mother's desire for revenge, the Salome of Wilde and Strauss is a creature with a will of her own. As a "bestial virgin Jewess," Salome the headhuntress is Salome the castrator, the quintessential devouring woman.[5] Several recent analyses of Wilde's *Salome* have emphasized the dancer's ambiguous gender. Because Salome is both a looked-at object of male desire and a woman who assumes the masculine prerogative of looking at her sexual prey, she also expresses Wilde's own homoerotic longings.[6] The fantasies that produced Salome and other symbols of female perversion have also been read as expressions of fear of the New Woman. Salome was a classic vamp, a sexual seductress who makes her allure the cause of male destruction. The sexually perverse vamp, along with the mannish woman and the androgyne of indeterminate sexuality, were other figures of the misogynist cultural landscape of the late nineteenth and early twentieth centuries.[7] Salome symbolized woman's volatile eroticism, even women's pent-up hostility toward men who thwarted their desires.

But the fascination with the Salome story did not end with Wilde and Strauss. Most literary critics miss Salome's transformation into a pliant figure of entertainment.[8] Once released from the realm of high culture, Salome took on a number of new forms, sometimes tripping over herself in one parodic version after another. The story evolved into what literary critics call an open text. Salome with all of her ambiguities and excesses was revised and subjected to varied uses as she wended her way from the high arts of painting, literature, drama, and opera onto the vaudeville and revue stage, into the movies, and then back again into literature and opera.

Salome was not just a male creation. Nor was she simply an erotic spectacle for men's voyeurism. She was also an important resource for women performers and audiences, a vehicle for female self-expression and sexualized assertiveness. That is part of the reason why the name of Sarah Bernhardt and the idea of Salome were closely linked in the popular imagination. Oscar Wilde considered the actress ideal for the role of his heroine, while Bernhardt herself embraced the play, lending what Wilde called the "glamour of her personality" to his "poem."[9] Bernhardt put the play into rehearsal in London before it was censored, and later planned to produce it in Paris. Why she dropped the project remains something of a mystery, although one of her biographers speculates that the character of Salome was so blatantly lustful, decadent, and unsympathetic—so incapable of generating pity—that in the end even an actress as brazen as Sarah Bernhardt ultimately found the role too risky for her career.[10]

Yet Bernhardt's name remained firmly implanted in what one historian calls "the Salome tradition."[11] And it is no accident that other ambitious and daring female performers of her day, especially the rising stars in European modern dance and American popular theater, expressed themselves through this powerful figure.[12] Taken out of its narrative context and performed as a solo piece, the "Dance of the Seven Veils" became a female-dominated scene.

Salome helped launch several theatrical careers and added new dimensions to the reputations of more established female performers. The role proved powerfully attractive to the daring women of the American popular theater—Gertrude Hoffmann, Eva Tanguay, Aida Overton Walker, and Fanny Brice—each of whom creatively manipulated the image of the Salome dancer to call attention to herself. Salome was a symbol, a role, and a mask for women. She was a sign of what society found both terrifying and exciting. She was a figure to be watched, and those who seized the image were inviting the public to look at them in new ways.

Salomania both reflected and contributed to the early twentieth-century passion for Orientalia. Contemporary Western fascination with the East (both the Middle and Far East) as a kind of primitive, erotic, and mysterious land where images of spirituality mixed with fantasies of unbridled sexuality permeated both high and popular culture at the turn of the century, inspiring everything from best-selling novels like Robert Hichens's *The Garden of Allah* (1904), to stage designs and department store displays, to dance styles and movie settings.[13]

Orientalism, an interest derived from the ascendancy of Western imperialism and colonization, provided a vehicle for representing the unruly New Woman in the costume of exotic Eastern otherness. As women struggled for social, political, and sexual emancipation, painters, writers, composers, and performers turned to the East and to antiquity as settings for orgiastic excess, decadence, and the feminine lust for power.[14]

European and American women found Orientalist dance an especially powerful mode of self-expression in the late nineteenth and early twentieth centuries, no doubt because in some colonized parts of the world sensual dances had been part of traditional cultural practices.[15] And most of the pioneers of modern art dance in Europe and America, such as Loie Fuller, Ruth St. Denis, and Ida Rubenstein, included Salome and other examples of Oriental exoticism in their repertoires. Ruth St. Denis in particular became known for her ability to combine "artistic spirituality" with overt eroticism in movements that allowed her to express herself through the sensual racial exotica of the East.[16] In a society that still considered overt female sexual expressiveness a form of scandal and even abnormality, the spectacle of the solo dancer, not to mention the white woman as Oriental erotic dancer, was a radical sight. It was radical too because the right to be sexually expressive along with the right to work and to vote was an off-stage political issue for younger women who, after 1910, would identify themselves as feminists. Taking their cues from the entertainers of the popular stage and screen as well as the urban working-class women who were practicing new forms of sexually expressive public behavior, self-dramatizing middle-class feminists demanded a loosening of older moral ideologies and an end to strict distinctions between good and bad, pure and sinful women.[17]

"Salomania"

Salome was Americanized on the vaudeville stage, where she served as an important vehicle of female self-expression and sexualized assertiveness, and as a malleable tool for playing out the anxious comedies of gender and race. Thus the Salome epidemic provides a remarkably vivid example of the highly volatile interanimations of race, ethnicity, and sexuality in early twentieth-century America.

Salomania was generated by several theatrical events, beginning with the premiere of Richard Strauss's opera in New York. Strauss's *Salome* opened at the Metropolitan Opera House and played a single performance on January 22, 1907, before the Met's high-society board of directors (among them J. P. Morgan, W. K. Vanderbilt, and August Belmont) shut down the production, citing its "moral stench." Rumors had it that the displeasure of Anne Morgan, daughter of the capitalist, had played a part in the decision.[18] Apparently, it was not the "voluptuous dance of the Seven Veils" that offended the opera's backers. As a critic for *Theatre Magazine* maintained, Salome "in her transports of rage and gross sensuality is no less respectable than the . . . Mrs. Warrens and other red-light heroines of the contemporary stage." Rather, it was Salome's perverse violence, the "repulsive grewsomeness [sic], the shuddering horror of the woman fondling a decapitated head," that had "sickened the public stomach."[19]

Whatever its exact causes, this act of censorship had productive consequences. For as one critic put it, the American habit of "trying to suppress such things" meant they would always "crop up again in various forms to plague the suppressors."[20] It did not take very long for the plague to spread. After the Met banned the opera, promoters at the Lincoln Square Variety Theater invited the prima ballerina, Bianca Froelich, to perform her censored "Dance of the Seven Veils" on the vaudeville stage, whereupon, despite her high-culture credentials, she was quickly labeled a "cooch" dancer.[21]

Cooch or cootch dancing—the belly dance craze that caught on in the 1890s with the appearance of various "Little Egypts" at world fairs and amusement parks—was the perfect niche for American popular theater's first appropriation of Salome. Even before Bianca Froelich had moved her Salome dance from the opera to the variety stage, critics had noted her resemblance to those "unforgotten dancers of the [Chicago World's Columbian Exposition] Midway Plaisance."[22] Froelich's Salome dancing at the Metropolitan Opera reproduced the "scandalous exposure" and "seductive intent" of the "Little Egypts [of] a few years ago," wrote one critic. "Even if there were more refinement of terpsichorean art in her last night's [opera] exhibition, it only served to make vice more alluring." With her performance of the "Dance of the Seven Veils," the Met's Salome had reached "the acme of lasciviousness."[23]

Where high-culture operatic dance left off and lowbrow erotica began is beside the point. The public's fascination with dancers who did the erotic "hootchy-cootchy" paved the way for what one journalist called an epidemic of Salome-dancing by music hall and vaudeville performers of every description.[24] The epidemic was in part attributable to the antics of La Belle Dazie, whom Florenz Ziegfeld, Jr. hired to perform a version of Salome's Dance of the Seven Veils in the *Follies of 1907,* which featured a satire on the Met fiasco. Only the year before the dancer had orchestrated a massive transatlantic publicity stunt, posing as the "veiled mystery of the stage," Le Domino Rouge (Red Mask). From June 1905 to May 1906, the ballet dancer appeared on stage and off wearing a red mask, while the public and the press engaged in wild speculation about her true identity. The guessing game about her Parisian or Russian nationality finally came to a halt when Domino Rouge unmasked herself at Weber & Fields Music Hall, revealing that she was actually Daisy Peterkin from Detroit, or, as she now preferred to be called, La Belle Dazie.[25] Compared to her earlier exploits as the mysterious Domino Rouge, Dazie's appearance as Salome in the *Follies of 1907* generated relatively little public commotion. In the skit, her Salome dance is interrupted by the police, who arrest her and later join her in a "can can" dance at the finale.[26] By far Dazie's most important contribution to Salomania was the dancing "school for Salomes" she opened at Ziegfeld's rooftop theater. By the summer of 1908, an estimated 150 newly minted Salomes from Dazie's school were descending upon the vaudeville circuit every month.[27]

Many of them found work as cooch dancers in the variety theaters along 14th Street in Manhattan.[28] This "vulgarization of Salome," one observer insisted, amounted to "the poetic vengeance which the fates have granted to the spurned composer and the dead poet." The "New World . . . which would not accept the Salome of art, has now riotously welcomed the Salome of the dance hall."[29] Even the fashion industry rode the wave of Salomania to push a fabric called Salome silk as the perfect dress fabric for a "bridge" or "luncheon gown."[30]

Female Visions of Salome

In the world of commercialized popular entertainment, Salome was a hot number. Every major vaudeville theater in and outside of New York City eventually featured at least one. But none was as scandalous and caused as much national furor as that offered by the multi-talented Gertrude Hoffmann—dancer, choreographer, and mimic extraordinaire. Her "Vision of Salome" was the biggest hit in the history of Hammerstein's Victoria Theater, a vaudeville house whose popularity had long rested on its willingness to offer adventurous New York audiences a taste of the bizarre and the sensational.

In May of 1908, Gertrude Hoffmann sailed for London on what the press called "a mysterious mission for the House of Hammerstein." It was a mission that would benefit both her and the impresarios. Her charge was to watch dancer Maud Allan perform her "Vision of Salome" at London's Palace Theatre, and return to New York with an imitation.[31] The Hammersteins had complicated motives for sending Hoffmann to London. Always at the forefront of theatrical public relations schemes, the flamboyant impresario Oscar Hammerstein, a German-Jewish immigrant cigar maker turned entertainment mogul, and his ambitious son Willie were determined to cash in on the Salome scandal at the Metropolitan Opera House. In 1906 Oscar Hammerstein had founded a rival institution, the Manhattan Opera House, through which he planned to upstage Heinrich Conreid and his prestigious temple of New York highbrows. In the ensuing "opera wars," Hammerstein had launched his first offensive by promising to open the 1907 season with Strauss's *Salome*. Though Conreid had beat him to it, the closing of the Met production gave him further ammunition. Seizing the moment, Hammerstein told the press of his plans to resurrect the opera the following season with beloved star Mary Garden in the title role—a feat he did not accomplish until 1909. Meanwhile he allowed his son Willie, manager of the Victoria Theater, to hire Gertrude Hoffmann to help them upstage another rival, vaudeville producer William Morris, who was at that very moment arranging an American tour for London's wildly popular Salome dancer Maud Allan.[32]

Canadian-born and California-raised, dancer Maud Allan was the toast of London. Her "Vision of Salome" won a following not only among popular audiences at the Palace Theatre, but also among British and European nobility, including society women who saw in her art dances a daring new style of female expression and comportment. But the British had a love/hate relationship with Allan. Her supporters celebrated her artistic vision, while her detractors remonstrated against her unorthodox use of a biblical character.[33]

To imitate Allan, then, meant not only to copy her dance but to re-create the sensation and scandal that accompanied it. Gertrude Hoffmann, whose particular talent was satiric choreography, returned to New York with a mischievous rendition of Allan's "Vision of Salome," billed by publicity agents as "a faithful copy." For Hoffmann, however, a copy was never faithful. Rather, it was, like all of her imitations, a way of placing her own vision and her own critical perspective before the public. Already well versed in the practices of strategic self-presentation, Hoffmann had her own complicated agenda for Salome. Her "Vision" sought both to introduce the American public to modern art dance and to satirize the arty spiritualism of the modern Orientalist dance style itself.[34] Salome also provided Hoffmann a way to flaunt female naughtiness, to expose men's lust for erotic spectacle, and to ridicule the prudishness of America's self-appointed moral censors.

Hoffmann's "Vision of Salome" premiered at Hammerstein's Roof on July 4, 1908.[35] Part art and part cooch, the dance slyly exposed the aesthetic conventions of both. Advance publicity hype about the erotic daring of Hoffmann's performance shaped the conditions of reception, as it also had for Maud Allan in London. So did the kind of moral outrage that led to the censorship of the Strauss opera at the Metropolitan.

Early reviews of Hoffmann's performance emphasized the violence, excess, and "wild abandon" of her dance.[36] And like Allan's critics, Hoffmann's reviewers strained hard to combine sensationalism with evidence of some redeeming artistic merit in this "Vision of Salome." Sam M'Kee, theater critic for the *New York Telegraph*, provided one of the most detailed descriptions. While the orchestra produced its "eerie strains," he reported, a drop curtain rose and "disclosed rich tableau curtains that parted slowly on a production, beautiful, complete and possessing a sort of barbaric grandeur." Hoffmann's Salome was "beautiful in face, in form, in limbs. Her grace is such that the word might well have been coined to describe her sinuous figure as it slowly weaves its way . . . toward the footlights." Most of his attention (and the audience's) was drawn to Hoffmann's encounter with the infamous decapitated head. Describing the climax of Hoffmann's dance, M'Kee wrote:

Suddenly she turns and sees the head of John the Baptist. She takes it with a combination of eagerness and aversion. . . . places the head before her and in wild abandon as if to conquer her loathing begins a tempestuous dance. She is garbed with draperies and with gewgaws of a bloody age, but . . . the effect is as if she were bare . . . The violence of the excess of abandon is such that Salome falls exhausted, but . . . writhes her way toward the head. Once more she seizes the head and once more her wild mood possesses her, but this time the effort results in a swoon.[37]

Critics debated whether Hoffmann's dance was more or less scandalous than Bianca Froelich's performance at the Metropolitan Opera. "All of New York's experts in Orientalism were present and declared that it was a perfectly modest affair, but very exciting," announced one critic who defended Hoffmann's "semi-nude sensation" at Hammerstein's Victoria Roof that July.[38] But others disagreed, arguing that compared to the spasm of Hoffmann's quivering "nude" figure in its "physical raptures" over the head, Bianca Froelich's dance looked like "the revery of a nun."[39] As one disgruntled critic pointed out, that was exactly why audiences flocked to see Hoffmann's performances. "Of the countless thousands who have enjoyed witnessing the Salome dance of Gertrude Hoffmann, scarcely one in ten knows the dramatic historical story from which the dance is derived. Scarcely half know why the 'Head' is placed on the stage, or indeed whose head it is."[40]

Hoffmann used her "Vision of Salome" to enlighten, confound, and satirize the phenomenon of Oriental dancing and her own role in it. Deliberately keeping her critics off balance, she milked Salome's potential to offend public taste while defending her performance as "artistic" expression.[41] At the same time, "Gerty" played her role with tongue-in-cheek, relying upon what critic Ashton Stevens called her "incorrigible humor" and her sly smile to provoke and tease her audience.[42] Her staging of Salome conformed to even as it poked fun at the expectations of what Broadway insiders called the "baldheads" or "tired business men" (TBMs for short), who came to the theater largely to gape at barely clad dancers and show girls. But Hoffmann turned the baldhead's gaze into the target of humor. She joked to journalist Heywood Broun that it was necessary for her to dispense with some of the "preliminary arm motions" used by Maud Allan and go directly to her erotic stage business. "You see," said Hoffmann, "it's hard to draw a man's attention away from his beer and his cigar . . . and I have to get down to cases very rapidly."[43] In her self-conscious use of humor she seemed to knowingly make an outrageous spectacle of herself and have fun watching the audience watch her do it. Her coy humor is reminiscent of the antics of British feminists, who, during the height of Maud Allan's popularity in London, published a playlet called "Salome and the Suffragettes." In this bit of feminist satire, the suffragettes hold Allan (who was actually known to oppose woman suffrage) hostage until the British Parliament and Prime Minister Asquith agree to give women the vote. The point of the play is that men will sacrifice anything, even their right to control politics, in order to watch the Salome dancer's writhing body.[44]

Welcoming press coverage that emphasized the orgasmic violence and lust of her performances, Hoffmann was only too happy to see her dances discussed in terms usually reserved for lurid crime reportage. Indeed, she had stirred up so much expectation about the sexual titillation of her Salome act that some local audiences during her road tour were actually disappointed to find, as a reporter from Cleveland put it, that the performance itself was "rather ridiculous and tame," more silly than naughty. "She steps down from a dais . . . Then she begins to claw the air. . . . She breathes heavily, as though from pneumonia. She jerks as in hydrophobia," he complained. Around the head of John the Baptist ("which looked more like a washbowl"), Hoffmann "hops and skips and falls and crawls and grovels and grunts and that's about all there is of the Salome dance."[45]

As much as any other aspect of Hoffmann's Salome, it was her costume, or lack thereof, that fueled controversy.[46] Like Maud Allan's, and indeed like the dress of most of the other Salome dancers, Hoffmann's costume had circular breast plates made of coiled strands of pearls, complete with large nipple-like jewels at the center. Strings of pearls and jewels were suspended from the breast plates to drape over the sides of her torso, and a large jewel accentuated the center of her belly. A black gauze skirt hung from a jeweled waistband attached at her hips. Underneath she wore short white "trunks," but her legs and feet were bare. Bare feet, the trademark of Oriental dancers including Little Egypt, seems to have been a crucial aspect of Salome's erotic charge.[47]

Hoffmann skillfully maneuvered a massive public relations scandal around her "obscene" attire. When she ended her engagement at Hammerstein's Victoria theater and took her act on the road, Hoffmann and her press agents used the costume scandal to provoke local vice reformers and censors in Iowa, Ohio, and Kansas. "My costume," she told a reporter in Columbus, Ohio, "consists of one pair of six-inch trunks, two jeweled saucepans, a black net skirt and ropes of pearls. Yes, I wear a jeweled snake in my hair which falls over my shoulders."[48] In Kansas City, where, according to newspaper reports, a Supreme Court judge had announced that Hoffmann "has the Right to Pack it [her costume] in a

Thimble Case and Go," the Court issued a temporary injunction against her performances. And according to reports from Des Moines and Council Bluffs, Iowa, Hoffmann's costume and dance had led certain senators to introduce a bill dealing with the subjects of "High Kicking and Gauzy Raiment." In Columbus, Ohio, it was even rumored that members of the Women's Christian Temperance Union had approached the governor of that state to call out the National Guard to keep Hoffmann off the stage.[49]

Back in New York for another run at Hammerstein's Victoria in the summer of 1909, Hoffmann stoked the fires of her costume controversy, hiring Dan Slattery, the "recently deposed . . . secretary to recently deposed [New York] Police Commissioner Bingham," as her press agent. Together they engineered her arrest at the Victoria Theater on indecency charges.[50] This timely piece of publicity brought her record-breaking attendance at subsequent performances, before which she was required by the court to dress for her act under the watchful eye of Mrs. MacMahon, matron of the West 47th Street police station.[51]

By the end of 1908 the popularity and financial success of her "Vision of Salome" had given Hoffmann the courage to make ever more grandiose claims for her own cultural significance. "Miss Hoffmann wants the world to know her as the 'Divine Gertrude'," announced a Chicago reporter after Hoffmann told him she would upstage Sarah Bernhardt and steal her title. Describing Salome as her "opportunity," Hoffmann told him that "these dancing days" were "the mountain on which I am climbing to the serene heights of great effort and achievement."[52] If her actual achievement was perhaps more modest, the popularity of Hoffmann's Salome dance did make her a national celebrity, gave her the resources to establish her own production company, and allowed her a remarkable degree of independence in the world of popular theater.[53]

Salome was an archetype that reflected male desires, fears, and fantasies about women's eroticism spinning out of control. It was a parody of feminine excess. But its very excessiveness left it open for further parody. And no one knew that better than Eva Tanguay. Aware of the objectifying potential of the viewer's gaze, she used it to advantage in her Salome by turning her spectacle of energized sexuality into a kind of self-parodying overload.[54] Tanguay's performance strategy might be likened to the idea of the "female female impersonator"—one who takes the stereotypes of hystericalized femininity and wears them like a costume.[55] Like Mae West (for whom Tanguay was a model) as well as the late twentieth-century singer Madonna, Tanguay both identified herself with and sustained a mocking distance from her own stage characterizations. Her Salome exemplified that paradoxical stance.

On July 18, 1908, Tanguay announced to the public that she would "be Salome" at Percy Williams's Alhambra Theater in Harlem. "Surely, I have the figure for it," she told the press. "I have been reading the story and I shall be ready with my own interpretation."[56] Only months before, Tanguay had conducted her self-serving publicity feud with Gertrude Hoffmann when Hoffmann refused to stop impersonating Tanguay on the vaudeville circuit. Now, to upstage Hoffmann, Tanguay added her own mix of "creative hysteria" to the character.[57]

Billing herself as "The Real Salome," she told the press that every part of the production was under her personal control. As one reporter put it, "the New York public that has followed her from theatre to theatre knows it will see a Salome that is thoroughly original, besides being one they are fully prepared to like in advance."[58] What he meant was that her fans would like most anything she offered, so long as it was what Percy Williams of the Alhambra Theater called "Tanguayesque."[59]

Tanguay opened her Salome before a standing-room-only crowd, while outside on the streets throngs of people who could not get tickets awaited her arrival at the theater. "Eva Tanguay is Salome . . . she is her own Salome and she is the public's Salome," Sam M'Kee announced.[60] As Salome, Eva Tanguay "danced like one possessed, shrieking . . . in her happiness," one critic wrote, offering the public a chance to "gorge" on her "cyclonic" spectacle as never before.[61] With a headline that read "Little Eva in Oriental Twist, Funniest Thing in Sight," another critic told readers to "imagine the electrically eccentric actress going though her Salome stunts clothed in a warm smile and a girdle."[62]

Tanguay shared with her audiences the conviction that while Salome was the vehicle, Eva was the event. At the close of her act, while still dressed in her Salome outfit, Tanguay came back out on stage, and "ripped off two slices of [her theme song] 'I Don't Care'."[63] Then she put on a kimono and appeared once again before the audience as Eva. She told a reporter that putting on the kimono was her way of establishing herself as the real subject of her performances. Her desire, she said, was to "leave the audience [with] my own personality." "I don't care if it isn't good art to spoil a masterpiece you have just created," she confessed. "I made my first hit as Eva and I'm not going to have Eva sidestepping for any Salome."[64]

In September, when she performed her "Salome" at the Orpheum Theater in Brooklyn, Tanguay took out a half-page publicity advertisement in *Variety* with clippings from local reviewers. Among them was a "roast" from the *Brooklyn Daily Eagle,* which compared her Salome to "the war dance of an apache or the fetish of a South African Savage." This was accompanied by her claim, printed in large block letters, that "THIS CRITICISM 'Doesn't Bother Me.'"[65] Like Hoffmann, Tanguay manipulated the press to call attention to the sexually explicit nature of her Salome act (she told reporters that her costume was so tiny it could fit into the palm of her hand), while at the same time denying it contained any "vulgarity."[66] But Tanguay's performance actually undercut the titillation of her costume, or at least set the opportunities for sexual voyeurism against a formidable competitor: her punishing voice, an intrusive shrieking presence that effectively disrupted the erotic visual components of her dance. As critic Sime Silverman of *Variety* put it, unlike other "Salomers," Miss Tanguay was "the first to acknowledge 'Salome' had the power of speech," a power that apparently annoyed more than it shocked some audience members.[67] Tanguay's vocal mischief, complained another critic, was more offensive than the original work by Oscar Wilde. With her irritating voice she sang "unharmonious lines in a ragtime spirit, the syncopation of which was rhythmically wrong." But to criticize her, he concluded, "would be to shoot a zeppelin at a buzzard."[68]

Playing With Race and Sexuality

In Tanguay's hands, Salome's virulence became unruly playfulness. Making the spectacle of the *femme fatale* outrageous rather than terrifying, she turned the story into a vehicle for her own cyclonic personality. In creating her own vision of Salome, Tanguay had toyed with the idea of throwing the head of John the Baptist into a large fountain on stage and then swimming out to rescue it. Abandoning the concept of a "damp" Salome, she promised in its place to "pull something good."[69] Sam M'Kee, who called the performance "gorgeously barbaric," reported that when Tanguay looked at the head, "life seems to return to the dead face and the eyes to look at her in a reproachful way, and she swoons in terror at the awful sight."[70] Others noticed the severed head "seemed to wink an eye."[71] That the eye was actually winking was no optical illusion. "No sir, it's alive, John the Baptist is," she announced to a reporter; "he's a man . . . didn't it scare you when he moved his head and looked at me."[72] She had "hired a Negro boy with big eyes. I sat him on the side of the stage all covered up. As I began to dance," said Tanguay, "I uncovered his head which, to the audience, appeared to be resting on a silver tray. As I moved about the stage his huge eyes also moved, following me."[73]

It was a bizarre marriage of minstrelsy and sexual parody. Here, masked in humor, we sense the deeper psychological underpinnings of performance in an era when sexuality, race, and violence were linked together in the American imagination. The common practice of lynching or castrating black men for transgressing social hierarchies and taboos could be effortlessly translated into a "Negro boy" whose head is delivered to the white female dancer on a silver platter. Even in death his roving eyes follow her about the stage. In a period rife with murderous fantasies about black males' desires for white females, Tanguay enlisted racist stage conventions to push her parody of the unruly woman. "Little me—I Did It!," she bragged. "It's my original version of Salome."[74]

Her performance forces us to rethink the overly simplified notion that women's humor by definition explores social powerlessness in order to offer a subversive protest against it. "Making trouble," as one writer labels the subversiveness of women's humor, may be an apt description of how vaudeville performers used comedy to critique conventional expectations about women. But as Tanguay's re-working of Salome suggests, recent scholarly emphasis upon the dislocating, anti-hierarchical pleasures of female humor masks its ambiguities, tensions, and paradoxes.[75] For if the humor of subordinate social groups was expressed as resistance to the dominant culture, it was shaped and in many respects limited by the conventions and prejudices of its own time. The parodic versions of Salome played by women on the vaudeville stage expressed a range of social statements and ideologies, some transgressive, some conservative, all within a single performance.

Tanguay's addition of a black male prop to her Salome dance was actually of a piece with her earlier use of minstrel traditions.[76] In 1904 she had developed a comic routine called "Blonde in Black," which she later retitled "The Sambo Girl." In it she plays Carlotta, the mulatto Sambo

Girl who teaches women how to do the cakewalk.[77] It was but a short step from the mulatto cakewalker to the white pseudo-Oriental dancer who performed before the roving eyes of the black minstrel head.

Tanguay's professional relationship with the African American comedy team of Bert Williams and George Walker, with whom she shared a vaudeville booking in the summer of 1908, and her reputed backstage affair with Walker, did nothing to dissuade her from using black racial stereotypes in her Salome act. Ironically, it may have even encouraged her.[78] Indeed, Tanguay's provocatively racialized sex humor, with its undisciplined stage Negro and transgressive white dancer, was not unique, and it was no doubt inspired by the blackface comics who began to parody the Salome craze even before Tanguay got into the act.

At the height of the craze, white male comics with blackened faces and Oriental costumes burlesqued the female dancers then appearing at various vaudeville theaters around New York City. Most prominently featured in the summer of 1908 was the popular blackface comedy team of Bedini and Arthur. According to *Variety,* they "brought down the house" with a "screamingly funny" Salome burlesque in which Arthur, in blackface, oversized shoes, and Oriental drag played the gyrating figure of "Salami." The team was booked along with the various Salome dancers performing at vaudeville theaters around New York that summer. At the 125th Street Theatre in Harlem, Bedini and Arthur parodied the Salome dance of a famous contortionist called "La Sylphe" (a.k.a. Edith Lambelle).[79] At Hammersteins' Victoria, Arthur's blackface parody followed Gertrude Hoffmann on the bill. At the Alhambra Theatre, they shared the bill with Eva Tanguay and burlesqued her Salome act. And at the Fifth Avenue Theatre, which featured the Salome dances of "La Sylphe" and Eva Tanguay on the same bill, they followed both with what the press called a "laughable travesty."[80] That season *Variety* even published the lyrics to a coon song, "De Sloamey Dance," whose rhyming verse went: "Git a John de Baptist head: Say yo'se jes' arrived from France, an' go do de Sloamey dance."[81]

Soon Jewish immigrant comedian Eddie Cantor would join the Bedini and Arthur comedy team, adding his own blackface drag parodies of Salome, complete with a skirt that managed to fall off him at every performance. His burlesques played out the gender confusion that Wilde had introduced in Salome, and also exploited the theme of racial difference by layering black over Jew.[82]

Bedini, Arthur, Cantor, and their contemporaries who impersonated

Salome behind the mask of blackface worked in the tradition of nineteenth-century American minstrel stage, where white men in blackface and drag performed sexual caricatures in so-called wench roles, often playing "pretty plantation yellow gals." [83] Minstrel and burlesque performance styles had begun to merge in the 1870s, as blackface entertainments placed increasing emphasis on female impersonation, and burlesque comedy troupes added minstrel routines.[84]

Traditionally, the humor of blackface comedy ridiculed African Americans, and in the nineteenth century, when the early women's rights movement joined hands with the abolitionist cause, cross-dressed blackface minstrels made black and female aspirations alike into an anxious joke.[85] In the Progressive era, when an assertive generation of New Women and New Negroes were knocking at the doors of white male power, a hilarious Salome cloaked in the mask of minstrelsy, or more precisely made ridiculous through it, registered the fascination and fear that surfaced when women and blacks threatened to act out new social roles.

During the same season that Bedini and Arthur were performing their blackface Salome parodies at vaudeville theaters around New York, George M. Cohan and Sam Harris drafted the female impersonator Julian Eltinge (William Dalton) to appear as Salome with them. Eltinge, who was on his way to becoming the premier drag artist of the Progressive era stage, was a stocky man, but despite his 5'8", 178 lbs. physique, he managed to whittle his waist down to a mere 26 inches by use of a tight corset.[86] Salome's hyperfemininity seemed ready-made for Eltinge's appropriations.

He first performed his Salome routine in early August 1908 in New York. In addition to Eltinge, the Cohan and Harris show featured other popular blackface performers, including George "Honey Boy" Evans and Eddie Leonard and the Golden Boys in their "plantation act."[87] Eltinge and "Honey Boy" Evans sang "Oh, You Coon" in blackface. Then they did a routine called the "Gibson Coon," in which Eltinge burlesqued the popular visual icon of the white New Woman, the Gibson Girl, wearing tan make-up. Playing his foil was "Honey Boy" Evans as the "millionaire coon gambler from Baltimore."[88]

But it was Eltinge's whiteface drag Salome that stole the show. "Just as a white man makes the best stage negro, so in this case, a man gives a more photographic interpretation of femininity than the average woman is able to give," wrote one reviewer. Eltinge delivered "a better 'Dance of the Seven Veils' than any woman has yet presented on Broadway."[89] The element of travesty in the act came, as it did with Eva Tanguay, in the treatment of the severed head. For this, Eltinge substituted the "'prop' heads of the presidential candidates and [Teddy] Roosevelt" for John the Baptist's.[90]

Salome proved to be a turning point in Eltinge's career, enabling him to move from minstrelsy to mainstream Broadway, where by 1910 he had become the dean of "glamour drag." The most beloved male impersonator of beautiful white womanhood, Eltinge emerged as leading expert on female fashion and cosmetics. But he constructed his off-stage persona as a manly man, and attracted a large following both among heterosexual middle-class women and male homosexuals.[91] His sexual ambiguity and the drag campiness of his transvestite Oriental dancer had a special appeal to members of Manhattan's gay subculture, among whom Salome became a popular nickname.[92]

It was one thing for a white man or woman to appear as Salome in the tradition of the minstrel show, and quite another for an African American woman to assert her right to perform an artistic version of Salome's dance. But Aida (Ada) Overton Walker was determined to try. In American popular culture, the part of exotic foreign dancer was clearly imagined as a white woman's role. Indeed, the sexual tension in the image of Salome seemed to reside in the idea that the costume and mask of the Oriental dancer permitted a white woman to release herself as an erotic spectacle. Like audiences for blackface entertainments, those who came to appreciate the transporting qualities of Eastern exotica preferred the *performance* of foreign otherness to the real thing. The Oriental aspect of Ruth St. Denis, who brought her art dance version of Salome to New York in 1909, is a good example. Though St. Denis strove to heighten the authenticity of her dance by wearing dark body paint when she performed, audiences knew and valued the fact that off stage, she was really white.[93] For a non-white woman to perform the role of the erotic siren, certain adjustments were necessary to lessen the threat.

No one knew that better than Aida Overton Walker, the preeminent African American singer and dancer of the pre-WWI era. Born Ada Wilmore Overton in Manhattan in 1880, by the age of sixteen she had signed on as a member of Madame Sissieretta Jones's "Black Patti's Troubadours," an all-black traveling show which combined serious music with elements of minstrel farce. In 1898 she joined the black vaudeville comedy team of George Walker and Bert Williams, whose show,

"Senegambian Carnival," featured Aida Walker doing a modern ragtime rendition of the cakewalk (said to be an old plantation dance in which promenading slaves mockingly imitated white cotillions). Walker's graceful cakewalk became the newest rage among fashionable white New York society women in 1903, some of whom recruited this "graceful young negress," as the press called Walker, to teach them "the Art of Terpsichore."[94] From 1902–03, Aida, her husband, George, and his partner, Bert Williams, starred in the musical comedy hit *In Dahomey*—a show that not only played on Broadway, but traveled to London, where it was given as a command performance to the Royal family at Buckingham Palace.[95]

Fame and the accolades of white nobility did nothing to mitigate the tremendous obstacles that racism placed in the path of African American performers. Telling the press about the "color line" in musical theater, Aida Walker spoke eloquently of "the limitations other persons have made for us." The white public did not have "the faintest conception of the difficulties which must be overcome, of the prejudices which must be soothed, of the things we must avoid whenever we write or sing a piece of music, put on a play or sketch, walk out in the street or land in a new town." No white person "can understand these things," she said. "Every little thing we do must be thought out and arranged by negroes, because they alone know how easy it is for a colored show to offend a white audience."[96]

Most likely to offend was a real love story involving black people. Citing the "particular prejudice against love scenes enacted by negroes," Walker complained that "in all the ten years I have appeared in and helped produce a great many plays of a musical nature, there has never been even the remotest suspicion of a love story in any of them." Conversely, she observed, "during those ten years I don't think there has ever been a single white company which has produced any kind of musical play in which a love story was not the central motive."[97]

This absence of love scenes reflected a tendency to portray blacks as a debased people—a people incapable of sharing in the same emotions, the same sentiments, the same values as whites, including true love and stable families. The sexual exploitation of black women by white masters left a lasting cultural stigma against which African American women would continue to struggle in defense of their moral integrity.[98] In the face of this "particular prejudice," Walker had consistently aimed to uplift the image of black women. Without sacrificing the energetic physicality that audiences associated with popular African American dance styles, her choreography also placed a high premium on what contemporaries called feminine grace.[99]

Given white prejudices against black love stories, it is hardly surprising that the character of Salome presented Aida Walker with a special kind of challenge and a special kind of risk. Salome's love was wanton and debased, and Salome's dance was highly sexualized. How would a woman who was especially sensitive to the public image of African Americans, including the ways black performers might offend white sensibilities, play the erotic princess? There were other issues as well. The Salome dance had originated in the high-culture world of European literature and opera. And despite its new incarnations in the low- and middlebrow arenas of the dance hall and the vaudeville stage, it still seemed like something of a racial transgression for a black woman to play what some commentators called a classical role.

Walker's strategy was almost the opposite of that of the white Salomes of the vaudeville stage. Rather than hype the sexual prurience of the dance, she characterized her black Salome as more artistic than erotic, more spiritual than sensational, and to a remarkable degree reviewers were prepared to see her in the way that she had intended.

On August 27, 1908, Walker performed her Salome dance for standing-room-only crowds at Brooklyn's Grand Opera House in a Williams and Walker musical comedy called *Bandanna Land,* a show with an unrelated plot. The press made much of this first black Salome, and reviewers were quick to contrast her cleaner, less suggestive version with the vulgarity of white Salome dancers. A reporter for the *Brooklyn Eagle* claimed that the "chocolate colored variety" of Salome was "gracefully performed" despite "the usual lack of clothes," and decided that the light applause for Walker indicated only that New York audiences "are growing weary of Salome's of every sort."[100] But many spectators may have been unprepared for a Salome dancer, especially a black woman, who emphasized grace over sexual abandon.

When *Bandanna Land* opened at Boston's Orpheum Theatre in September, for example, one review complimented Walker for "poetry of motion," going so far as to call her the "'Mlle. Genee' of her Race," a reference to graceful, classically trained Danish ballerina, Adeline Genee, who became a famous star of the American musical stage. Stressing the originality of Walker's conception of Salome, the critic went to great lengths to distinguish her from the vaudeville Salomes then appearing in New York. "She does not handle the gruesome head, she does not rely solely upon the movements of the body, and her dress is not quite so conspicuous by its absence," the reviewer noted, adding that her costume consists of a "full covering of the body and limbs," except for bare feet and shoulders. One notable "phase of her art" was the "fact that she acts the role of 'Salome' as well as dances it."

Acting, a more respectable way of being female than dancing, carried certain high-art connotations, and this critic was quick to laud Walker's ability to express "the emotions which the body is also interpreting, thus making the character of the biblical dancer lifelike."[101] "Grace it has in abundance," wrote a Chicago critic, who noted that Walker dispensed with the "hoocha-ma-cooch effect which adds a suggestion of sensuality to the exhibitions of other Salomes."[102]

The sheer politeness of these reviews seems especially remarkable. Along with the genuinely graceful style of Walker's performance, it also seems clear that some critics used the theme of a black woman's modesty to implicitly critique the unruly sexual vulgarity of the white Salome dancers. Whatever the precise reasons, many reviewers were ready to grant Walker some of the respect she craved.

But there was more to *Bandanna Land* than Aida Walker's graceful Salome and her lifelike acting. For as one review from Chicago put it, *Bandanna Land* actually had "two dusky Salomes."[103] The other was Bert Williams, who performed a burlesque of the dance in what one observer called his "inimitably funny and grotesque style."[104] Just as the white Salomes of vaudeville had been followed by blackface parodists, so too this black Salome was to have her comic imitator. Williams's two-minute routine delivered a double parody: one of the Salome craze, the other of the stereotypical image of black men as watermelon eating buffoons. "With his fine sense of travesty," wrote a reviewer, "the colored comedian turns the whole silly affair [of Salome dancing] into a hearty, healthy laugh." Williams's "awkward preparations; the deliberate removal of his huge shoes [part of his signature costume] that he may dance in stocking feet; his lumbering undulations in cheesecloth skirt; his comedy fall in imitation of the emotional abandonment of the other imitation Salomes; his immediate concern for his skirts, which he readjusts before he finally lies prostrate, and then his laborious dragging of his huge body toward the stand upon which the watermelon rests—is all delightfully foolish."[105] Although neither Aida Walker nor the reviews made mention of it, the travesty perhaps made her look a bit foolish too.

These liberties taken with Salome on the popular stage had so Americanized and domesticated the figure that when impresario Oscar Hammerstein revived the Strauss opera at his Manhattan Opera House in the Spring of 1909, with Mary Garden in the title role, what had been an offensive text in 1907 now seemed perfectly acceptable to the moral guardians of highbrow. Vaudeville, *Theatre Magazine* noted with more than a little irony, had made Salome safe for the opera. "Irreverent as it may seem to lug it in here," the magazine's editor insisted, it was the deluge of Salome dancing on the vaudeville stage that made the "decadent longing of the daughter of Herodias" tolerable to opera-going audiences. "Don't smile at the suggestion that vaudeville has anything to do with the public's grand opera taste—for there is more than a modicum of truth in it."[106]

The ironies did not stop there. As the cultural elites were busy reappropriating Salome for the world of high art, the "Dance of the Seven Veils," despite its notorious history on the vaudeville stage, was suddenly designated as a classical dance. Now the idea that an African American performer like Aida Walker might offer the dance once again created another level of controversy.

So long as Walker performed her Salome as part of a black musical comedy called *Bandanna Land,* the public was prepared to appreciate the modesty and grace of a colored woman's dance and was more than ready to contrast Walker's version to the vulgarity of "the Salome plague" in vaudeville. But once it was announced in early August of 1912 that Walker had been invited to revive Salome's dance as a piece of classical art at Hammerstein's Victoria Theater, a strange and revealing shift in the terms of publicity and reception occurred. The Hammersteins were well aware that Walker's color was sure to spark enough controversy to make her a big box office hit in the Salome revival. Most African American performers, including hugely successful artists like Walker, operated largely within a segregated world limited to second-rate theaters serving a black clientele. Willie Hammerstein, Percy Williams, and Florenz Ziegfeld, Jr. were among a handful of white producers in the prewar era who featured black talent in mainstream entertainment venues, but even Ziegfeld only had room for one black performer: Bert Williams.

Stressing the novelty of allowing a black woman with ties to the world of African American entertainment to perform what was now called a classical dance, publicists and critics ignored the past five years of

Salomania on the American vaudeville circuit, including Gertrude Hoffmann's run at Hammerstein's Victoria. They conveniently forgot how even high art performers, like the Metropolitan Opera's Bianca Froelich, had been labeled as cootch dancers during the Salome epidemic. Rather, what concerned the press was exactly what Hammerstein had set out to tell them: Aida Overton Walker was the first colored performer who has "ever attempted to execute classical dancing."[107] For as one of his press agents put it, "Mr. Hammerstein, after witnessing several performances of Miss Walker surrounded by a company of real negroes," was so impressed with the "artistic mannerisms of this colored artist" that he came to the conclusion that she was "capable of graduating from this environment." Hammerstein had the audacity to deviate from "all traditions in theatrical history" by presenting a colored artist as "an exponent of this classic style of dancing."[108]

The transgression was not lost on the critics. *Stage Pictorial* quickly announced that "a Salome of color" was "a direct smash in the face of convention." Although Walker was "a prima donna at the head of several companies of colored performers and has won considerable popularity in vaudeville," her classical role would "surprise theatergoers."[109] It was a rare critic who caught the ironies of color in controversy surrounding Walker's "dark skinned Salome." Noting that "Miss Walker is the only colored artist who has ever been known to give this dance in public," an article in the *New York Telegraph* pointed out that this was actually quite strange, considering that "the original Salome's skin may have been a hue resembling that of Miss Walker's."[110]

In the end, Aida Overton Walker, who died in 1914 at the age of 34, was unable to transcend the categories to which black performers had been consigned.[111] Perhaps it was the still-fresh memory of Bert Williams's Salome burlesque in *Bandanna Land,* but, more likely, it was the inability of white critics like *Variety's* Sime Silverman to appreciate black performers outside of certain racially specific entertainment contexts. Thus to Silverman, Walker's Salome of 1912 was just another form of low comedy. As he saw it: "Ada Overton Walker's single-handed 'Salome' was funny at Hammerstein's Monday . . . Miss Walker did it the same way Tuesday, it was just as funny." The music, on the other hand, was "all wrong." Instead of "heavy classic stuff," Sime argued, "the bunch should have been playing 'Robert E. Lee.' Ada could just tear that tune to pieces as 'Salome' for she is the best 'Salome' 'Tommy' dancer who ever hit Broadway on a warm day."[112] A Tommy dancer was one who did the "Texas Tommy," a highly acrobatic routine first performed by black dancers in the cabarets, nightclubs, and vaudeville houses of the prewar era, and later copied by whites.[113]

When an African American woman took the part of Salome, it was assumed she would be doing some kind of funny "business." Given the marginal position of Jews in American society in this period, the same expectations might have held. In fact, however, Jewish women's ability to manipulate the Salome role was far more complex.

Although Sarah Bernhardt was so closely identified with the Salome figure, the first recognizably Jewish performer to engage Salome in the United States was Fanny Brice. At different points in their careers both Aida Walker and Fanny Brice had tried but failed to be taken seriously as something other than ethnic performers. While Walker was seen as too "dark," Brice was labeled "too New York" and "too Jewish" to be fully acceptable to non-Jewish audiences.[114] Yet it is significant that while Walker had used Salome to try to transcend her identification with race comedy, Brice embraced the role as an opportunity to develop her persona as a Hebrew caricaturist.

Born Fanny Borach to Hungarian Jewish immigrants in 1891, Brice had spent much of her early life in Newark, New Jersey, but took every opportunity to mythologize her childhood roots as a Lower East Side New York ghetto girl. When Brice was in her teens the family moved to Harlem, where Fanny performed sentimental ballads and coon melodies at Keeney's variety theater. Brice made it to Broadway fame in 1910, when she was a featured ethnic comic in the Ziegfeld *Follies,* but only after what she called her "Jewish comedy song"—"Sadie Salome"—had enabled her to develop some of the tools of her signature style of Hebrew impersonation.[115]

Before Fanny Brice took Salome in hand, the Jewishness of the character had not been prominent in the American public discourse. In contrast to the anti-Semitic overtones of European high-culture traditions of Salome, Americans emphasized her more amorphous Oriental associations. If they identified the image of Salome with Jews, it was more to the remote Hebrews of the Bible rather than to recent Jewish immigrants from Eastern Europe. On the American stage the most prominent Jewish female stereotype was that of the *belle juive,* with her aura of feminine mystery and sexual allure. The *belle juive* was more tragic than treacherous. Like Bernhardt's Leah, she displayed the womanly qualities of noble self-sacrifice.[116] In contrast, the European Salome was a grotesque variation on a Jewish historical type—a monstrous figure representing a degenerate race.[117] On the American stage, she had no equivalent.

Thus when Fanny Brice entered the world of American popular theater in 1909, the idea of a destructive Jewish vamp or femme fatale had been absent from it, and even Salome was not understood as peculiarly Jewish by American audiences. In American popular stage comedy, there were *belles juives* and scolding, overbearing, and aggressive Jewish New Woman characters often played by Gentile women. Mainly, however, it was male rather than female Jewish types that dominated the popular stage of the Progressive era.[118]

Fanny Brice turned Salome into a Jewish immigrant daughter and made both her own and the character's ethnicity the point of comic departure. An American-born child of immigrant parents, Brice spoke no Yiddish, but she used a fake accent to turn her Sadie Salome into a stereotypical Lower East Side ghetto girl. Following the lead of vaudeville's male comics who performed humorous renditions of Eastern European Jewish immigrant street types, Brice's parody created a hilarious contrast between the dancing femme fatale and the awkward ethnic mannerisms with which she portrayed her.[119]

Brice first performed her routine Sadie Salome in a burlesque show called *College Girls*. Using Edgar Leslie and Irving Berlin's Tin Pan Alley tune of 1909, "Sadie Salome, Go Home!" she created a sight-gag called Sadie Cohen, a nice Jewish girl who leaves her happy home and her conservative boyfriend Moses to become "an actress lady." On the stage she's all the rage as a "Sa-lo-my ba-by." Wearing a heavily starched and obviously itchy sailor suit instead of the harem costume of most vaudeville Salomes, Brice rolled her large green eyes for comic effect, and used hilariously awkward physical movements to turn the legend of Salome's threatening sexual perversity into a scene of comic incongruity.[120] Conveying the pleading of Sadie's disgraced boyfriend Moses, Brice intoned in heavy Yiddish accent: "Don't do that dance, I tell you Sa-die. That's not a bus'ness for a la-dy. Oy, Oy, Oy, Oy,—where is your clothes? Sa-die Sa-lome, go home!"[121]

Brice's routine poked fun at Salome dancing and criticized the silliness of stage-struck girls like Sadie (and Brice herself) who were taken in by the fad.[122] Moreover, by layering her Sadie Salome with complicated self-deprecating Jewish meanings, Brice displaced the stereotype of one kind of Jewish woman (the decadent and degenerate Jewess of European Orientalist fantasy) with another (the unsophisticated and awkward ghetto girl of Progressive-era urban America).[123] Both were cultural outsiders, one coded as a powerfully mysterious exotic of the mythical past, the other as a relatively powerless ethnic outsider of the present.

The Brice interpretation involved some important reversals. With the exception of Aida Walker, most of the Salomes of the popular theater had been white American women masquerading as dangerously voluptuous and exotic Oriental others. Brice's Sadie, on the other hand, is an immigrant who has taken up the godless sex-crazed ways of American mainstream popular culture, including its Salome dancing. In this reappropriation, the newcomer becomes corrupted by the exotic foreignness of American popular culture.[124]

Mixing sexual and ethnic themes, Brice would use Salome to launch a career in which she burlesqued both the artistic pretensions of high culture (modern dance, ballet, and other kinds of contemporary theatrical fare) and the histrionic excesses of theatrical and cinematic *femme fatales*. Among the later was a routine called "I'm Bad," in which she parodied the movie vamp Theda Bara.[125]

We can never know with any certainty how the predominantly middle- and working-class, mixed-sex audiences interpreted the performances of Brice, Walker, Hoffmann, and Tanguay. Clearly, the self-conscious humor of these dancers and comics offered a range of positions with which to identify. And their play with Salome draws our attention, once again, to the ways in which women's theatrical experimentation produced ambiguous ideological statements. In the era of the New Woman, playfulness, parody, and burlesque constituted the core of an expressive culture that could be used to achieve mocking distance, to criticize, or to conserve—or simply to be enjoyed for its own sake. Motivated by the desire for self-expression, for celebrity, for money, and, especially in Walker's case, for social change, the vaudeville Salomes both exploited and critiqued some of the predominant gender and racial typologies of the day.

The Death of Salomania and the Rebirth of Salome

By the outbreak of the First World War, the epidemic of Salome dancing had largely subsided. In 1913, when Frederic La Delle published his illustrated "Course of Instruction," *How to Enter Vaudeville,* Salome was listed as just one of 90 common stage types who, along with the Soubrette, the Spanish dancer, the Cow Girl, the Indian Maid, the Gypsy, the Juvenile, the Tramp, and the Dutch, Negro, Coon, Irish, and Hebrew, were stock figures in the ethnic and gender stereotypes of the popular stage. Salome had become both a costume and a set of associated gestures that any aspiring vaudevillian with a degree of originality and individual judgment—what La Delle called that "something different"—could try on for size.[126]

Nevertheless the idea of Salome as a powerful symbol of female transgressiveness remained very much alive as a cultural resource. As the domestic hysteria surrounding America's entrance into the First World War began to mount, and as the American suffrage movement shifted into high gear, popular culture breathed new life into the figure of Salome. Nineteen eighteen was a banner year for Salome revivals. As in the prewar Salome craze, sexuality and humor went hand in hand. In the fall of 1918 at New York's Winter Garden Theater, the Shubert brothers opened the seventh edition of their annual musical revue, *The Passing Show.* Like other musical revues of the era, this was a comic extravaganza—a satirical romp through the social, political, cultural, and theatrical landscape of contemporary urban life. The show featured topical skits, interpolated by the singing and dancing spectacle of revue's best-known feature, "glorious girls." But the girls of this 1918 revue were as troubling as they were glorious. Though the program promised "a tidal wave of laughter" a "flood of fun" a "Niagara of Beauty," and a "Cascade of Melody" in its cacophonous representation of modern womanhood, it also displayed the deeper strains of wartime political and sexual struggles. On this bill were "Alluring Vampire Girls," "Nubian Slave Girls," and "Salome," whose violent sexuality was enlisted to serve to interests of patriotism.[127]

The show burlesqued the story of Salome by changing the setting to America's home front during World War I, working in jokes about war bonds, German spies, and Liberty Loans. The story also became a vehicle for satirizing contemporary politics and moral codes. Fearing that Salome's dancing might bring out the censors and spoil his evening, "Americus" (the Shubert's version of Herod) turns the Salome story upside down by begging her *not* to dance and promising her "all the treasures of the world"—in this case all of the commodities in short supply during World War I—if she will only not dance. His song implores:

I've an egg that I keep in my safe locked up,
. . . and a half pound of steak right from Tiffany's store,
and a pint of gasoline . . .

I've a lump of sugar and some coffee beans. . . . .
These treasures so rare I will give them to you. . . .
If you'll promise not to dance.

But Salome, who has earned the nickname "Miss Spearmint" because she's so "Wrigley," does dance and ends by asking for the helmeted head of Kaiser Wilhelm—the "man who put the germ in Germany." One edition of the revue had Salome calling for the head of anti-war Senator Robert La Follette—"the man who put the 'sin' in Wisconsin."[128]

The war and postwar years also saw the renewal of more serious treatments of the Salome story and its revival as a tale of women's disruptive and deadly sexual power. It was a renewal in which Eastern European Jewish women were important participants. Film actresses Theda Bara and Alla Nazimova, as well as the self-theatricalizing immigrant writer Anzia Yezierska, restored something of the flavor of foreignness and Oriental mystery to the figure of Salome in the years between 1918 and 1923.

With the release of Fox studio's full-length feature, *Salome,* in 1918, the non-opera-going public was treated to a riveting narrative account of Oscar Wilde's Salome story, with the "sinful" and brooding "vampire woman" of the movies, Theda Bara, in the title role.[129] Billed as "the wickedest woman in the world," Bara was really Theodosia Goodman of Cincinnati, daughter of a Polish Jew.[130] Beginning in 1915 with a film called *A Fool There Was,* Fox studio featured her as the "ruthless siren" in a series of sensational melodramas about women who mercilessly destroy the lives of men—titles like *Sin, The Devil's Daughter, Cleopatra, The Serpent, Gold and the Woman,* and *Destruction.* By 1918, the name Theda Bara had become part of the national cultural vocabulary. As a Cleveland reporter put it, the term "bara-esque" had become a synonym for erotic danger: "to be a vampire now is to be a Thedabara."[131]

It seemed only logical, therefore, that Bara, the bad woman and "love pirate" of Progressive-era movies, a star who claimed that even so "great an artist as Sarah Bernhardt" had never quite "realized the emancipation of passion," would play Salome.[132] "As *Salome* I tried to absorb the poetic impulse of Oscar Wilde," wrote Bara. "I tried to interpret the extraordinary, the hopeless moral disintegration of a woman's soul," with "sincere artistic effort."[133]

But Bara also claimed that Salome had social significance for contemporary women. "It may be," she claimed, "that in every woman there is *Carmen* and *Cleopatra, Juliet* and *Salome.* In me they are frankly destined."[134] Only three years before the release of *Salome* Bara had claimed that her "vampire" roles symbolically redressed the unavenged wrongs and unredressed grievances of her sex. Asserting that "women are my greatest fans," she insisted that "downtrodden wives write me to this effect." In playing the vamp, "I am in effect a feministe."[135]

In 1918, just before *Salome* hit the screen, the *New York Telegraph* published more of Bara's analysis of why good women, even model wives and mothers, flocked to see her pictures. The "vampire," she said "is a sort of revenge for the disappointments and dullness of life." The vampire's invariably tragic end, Bara claimed, was "sort of a compensation for the woman whose sense of justice would be outraged if sin were to triumph in the end," for "you can't have your cake and eat it too, no matter how clever or charming you may be."[136] And when a St. Louis film review board attacked the "overbold and underclad" nature of the *Salome* film, Bara railed against the hypocrisy of the "present-day viewpoint which makes it 'sinful' for a woman to expose parts of her body on the stage or screen," but "conventional for her to do it at a bathing beach." Those critics who only went looking for signs of immorality, she said, missed the powerful moral lessons of the film. "Salome," she insisted, was not an "inspiration" to wickedness, but a "deterrent."[137]

Four years after Bara's film, on the heels of her Broadway debut in Ibsen's *Hedda Gabler,* Russian Jewish immigrant actress Alla Nazimova starred in a modernist art film version of *Salome.* The movie, which *Photoplay* called "a hot house orchid of decadent passion," had exotic sets (designed by Natacha Rambova—Rudolph Valentino's second wife) based on the notorious illustrations of Aubrey Beardsley, and bizarre Oriental-*moderne* costumes, not to mention a cast that included dwarfs, men in drag, and blacks playing slaves. Like Theda Bara, Nazimova defended her character, insisting that Salome was "the one pure creature in a court where sin was abundant." And "if in her ignorance she destroyed her idol, she was not the first woman to do that, nor the last." Then, in a kind of pseudo-feminist gesture, Nazimova linked the legend of Salome to the desires of modern women, insisting that "the feminine instinct within Salome to command and rule that which she loved persists in the race from the legend of Eve to the newest divorce story in the latest issue of today's newspaper."[138]

Nazimova and Bara's application of the Salome story to contemporary female behavior was an important shift in direction. For while the vaudeville performers had used the Salome dance as a vehicle for their own stage personalities and as an affront to sexual prudery, none but Brice had called attention to Salome's off-stage counterparts. With the publication in 1923 of Anzia Yezierska's first novel, *Salome of the Tenements* (and its cinematic incarnation in 1925), the dancing *femme fatale* turned, like Brice's Sadie, into the immigrant daughter trying to establish her own individual identity in America. Whether the Russian Jewish immigrant writer had seen Brice's routine or the films by Theda Bara and Alla Nazimova is unclear. What is certain, however, is that the figure of Salome emerged as the powerful alter-ego for Yezierska's first fully developed fictional heroine, Sonya Vrunsky.

The story of a mismatched love affair between an ambitious ghetto girl and a millionaire philanthropist, *Salome of the Tenements* was in part based on the marriage of Yezierska's friend, the Jewish immigrant writer and labor activist Rose Pastor, to the wealthy Socialist do-gooder Graham (J. G. Phelps) Stokes. But like all of Yezierska's fiction, it was also autobiographical, telling the story of her own tempestuous romance with the WASP intellectual and reformer John Dewey.[139] In this novel Yezierska uses the Salome story to contrast the passionate, sensual hunger of the Eastern European Jewish heroine Sonya (Salome) with the cold, overly rational, sexually repressed saintliness of the high-born settlement house worker John Manning (John the Baptist). Her Sonya/Salome "was an electric radiance divinely formed of flesh and blood . . . She has the figure of a born dancer, of a Bernhardt in her youth." Like the great tragedienne she seeks to emulate, Sonya was a star on "her own small stage." In her "intensity of emotion," she was "rapacious" in her desire to "absorb the austere perfections of the Anglo-Saxon race." Using her beauty and guile, Sonya, the "oriental mystery" of tenements, wins John's love. But the paternalistic disregard of this "frozen philanthropist" for the true needs of the Jewish ghetto dwellers, and his ultimate rejection of her "hot blooded" physical passion, bring down her wrath. In the end, the scorned Jewish temptress returns to "her people" in the East Side ghetto, choosing repatriation over assimilation to the "abnormal repression" of Anglo-Saxonized femininity.[140] Yezierska rescues Salome's reputation, gives her a more empathetic identity, and invites her readers to identify with her idealism. By making Salome/Sonya into a fierce defender of her people, and turning her deadly will into a source of positive ethnic female energy, the writer shows her readers a model of what a passionate Jewish feminist might look like.

With the publication of Yezierska's novel and the release of the two films, Salome in America had come full circle. When she first hit the vaudeville stage with a vengeance in 1908, Salome was a hyperbolic vehicle for the promotion of women's stage personalities as well as a screen for projecting the cultural anxieties about sexuality and race. Even when the figure lost some of its ludic mobility as she moved from the fluid medium of live theatricals to the more tightly scripted narratives of film and back into the realm of literature, her meaning was never fixed or static.

Salome was a powerful figure, and performers and writers of both sexes and from many artistic traditions appropriated her for their own purposes and derived a kind of license from the character itself. What began in the high culture of literature, painting, and opera as a vision of the *femme fatale,* eventually came to serve as vehicle for Gertrude Hoffmann's knowing smile, for Eva Tanguay's hyperbolic joke, for Aida Overton Walker's bid for respectability, for Fanny Brice's self-deprecating ethnic satire, and Anzia Yezierska's search for an acceptable way of being an independent Jewish woman in America. By using Salome to assert the force of their own personalities and critical perspectives, they not only refracted and reorganized a powerful cultural stereotype of the bad woman, they experimented with new and more complicated ways of representing female assertiveness. In the first two decades of the twentieth century, that kind of experimentation was taking place on both sides of the footlights.

1. Sarah Bernhardt symbolized brazen female egotism and self-assertiveness, and became a model for other actresses and an icon for American suffragists seeking their own limelight. 1880 photo.

2. In *La Dame aux Camélias* Bernardt played the tubercular courtesan Marguerite, one of many roles in which she is both sexually sinful and morally redeemed. 1896 photo.

MME. SARAH BERNHARDT,
WHO COMES TO THIS COUNTRY
EARLY NEXT MONTH FOR A
LIMITED ENGAGEMENT.
From a Recent Photograph
Bearing Her Autograph.
(Photo by Sarony
Studio.)

COPYRIGHT 1896 BY N. SARONY.   No. 11

3. Here Sarah Bernhardt poses as the fiery femme fatale and former courtesan, Empress Théodora. The actress turned all her stage roles into vehicles for her own flamboyant personality. Photo c. 1884.

4. In her famous 1910 working-girl comedy, *Tillie's Nightmare,* Marie Dressler played her signature stage role: the fat, acrobatic, and hilariously awkward woman who longed for love and respectability in a society that glorified passive slender female beauty.

5. Marie Dressler designed her own costumes as hilarious parodies of cumbersome and constraining turn-of-the-century feminine fashions. Photo c. 1900.

6. With her loud and unmelodic voice, wildly energetic physicality, and audacious self-promoting style, comic singer Eva Tanguay honed an image of defiant female eccentricity that had a special appeal to female audiences. Photo c. 1909.

7. Trixie Friganza, a musical comedy and vaudeville star from the early 1900s to the 1920s, was the queen of "fat" comedy. Her self-deprecating humor focused on the trials and tribulations of those who did not conform to popular ideals of womanhood. Photo c. 1920s.

8. Singing comedienne Nora Bayes challenged the idea that women had to be unattractive and grotesque in order to be humorous. Bayes also challenged marital stereotypes by billing her husband, songwriter and pianist Jack Norworth, as her "assistant." Photo c. 1908.

9. Teenage mimic Elsie Janis rose to popularity by imitating and satirizing her contemporaries on the vaudeville and Broadway stage. To imitate was not merely to copy, it was also to make a spectacle of one's self. Photo c. 1905.

10. Cecilia Loftus, "The Mimetic Marvel," here imitates Sarah Bernhardt. The imitation craze revealed turn-of-the-century fascination with mimetic technologies such as cameras and phonographs. 1898 photo.

11. Imitations enhanced the celebrity of the initator and the imitated. In 1910,
Tanguay invited other performers to "Give an Imitation of Me."

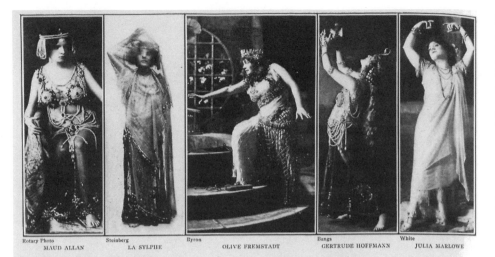

All Sorts and Kinds of Salomes

SALOMANIA is not a new craze. Mary Garden, who is now impersonating the Daughter of Herodias in Strauss' vivid music drama at the Manhattan Opera House, is only the descendant of a long line of scantily-clad Salomes that have cropped up from time to time during the last two thousand years.

Medieval legend depicts Salome blown upon by the Mighty Breath for having caused the Prophet's death by her dancing, and by way of punishment being whirled into space, where she is doomed to dance and whirl forever. Thus Salome joined the "furious host," a roaming band of banished spirits which haunted medieval Europe with their restlessness. Berchard of Worms reports with twelfth century gravity that fully one-third of the whole world worshipped her. We still seek her shrine, but we do not always worship.

Salome, as we know her to-day, has evolved gradually from the brief accounts given of her in the Bible, and she has inspired poets, painters, dancers, dramatists and composers. The subject "Salome Dancing" has appealed particularly to artists of all ages, from the fourteenth century manuscript which reveals her "vaulting before Herod" on her hands, to several pictures by the old masters.

The numerous versions of the story are conflicting. Some, based upon the meager Biblical account, are historical, while others follow the Oscar Wilde dramatic poem, vivid in the color of its word-painting and unpleasantly morbid in its imagination. Historically Salome was a "korasian," which in the Hebrew means "damsel," innocent of evil motive, but the victim of her wicked mother's revenge. She is terror-stricken at the sight of the head of John the Baptist, and remorseful. Renan in his "Life of Jesus" suggests the interpolated love of Salome for the Prophet, and in Flaubert's "Herodias" the motive is further emphasized. Sudermann's "Johannes" deals with this theme more gently, while in Wilde's version Salome is imbued with a revoltingly morbid motive for her crime — sexual passion for John the Baptist.

Some fifteen years ago, Sarah Bernhardt presented the Wilde drama at the Palace Theatre in London, but the censor prohibited it after the first performance. Oscar Wilde later tried to sell her the drama, which she refused.

12. "Salomania," the epidemic of Salome dancing, swept the nation in 1908. On the vaudeville stage, dancers of every description used the power of the character as a vehicle for their own personalities and theatrical aspirations.

GERTRUDE HOFFMANN   SALOME DANCE No. 7.

COPYRIGHT
1908
BY F.C.BANGS

13. Gertrude Hoffmann defended her vaudeville dance, "Vision of Salome," as art while hyping its sexual lewdness. Here she poses with the gruesome "head." 1908 photo.

14. Aida (Ada) Overton Walker was vaudeville's first black Salome. She tried to use the role to overturn racial stereotypes and gain respect as a "classical" dancer. 1912 photo.

15. In the 1910s activists in the modern suffrage movement tried to dramatize their cause and counter the image of suffragettes as "unsexed" or manly. Hence they chose actress-like speakers such as the attractive and charismatic attorney Inez Milholland Boissevain, here leading the 1913 suffrage parade in Washington, D.C.

16. The lines between acting and activism were further blurred by anarchist Emma Goldman, who turned politics into a form of theater with her fiery monologues. 1919 photo.

17. Members of the modern suffrage movement emphasized uniformity of dress and dignified marching in their annual street parades. Yet some commentators compared activists, as in this 1912 New York City parade, to squads of Broadway chorus girls.

18. In Broadway musical revues of the 1910s and 1920s, chorus girls became ornamental objects, as in this Ziegfeld *Follies* show. Women and things and women as things were central themes of these revues. (HRC)

19. Elaborate headdresses, like these battleships from the Ziegfeld *Follies of 1909*, were a staple of Broadway revue costumes of the pre- and post-WWI era.

20. Fashion and eroticism as well as absurdity and excess were important aspects of the Broadway revues of WWI era, as in this *Ziegfeld Follies* ensemble.

21. Precision dancing, which featured geometric formations of chorus girls arranged by height and specialty, mirrored early twentieth-century industrial culture. In contrast to the distinctive personalities of actresses and comics, these line dancers functioned as a disciplined female mass, as in this scene from the *Ziegfeld Follies of 1916*.

22. Ned Wayburn, the "chorus king" of the Broadway revue, was known as an "efficiency expert in girls." In an era of feminist self-assertion, Wayburn insisted that his ideal line dancer was a female "automaton" designed "to please." Photo c. 1917.

23. Strong female personalities like the comic Fanny Brice had to compete with the legions of beautiful young chorus "girls" who populated Ziegfeld's shows. Brice (in stripes) performed Yiddish-inflected send-ups of popular female stage dancers and screen vamps. She is pictured here with Grace Tyson and Billie Reeves in a scene from the *Follies in 1910*.

24. As the aggressive New Woman of the early twentieth century demanded political, economic and sexual equality, Broadway producer Florenz Ziegfeld Jr. advertised his alternative: a standardized female product called the "Glorified American Girl." Chorus girl Olive Thomas is pictured here in a scene from the *Midnight Frolic of 1916*.

25. Musical revues of the 1910s and 1920s tried to obliterate the New Woman's political and sexual threat. "The Rotisserie" number in *Artists and Models,* a 1925 Shubert revue, turned passive chorus girls into "broilers" that could be trussed, cooked, and eaten by men.

26. From 1900 to the early 1930s, the chorus girl was seen as the reflection of a new generation of striving urban women. Variously depicted as a sexy "chicken," a modern Cinderella, a ruthless "gold digger," an outrageous spectacle, and a heroic working-girl, she symbolized the emergence of modern women into the twentieth century. Ina Claire plays the predatory chorus girl in Avery Hopwood's *The Gold Diggers* (1919).

27. By the end of the 1920s, women found fewer opportunities to engage in self-styled theatrical irreverence and creativity. Mae West, who successfully moved from vaudeville to Broadway in the 1920s and then to sound comedy in the 1930s, was a brazen vestige of an earlier era. She is pictured here in her controversial Broadway play of 1928, *Diamond Lil*.

"The Eyes of the Enemy"

FEMALE ACTIVISM AND THE
PARADOX OF THEATER

5 In February of 1914, when the famous anarchist Emma
Goldman was lecturing on the "Social Significance of
Modern Drama" at the Berkeley Theater on 42nd Street
in New York, she received what she called "a bit of interesting news." A representative from Hammerstein's
Victoria—the same vaudeville theater where, just a few
years earlier, Gertrude Hoffmann and Aida Overton Walker performed
their controversial visions of Salome—approached Goldman to ask if
she might "consider the vaudeville stage."[1]

Hammerstein's wanted her for one week and was willing to pay
$1,000 for the engagement. The suggestion threw her into a quandary.
Torn between her desire to pay off her financial debts "and drift for a
year in peace," and her contempt for commercialized entertainments
like vaudeville, where her political speeches would be "sandwiched in"
between dancers, acrobats, and trained dog acts, she initially dismissed
the proposal as ridiculous. "The only thing that would counteract my
disgust would be a large money consideration," she wrote to her lover
and political comrade Ben Reitman. "If I could get 5 weeks [at] a thousand dollars a week, or several months at $500 per week I would take it
. . . But if I am to sell my soul, it will not be for little."[2]

Given Emma Goldman's status as a political celebrity, the invitation to
be a two-a-day act on the vaudeville stage is hardly surprising. Outside
the theatrical profession itself, few women of her day had as much name
recognition as Emma Goldman—"the most dangerous woman in America."[3] Mention of her name, which was associated with "free love and
bombs," was, as one of her friends recalled, "enough . . . to produce a
shudder."[4]

But it was not just Goldman's reputation that attracted the attention of the impresario: it was also her self-dramatizing personality. Of all the famous female left-wing orators of the pre-WWI era, Goldman was the most self-consciously dramatic. To many of her contemporaries, writes one of her biographers, Goldman seemed "almost a figure of the theatrical world."[5] Politics was for her a form of theater, and theater a medium of political expression. During her annual cross-country lecture tours, which began in the 1890s and lasted until her deportation in 1919, she was arrested numerous times on the grounds that her inflammatory speeches posed a threat to public order. Huge crowds of admirers as well as detractors came to hear her denounce capitalism, militarism, organized religion, and the state, and to defend women's right to sexual freedom and birth control. "I demand the independence of woman," she declared, "her right to support herself; to live for herself; to love whomever she pleases, or as many as she pleases."[6]

Goldman's high-minded disdain for the popular stage notwithstanding, her style of political activism actually had much in common with the professional strategies of the female stars of vaudeville. Like Eva Tanguay and Gertrude Hoffmann, Goldman was a "headliner" whose success built on her ability to showcase her strong personality. For her, personality was a form of political communication. "After all," Goldman wrote to a fellow anarchist in 1906, "it is more important to do propaganda with one's personality than with words."[7]

Like the vaudeville headliners, Goldman was a new kind of public woman, whose influence grew in many respects from her skillful efforts at self-mythologizing and her shrewd manipulation of the machinery of public relations and mass media. Her lectures were never spontaneous. They were carefully orchestrated for maximum public exposure, extensively promoted and advertised, and given advance publicity in the commercial as well as the radical press.[8]

The offer from Hammerstein's Victoria was neither the first nor the only time that the spectacle of women's activism was imagined as a form of entertainment. In 1906, when the fiery Socialist orator, Elizabeth Gurley Flynn, was still a high-school student in New York City, she and several other comrades (including her father) were arrested after they spoke at a rally at the corner of 38th and Broadway, then the heart of the theater district. In the aftermath of Flynn's arrest, Theodore Dreiser published an article in *Broadway Magazine* (a theater journal) describing her "eloquence, her youth and loveliness" and calling her "An East Side Joan of Arc." He was not alone in viewing Gurley Flynn's performance and arrest through the lens of the theater. The famous Broadway producer David Belasco sent Elizabeth and her mother tickets to his popular play, *The Girl of the Golden West*. After the matinee they were escorted upstairs to Belasco's office, and the producer "asked with an amused twinkle in his eyes, had I ever thought of being an actress; he was thinking of producing a labor play and I might be good material to appear in it." To which she replied: "Indeed not! . . . I don't want to be a actress! . . . I'm in the labor movement and I speak my own piece!"[9]

As Goldman and Gurley Flynn both knew, politics and theater were not the same. Theater licensed female transgression so long as it could sell it as entertainment. Female activism, however it might take on the look and feel of theater, had vastly different agendas; its sharply defined social and political goals carried potentially revolutionary consequences. Nevertheless, Hammerstein's invitation to Goldman and Belasco's summons to Gurley Flynn symbolized a broad cultural shift in which acting and activism, theater and politics, began to blur. As women on both sides of the footlights were making spectacles of themselves in public, being political and being theatrical became mutually reinforcing aspects of a new style of femininity. As politics and theater became zones of cultural convergence, the perceptual effect was similar to that produced by the machine known as the stereopticon—a popular device of the late nineteenth and early twentieth centuries which created a dissolving view from two discrete images. The result was that in the popular imagination two pictures of female spectacle began to blend and merge as the eye of the spectator pulled them together, building image on image. As a consequence, images of the female activist and suffragist were layered with aspects of the stage, and the representations of women in the theater were refracted through the changing nature of women's off-stage behavior.

Being Theatrical

As a mode of communication and persuasion, theatricalized political spectacle has a long history in the United States. Elaborate parades, military, labor, and temperance processions, street burlesques and charivaris, and other festive enactments of political propaganda, not to mention open-air speeches, were all part of the political culture of nineteenth-century America.[10]

Up until the end of the nineteenth century, street theater was largely perceived as a male affair. Women served as allegorical figures representing traditional domestic roles in male political spectacles. Unless they were under the protective escort of a man or costumed as symbols of purity or patriotism, respectable women were often excluded from election parades. But the exceptions were many and growing more numerous. Self-identified female radicals, and so-called platform women in the temperance, suffrage, populist, and labor movements, whose mass meetings and demonstrations brazenly challenged gender norms, were a conspicuous part of the spectacle of late nineteenth-century political life.[11]

After 1900 mainstream political parties came to depend less and less upon rituals of street spectacle and public display. But other organizations, including civic groups and women's groups, came to rely upon them more and more.[12] At the same time, the mainstream political parties, the radical left, and the woman suffrage movement all turned to modern political methods, most importantly the use of media-driven publicity strategies.[13]

In the years between 1907 and 1919, the woman suffrage movement adopted what one observer called "unconventional maneuvers" and spectacular methods of political activism.[14] Suffrage organizations staged elaborate street parades and pageants, delivered open-air speeches and held outdoor rallies, arranged auto, trolley, and train tours (called suffrage specials), put on street dances, outdoor concerts and demonstrations, launched hot air balloons, performed shows in vaudeville theaters, wrote and performed pro-suffrage comedies, satires, and dramas, made movies, gave speeches during intermission at theaters and movie houses, put up billboards, electrical signs, and window displays, manufactured and sold buttons, badges, clothing, and other consumer goods designed to promote the cause, and used every conceivable form of publicity stunt to call attention to their campaign.[15]

The "big spectacle" in the modern American suffrage campaign owes much to the legacy of radical civil disobedience on the part of Susan B. Anthony and other nineteenth-century suffragists. But especially influential was the example of the militant methods of the British suffragettes. Their strategy involved the disruption of political business as usual by means of publicity-getting spectacles that included heckling cabinet ministers, mass demonstrations, and arson and property destruction, which led to still other sources of publicity—arrests, imprisonments, hunger strikes, and the drama of the protagonists' eventual release from prison. It was a campaign that relied heavily upon images of female martyrdom, and it was cloaked in the rhetoric of righteous moralism.[16]

A number of key American suffrage activists, including Harriet Stanton Blatch and Alice Paul, had close relationships with the British militants, participated in some of their early organizational activities, and though they eschewed their violent tactics, they admired the militants' courage and learned from their ability to generate media publicity.[17] The younger American suffragists, Blatch among them, were also influenced by their ties to the labor and socialist movements. The cross-class alliances they formed in the Women's Trade Union League and Blatch's Equality League of Self-Supporting Women familiarized middle-class suffragists with more aggressive styles of working women's street protest in an era of well-publicized industrial strikes and uprisings.[18]

Although the socialist and anarchist left had a complicated relationship to the suffrage movement—Goldman, for example, was a bitter critic of what she saw as the suffragists' narrow ideological premise—the wider radical subculture of the American left nevertheless provided the suffragists with examples of flamboyant, crowd-captivating labor and political organizers. Among them were celebrity speakers Mary Harris ("Mother") Jones, Kate Richards O'Hare, Elizabeth Gurley Flynn, Voltairine de Cleyre, and, of course, Emma Goldman. From the 1870s to the era of the First World War, left-wing radicals of every sort—Populists, Socialists, anarchists, and labor organizers—specialized in head-line-grabbing styles of fearless agitational politics which included, in addition to picket lines and open-air and indoor mass meetings, flagrant acts of civil disobedience leading to arrest and political martyrdom.[19]

But just as critical in influencing the flamboyant campaign methods of the modern suffrage movement were the new institutions of urban commercial spectacle—the new journalism, advertising, and, most importantly, the popular theater. Popular theater, the central instrument of spectacle in this larger commercial culture, provided some of the key conceptual and visual vocabularies for the emerging style of female political conduct.[20]

The relationship between theater and female activism was expressed and perceived in several overlapping areas. First, the stage and the female performer became increasingly important symbols and resources for the conduct of women's politics, particularly in the early twentieth-century suffrage campaign. Second, the experience of the popular theater influenced the way the public saw and understood new styles of women's political behavior. Finally, the institution of the theater deflected the rising tide of female activism by translating it into the familiar idioms of the popular stage.

For the suffragists the result of this connection was paradoxical. Suffragists wagered that the serious political purposes of their movement could be communicated by using the popular stage and the larger commercial culture for their own ends. This strategy proved indispensable as the means for drawing attention to their cause. What they did not anticipate was how their turn to theatricalized spectacle would also make them vulnerable to adversaries who wished to undermine their political message.

When the suffrage campaign entered the twentieth century, organizers developed a sometimes contentious blend of old and new strategies. The National American Woman Suffrage Association (NAWSA) with which many of the state suffrage groups were affiliated, combined traditional methods of education and petitioning with newer organizational tactics. Beginning in New York at the city and state Level, NAWSA organizer Carrie Chapman Catt and her co-workers created their suffrage "machine" in 1909—a highly efficient political structure that was to be a better version of Tammany. Eventually, this group took the name of the Woman Suffrage Party. After 1910 Catt developed a highly centralized suffrage organization at the national level, complete with a dedicated corps of professional organizers, many of them college-educated women, who traveled the country working on various state referenda campaigns for the vote. By 1914 NAWSA had even established a professional lobby to work on behalf of a constitutional amendment securing woman suffrage.[21] These were also the years when the suffrage movement split over tactics. After 1913, a number of the more militant members of NAWSA left the organization to work with Alice Paul in the Congressional Union, an organization with a stronger feminist and working-class identity and one dedicated to directing its political energies exclusively toward the passage of a federal constitutional amendment.[22]

Though they differed in their larger organizational strategies, by 1912 the major American woman suffrage associations at the state and national levels agreed upon one thing: if their movement was to succeed it needed publicity. The goal was to get the activities of the suffrage campaign on the front page of every national newspaper and to keep it going until the vote was won. "As this is an advertising age," announced militant Harriot Stanton Blatch in 1912, "leaders of any movement do well to study . . . the methods of the [theatrical] press agent."[23]

Blatch spelled out the central premise of the campaign: "We all believed that suffrage propaganda must be made dramatic."[24] "We . . . believe in standing on street corners and fighting our way to recognition, forcing the men to think of us," announced a 1909 suffrage manifesto; "we glory . . . that we are theatrical."[25]

Being dramatic and theatrical meant being in the limelight. "For centuries," explained New York suffrage activist Gertrude Foster Brown, women had "been taught that self-distrust and shrinking from publicity were the most admirable of womanly qualities—'womanly modesty' was the phrase that covered it all, and this was thought to be the supremely desirable feminine characteristic." Brown spoke for a suffrage movement that was now dominated by a younger generation of middle-class activists when she said that the suffragists refused to be "timid" and were "now demanding a startling change."[26]

That startling change was the willingness to make a spectacle in public. Like women of the theater, suffragists would use their voices, bodies, and personalities to draw attention to themselves. From Boston to New York to Philadelphia, extending to the cities of the West, publicity stunts and street spectacles of every kind kept the cause before the public eye and the media. Among the most innovative and daring advertising tactics was the so-called Voiceless Speech. In 1913, Anna Constable, a member of the New York City Women's Political Union, was arrested after she rented a window in a Fifth Avenue shop, where, in full view of the street, she stood at a large easel, displaying "the wisdom printed in large letters on each one of the three dozen . . . thick pasteboard cards." Although store owners were only too happy to accommodate the suffragists, the police claimed that the gathering crowds blocked the sidewalks, disrupted traffic, and created a disturbance.[27] Year by year the press coverage of suffrage spectacle increased, and by the outbreak of the war in Europe these political theatricals, along with giant suffrage parades and pageants with tens of thousands of participants and as many spectators, had become major media events, with journalists and photographers covering their every twist and turn.

Being theatrical also meant scene-setting, and, most importantly, it meant image-making. Crucial to the publicity strategy of the suffrage campaign was the effort to create a new look for the suffrage activist, one that would appeal to a broad cross-section of the American people.

Observing the power of half-tone photography, theatrical press agentry, and advertising, suffragists learned how to use the apparatus of modern image-making to undercut traditional forms of gender prejudice.[28]

To fight the war of images and win the confidence of the public, the movement had to combat the long history of anti-woman suffrage representation in the popular culture. In popular iconography, the enemies of woman suffrage depicted the emancipated New Woman and the suffrage activists as unsexed, mannish, and domineering women. They were portrayed as spinsters who could not or would not marry or as married women who neglected their homes and children, henpecked their husbands, and generally inverted the natural order of gender relations. Thus American and British suffragists who fought the war of images, had to struggle for control over the very concept of femininity.

Both anti- and pro-suffrage forces struggled to assert their authority over the definition of the so-called womanly woman.[29] The American woman suffrage movement presented the female voter as a womanly woman engaged in maternalist reform. She emerged in the ideology as a selfless social mother or municipal "housekeeper" who would clean up political corruption and bring morally uplifting values to social life. The womanly woman was also an enlightened consumer who could be trusted not only to make wise choices for her home and family but also to choose socially responsible candidates for public office.[30]

Suffragists faced a special challenge in contending with the concept of the militant activist. A label for deviant femininity, it connoted a package of incongruent associations which included masculinity and shrieking, virago-like female hysteria.[31] One strategy was to domesticate her image, as Mary Holland Kinkaid's article and photo spread tried to do. Touting "The Feminine Charms of the Woman Militant," Kinkaid emphasized the "personal attractiveness and housewifely attainments," "exceptional charm," "beauty and talent" of the leaders of the modern suffrage campaign.[32] In England and America suffrage strategists also translated the female militant into a powerful and affirmative figure— Joan of Arc, the heroic symbol of woman's willingness to fight and sacrifice for a righteous cause. Both American and British suffragettes made frequent reference to the martyred figure, and incorporated her image in their pageants and parades.[33] The image of the righteous female militant also encompassed that of the courageous female wage earner, whose economic and family security, it was argued, would be protected by woman suffrage.[34]

But of all the new suffrage campaign images, none was as modern and ultimately as problematic for the movement as the notion of the pretty and charming "new" New Woman, a young and stylish version of the American girl of popular culture, whose physical allure and fashionable exterior meant to soften the threat of her political aspirations.[35] More was at stake than just the public relations value of the pretty suffragist. The younger members of the suffrage movement believed physical allure and stylishness were perfectly compatible with political commitments. Both were part of a modern female identity. As Lydia Commander proclaimed, "Women are no longer to be considered little tootsey wootseys who have nothing to do but look pretty," but then she added what became the critical piece of feminist revision: "They are determined to take an active part in the community and look pretty too."[36]

As they exploited the public relations value of advertising, film, and street theater, the younger generation of suffragists worked to recast the woman citizen variously as mother, worker, consumer, "municipal housekeeper," womanly woman, and modern girl—feminine, stylish, fashionable, and pretty.

Actresses and Activism

When feminism (with its emphasis upon individual self-realization) and suffrage activism (with its focus on political equality) began to converge in the early twentieth century, both the actress and the institution of the theater provided a number of other symbolic possibilities for the women's rights movement.[37] Actresses would be recruited to advocate votes for women, and suffrage organizers frequently borrowed concepts from the stage as they strategized their new style of campaigning.

Given the taint of moral equivocacy that some still attached to the acting profession, and the increasingly daring and controversial performances by women on the popular stage, it may seem surprising that actresses played an important role in the suffrage campaign's efforts. But as urban society began to adopt more playful and experimental modes of personal and social expression, stage performers became a more positive symbol of modern times. Celebrities, whose professional and personal lives were intensely interesting to the public, provided vicarious forms of pleasure and fantasy.[38]

The actress figure was also an important source of inspiration to a generation of young women who were moving into the world of paid labor and professional life. Actresses were among the few working women able to command salaries as high as, and often higher than their male counterparts. Moreover, as representatives of an independent female life style and as symbols of feminine assertiveness, they exemplified a modern way of being female. "The actress," wrote British playwright Israel Zangwill, "has long appeared to the crowd as the ideal image of freedom and spontaneity, and indeed as a pioneer of public work and wages for women . . . free from many old-fashioned crampings and conventions." The stage, he pointed out, was "the sphere which women adorn equally with men, if not indeed with superior luster." To tell the actress that her place was in the home, he observed "would scarcely occur even to the most bigoted defenders of the hearth."[39]

As much as anything else, however, it was the craft of the actress that had both symbolic and strategic importance to suffrage organizers. To Harriot Stanton Blatch, the actress's powers of persuasion—her capacity to move the hearts and minds of the audience—made her vital to the suffrage cause. In a speech before the Actresses Committee that gathered to pledge their support for the 1912 New York Suffrage Parade, Blatch declared: "People must be appealed to through the emotions." For "this reason, your profession is the greatest in the world."[40]

In the "greatest profession in the world" there was no more famous figure than the larger-than-life Divine Sarah Bernhardt. Beginning in 1910, when the votes for women campaign first appropriated her celebrity for their cause, Bernhardt allowed the suffragists to bask in her reflected glory. That year, at the age of sixty-six, she made one of her legendary "farewell to America" tours, accompanied by her dashing and handsome twenty-seven-year-old lover and leading man, Lou Tellegen. When her ship docked in New York, members of a group calling themselves the Joan of Arc Suffrage League were on hand to greet her.[41] Bernhardt, who had first played the role of Joan of Arc in 1890 and was scheduled to perform it again on her American tour, must have seemed to the suffragists like a living embodiment of this heroic symbol of their campaign.[42] Carrying yellow pennants (the official color of the suffrage movement), members of the Joan of Arc Suffrage League, whom one reporter called "a hundred stern-looking women," presented Bernhardt with a large bouquet of chrysanthemums (their official flower) and crowded around her, shouting "Speech, sister, speech." Although sister

Bernhardt had graciously accepted an invitation to become an honorary member of their organization, she refused their requests for a speech after she arrived.[43]

Bernhardt's next farewell tour (1912–13) served as a rallying symbol for the New York Woman Suffrage Party's effort to get the franchise on the state ballot, and it provided the actress with still more opportunities for publicity. Arriving in New York City on May 4, 1913, in time for a scheduled suffrage parade, Bernhardt defended votes for women and cast aside her earlier reluctance to speak out openly in support of the suffrage cause. "I believe in the independence of women. I am for the vote," she told a reporter for the *Evening World.* "Perhaps," added Bernhardt, "the methods of the militants in England are necessary. I do not know. But I do know that women who starve themselves to death for an idea [a reference to jailed British suffragettes who went on hunger strikes] are not objects of ridicule. They interest me; they touch me very much!"[44]

Well before they approached Bernhardt, the New York suffragists had seized every available opportunity to publicize the involvement of prominent stage women in their campaign. The New York Woman Suffrage Party and other local and state groups were ideally positioned to take advantage of the publicity benefits that came from linking their cause to the theater. The hub of modern advertising, fashion, commercial culture, and popular theater, Manhattan—the most "cosmopolitan campaign center," as journalist Bertha Damaris Knobe called it—"naturally sets the spectacular pace" of the movement.[45]

There, in the heart of the Great White Way, New York City suffrage organizers called upon the names, talents, and resources of the popular theater and the larger commercial culture to represent and sell their cause. In March of 1909, for example, New York City suffragists announced a new phase in their campaign. "Henrietta Crosman, the actress, has joined their ranks," reported the *New York Times,* "and New York State is to be placarded with woman suffrage posters." Not only were Crosman and her mother "earnest workers" for the cause of woman suffrage, according to the *Times,* but the actress was also busy "preaching the doctrine to members of her profession and making converts."[46] In 1912 the Women's Political Union held a tea in honor of the Actresses Committee (which included Ethel Barrymore, Constance Collier, Gertrude Elliott, and Flora Zabelle), a group that had pledged their support for the upcoming New York Suffrage Parade.[47] The strategic value of such events could hardly be overstated. Fundraising teas and parties for luminaries of the New York stage drew "enormous crowds," recalled New York activist Gertrude Foster Brown. The "leading theatrical stars loved the publicity these occasions gave them and the public loved the opportunity to talk to their favorite actresses."[48]

Actresses lent both occasional and formal support to the American suffrage campaign. Professional and amateur actresses joined together to speak, hold fund raising events, perform plays, and march in parades for women's votes.[49] The involvement of actresses in the cause had its earlier parallel in England, where hundreds of politically minded theater women, mainly from the legitimate stage, formed the Actresses Franchise League in 1908. Using their expertise as public speakers, they toured the country to appear at suffrage meetings, offered special classes to train inexperienced women in the art of public speaking, performed suffrage plays and pageants, and raised funds for the movement.[50]

In the United States the most prominent of the suffrage theater groups was Marie Jenney Howe's Twenty-Fifth District Players, a theatrical stock company composed of Twenty-Fifth Assembly District members of the New York Woman Suffrage Party. In addition to Howe (the founder of the radical Greenwich Village feminist club "Heterodoxy"), the Players included popular Broadway actress Mary Shaw, Fola La Follette, charismatic daughter of the Wisconsin senator (both members of Heterodoxy) and Caroline Caffin, who wrote on modern dance and vaudeville.[51]

By 1909, the interest in woman suffrage had grown so evident among members of the American theatrical profession that the trade journal *Billboard* published the hyperbolic headline: "Women of the Stage All Desire to Vote," and "Whole Bunch Now Interested in Politics."[52] Desiring the vote and working to help the suffrage campaign were not, however, the same thing. While many if not most female performers may have agreed in principle with the idea of woman suffrage, and while dozens of actresses openly marched in parades or worked in other ways to help the suffrage cause, many remained on the sidelines of the suffrage campaign and its controversies—sympathetic but not visibly active in a way that would attract the attention of the media. The more politically active personalities included vaudeville and musical comedy stars like Elsie Janis, May Irwin, Hattie Williams, Trixie Friganza, Lillian Russell, Olga Nethersole, and opera singers Mary Garden and Nellie Melba.[53]

Few actresses were as clear and forthright about their commitment to the cause of woman suffrage as Mary Shaw and Lillian Russell. An early convert to the cause of women's rights, Mary Shaw, star of legitimate drama and vaudeville, acted in some of the major proto-feminist dramas of the prewar era, including Ibsen's *Hedda Gabler* and George Bernard Shaw's controversial "red light" play, *Mrs. Warren's Profession,* for which she and the other members of the New York cast were arrested on opening night in 1905 and charged with offenses to public decency.[54]

Observers at the time had difficulty distinguishing where Miss Shaw's stage career ended and her political commitments began. Certainly she was among the most outspoken female intellectuals on the American stage, an outspokenness that was often directed to the question of women's issues.[55] In 1909 Shaw performed the leading role as suffragette Vida Levering in the New York debut of Elizabeth Robins's English suffrage play, *Votes for Women,* at Wallack's Theater, thus launching the first significant commercial production of a pro-suffrage play in the United States.[56] She was also one of the few American actresses to move beyond the endorsement of suffrage and publicly identify herself as a feminist. "I am not only a suffragist," she announced in 1915, "I am a feminist, and have made up my mind that some inherent force is pushing women forward to a higher civilization."[57]

Yet even an outspoken feminist like Shaw sometimes found it necessary to hedge on the political significance of her dramatic roles. While the press noted that "all the suffragettes in New York society turned out en masse," to welcome Mary Shaw on opening night of *Votes for Women,* the actress was deliberately coy about the meaning of the event.[58] Having faced the political backlash surrounding *Mrs. Warren's Profession,* she was quick to insist that "my interest in [the play] *Votes for Women* is purely that of an artist." But in the end she left little doubt where she stood. "I believe the psychological moment for the production of a play about woman's suffrage has arrived," Mary Shaw asserted, adding that this play accurately described "the mental condition of many modern women" on the suffrage question. "With ancient countries like Sweden . . . granting suffrage to women in one form or another; . . . with four or five states in our own country granting it and others about to grant it; with representative women in social and public life furthering it—-what more need be said?" she asked rhetorically.[59]

Comic opera star Lillian Russell, on the other hand, felt no need to hedge—a stance that was enormously beneficial to a feminist movement trying to counter the notion that voting would de-sex women. Russell's mother, Cynthia Hicks Leonard, was a well-known suffragist and Social-ist who entered the New York mayoral race in 1884. And when the New York suffrage movement was revived after 1907, Lillian Russell took every opportunity to publicly identify herself with the cause of equal suffrage, speaking out at meetings, holding fundraisers, marching in pa-rades, and, following in her mother's footsteps, proposing herself, in 1915, as a worthy candidate for mayor of New York.[60]

Actresses who lent their names to the suffrage campaign had mixed motivations. Given the publicity value of suffrage activism in the prewar and wartime years, it is sometimes difficult to untangle their political principles from their own professional interests. It certainly did not take comic Trixie Friganza very long to sense the publicity value of declaring she had become a suffragette. In October 27, 1908, Friganza told New York City reporters that she had contributed money to the campaign and intended to make a speech on behalf of votes for women at a rally on the steps of City Hall. "I do not believe any man—at least no man I know—is any better fitted to form a political opinion than I am," Friganza insisted.[61] But when she appeared at the suffrage "hubbub" at City Hall decked out in a yellow Votes for Women sash, one cynical re-porter claimed it was "really for Art's sake"—to call attention to herself rather than the cause of suffrage. "The violence of her longing for women's rights," he carped, "is revealed by the fact that her press agent managed the affair."[62]

Popular female performers like Friganza had a complicated and some-times ironic relationship to the world of off-stage female politics. While they supported the principle of votes for women, the publicity they gained in coming out for suffrage cut two ways. On the one hand, it could keep them in the public eye, which was critical to their profes-sional success. On the other hand, there were certain risks involved in taking sides in a divisive political campaign—especially a campaign where women engaged in controversial, and what some considered "militant," methods of street spectacle.

The female comics were particularly vulnerable to these ironies. Trixie Friganza, for example, had no trouble making a grotesque spectacle of herself before vaudeville audiences. Her feminist stage humor built on self-deprecating and satirical fat woman comedy, which aimed to make common cause with oppressed members of her sex. But nobody laughed when she acted up off stage for overtly political purposes. Press coverage of her participation in the 1908 City Hall rally was anything but flattering: "Mrs. Loebinger, the leader of the [suffrage] forces, and Miss Friganza refrained from chaining themselves to the desk of the mayor . . . They bravely mounted a ladder in Chambers Street . . . and would have harangued the mob which had gathered there if the mob had permitted it." Only months after her participation in the hubbub, Friganza was busy distancing herself from the event. In January of 1909 she told reporters that she had "worked hard for the cause" but complained that the methods of the New York suffragettes were "a little too sensational." Every "effort seemed to be directed toward getting the names of certain leaders into the newspapers." She admitted that "I personally welcome publicity for being an actress, it is the breath in my nostrils," but cautioned that "misdirected publicity" was "not always valuable in advancing such a serious movement as . . . demanding votes for women." Much more effective, and much better for her own reputation, she might have added, were the "splendid business methods" of Jane Addams and other Chicago women who worked for a committee to establish municipal suffrage for women.[63]

Other performers too worried that their irreverence, so willingly embraced in the theater, would not be acceptable on the streets. Marie Dressler, for example, pontificated with stunning inconsistency on the subject of women's role in politics and society. "Personally, I am a staunch believer in woman's equality with man," Dressler insisted in 1913, but this was a "mental" and not a "physical equality." Woman, she argued, "was never devised to steer the ship of state or to go to the polls." Striving hard to portray herself as an old-fashioned person who believed that woman's "sphere is in the home," while at the same time defending her own path as a modern woman, Dressler insisted that talent, "artistic or otherwise," was the only justification for "a professional career."[64] Yet she also admitted that "I was seriously inclined at one period of my youthful career . . . to take up public life in some form or other . . . to seek some public career, if not in a sociological or political propaganda, at least to be the head of some mercantile concern," but decided that was "no career for a woman."[65]

Seeking to ally herself with the cause of women's rights while keeping some distance from the negative image of the movement, Dressler claimed in 1913 that she was "an anti-suffragist and above all an anti-militant."[66] But three years later, in February of 1916, she willingly added her name to the roster of woman suffrage supporters, starring in a pro-suffrage comic operetta called *Melinda and Her Sisters,* which was performed as a fundraising event at the respectable society venue of the Waldorf-Astoria Hotel.[67]

It was one thing for women of the theater to lend their celebrity to the suffrage campaign, and quite another to turn suffragists into crowd-pleasing performers. But that was exactly what some organizers believed was necessary to win the vote. Theater was an important source of inspiration, but it was not the only one. Contemporary oratorical conventions widely used by politicians, ministers, and other public figures also influenced suffrage speakers. Thus to address the need for skilled orators, the suffrage campaign set up courses of instruction to teach elocution and oratorical skills. At one such place Anna Howard Shaw lectured on "The Psychology of the Audience," and professional speakers and actresses instructed their charges on the art of speaking before a crowd.[68]

Yet increasingly organizers emphasized that speakers also needed the sine qua non of the modern stage: "personality." The professional actress was *a personality* in the sense of being a woman with an individual identity—which is how feminists understood the significance of the concept. But she also *had* "personality"—external qualities like charm and humor and beauty, and the ability to use all of these to captivate an audience.[69] In the campaign for woman suffrage, it was personality as style rather than personality as individualism or selfhood that mattered most.

These external qualities, Susan W. Fitzgerald explained at a National Suffrage Convention in April of 1910, were exactly what was required to effectively carry on the campaign in hostile territory. As Fitzgerald put it, suffrage organizers who held open-air meetings faced a different sort of challenge from those who used their voices to speak to indoor audiences. "The whole object of outdoor meetings is to catch the attention of the indifferent and uninformed person, and above all, to catch every sort of person." Like actresses, effective suffrage speakers needed "voices of good carrying power" and the ability to speak "with spirit and rapidity"; they needed to be "good-humored and quick to feel the spirit of the crowd." It was essential that "speakers must possess the dogged determination of 'making good' under any circumstances, and a power of adjustment to unexpected conditions and the demands of the crowd." Therefore, she insisted, "it is important to have speakers whose personality will interest from the start."[70] Moreover, they needed to be physically attractive. As Rose Young wrote in an article for *Good Housekeeping* in 1912, pro-suffrage speakers had to be "pretty," for "our men won't listen to any other kind."[71] Even the most militant of the suffrage organizations, Alice Paul's Congressional Union, chose its public speakers on the basis of their ability to project an image of beauty, youth, and intelligence.[72]

This, of course, was not an entirely new requirement. In the late 1860s and early 1870s, the glamorous and passionate Anna Dickinson was the most successful women's rights speaker in the nation. An aspiring actress who made a lucrative living as Queen of the Lyceum lecture circuit, Dickinson had abandoned the plain Quaker attire favored by other so-called platform women of her time in favor of fashionable and expensive Parisian gowns and elegant jewelry. According to Mark Twain, this appealing but earnest advocate of abolitionism and female rights had so much vim and energy, she "could compel the respect and attention of an audience, even if she spoke Chinese."[73]

The most popular suffrage campaigners of the early twentieth century were likewise attractive actress-type figures with pleasing "personalities." Indeed, the suffrage movement anointed as its standard bearers those women who had deliberately cultivated a stage-worthy public image. Fola La Follette, an aspiring actress who instead found her true calling on the suffrage lecture circuit, where she performed propaganda plays, was such a figure. "Miss La Follette in her personality, dress and style, runs counter to all the conventional traditional 'suffragists' who are the butt of the comic-joke maker and the caricaturist in Puck or Life," a 1910 report from the Massachusetts office of National American Woman Suffrage Association boasted.[74]

Equally if not more renowned as a suffrage celebrity was the beautiful attorney Inez Milholland. A member of the feminist club Heterodoxy and no stranger to the rough-and-tumble world of street politics, Milholland had campaigned with Christabel Pankhurst in London and had also been arrested for disorderly conduct during the 1909 New York shirtwaist makers' strike. Later she rode on horseback at the head of the May 1912 New York City Suffrage Parade and the 1913 Washington, D.C. parade, and traveled the country on behalf of the votes for women campaign. Yet what merited notice was her "forceful and attractive personality," and a "young . . . immediately attractive appearance," which proved to be an "agreeable surprise" to the men in the audience. Her "self-possessed" demeanor, said the writer for *McClure's*, enabled her instantly to center attention, allowing the clarity and power of her speaking to "carry her along" in front of the crowd.[75]

These talents proved especially critical as the suffrage movement brought its campaign into the commercial venues of popular entertainment. Indeed, attractive women with strong personalities and expert oratorical skills such as Milholland and La Follette were central to the success of the suffrage movement's most daring adventure in theatricality: the foray into vaudeville. Unlike Emma Goldman, who refused to sell her ideological soul by mixing politics with popular entertainment, Milholland, La Follette, and the combined forces of the New York suffrage campaign eagerly embraced the opportunity to exploit vaudeville's political potential.

The September 1912 Suffrage Week held at Hammerstein's Victoria Theater was the best-publicized theatrical event of the New York State suffrage campaign. In their eagerness to exploit the box office value of political controversy, Hammerstein and other theater owners had vied for the opportunity to host the event. Woman suffrage, a theme of "universal interest" to vaudeville audiences, as one observer put it, was sure to draw a huge audience. But it would be an audience divided between pro- and anti-suffrage patrons and accustomed to comedy acts that played "both sides of the question."[76] As one hostile reporter for *Variety* saw it, Hammerstein's week-long exhibition of the "trouser movement" would appeal to the "150,000 women in New York and vicinity who have had cause to complain either because they have no husbands or because they don't like the way their husbands run things."[77]

This was not the first time that publicity-seeking vaudeville theaters and publicity-seeking suffragist activists exploited each other's goals. In the fall of 1908, with the cooperation of vaudeville impresario Percy Williams, who hoped that each woman voter would stay for the matinee performance at his theaters, a New York City suffrage organization identified by the press as the National Progressive Woman Suffrage Union set up mock "suffragette polling booths" in the lobby of Williams's Orpheum, Alhambra, Crescent, Greenpoint, Novelty, and Gotham theaters so that women might "cast a vote" on election day.[78]

Hammerstein's Victoria Theater, where the Suffrage Week was to take place, specialized in presenting bizarre and unusual shows, including so-called freak acts. In 1902, for example, the Victoria featured both the famous young murderess Florence Burns (one of a series of "shooting stars" to appear on Willie Hammerstein's stage) and the famous temperance crusader Carrie Nation, who recreated her legendary hatchet attack of a Kansas saloon before a hissing audience.[79] Despite the risks of unflattering associations with previous star turns, a political campaign determined to capitalize upon free publicity could hardly find a better venue than the Victoria. Not to be outdone by his rivals, and with the blessing of the New York campaign, Percy Williams also sponsored an all-woman-suffrage show at the Colonial Theater under the direction of vaudeville headliner Emma Carus, and Keith and Proctor's staged a "Suffragette Bill" at the Fifth Avenue Theater. Other New York theaters invited suffragists to give political speeches during intermissions.[80]

The National American Woman Suffrage Association promoted Suffrage Week in vaudeville with all of the fanfare that might precede the opening night of a major Broadway extravaganza: "Big Suffrage Week at Hammerstein's: 500 Suffragists on the Stage—Great Question Presented in Theatrical Form—Souvenirs for Everybody."[81] Using the language of the popular theater, the *Woman's Journal* referred to suffragists participating in the event as stars and headliners who would be performing turns and acts, and congratulated the campaign on its big break into the theatrical mainstream.[82]

Suffrage Week opened at the Hammerstein's theater on September 9, 1912. Twice a day, at 3:30 in the afternoon (in the prime spot following the intermission) and later at 9:30 in the evening, representatives from various New York suffrage organizations, including the Men's League for Equal Suffrage, performed their turns, delivering speeches and offering elaborate spectacles and dramatic recreations of suffrage events.[83] Meanwhile, an outdoor audience would assemble on the Broadway and 42nd Street side of the Victoria Theater to listen to pro-suffrage street speeches by actresses Mary Shaw and Beatrice Forbes-Robertson.[84]

While the stage spectacles were certainly eye-catching, it was the charming and attractive young suffrage celebrities like Fola La Follette and Inez Milholland who got the loudest applause.[85] As a reporter for the *Dramatic Mirror* put it, "Inez Milholland made such an unqualified hit by her beauty alone that no man in the house would have dared vote otherwise than as she wished."[86] "A few men left [the theater]" during the suffrage show, reported the *Woman's Journal*, "but most of them listened, with just about the same degree of interest they gave to the Indian love scene and the facetious monologue preceding the suffrage turn."[87]

From a publicity standpoint alone, Suffrage Week in vaudeville was deemed an unqualified success. In a mood of self-congratulation, the *Woman's Journal* reported, that "there is really no opportunity for anyone who comes anywhere near 42nd Street, Broadway and Seventh Avenue not to know that votes for women is the most interesting thing in the neighborhood."[88] "Theater nights" soon became a popular tactic among New York City suffragists, who in 1915 managed to convince all but three Manhattan theaters to allow them to make political speeches between the acts.[89]

Seeking to cultivate an image of themselves as young, modern, fashionable, and feminine, New York suffragists also mined the public relations potential of other related institutions of commercial culture. Tin Pan Alley music, for example, supplied the inspiration for a suffrage fundraiser held on New Year's Eve of 1913 by the 27th Assembly District of the New York Woman Suffrage Party. Advertised as a "UNIQUE ENTERTAINMENT AND DANCE," it included adaptations of popular dance crazes: the "Suffrage Trot," the "Voters' Dip," and the "Anti-Glide-by."[90] Fashion and consumerism provided still other commercial avenues for pro-suffrage publicity. Suffragists designed and marketed their own hats, blouses, fans, pins, buttons, dolls, and cups, and, in 1912, designated Macy's department store as the official headquarters for the sale of suffrage parade outfits and accessories.[91]

However, no aspect of suffrage publicity and spectacle was quite as effective as massive street parades. They followed a long tradition of political street spectacle but also echoed aspects of the contemporary stage, especially the musical theater, with its emphasis upon large-scale productions, well choreographed movement, costuming, and female beauty en masse. The New York City suffrage parade of 1910 established the pattern for all future events. Banner-, flag-, and placard-carrying suffragists representing different organizations and political districts rode or marched through the streets, donning an array of suffrage colors and costumes.[92]

Harriot Stanton Blatch of the New York-based Women's Political Union had pushed the movement to modernize its image and exploit the dramatic possibilities of spectacular street parades. This aesthetic arbiter and chief choreographer was convinced that "mankind is moved to action by emotion, not by argument and reason." What could be more stirring, she asked, than hundreds of women carrying banners and "marching—marching—marching!" Through mass parades of women "the public would be aroused, the press would spread the story far and wide, and the interest of our own workers would be fired."[93] Warned by both the New York State Suffrage Association and the National American

Woman Suffrage Association that the negative publicity of women's street parades "would set back suffrage fifty years," Blatch nevertheless pressed forward with her plans for the May 21, 1910, event, which the press hailed as "the greatest suffrage parade and demonstration ever seen in New York."[94]

Answering critics who believed it was safer and more dignified to have an automobile parade than a suffrage march, Blatch insisted that women needed to "march on their own two feet out on the streets of America's greatest city." Only by marching could women prove they had sufficient discipline to be trusted with political power. But for Blatch and the other parade organizers marching was an aesthetic as much as political act, something she emphasized by encouraging parade participants to attend classes that would instruct them in "the art of walking." Unlike the picketing of industrial strikes, where courage took precedence over visual form, the organized marching of the suffragettes was supposed to be courageous *and* visually attractive. As Blatch explained: "The enemy must be converted through his eyes. He must see uniformity of dress. He must realize without actually noting it item by item, the discipline of the individual, of the group, of the whole from start to finish. He must hear music, as must each marcher, too, music all the time, if the beat, beat of the feet were to be kept in time and tune with the beat of the heart."[95]

Both the suffrage marches and the larger civic pageantry craze that began after the turn of the century and reached its peak in the Progressive era were influenced by some of the same principles that guided choreographers of the Broadway stage, particularly the "laws of velocity and precision" popularized by nineteenth-century French drama theorist Françoise Delsarte. Delsartian poses, gestures, and precision provided the underlying visual vocabulary for morally uplifting scenes of civic and suffrage pageantry and for the purely commercial choreography of Broadway shows like the Ziegfeld *Follies*.[96] These laws dictated a formula for exact movements for the head, hands, arms, and legs that represented idealized emotional, artistic, and intellectual states such as remorse, calm, accusation, and reproach. Described by dance historian Ann Daly as "an updated substitution for Victorian strictures," the Delsartian system aimed to convey the collective expression of universal ideas rather than individual feelings.[97]

Unlike the mass spectacles of the Broadway stage, however, where pretty chorus girls provided a feast of sensuality, the political spectacles of the suffrage parades, with their properly attired women in head-to-toe white frocks, aimed to project what Blatch called "dignity above all else."[98] The purpose of the suffrage parades was to transform the perceived threat of women's political power into a visual spectacle of moral heroism and beauty.

To create an appearance of dignity, the Women's Political Union gave participants in the New York Suffrage Parades strict printed instructions on what to wear, how to move, and how to get into formation. They specified: "'Dress': if possible white or light dress, small special [white straw] hat (not obligatory) and low heeled shoes. 'Bearing': head erect, shoulders back, eyes to the front; no talking or laughing; keep step; obey your marshal, remember you are marching for a principle."[99]

The success of these parades as staged publicity and propaganda events could hardly be doubted. Following the May 9, 1911 parade, an editorial in the *New York Times* admitted that prior to the event "there was a good deal of talk to the effect that it was either ridiculous or shocking, or both, for women to display themselves on the public streets," but judged that "those who watched these paraders and noted their quality and demeanor, found little cause for laughter or scorn." On the contrary, "the comment one hears on the demonstration" suggested that it gave "no small number of their antagonists the first convincing reason for taking the suffrage movement with something of the seriousness which was shown by the women who marched."[100]

The 1912 New York City parade exceeded all expectations. A solid line of 20,000 marching women extended from Washington Square in lower Manhattan, where the parade began, all the way to Carnegie Hall on 57th Street, where it was to conclude, while an estimated 500,000 spectators overflowed the sidewalks and spilled into the streets. In certain places along the route the crowds of onlookers were so dense that police had trouble keeping a free path for the parade.[101] This "white garbed army," as the press called the marchers, was composed of separate divisions of Professional Women (doctors, lawyers, writers, musicians, artists, librarians, lecturers, and social workers), Industrial Workers (milliners, dressmakers, shirtwaist makers, laundry and domestic workers), Business Women, divisions representing the Women's Trade Union League, and Socialists. Each entered the parade from different points along its route. Unintegrated into any of the working-class and professional categories was what the press called a "colored women's division," which marched with a party of young women from a local high school. Finally, there was a "men's division."[102] It was a "parade of contrasts," wrote a reporter, of women "who work with their heads and women who work with their hands and women who never work at all."[103] "The paraders were well worth looking at," noted an article in *Current Literature*. "Many were young and attractive, nearly all were becomingly gowned, all stepped out like women unafraid."[104]

In the aftermath of the 1912 event, one thing had become clear to Blatch and her colleagues: this new form of women's political spectacle was "becoming respectable." By that she meant that the local newspapers as well as major national print media were giving them excellent coverage, complete with elaborate photo spreads and even advance publicity articles. And many women who had previously declined to participate or bitterly opposed the parades on principle "now marched as a matter of course."[105] Whether the public agreed with the idea of woman suffrage or not, they could not ignore the campaign. The parades had demonstrated both the idealism and the formidable organizational powers of the suffrage campaign, as well as the organizers' capacity to translate both into carefully orchestrated displays of women's political will.

But could the movement's organizers make one kind of female spectacle without risking that it would be read as another? Could they, as historian Lisa Tickner has argued in the case of the British suffragettes, produce a spectacle in which they invited the "gaze of onlookers" without having to "passively endure" the consequences?[106] In the American case, the answer was no. Suffragists could remake their image for public consumption, but the "eyes of the enemy," as Blatch had put it, were already conditioned to see women in a particular way—conditioned in part by the theater itself.

The Paradox of Theater

An institution that had always exercised considerable influence on the way society looked at women, theater proved to be a useful ally to the suffragists. But it also provided some of the distorting metaphors and concepts that shaped the public's perception of the campaign. For as journalists and Broadway producers swooped in to interpret and exploit suffrage as spectacle, their points of reference, not surprisingly, often came directly from the world of popular entertainment. Translating the display of female political assertion into theatrical images that were palatable to male members of the audience, the press and the Broadway establishment undercut the serious political message of the suffrage campaign.

Even the friends of suffrage unwittingly contributed to this. As early as 1909, in an article called "Actress Versus Suffraget" published in an American magazine (*The Independent*), British playwright and suffrage supporter Israel Zangwill had argued that "as far as feminine fascination is concerned," in the "popular imagination" the "suffraget" was "indistinguishable from the typical actress." For the "typical suffraget" was "no longer the unsexed virago, the unhusbanded surplus, the [be]spectacled bluestocking. Manliness does not go even with militancy." Rather, he argued, like the actress, the "suffraget" was now "a young and pretty girl." The major difference was that, unlike the actress, the "suffraget" speaks "not to pleasure her audience, but to win it from its prejudices." Thus she was more likely than the actress to face "enemies rather than friends."[107]

Well-paid professional actresses, however, were not the only kind of young and pretty women on the Progressive-era stage. More commonly, the press compared suffrage marchers to the sexy and sumptuous chorus girls of Broadway. To understand and explain the new phenomenon of suffrage spectacle, a *New York Times* editorial of 1911 invoked the most famous show in the history of American musical theater, *The Black Crook*. A musical extravaganza featuring 200 shapely and daringly clad chorus girls in tights, fantastic sets, and an array of dazzling special effects, *The Black Crook*, which opened in 1866 and was revived eight times, toured the nation in the years between 1868 and 1892. Reminding readers that "forty-five years ago" the "Amazons in 'The Black Crook,'" had proved that women were "our best marchers" and knew how to create a harmonious "spectacle," the writer declared that "good marching is always worth looking at."[108] The mixture of awe and anxiety provoked by parading female armies registers in the writer's use of "Amazon." The name of mythical female warriors and the slang term for large and imposing chorus girls who performed military drills and marches in theatrical extravaganzas like the *Black Crook*, it was also an epithet for a frighteningly assertive woman.[109]

The reference to marching chorus lines is hardly surprising, considering that the huge publicity parades of the suffrage campaign coincided with the moment in the popular theater when the mass spectacle of women was growing more and more elaborate and increasingly influential in shaping feminine images. More important, the theater and the suffrage movement were among the few places where the organized massing of women for common purpose took place with any regularity. True, women's colleges and schools, factories, picket lines, department stores, and public parks all had their female masses. But it was the producers of Broadway chorus girl spectacles and the organizers of suffrage parades who helped generate a metaphor that was not widely used outside of either context: the parading female army. As different as they were in social composition and purpose, both kinds of female armies were still relatively unfamiliar sights. And both were deeply intriguing phenomena that generated complex emotional reactions ranging from sexual titillation to outright fear.

Thus beneath the glib *New York Times* account lurked a more ominous image of a massed female army whose purpose was not only to entertain but to seize new forms of power. The writer had to admit that unlike the popular Amazons of the theater, suffragists marched "under the searching eyes of a crowd which will not all be sympathetic." Many people will "watch them with derision, many more with mere curiosity, comparatively few with perfect sympathy."[110] Even the famous magazine illustrator Charles Dana Gibson, whose beautiful and haughty girls were themselves Amazonian in scale, once confessed that he found "a mass of women" marching in the streets to be "rather terrifying." Not only did they "lack the swing of soldiers," but they were not subject to "the careful selection a stage manager uses in picking a chorus."[111]

The overriding tendency of the press and the Broadway establishment, however, was to absorb the Amazonian threat of the female army into the more pleasurable image of Broadway beauty chorus. When the New York woman suffrage movement announced its plans to feature "Twelve Tall Beauties to Form a Living Flag" in their 1915 parade,[112] the *New York Times* reported the announcement in a facile tone that suggested a casting call for the chorus of the Ziegfeld *Follies*: "Big Demand for Tall Girls—Statuesque Beauties to Carry Banners," read the headline to an article on the upcoming event.[113] The actual parade, which took place on October 23 and featured more than 25,000 marchers and an estimated 250,000 "admirers," was written up as "a comely dignified show"; the press lauded "the bewitching squadron of female cavalry" and the "well ordered series of pictures of seemly movement, more poem than procession." While not forgetting "the evident earnestness" and "grave sobriety of the event," the reporter nevertheless felt compelled to stress the "aesthetic side" of this "spectacle with a purpose."

"Has there been before . . . such blaze and brilliance of hue" as to turn Fifth Avenue "into a sort of theater of enchantments?"[114]

Unsurpassed in its determination to reinvent the suffrage paraders as Broadway chorus girls was the 1912 edition of the Ziegfeld *Follies*. Here the satiric burlesques of the suffrage campaign substituted women's political ambitions with a more palatable female weapon: beauty.[115] "The Palace of Beauty" scene featured some of the same female figures of myth and history that suffrage pageants also drew upon such as Joan of Arc and Columbia, but added temptresses like Venus and Cleopatra.[116] The character Columbia said it all when she remarked: "We have been trying for three hours to find the most beautiful woman in the world. Why not elect *her* President?" The scene climaxed with a dazzling Parade of Women. To the sounds of a Sousa march, a line of chorus girls dressed to represent squads of Lady Policemen, Lady Soldiers, and most important, Lady Voters appeared on stage. Bringing up the rear of the parade was the figure of Columbia on a white horse, followed by clowns, acrobats, and animals. The Lady Voters carried banners which read:

"For President. Our Lillian"
"For Vice Pres. The Pink Lady"
"Vote for the Merry Widow"
"Our Emblem the Chicken."

"Our Lillian" referred to the iconic Ziegfeld Girl, Lillian Lorraine, who as The Twentieth-Century Girl took the prize as the most beautiful woman in the world.[117] One did not have to be a Broadway insider to get the references to long-running shows like *The Pink Lady* (1911) and *The Merry Widow* (1907), or to recognize that "chicken" was a popular slang word for a beautiful and sexually alluring chorus girl. If these theatrical metaphors and satires made suffragettes seem more attractive than dangerous, they also worked to ridicule the goal of women's political efficacy. Ultimately, however, it was not the newer image of the pretty chorus girl but the older concept of the dominating hen and menacing Amazon army that proved most troubling to the suffrage campaign's efforts at image-making.

Broadway made its own contributions to this problem. Popular shows like Lew Fields's 1911 musical comedy *The Never Homes* equated the suffrage leader with the one theatrical figure capable of holding center stage because of her excessive and unattractive behavior: the funny woman. A pull-no-punches lampoon of the comedic girth of the funny suffragette, the play was set in a small town "on the outskirts of No-where," on the eve of an election. It starred the notorious female imper-sonator George Monroe, famous for his role as a fat, obnoxious Irish cook.[118] In *The Never Homes* he plays the sight-gag Patricia Flynn, a ro-tund, bossy character who becomes town's new fire chief after the candi-dates on the "Super-Suffragette Ticket" win the election and the hen-pecked men willingly give up their power. Suffragettes take over all of the municipal positions, including the police department, and man the fire stations with women who are too busy having tea parties and mak-ing taffy to be bothered putting out fires.[119] In the end, however, the war-ring sexes are reconciled as an epidemic of love descends upon the town, and the suffragettes return the city government to its rightful rulers.[120]

A wider range of theatrical types came into play in the Shuberts' *Pass-ing Show of 1913*, which combined the funny suffragette with the sexy stage dancer in a satire of recent campaign events. The show featured a scene in which the White House is seized from the Democrats by Mrs. George Monroe Potipher Crankhurst—whose name was a pejorative medley of the militant English suffragette Christabel Pankhurst with George Monroe who had played the bossy suffragette fire chief in *The Never Homes,* and the seductive wife of the biblical Potipher. The convo-luted plot included scenes in which the newly inaugurated Suffragette President (Mrs. Potipher) brings a motley suffragette army to revolu-tionary Mexico. Later she reappears as the proprietor of the "Oriental Suffragette Cafe," where a suffragette harem performs a nightly program of risqué cabaret dances![121]

More pointed and less charitable was the Ziegfeld *Follies of 1913,* whose song "Ragtime Suffragette" was an unapologetic diatribe against "shouting" women, "Ragging with bomb-shells and ragging with bricks, / Hagging and nagging in politics." As the lyrics put it: "Ragtime suffra-gette, / She's no household pet! / While her husband's waiting home to dine, / She is ragging up and down the line." The solution to the "noise" and "crash" of the suffragette demonstrations and speeches was the re-tort: "Why don't you go home and bake a cake?"[122]

The dark humor of this musical satire, which inverted actual events to make female marchers perpetrators rather than victims of violence, un-derscored the mounting levels of public anxiety produced by the specta-cle of suffrage activism in the nation's capital that spring. On March 3, 1913, the day before the inauguration of President Wilson, suffragists from all over the nation converged upon the capital to put on a political show of their own. Organized by the National American Woman Suffrage Association (NAWSA), the pageant and the parade that followed aimed to allay the fear that the vote "would make women less womanly." As the *Woman's Journal* explained: "To those who feared that in becoming politically free woman will become coarse and mannish looking, to those who fear the loss of beauty and grace, art and poetry . . . the pageant offered the final word, the most convincing argument that human ingenuity can devise."[123] Designed by Hazel MacKaye and staged on the steps of the Treasury Department, the pageant began with the figure of Columbia descending a flight of stairs while a giant American flag was unfurled. Columbia was joined by a group of suffragists dressed in classical-style gowns, posing as the allegorical figures of Justice, Charity, Liberty, Peace, Plenty, and Hope, accompanied by groups of female attendants whose colorful and elaborate costumes and props elaborated the themes of the pageant.[124] Professional singers from around the country also participated in the pageant and the parade that followed. Among them were prominent members of the Metropolitan Opera Company, whose Mme. Nordica had agreed to play the part of Columbia in the pageant.[125]

Following the pageant, an estimated 5,000 women paraded down Pennsylvania Avenue in military formation, carrying standards representing every state in the union. Some rode in automobiles, others sat atop floats, most marched past the 500,000 onlookers who lined the streets. Bands played and hundreds of yellow suffrage banners fluttered in the breeze. Bringing up the rear of the parade was the stately figure of Inez Milholland, mounted on white horse and dressed in a white suit, riding boots, and a white cloak. Yet neither her presence, nor the beauty of this spectacular Delsartian-style pageant and parade, nor the presence of professional actresses was enough to dispel the hostility of some onlookers. The suffrage procession had barely gone one block before part of the crowd turned violent, physically attacking the women marchers, spitting upon them, and yelling obscenities. Local police were unwilling to protect the suffrage marchers, and order was restored only after Secretary of War Henry Stimson called in troops.[126]

When a Senate subcommittee convened later that month to investigate the causes of the violence and the failure of police to restore order, it became clear that the suffragists' emphasis upon nonthreatening beauty, an emphasis that the press had helped magnify, had created audience desires that could not be fulfilled. In her testimony before the Senate, Janet Richards, one of the marchers who braved the "hooting and jeering" men in the mob, reported that along the lines of the parade route "men in the crowd shouted 'These are nothing but hens, we came out to see chickens.'"[127]

Context was critical. In New York City, the center of the nation's theater industry, female activism could be more readily accommodated by a public accustomed to sophisticated and irreverent forms of entertainment. In the nation's capital, on the eve of a presidential inauguration, spectators apparently could not detach the suffrage performance from its immediate political milieu. Masses of women had joined together at the site of American political authority and were threatening to upstage the President himself. No amount of beauty, poetry, and grace could hide that fact.

"Nationally Advertised Legs"

HOW BROADWAY INVENTED
"THE GIRLS"

6 The acerbic theater critic George Jean Nathan remarked in 1921 that if all it took to mount a successful musical show was a good score, a good libretto, and imaginative scenery and costumes, Broadway producers "would all be millionaires." The "trouble," he observed, lay in finding "the girls" and "presenting them to the best advantage." "The girls" had to be "dredged up and exploited," but the real trick was how to do it properly. Hiring these "appetizing ornaments is only half the business." Once a pretty girl has been discovered and "landed," "it is necessary theatrically to authenticate her." To preserve or heighten a "pretty girl's prettiness," her looks had to be "craftily and adroitly handled."[1]

Nathan's remarks bring us face to face with a central paradox of popular theater, namely, that it simultaneously magnified and diminished the idea of female agency and individuality.[2] At precisely the moment when women seemed increasingly to move beyond men's control, Broadway producers, critics, and press agents invented a fantasy world in which men dictated and managed the terms on which women might be seen in public. In contrast to the creative and self-authenticating strong personalities like Sarah Bernhardt, Cissie Loftus, Gertrude Hoffmann, Eva Tanguay, Aida Overton Walker, Nora Bayes, and Marie Dressler, "the girls"—as female chorus performers were known—were "ornaments" produced and "handled" by men. Thus if theater provided the space for assertive self-spectacle *by* women, it also permitted Broadway producers to make spectacle *of* women by presenting them as alluring and nonthreatening objects. The musical revue thus provides an ideal laboratory for understanding the dynamic tension between women's determination to use spectacle to amplify their voice in public culture, and

155

theater's competing tendency to turn female spectacle into a symbolic reassertion of male mastery.

In the period from 1910 to the end of the 1920s, producers of the modern musical revue positioned the young women of the chorus as literal and figurative products of the stage, luxurious goods in a scenic world of material opulence and plentitude. Incorporating the symbolic language of modern industrial and consumer culture, the Ziegfeld *Follies* and other Broadway revues, in concert with the advertising industry, objectified the female body in a distinctly modern way.

No Broadway producer was as closely associated with "the girls" as Florenz Ziegfeld, Jr. In part this is because Ziegfeld himself worked assiduously to cultivate his own cultural myth as the man who was most responsible for glorifying female beauty on stage. While other producers of Broadway musical revues had costumes that rivaled Ziegfeld's and some even had better lighting and scenery, only Ziegfeld was said to possess what George Jean Nathan called the magical touch of an artist who could convert "costumes, lights and girls" into a "fluid beauty" unsurpassed in the history of the Broadway musical show.[3]

But long before Ziegfeld established himself as the chief arbiter and manufacturer of modern stage beauty, there was George Lederer, whom Nathan called the "super-Ziegfeld" of the early 1890s. Lederer started his performers on their careers of beauty. "He dug them out of obscure choruses; his alert eye detected them in out-of-the-way restaurants, in the auditoriums of provincial theatres, in the crowded waiting-room outside his office . . . and led them into spotlights that were soon to flash the news of their beauty across America."[4]

Such depictions, echoed with increasing frequency in the first two decades of the twentieth century, proclaimed that no specific talent or self-determination propelled the girls of the Broadway chorus to their place on the stage. They existed only as obscure raw material to be detected, authenticated, trained, and led by producers like Lederer and Ziegfeld. Yet this was hardly the case. Chorus performers had to do more than look pretty on stage. They had to dance and sing and move with grace and agility; they had to have ambition and tenacity. But those facts were obfuscated by the rhetoric of the Ziegfeld touch.

Ziegfeld was only the most self-promoting among the revue producers who invented this twentieth-century version of the girls. In addition to Ziegfeld and his imperious dance director Ned Wayburn, the authenticators of beauty included an influential group of imitators and rivals. Not only did these producers vie for audiences, but they also vied for performers. The expression "Please don't 'Ziegfeld' me" referred to the producer's reputation for making flattering monetary offers to women under contract with his competitors.[5]

Ziegfeld's chief rivals were the Shubert brothers (Sam and Lee) whose ongoing revue, *The Passing Show* (with annual editions from 1912 to 1924), aimed to steal some thunder from the *Follies*. Others included George White and his *Scandals* (with editions from 1919–1939), John Murray Anderson and his *Greenwich Village Follies* (1919–1928), and Earl Carroll and his *Vanities* (1923–1931).[6] Black producers also gave Ziegfeld a run for his money in the early 1920s. Flournoy Miller and Aubrey Lyles's celebrated *Shuffle Along* (1921) and three 1922 shows with all black casts: *Strut Miss Lizzie,* the *Plantation Revue,* and *Liza,* introduced new dance styles, helped launch the careers of talented performers like Florence Mills and Josephine Baker, and won the admiration of black and white audiences and critics alike.[7] But the competition, whether from black or white producers, did nothing to upset Ziegfeld's vaunted reputation.

The notion of the Ziegfeld touch also obscured the part that other women (besides "the girls") played in the production end of Broadway musical shows. Well-known and widely acclaimed costume designers such as "Lucile" (Lady Duff Gordon) and Cora McGeachy had a huge impact on the look of the Broadway revue.[8] However, that fact did nothing to disturb the powerful myth that chorus girls were the product of Ziegfeld's magic. Women other than chorus girls also appeared as featured performers in Ziegfeld's shows: solo specialty dancers and singers such as Gilda Gray, Ann Pennington, Evelyn Law, Marilyn Miller, and Bessie McCoy, and comics such as Fanny Brice, who performed in seven editions of the *Follies* between 1910 and 1923. Yet even the most celebrated solo dancers and comics could not by themselves satisfy audience expectations of the Broadway revue. It was the combination of comedy, dancers, and especially "the girls" that distinguished musical revue from other entertainments.[9] One New York critic summed up the views of many of his contemporaries when he wrote that in mounting the *Follies of 1919,* Ziegfeld had reached "the zenith of feminine loveliness, musical charm and comedy perfection." In the end, however, it was "the exquisite material" of Ziegfeld's "bonbon choruses" that captured his attention. Ziegfeld had gathered: "Girls of every type and setting, girls of every charm and grace—just girls, girls, girls; bevies and bevies of wondrous, beautiful" girls.[10]

Ziegfeld's reputation as what one writer called "ruler *de facto*" of the

Broadway "Beauty Trust" did not emerge all at once.[11] Born in Chicago in 1867, Ziegfeld was the son of a German Lutheran immigrant father and a French Catholic mother. Legend has it that while his conservative father ran the Chicago Musical College out of the family home, young Florenz found himself continually seduced by turn-of-the-century popular entertainments—Buffalo Bill's Wild West shows, vaudeville, and the music hall acts he saw on his first European trip in 1892. By 1906 he had channeled his enthusiasms into a Broadway career, making a name for himself and his star performer Anna Held in a show called *The Parisian Model.*[12] With the backing of the powerful Klaw and Erlanger Theatrical Syndicate, he produced the first edition of the *Follies* in 1907 and staged twenty-one more editions between 1908 and 1931.

Unlike a vaudeville show, which was a series of unrelated acts using only minimal scenery, the Broadway revue was an integrated production staged on a grand scale. By the 1910s the Broadway revue had evolved into a fast-paced conglomeration of satiric comic sketches and parodies, songs, solo dances, and elegant chorus production numbers with elaborate three-dimensional scenery, colorful lighting, dazzling costumes, and sophisticated special effects.[13] The typical revue had two or three acts held together by a loosely connected plot. Each act contained about ten, and sometimes more than twenty separate scenes. Many were set in exotic locales or extravagant urban settings and featured groups of chorus girls in tableaux, promenades, parades, and dance numbers. Every show contained a finale which included the entire cast.[14] Broadway revues in the late 1910s and early 1920s had between 50 and 60 chorus girls, but in some shows they numbered as many as 100. In addition to the regular chorus (they were listed on the program as "dancers") revues featured a separate category of chorus performers called Show Girls. In the Ziegfeld *Follies* these included the famous leading beauties—Lillian Lorraine, Jesse Reed, Kay Laurell, and Marion Davies—women who held center stage in lavish production numbers and whose comely faces and half-undressed bodies circulated via advertising posters, publicity photographs, and sheet music promoting the so-called Ziegfeld Girl.[15]

With each edition of the *Follies* the scenic effects, costuming, and chorus numbers became more extravagant, and by the end of World War I the costliness of these shows became part of the Ziegfeld legend. The "Episode of the Chinese Lacquer" in 1917 was a striking and perhaps representative scene created by set designer Joseph Urban. It opened with sensuous showers of colored water and an elegant set composed of a "fruit festooned" roof-top parapet overlooking a backdrop painted to look like moon-bathed lower Manhattan. But the scene was quickly transformed to a semi-darkened stage. There, against a black backdrop, fifty chorus girls dressed in Chinese costumes performed an elaborate routine, climbing in unison upon three red and gold ladders fitted with incandescent rungs. Another spectacle scene, performed to the song "The Garden of Girls," began with the sprinkling of flower seeds on the stage. Then girls dressed as different varieties of flowers emerged from a trap door. Behind them hung an opalescent backdrop that appeared to be studded with thousands of imitation pearls. As the backdrop lifted, two goddesses appeared in a sea of giant shimmering soap bubbles. Then the audience saw a patriotic finale in which the figure of President Wilson reviewed a troop of female soldiers who performed precision drills in front of a painted eagle. At the end of the scene, a mechanical set gave the illusion of a fleet of American warships sailing toward the audience.[16] The 1923 edition of the *Follies* featured a tableau spectacle called the "Maid of Gold," designed by the French artist Erté. Originally, show girl Murial Stryker was supposed to have her entire body covered in metallic gold paint, but health hazards dictated that she wear a gold lame dress instead. When the tableau opened, a black curtain hid the scene. Then, one by one, chorus girls representing "the desires of man" (luxury, glory, pleasure, wealth) came through the curtain. When the curtain finally parted, it revealed two large black staircases elaborately decorated with gold designs and festooned with huge gold acorns. Chorus girls dressed in "one tremendous gold garment which binds them together" descended the staircases to form a semicircle. The black velvet curtain at the back of the two stairways parted to reveal "Wealth" encased in a "tremendous crinoline"—a visual effect created by kneeling chorus girls wrapped in the long gold veils of her garment. Eventually they unfurled themselves and performed an elaborate dance routine.[17]

"A Certain Riotous Irreverence"

These sumptuous and expensively staged chorus girl spectacles distinguished Broadway revues from other forms of urban entertainment. But so did the deliberateness with which the chorus girl numbers and the comedy routines of Broadway revues announced and celebrated their own claims to innovation, knowingness, and what contemporaries called "smartness." At their best, wrote theater critic Rennold Wolf in 1914, these satiric Broadway revues had "no reverence for sacred conditions or established favorites, either in the theatre or in persons."[18] Praising the Shuberts' *Passing Show of 1912,* one theater critic similarly observed that like all good musical revues, this production had "a certain riotous irreverence that takes a fling at everybody and everything that happens to be of topical interest."[19]

The modernist iconoclasm of the Broadway revue had its analogue in the so-called smart magazines—*The Smart Set, Vanity Fair,* and *The New Yorker.* Like the producers of musical revues, the editors and writers for these urbane middle-class magazines shared a general optimism about the "promise of American life." But along with the Broadway producers they rejected the uplifting, self-improving tone of the Great Books or *Reader's Digest,* and the do-goodish stance of the era's professional reformers, preferring instead ironic distance—what *Vanity Fair* editor Frank Crowninshield called "the mock-cheerful angle of the satirist."[20] Emblematic of middle class urbanity, magazines like *The Smart Set,* under H. L. Mencken's editorship from 1914, enshrined "cleverness" as a modern virtue. Clever people knew how to size up the world and prick its pretensions, even their own. Writers, editors, and readers of the "smart" magazines understood, as historian William R. Taylor puts it, "that it was clever to laugh at oneself, just as it was clever for society people, without yielding an inch of status," to joke about their own customs.[21] In a similar fashion, revue comedy sought not to reform society but rather to point out the excesses and idiosyncrasies of the day.[22]

The audiences for the smart magazines and the Broadway revue also had much in common. Unlike vaudeville with its 25 and 50 cent tickets, the *Follies* musical revues attracted relatively well-to-do patrons eager to flaunt their sophistication. But the running joke in the theatrical world was that these shows catered to the Tired Business Man or TBM and his wife or girlfriend. Though discounted tickets could always be found, the seats usually cost between $1.00 and $2.00, and much more on opening night, when the *Follies,* which became something of a New York institution by the mid-1910s, drew the cream of New York society.[23] "Those who constitute New York's summer edition of 'Who's Who,'" observed a critic in 1915, "would as little think of missing a 'Follies' premiere as would their prototypes of the winter a Caruso Metropolitan first night."[24]

Those who produced the smart magazines and musical revues were sometimes, but not always, college-educated members of the middle and upper middle class. Yet musical revue was also the creative product of cultural outsiders, of first- and second-generation immigrants and African Americans who wrote its songs, performed its comedy routines, and served as its directors and producers—people like Fanny Brice, Bert Williams, Eddie Cantor, Irving Berlin, the Shubert brothers, and to some extent even Florenz Ziegfeld, Jr., that is, self-made individuals who (like some members of the audience) had not grown up in the society lampooned in revue comedy. These outsiders contributed a democratizing influence to the stylish irreverence of the revue. In addition to ragging the highbrow classics, the *Follies* featured noncomedic modern dance, ballet, and popular dance as well as elaborate fashion and costume parades that made this form of entertainment a source of cultural education as well.[25]

Above all the *Follies* symbolized the modernist sophistication of New York City. "Among those green peacocks and gilded panels, in the luxurious haze of the New Amsterdam [Theater]," Edmund Wilson observed, "there is realized a glittering vision which rises straight out of the soul of New York. The *Follies* is such a fantasy, such harlequinade as the busy well-to-do New Yorker has been able to make of his life. Expensive, punctual, stiff, it moves with the speed of an express train."[26] Nevertheless, if these shows were fundamentally about the world of middle- and upper-class New Yorkers, their reach was not limited to that small island of modernist sophistication. After their summer season on Broadway, the *Follies*, *The Passing Show*, and other revues typically went on the road to play in major urban centers across the nation.

The girls constituted more than a scenic backdrop for the "glittering vision" and "riotous irreverence" of revue's modernism; they were a crucial aspect of it. The point was not so much the willingness of the Broadway musical revue to display women's bodies for show, which is something that painters, artists, and popular entertainments had been doing for centuries. Rather, what made the girls essential to the modern ethos of revue was that they were girls and not women, grown-up daughters perhaps, but certainly not wives or old-fashioned mothers. America, the nationally syndicated cartoonist Nell Brinkley announced in 1916, was now living in the "Day of the Girl."[27] The revue helped the sexy young female achieve her iconic status in the visual culture of the modern age. From the Ziegfeld *Follies*, which, as one reporter put it, was preoccupied with GIRL in "all her moods and tenses,"[28] to the lovely Seaside Girls of British popular culture, and "les girls" immortalized by Jules Cheret's poster ads for Parisian cafes-concerts, youthful femininity symbolized the transatlantic rebellion against the constraining influences of the old order.[29]

It was also no accident that as the aggressive New Woman of the early twentieth century stepped onto the public stage, Broadway expressed and satirized the growing awareness of female ambition by making passive beautiful girls its central cultural fantasy. In the revue this modernist fantasy of the girls revolved around the themes of sexual spectacle, commodities, male connoisseurship, and managerial efficiency. Each theme played on the concept of desire—the desire to look at female beauty, sexual and material desire, and the desire to control women.[30]

"Tastefully" Displayed

In the collective popular memory of the Ziegfeld *Follies*, what stands out most clearly is the spectacle of female sexual display. In 1927, for example, dance critic H. E. Cooper remarked that "each successive edition of the *Follies* . . . has seen the settings grow more elaborate, the costumes less evident."[31] However, unlike the Salome dancer's dangerous sensuality which represented an uncontrollable dynamic force, the sexual exhibition of the girls aimed to achieve the opposite effect: their eroticism was understood to be artfully managed by men, and in place of the passionate abandon of female self-expression, revue choreography emphasized impersonality, control, and repetition.

Although theater historians disagree about the amount of nudity in the Broadway revues of the 1910s and 1920s, one writer argues persuasively that the "possibility of nudity was ever present."[32] But critics made frequent reference to the painterly tastefulness of *Follies* undress. One writer noted that the pictorial talent of Viennese set designer Joseph Urban (in the *Follies of 1915*) "proves it is quite possible to titillate the senses in really artistic fashion. A mere display of bare shins, no matter how carefully selected and whitewashed, becomes an awful bore after a few moments, no matter how many thousand pretty young females you collect in one place . . . But here they are displayed not only tastefully but brilliantly." Not only were their costumes in good taste, but the show avoided "blatant, obvious display of nudity" in favor of "a cleverly designed background for the pulchritude on view."[33]

The tolerance for bare bodies varied from one city to the next. Prior to the 1920s, Chicago and Boston still required chorus girls to cover their legs with tights.[34] New York City censors were more lenient. Some nudity (mainly bared breasts) was permitted in New York so long as the performer remained motionless on stage. This was normally confined to *tableaux vivants* (living tableaus). The most famous of these were staged by designer Ben Ali Haggin and featured semi-nude girls posed statue-like in elaborately rendered scenes reminiscent of classical art works.[35]

More overtly sexual were musical numbers in Ziegfeld's intimate cabaret entertainments, *The Midnight Frolics*. Critic Rennold Wolf described the *piece de resistance* of the 1915 *Midnight Frolic*—a transparent glass runway about ten feet over the heads of the first two rows of tables, illuminated with colored lights: "When the entire Ziegfeld chorus, attired in filmy skirts and not much more of anything else, slowly filed along this glass pathway, the effect upon those underneath was startling."

Enhancing the impact, "and to preclude the possibility of any obstacle of vision," continued Wolf, "a series of blowers had been stationed along the route, thus lifting the skirts to dangerous heights."[36] The same show, as reporter Stella Flores enthusiastically described it, featured a bevy of "balloon girls" who allowed the "men of wealth and high social position" sitting in the first rows to "reach out with their cigars trying to touch the balloons and make them pop."[37]

Sexual display, whether semi-nude or artfully erotic, enhanced the Broadway revue's irreverent and naughty smart-set cachet. Yet clothes were at least as important to the look of the girls as the intimation of undressed bodies. As theater historian John E. Hirsch has demonstrated, while Ziegfeld and his competitors continued to insist that legs of the girls were the raison d'être of revues, the other stars were the costumes.[38] Yet what seems like a paradox turns out on closer examination to be an important relationship between clothes as eroticized commodities and women as sexualized objects.

No one made this relationship more obvious than the famous London fashion designer, "Lucile" Lady Duff Gordon, who from 1915 to 1921 served as one of the principal designers for Ziegfeld's *Follies*.[39] Her gowns and fashion shows deliberately blurred the lines between fashion, eroticism, and theater. Lucile gave erotically charged names to her "emotional dresses": "Terrible Temptation," "Enchantment," "Call of the Wild," "The Discourager of Hesitancy," "The Sighing Sound of Lips Unsatisfied," and "Red Mouth of a Venomous Flower."[40]

Known as the inventor of the so-called mannequin parade or live modeling show, Lucile opened a salon in New York City in 1910. Her fashion shows featured dozens of tall "glorious, goddess-like girls," and attracted what one reporter described as "the most stylishly dressed of New York women, leaders of fashion, leaders of suffrage, leaders of music, leaders of dramatic art."[41] Given both the social prestige of Lucile's clientele and the erotic luxury of her creations, it was little wonder that Ziegfeld recruited both her gowns and her mannequins for his revues. Indeed, the gowns Lucile designed for London and New York high society women were often identical to the ones she later produced for Ziegfeld's revues.[42]

Lucile's designs gave added ammunition to the defenders of bare bodies on stage. Theater critic Louis V. De Foe admitted in a 1919 article that Broadway's "exploitation of nudity" was both "frequent" and "calculated," and ranged from the "sensual loveliness" of the "scantily draped" beauties of the *Follies* to the "flagrant undress" of the Shuberts' Winter "spectacle" (a reference to *The Passing Show*). But in a coy justification of the revue, De Foe insisted that "the undress of the chorus girl scarcely exceeds that of the ladies in the [theater] boxes and stalls." The only real difference "is that the ladies in the boxes began to undress first," meaning that they put on their low-cut gowns before they arrived at the theater.[43] While it is doubtful that the "ladies in the boxes" agreed with this estimation, there was little doubt that the incorporation of high fashion and elaborate costuming into the Broadway revue was intended in part to appeal to them. This was after all a period when theater, fashion, and sensual display were becoming familiar ingredients of middle-class women's urban experience.

The modern department store made the connections among them explicit. Outside of the stage itself, no urban institution was as instrumental in establishing the cultural circuitry between theater and fashion. Using light, color, mannequins, and a backdrop of sensual and exotic decor, department stores turned the display of goods into a form of theatrical entertainment. With elaborately designed indoor spaces and sumptuous plate glass show windows to capture the attention of pedestrians, department stores arranged their wares into a visually enticing consumer spectacle.[44] Women shoppers were also part of the spectacle. The conspicuous display of society women—that "army in furs and feathers"—were there to be seen as well as to see.[45] One journalist summed up the implications of this growing association between women and shopping when he remarked in 1907, echoing Thorstein Veblen, that woman had become the show in "successful America," an ostentatious spectacle of her husband or father's material achievements.[46]

But as a factor in the making of modern conceptions of gender, the modern department store was very different from the Broadway musical revue. While the Broadway revue attracted a mixed-sex audience, it also catered to the tastes of the Tired Business Men. By contrast, the modern urban department store cultivated an audience that consisted primarily of female consumers. As historian William Leach puts it, the department store was a "land of desire" where despite male managerial rule, women experienced a new kind of freedom and self-confidence in their pursuit of material pleasure.[47] Moreover, if the department store and the revue celebrated and promoted conspicuous consumption and female spectacle, one difference was that the revue also went out of its way to satirize both of these.[48] A good early example is the "Hat Song" from a production number in the Ziegfeld *Follies of 1908,* which burlesqued the growing circumference, weight, and elaborate adornment on the latest women's headgear:

> The girls who have a passion
> For following the fashion
> Now carry all their burdens on their heads.
> You see them out parading
> So gaily promenading;
> With hats about the size of folding beds. . . .

The refrain mocked:

> Big hats and bigger hats
> And the biggest hats of all.
> The kind of thing
> They wore last spring
> And the freak they'll wear next fall.[49]

Satire aside, in revues like the *Follies* the girls themselves were often indistinguishable from goods on display. Revue thus positioned the modern female as desiring consumer and consumable object. In equating girls and goods, the *Follies* and other Broadway revues had much in common with another modern consumer industry: advertising. Both contributed to a modern visual iconography in which women symbolized material abundance, the technology that fueled it, and the commodities that resulted from it. Simultaneously acknowledging and undercutting the concept of independent female agency, the visual representations in the popular theater and in advertising merged the female form with material objects.[50] The displayed female body helped sell commodities, but it was also a commodity in its own right.

Popular theater supplied female images; the advertising industry moved in to exploit their commercial value. At the turn of the century, famous actresses and singers were recruited to sell a number of products. For example, images of "the immortal" Sarah Bernhardt appeared in advertisements for Lowney's Chocolate Bonbons in the 1890s, and between 1903 and 1905 Metropolitan Opera star Lillian Nordica was the poster-woman for Coca Cola, appearing not only in magazine ads but as the logo on the company's serving trays and calendars. In neither place did the product itself actually appear. Rather, the beautiful woman's image stood in for the thing she was there to sell.[51]

The later 1920s advertisements also featured women of the stage, but showed the products alongside them. The photographed face of Alla Nazimova helped sell Lucky Strike Cigarettes; an artist's rendering of actress Gertrude Lawrence in an elegant designer gown appeared in an ad for Elgin Watches.[52] Also in the early 1920s advertising iconography moved toward more streamlined and rationalized representations of goods and people. Women's bodies and limbs were artificially elongated or bent into angular configurations that matched the modern look of the goods in the ads. Historian Roland Marchand observed that in advertising art, men with their "firmly planted stance" never appeared in these distorted physical shapes and postures. "Only women could appear so unserious and purely decorative." Thus the female figure, along with drapes and sculpture, turned into one of the design elements of the "depicted room." As in the earlier era, in some 1920s advertisements women replaced the goods altogether. For example, one for Fisher motor cars, which promised the "beauty and comfort" of Body by Fisher, held only the svelte figure of the fashionably dressed Fisher Body Girl.[53]

The popular theater had a similar history of representational practices. In the 1890s the bodies of chorus girls were staged to symbolize both material abundance and male technological triumphs.[54] In Imre Kiralfy's 1893 patriotic extravaganza *America,* the "Grand Ballet of American Inventions," there were Lightning Rod Girls, Sewing Machine Girls, Telegraph Girls, Phonograph Girls, [McCormick's] Reaper Girls,

Typewriter Girls, Electric Light Girls, and Telephone Boys (played by girls in drag).[55] These were, of course, highly ambiguous images. As Martha Banta has shown, female figures frequently appeared as allegories for technology and as icons of national progress in late nineteenth- and early twentieth-century America. These allegories drew on traditional notions of woman's virtues such as truth and moral goodness. Yet as Banta demonstrates, by the beginning of the twentieth century the "eternal moral verities" associated with the female figure were being replaced by a modern version of the female "idol"—a figure "fit for industry and business" and ready to be appropriated as a sexy pin-up girl on calendars and advertisements.[56]

We need look no further than the first six editions of the Ziegfeld *Follies* (1907–1912) to glimpse the theater's contributions to the making of this sort of female idol. Ziegfeld's revues staged sexually alluring girls as every conceivable product and invention of modern life. In a musical number built around the song "Take Me Round in a Taxicab," with its double-entendres about the taxi as a vehicle for transportation as well as backseat sexual play, the *Follies of 1908* costumed chorus girls as taxi cabs, outfitting them with headlights, red tin flags, "For Hire" signs, and meters on their shoulders that flickered "On" and "Off."[57] In the "Battle Ship" production number of the *Follies of 1909*, forty-eight chorus girls (each representing a different state in the union) were made to look like American naval warships. In the finale they appeared in headdresses that were life-like replicas of U.S. battleships and passed before the audience in a simulation of the U.S. naval fleet in review. As an added effect, their headdresses lit up to reveal illuminated portholes and searching spotlights.[58] The same edition of the *Follies* celebrated the triumph of the Wright brothers with a song called "Up, Up in My Aeroplane." In this number chorus girls dressed as airplanes accompanied show girl Lillian Lorraine, who was suspended from the ceiling in a "flying machine" from which she circled the theater while tossing American Beauty roses to the audience.[59]

Along with personifying chorus girls as man-made technological inventions, the *Follies* and other revues turned women into consumer products. "The girls" posed as every conceivable kind of luxury good, from cigarettes, candelabras, and jewels to playing cards and liquors. They even appeared as spices and salad ingredients.[60] These announced the perceived relationship between the idea of woman and the notion of conspicuous consumption. In addition, chorus girls frequently appeared as articles associated with fashionable and luxurious femininity: corsets, hats, parasols, handbags, furs, gloves, jewels, lingerie, bridal gowns, lace, and chiffon.[61] Legendary among these was the "Jewel Pageant" Lucile created for Ziegfeld's 1919 *Midnight Frolic.* Inspired by a Cartier bracelet that was then the rage among wealthy women in New York, Lucile staged a chorus processional in which young women posed as different precious stones in the bracelet: diamonds, emeralds, amethysts, rubies, dark emeralds, sapphires, and topazes. They entered the stage in that order so as to spell out the title of the song for this number: "DEAREST." The most spectacular of the girl jewels were the diamonds, swathed in what Lucile described as "filmy white chiffon, on which hung cascades of gleaming stones."[62]

Women as consumer objects became an especially prevalent theme in revues of the early 1920s. The outlandish nature of some of the costumes in these spectacles all but erased the distinction between women and material objects they represented, suggesting the absence of independent female identity. For example, in Ziegfeld's *Midnight Frolic* of 1920, chorus girls costumed by designer Charles LeMaire represented the theme of light and light fixtures. The girl who symbolized Electric Light was overshadowed by a towering headdress with a three-feet tall light bulb.[63] LeMaire repeated some of these themes in his costumes for the 1925 *Midnight Frolic,* in which show girl Babe Marlowe, hardly recognizable as Candlelight, was completely shrouded in a long caftan wired to make her arms stand straight out at her sides, while her head was covered by a giant candelabrum with five tall candles. Show girl Emily Drange, similarly unrecognizable beneath the weight of LeMaire's Lanternlight costume, was wrapped in a brightly spangled fringed gown made to look like an elaborately decorated base of the lantern. She supported at least a dozen Oriental lanterns from a wooden yoke attached to her shoulders, while her head balanced a giant six-tiered fringed headdress made to look like a lampshade.[64]

The New York extravaganzas were not unique: similar costume designs proliferated in Paris and London revues of the era. A scene from the Shubert brothers' *Passing Show of 1923,* for example, copied one from the Parisian *Folies Bergère* of that year, in which thirteen chorus girls formed a giant crystal chandelier, set alongside two huge crystal candelabras, and a proportionally sized goblet of sweets. Four nude women wearing crystal loincloths formed part of the chandelier, three protruded from each candelabrum, and three formed the base of the goblet of sweets. The American version, somewhat less elaborate, used girls to make the structure and contents of three chandeliers and a fruit basket.[65]

The studied excess of the revue's female-as-object stagings suggests a kind of tongue-in-cheek, wink-and-nudge perspective that can be read as the revue's efforts to expose and humorously parody its own visual codes and practices. Nevertheless, the implications for women in such self-reflexive stagings were hardly flattering. As the presumptive avatars of fashion and as erotic objects associated with other objects, they might be admired for their opulence and beauty. Yet they were clearly butts of a visual joke that reduced female identity to the status of an erotically charged consumer object.

"Nationally Advertised Legs"

It was one thing to represent the girls as eroticized jewels, candelabra, chandeliers, and sweets, and quite another to turn the girls themselves into a standardized entertainment product. Yet that was precisely what occurred. In 1920 Ziegfeld launched a concerted public relations campaign around the idea of The Ziegfeld Girl as "a masterpiece of stage production." By 1922, as one press release put it, The Ziegfeld Girl had become "an American institution," with the "prettiest" of the *Follies* "well-known nationally advertised legs."[66] So pervasive was the girls' product identity that a reporter for the *Chicago Tribune* joked that in the course of any year, Ziegfeld "sees and appraises the beauty of the most beautiful girls of America, for the same reasons that Mr. Heinz views and chooses America's most nearly perfect pickles."[67] Describing the girls in the *Follies of 1922* as if they were inanimate bolts of fabric, an enthusiastic New York theater critic wrote: "Ziegfeld is more than an exhibitor of feminine beauty, a window dresser of pulchritude. He knows how to unfurl it, to manipulate it so that its effect is doubled and tripled and the last drop of aesthetic pleasure seems to have been squeezed out of the material. In the current phrase of the day he makes beauty 'sell itself' to the spectators."[68]

Less upbeat was the commentary of novelist John Dos Passos. Reflecting upon the seductions of modern mass culture, he used the commodified image of The Ziegfeld Girl as a metaphor for the corruption of American values. In his 1925 novel, *Manhattan Transfer,* Dos Passos suggested the power of her status as an American commercial icon: "Pursuit of happiness, inalienable pursuit . . . right to life and lib-erty and . . . Faces of *Follies* girls, glorified by Ziegfeld, smile and beckon to him from windows . . . Every time he closes his eyes the dream has hold of him."[69]

The Ziegfeld Girl, like Heinz pickles, gained national product identity by measuring up to an advertised standard—in her case, Ziegfeld's "per-sonal standard of beauty." More than anything else, it was the myth of Ziegfeld's unique connoisseurship that created the concept of The Ziegfeld Girl.[70] Journalist Salita Solano echoed what had already become an axiom of the producer's self-promoting hyperbole when she wrote in 1917 that "as a collector of lovely, shapely . . . superbly young and pic-turesque" women, "Ziegfeld has no rival."[71]

Ziegfeld's genius was his uncanny ability to package titillation and naughtiness with the label of middle-class respectability, to blend ideal-ism and voyeurism.[72] With absolute confidence Ziegfeld boasted that from the 5,000 eager applicants for his cabaret revue he had personally selected "thirty girls," who "are the most beautiful women in the world." He explained the process: "On days of inspection the girls pass though my office in long lines. As they pass I say 'Yes' or 'No.' That is all. Those to whom I say 'Yes' go down to the stage and report to Mr. Wayburn. He knows that if I send them it is because they reach my stan-dard of beauty. He then tests their ability to dance."[73]

Ziegfeld proclaimed that his beauty standard made The Ziegfeld Girl different from the girls in other revues because she had to conform to his "established canons of perfection in loveliness."[74] Youthfulness was key, and most *Follies* girls were between seventeen and twenty-three years of age. "After twenty," said Ziegfeld's dance director Ned Wayburn, "a girl is good only for five years or so . . . This is partly because the work is exhausting, partly because new talent develops so rapidly and so abundantly," and partly, he might have added, because the sex appeal of girls in large part resided in the idea that they were young, dependent, and vulnerable rather than mature or sexually dangerous. Chorus girls were supposed to look playful, not threatening. As Ziegfeld explained it: "most people do not like the 'vampire' type of beauty" that some young women try to "imitate" but "prefer the charm of youth and happiness and health."[75]

Essential to projecting the look of youth and happiness was the smile. According to Ziegfeld, his chorus girls were "*taught* to smile," since smiling "was as much a part of their 'job' as the steps are." And if their steps had to convey "pep" and "action," overall chorus girls were never to appear so active that they seemed to challenge the concept of male mastery.[76] That may have explained why girls of small stature were especially popular among the male members of the audience. "Many people seem to regard size as an indication of age," he observed. "A very small girl seems young." To watch a little girl possessed of "a touch of impudence" was enjoyable to men in the audience: "we feel a good deal like a big dog playing with a kitten." Conversely, women in the audience were "'crazy' about the tall girls." A favorite was the stately six feet tall show girl known only as Dolores, whose "fine carriage" permitted her to "wear stunning costumes with superb effect."[77]

Although Ziegfeld would periodically revise his specifications for female perfection on stage, the "six chief points of beauty" he established in 1919 enumerated his criteria for chorus performers. Eyes "must always be large" and "must be blue or brown." Grey eyes, insisted Ziegfeld, "cannot be beautiful" because "they are too hard, too intellectual." They "are the eyes of the typical college girl," and "beauty and brains are not often found together." Nose "must be straight" and in proportion to the size of the rest of the face. Teeth had to be regular and straight. Hair had to be natural, not dyed. Ankles had to be slim and feet small. And a beauty had to have "a buoyant walk." There "is no standard as to size," Ziegfeld added, "symmetry is the thing."[78]

Ziegfeld further refined his beauty standard. In 1922 he announced that the right physical proportions for the girl of today's chorus consisted of the following: "Height—Five feet five and a half inches. Weight—One hundred Twenty-five pounds. Foot size—five." Even more precisely, "The height should be about seven and one-half times the length of the head. The head should be four times the length of the nose. When the arms are hanging straight at the sides they should be three-fifths of the body."[79]

By contrast, the formula set by J. J. Shubert, who maintained the beauty standard for *The Passing Show,* seemed relatively modest. As he told his stage manager, the show simply needed "pretty girls" who were "not too fat." As far as appearance was concerned the only other requirement was that they be "clean," "tidy looking," and "well groomed."[80]

The physical criteria for The Ziegfeld Girl, though exacting, were not totally undemocratic. Early in his career Ziegfeld insisted that neither class nor ethnicity was a barrier to a girl's chance for entering the *Follies.* Often he selected someone who "looked like a shop girl or an East Side

Factory Employee." But, he quickly added, in terms that would help make a legend out of the concept of the Ziegfeld touch, it was only because he was perfectly confident that such a girl "will be a stunning beauty before I get through dressing her."[81]

Like many other Americans of his generation, Ziegfeld believed in a kind of melting-pot theory of beauty. This was the idea, as writer Gertrude Lynch put it in 1904, that the American "melting pot" had produced a superior "amalgam" or ideal type from "varied sources."[82] In a 1919 article entitled "How I Pick Beauties," Ziegfeld endorsed the "theory that the American woman unites in her the finest points of all other nations." Hence, via circular reasoning, "it is not unreasonable to contend that the melting pot which fuses the mental characteristics of nations likewise blends their qualities of beauty." Indeed, he could prove that "there was a larger percentage of beauties in America than in any other country."[83]

But on Broadway, "beautiful" meant "white." Ziegfeld had commissioned several songs from J. Leubrie Hill's all black revue of 1914 *Darktown Follies* after it played on Broadway and had even hired *Darktown* dancer Ethel Williams to teach some of her routines to his own cast.[84] But except for Bert Williams, who joined the Ziegfeld *Follies* in 1910, non-white performers were excluded from revues. Not until the debut of all-black Broadway revues like *Shuffle Along* and *Strut Miss Lizzie* did glorified groups of partially clad and light-complexioned Brownskin Models and Creole Beauties become the rage on Broadway. Ziegfeld, who had a keen eye for what was new, popular, and controversial acknowledged and exploited this development in the *Follies of 1922*, where Gilda Gray (who was white) sang "It's Getting Dark on Old Broadway"—a song about the "pretty choc'late babies" who "shake and shimmie" everywhere on the "great White Way."[85] Yet at no time were black or Asian women permitted to tread the boards in Ziegfeld's shows.[86] Backstage at the Ziegfeld *Follies of 1925*, Edmund Wilson noted the contrast between the hidden "Negro wardrobe woman knowing herself handsome in another kind," and "all that white beauty, those open-eyed confident white girls in their paradise of bright dresses . . . all of them excited by the costumes and the music, proud to have been picked by Ziegfeld, happy to look like the covers of popular magazines."[87]

Whatever their ancestry, the white beauties of Ziegfeld's chorus displayed few obvious signs of ethnic difference. Ziegfeld voiced particular concerns about the suitability of Jewish chorus girls. While he acknowledged that "there are a great many pretty girls among Jewish people," and occasionally hired them for his shows, he insisted that "they mature early and lose their youthful slenderness. For that reason they do not last long as chorus girls." Conversely, a manager in search of "'show' material" could not afford to overlook the girl of Irish ancestry, for she was said to have "nice eyes, a good nose, and an expressive mouth."[88]

Ziegfeld claimed that his beauty chorus featured only *the American type.*[89] "Most of the pretty girls in our companies are Americans," he declared. "Not only are they native-born, but their parents and grandparents and remoter ancestors were also natives of this country."[90] Here he echoed the wartime and postwar hyper-patriotism and xenophobia that eventually resulted in the passage of restrictive new immigration legislation. Ziegfeld's public statements complemented the notions of eugenics crusaders and other racially inspired ideologues who insisted that undesirable mental and physical traits of certain foreign populations threatened to pollute the biological stock of future generations of Americans, so that only selective "breeding" would produce "racial betterment."[91]

Ziegfeld willingly capitalized upon the political mood of xenophobia and 100-percent Americanism. His 1917–1920 advertising campaign drove home the message when it proclaimed that the *Follies* was "A NATIONAL INSTITUTION."[92] It was not long before newspapers and electric signs on theaters advertised the "ZIEGFELD FOLLIES, A NATIONAL INSTITUTION, GLORIFYING THE AMERICAN GIRL."[93]

Observers were quick, however, to detect the cynicism and political opportunism of these slogans. "You don't hear so much of that old familiar French propaganda directed at all Americans to 'see Paris and die," wrote one critic of Ziegfeld's "Americanization movement." The new "American propaganda" dictated "the necessity to 'see New York and Ziegfeld's girls and die.'" The result, he concluded was that "Men may talk about the natural resources of the country, our enormous production of Ford cars . . . but in the last resort . . . it is girls, American girls as exhibited by Mr. Ziegfeld, about which the conversation centers."[94] "Lest I suspect myself of treason to the youth and charm of the lovely 100 per cent Americans in the exhibit," wrote another New York critic who had just gone to see the *Follies of 1922,* "I hasten to an attitude of patriotic admiration. Our comely countrywomen of the current *Follies* are as alluring a lot as ever Mr. Ziegfeld haremed in his brilliant seraglia."[95] Dance critic H. E. Cooper dismissed Ziegfeld's campaign as a "clever manipulation of the American mind." Realizing "the natives' pride in their own product," Ziegfeld "played up 'American' girls" but in truth "threw open the doors to any possessor of pulchritude regardless of where she came from." As a result of this deception, Cooper observed, Ziegfeld's revue became "a national institution on a par with Congress, Prohibition and the latest divorce suit," and "the very promising motto, 'Glorifying the American Girl,'" was "incorporated into the popular vocabulary."[96]

Others saw the glorification campaign as a way of coming to terms with the sexual anxiety of the era. Edmund Wilson commented in 1923 that

> Ziegfeld's girls have not only the Anglo-Saxon straightness—straight backs, straight brows and straight noses—but also the peculiar frigidity and purity, the frank high-school-girlishness which Americans like. He does not aim to make them, from the moment they appear, as sexually attractive as possible, as the [Parisian] Folies Bergère, for example does. He appeals to American idealism, and then, when the male is intent on his chaste and dewy-eyed vision, he gratifies him on this plane by discreetly disrobing his goddess.[97]

"An Efficiency Expert in Girls"

Ziegfeld ruled Broadway's Beauty Trust. But dance director Ned Wayburn was Broadway's answer to Frederick Winslow Taylor, father of the early twentieth-century scientific management. An advocate of rational control and human engineering, Taylor was known as a visionary and idealist who led the quest for mastery and order in a world filled with change and uncertainty. But where Taylor focused on rationalizing modern industrial production, Wayburn concentrated on engineering the chorus line. "Mr. Wayburn," a press release announced in 1922, "has made the selection of girls . . . an exact science. He is an efficiency expert in girls." Wayburn, the announcement claimed, remodeled girls for the stage and served as "the principal source of supply, not only for Ziegfeld but for other producers that are particular about legs." Wayburn "has a ready market for his product." And that "product" was none other than "the development of the Ziegfeld Girl."[98]

The choreographer's family background profoundly influenced his approach to the girls. Both his father and grandfather were inventors and manufacturers of industrial machinery, and as a young man Wayburn studied mathematics and mechanical drawing, working for a time as architectural draftsman before entering his father's business. Only later did he take up a career in the musical theater.[99] Known as "The Chorus King," over the course of his career Wayburn staged and choreographed more than 300 musical shows—on the vaudeville circuit and in revue and musical comedy for Ziegfeld, the Shuberts, Lew Fields, Charles Dillingham, and other Broadway producers—as well as producing revues of his own. From 1915 to 1923 he worked almost exclusively for Ziegfeld, assuming the title of "producing director."[100]

Rather than emphasize artistry, Wayburn talked of the female chorus in business terms—the business of beauty. "In our [dancing] school," a reference to his private training studios for stage dancers, "neither sentiment nor art enters the question—it is purely a commercial proposition with us . . . we make it a business to produce beauty."[101] The full-page advertisement he placed in *Variety* in 1924 used an industrial reference to make the point vividly clear: "NED WAYBURN STUDIOS OF STAGE DANCING—MANUFACTURERS OF DANCING STARS."[102]

On Broadway Wayburn was best known for the geometric precision of his dance routines and for his heavy-handed managerial style. Wayburn arranged his dancers into aesthetic spectacles that mimicked the rhythms of industry, glorified its productive capacities, and played to the desires of its consumers. This is hardly surprising, given the increasing visibility of young females in the industrial labor force. For just as well-managed laboring bodies could be orchestrated to fill the needs of industrial production, so too carefully selected and rationally disciplined bodies of chorus girls could be trained to the specifications of highly controlled theatrical spectacles.[103]

Such fantasies of rationally controlled female bodies emerged most forcefully in the early twentieth-century vogue for precision dancing. Although early Broadway show dancing built upon a number of classical and vernacular dance traditions, including the geometry, symmetry, and hierarchy of ballet and military drills, folk dance, American minstrelsy, and hybrids such as tap dance, modern Broadway choreography of the 1910s and 1920s pushed those traditions into a distinctly modern form: the dance routine performed en masse by the chorus.[104]

Precision dancing amounted to a codified series of steps, kicks, moves, glides, and hops performed by a line or other geometric configuration of chorus bodies. Born in the early Progressive era under the influence of choreographers like John Tiller, Ned Wayburn, and Gertrude Hoffmann, and powerfully reworked in the Depression staging and camera optics of Busby Berkeley, precision choreography synchronized limbs and bodies into precise series of steps and movements to manufacture elaborate stage pictures.[105] Here was Broadway's equivalent to the classical corps de ballet—matched sets of young women kicking, tapping, and marching to the jazzy rhythms of the twentieth century.

Watching the Ziegfeld *Follies of 1922*, New York critic Alan Dale marvelled at "fifteen of the cutest, winsomest, and prettiest lassies," who "were 'glorified' Ziegfeldianly," and noted that "they had all been marvelously matched, and were as alike as peas in a pod." In one number they appeared "in one recumbent mass, with their feet in the air. There we saw operating automatically 150 toes . . . 30 knees, 30 insteps . . . 30 ankles . . . and 30 exquisite calves. . . . There it was . . . but we saw nothing but the feet of the 'performers.'"[106]

This kind of choreography grew out of an exuberant faith in the potentials of technology and human engineering for modern society. It reflected the fact that the engineer had become something of an American cult figure in the years between 1890 and the 1920s.[107] Thus it was no accident that Ned Wayburn, with his background in the manufacture of machinery, became the most influential of the Broadway choreographers and the most important American contributor to the vogue for precision dancing.

Wayburn codified chorus routines into the forms that would eventually be adopted in musical films as well. By 1908 he had developed two main structures for chorus staging—the formation and the frame. The chorus was frequently used as a form of scenery to frame the action of featured solo performers and stars. He placed the chorus in semi-circles, Vs, Ws, or lines to focus audience attention on the featured performer(s) within the frame.[108] The formations, on the other hand, were self-contained—geometric shapes formed out of the bodies of a group of dancers. The shapes themselves—commonly rectangles and parallelograms, circles, ovals, or ellipses, inverted Vs and straight lines—were not wholly visible to the seated audience and were best seen from above. These optical formations influenced subsequent choreography on the stage and screen.[109]

The "Laceland" number he choreographed for the Ziegfeld *Follies of 1922* showcased this kind of elaborate geometry. "Laceland" depicted fancy lace garments, featuring chorus girls as lace weavers, romantic dreamers, and lace-adorned brides. In dance historian Barbara Cohen Stratyner's reconstruction, it began with a precision dance by eight girls carrying lace parasols. When they moved to the back of the stage, sixteen other girls formed a frame for the female solo singer. They were followed by a ballet soloist accompanied by a group of twelve identically dressed girls in short lace tutus and Dutch lace caps. As this group moved to the upper floor of a staircase system, thirty-six more identically dressed chorus girls formed a frame behind a second ballet soloist, who was dressed to resemble a butterfly with eight-foot wings. Ten more girls then entered the stage moving through a formation of kneeling girls to a song that introduced the theme of lace in a bride's trousseau. The ten girls then advanced to the middle level of the staircase and used their sashes to create a lace frame above the other dancers. By then the precision dancers had formed a straight line on the upstage part of the floor. Two rows of other girls were kneeling along each side in "dying swan poses." One group of girls formed a semicircle on the stage floor, which was paralleled by a semicircle of other girls up on the staircases.

Then came a wedding processional featuring eight tall show girls posing as lace items from a bride's trousseau: stockings, parasol, handkerchief, veil, fan, and a wedding gown with a twenty foot train. Finally, when the stage was filled with white lace costumes of fifty-four chorus girls and eight soloists, the lights were darkened. The only thing the audience could see was the parts of the costumes that had been treated with a glow-in-the-dark phosphorescent paint.[110]

"Laceland" was typical of many *Follies* chorus extravaganzas that created a thematic tension between the romantic extravagance of its feminine visual splendor and the rigid geometry of its choreographic frames, formations, and straight lines. Here as elsewhere in Ziegfeld's revues, the scene both exaggerates feminine material excess and disciplines it with the visual language of geometry and engineering.

Ned Wayburn's interest in symmetry and geometric formations, like that of other choreographers of his day, was influenced by several traditions. One was the pattern established in post-Civil War era ballet spectacles like *The Black Crook*, which featured marching legions of hefty chorus-girl "Amazons." The other was the minstrel show which also emphasized symmetrical stage formations.[111] Wayburn's dances were also inspired by some of the same Delsartian "laws of velocity and precision" that guided the choreographers of suffrage parades and pageants.

Delsartian principles, with their emphasis upon universal ideals rather than individual expressions of feeling, Wayburn explained in 1912, were ideal for the modern revue chorus, for they provided Broadway dancers with a standardized system of "rhythmical movement, gesture, and facial expression," which could be "simultaneously employed" by "60 trained personalities emphasizing the same idea at the same moment."[112]

Equally important to the development of Wayburn's precision choreography were his adaptations of popular forms of nineteenth-century social dance stage movement—the cotillion and the military drill.[113] For Wayburn (and later for Busby Berkeley, who had attended a military academy and served as wartime entertainment officer under General Pershing in France before he went on to work as a Broadway performer and dance director), drills which emphasized ordered steps and symmetrical paths of movement for paired dancers of the same height and physical proportions became an organizing principle.[114]

This technique was not unique to the staging of American chorus girls. Wayburn's counterpart in England, and no doubt a model for his own public persona, was Manchester merchant John Tiller, who bragged that his standardized female precision dancers were "utterly without temperament, thoroughly disciplined, and available to any producer." Using a military/industrial model, Tiller trained what he called "squads" of dancers who could be "imported from England, sight unseen, in groups of twelve or sixteen," by theatrical producers all over the world.[115]

As Tiller's comments suggest, the penchant for configuring groups of young women into precise geometric formations was not just an outgrowth of stage and social dance traditions. It had a political dimension as well. It reinforced the traditional notion that chorus girls—and by extension women in general—lacked definite individuality and thus lent themselves to deployment *en masse*. And it offered a reassuring antidote for the more ominous tempestuous female masses—the hefty armies of Amazons of the nineteenth-century stage and the militant armies of marching suffragists and industrial pickets—by substituting the highly controlled movements of glorified girls.

Thus to refer to the chorus as "small armies of femininity," as one reporter did in 1913, was to comment not only on the aesthetic principles that shaped the movements of the revue chorus, but also to represent chorus girls not as individual women but as rigorously disciplined identical types.[116] One American critic expressed this fantasy about females as compliant nonentities when he wrote in 1911 that "the members of the chorus, as a general rule, are incapable of independent playing. They are *parts of a whole* and are theatrically useless when not surrounded by other *particles.*"[117]

"As Any Automaton Designed to Please"

In his staging and rhetorical posturing, Wayburn rejected the power, freedom, and self-expression of the autonomous dancer represented by women as diverse as Eva Tanguay and Isadora Duncan. Instead, he portrayed the girls variously as rarified ornaments, performing machines, and obedient soldier-like puppets. He deliberately and gleefully heightened the discursive power of these images by promoting himself as the individual most responsible for engineering, manufacturing, and managing the perfect Broadway chorus girl. The sexual politics of his choreography and his self-promotion were no more clearly stated than in his 1920 declaration: "Ever since I have been a producer of girl shows I have had to create the chorus girl. She is a creation as completely thought out, moved about, wired and flounced, beribboned and set dancing, as any automaton designed to please, to delight, to excite an audience." Wayburn insisted that his goal was "to invent groupings of girls that could be moved [about] artistically, to set them climbing up golden stairs, or dancing and marching about . . . constantly increasing the procession of beautiful girls so that they will overwhelm the imagination of the audience with sheer sensuousness of spectacle, and dazzle it with the universal text of the theatre—woman."[118]

By claiming to have created a desirable dancing female automaton, Wayburn brought the story of Pygmalion and Galatea—a story that the New Woman had rebelled against—forward into the industrial and consumer age.[119] He attempted to merge, glorify, and symbolically assert control over two forces that were capable of provoking desire as well as fear—the machine and the display of female sexuality.

Yet even Wayburn's claim of inventing passive female performing machines was hardly novel. As we have seen, late nineteenth-century advertisement and theatrical spectacles regularly merged women and technological inventions in ways that emphasized the male inventor and the beautiful machine. Moreover, nineteenth-century Americans viewed machines not simply as utilitarian devises but as eye-pleasing spectacles worthy of public exhibition and adulation. Perceived as objects of art as well as of industry, nineteenth-century machines were elaborately adorned with decorative motifs, embellished to satisfy a hunger for beauty as well as utility.[120]

But the modern Broadway revue was thus something of a reversal of form: instead of showing machines with feminized decorations, decorative young women were turned into displays of mechanical precision. The eroticized body parts (breasts, midriff, and legs) were exposed to the public gaze but broken up (dismembered) into components moving to the routines of precision choreography. The effect, a number of commentators argued, was to de-eroticize the young female dancers, or at least to make their sexuality more abstract, less accessible, and by definition less threatening. Erotic display could be incorporated into the impersonal repetitions of modern mass production for those who relished the system. Even those who feared being dominated by machines (and by women) might find it amusing to watch women stand in for machines that could then be controlled by men.[121]

These simultaneous cultural fantasies of the sexualization of technology and the female as machine became a self-conscious aspect of modernist expression and not just in musical revue.[122] Among avant garde artists, especially the Dadaists in Paris and New York, the ambivalent fascination with America's commercialized machine-age culture inspired a number of playful, iconoclastic commentaries on the connections among women, machines, and erotic desire.[123] French artist Francis Picabia, who along with Marcel Duchamp helped shape the direction of the New York avant garde, created a number of machine women. Picabia's 1915 drawing "Fille née sans mère" (Girl born without a mother) has been described as a series of disconnected springs, rods, and tangled wires that took the form of a machine devoid of a working function.[124] Paul Haviland of the Stieglitz circle elaborated on the themes of Picabia's drawing, observing that "man made the machine in his own image. She has limbs which act; lungs which breathe . . . a nervous system which runs on electricity. . . . The machine is his 'daughter born without a mother.' That is why he loves her." This machine-girl, noted Haviland, remained at the "dependent stage." "Man gave her every qualification except thought. She submits to his will but he must direct her activities. Without him she remains a wonderful being, but without aim or anatomy."[125]

If Picabia's girl-machine denies female agency, then his other 1915 machine-woman, the phallic New Woman, "Voilà Elle" (Here She Is), is a grown-up *femme fatale* that "paradoxically" desires "to be dominated" like a "mindless" machine.[126] More famous still was the threatening mechanical sexuality of Marcel Duchamp's "The Bride Stripped Bare by Her Bachelors, Even (Large Glass)" (1915–1923). This work, which he began in New York in 1915, allowed the machinery of the Bride to communicate with and electronically control the Bachelors who are never actually permitted to reach her.[127]

But while Duchamp and Picabia simultaneously criticized and expressed their fascination with American commercial culture, Wayburn was a prolific contributor to that culture. He saw his mission not as an ironist but as an engineer, whose job was to train, order, and rationalize the girls. In some respects his modernist girl-machine fantasies harkened back to older mechanical entertainments. Automata had played an important part at traditional European court spectacles. And by the late 1840s, Parisian audiences flocked to automaton houses to watch mechanical dolls mimic human movements. Closer still were the nineteenth-century romantic ballets such as *Coppélia* (1870), which reversed the paradigm; instead of automatons as human-like entertainers, ballet dancers mimicked automatons who threaten to exceed the controls of their creators.[128]

Reducing Them to "Mere Mathematics"

But Wayburn made it clear that in his training and choreography he literally and figuratively sought to keep women in their proper places. To implement his system, Wayburn needed dancers that had enough "mental calibre" to learn his routines, but not enough to make them too independent or rebellious. If a girl was "too intelligent," he claimed, "she may not be teachable."[129] Discussing his fifteen years' experience as a trainer of chorus girls, Wayburn announced in 1912 that "the only way to handle women—or at least the women I train on the stage—was to reduce them to mere mathematics." "All women who come under my direction are classified by letters. They are either A, B, C, or D." After picking out and assembling "as many of the four types" as needed, training began. "We drive it into their minds that there is only one number in the world and that is eight. They stand in eight different ways and they move in eight different directions—or in multiples of eight."[130]

Combining the principles of modern engineering with the traditions of ballet, Wayburn selected, trained, and staged his girls according to a hierarchical rating system based on height, weight, and dance specialty. By 1913 he had arrived at the following classifications:

"The A Girl": 5'7" and upward.
"The B Girl": 5'5" to 5'7".
"The C Girl": 5'2"–5'6".
"The D Girl": 5'–5'5".[131]

"A" girls or show girls were not dancers per se. Their function was largely decorative. Taught to pose and walk in processionals and mannequin parades, their tall elegant frames were considered ideal for showing off the elaborate costumes and cumbersome headdresses designed for the *Follies*. "A" girls were also associated with the so-called Ziegfeld Walk, which has been described as "a slow promenade" (usually down a staircase or a series of platforms) with bodies held at an oblique angle to the audience. B, C, and D girls (who typically appeared on stage in groups of twelve, sixteen, or twenty-four) were the actual dancers. A separate category of the very shortest E girls did only precision dancing.[132]

This rating system also had social connotations. In a 1913 interview with Mary Morgan for an article in *Theatre Magazine,* Wayburn described the "A type" as "a tall good-looking girl, of brains, education and refinement, what we might call a 'well brought up' girl. There's a subdivision of this type. It is the road show girl. She is tall and good looking, but has less apparent breeding. She will do for the road, but is not quite up to the standard of New York." The "'B' girl," a "grown-up dancer, has the attributes of the show girl but can dance too, which is very useful. She is good cement, filling nicely into gaps, but a shade less dainty in appearance than the 'A' girl." The "C girl is much like the 'A' girl but smaller and younger . . . an undeveloped 'A' girl. She and the 'B' girl are very useful for the picture dances." Finally, the "'D girl' is a dancer. She is small, healthy, and trained for vigorous dancing."[133] A Broadway chorus, said Wayburn, could not permit any "mutts" or "hicks," and "there is absolutely no room for the blockhead or the girl utterly lacking in mental refinement."[134] As a *New York Times* reporter put it in 1915, Wayburn had assembled "the most complete directory of chorus girls in existence. He has listed the names, addresses and measurements of 8,300 girls," all "divided into classes."[135]

Reducing young women to "mere mathematics" required the discipline of a factory manager and the determination of a General. Wayburn announced in 1911 that the producer of girl shows bore "the brunt of a far more sanguinary encounter than the Battle of Gettysburg, and yet lives to tell the story."[136] Training chorus dancers to perform with the "mathematical precision of a military parade" required discipline that was "army-like" but more severe. "It is system, system, system with me. I believe in numbers and straight lines. I learned to value both when I was a mechanical draughtsman."[137] Reporter W. T. Gentz found "nothing fictitious" about "the air of military discipline." Wayburn taught his girls to move and behave with "machine-like" precision. "A minute's observation of Ned Wayburn in action compels admission that here is the most exacting martinet of the theater." Wayburn's "words," he observed, "are the lash of the ring-master"; his "directions" to the chorus were "uttered with the distinctiveness of a Gattling gun."[138]

To be sure, discipline and hard work have long characterized professional dance culture, especially ballet. Other Broadway choreographers were also known for their demanding training methods. But none even approached Wayburn's emphasis upon military discipline and managerial control—not even the cane-tapping Czarina of Broadway, as the Viennese-born ballerina and choreographer Albertina Rasch was known. She choreographed for George White and Florenz Ziegfeld in the mid to late 1920s, sending her well-drilled units of six to twenty Albertina Rasch Dancers to perform in vaudeville shows and musical revues, though she is better known for her staging of MGM movie musical numbers in the 1930s.[139] In the 1920s Rasch's dance troupes performed "uniform precision" work in toe dance routines adapted to the syncopated rhythms of jazz. But Madame Rasch, as her dancers addressed her, eschewed the rigid geometry of Wayburn's industrial style tap lines. Instead, the movements of her dancers were described as "supremely charming and unmechanically graceful." And her directorial style, while sharp and commanding, emphasized exacting dance technique rather than the creation of female automatons.[140] The same was true for dancer and later choreographer Gertrude Hoffmann. Like Wayburn, Hoffmann specialized in the training of precision line dancers. She too emphasized discipline and visual geometry, supplying troupes of Gertrude Hoffmann

Girls to Broadway and European revues and cabaret acts.[141] Early in her career as a choreographer, Hoffmann had bragged to a reporter about her efficient methods for rehearsing the chorus. But she attributed her success to the fact that she was a woman directing other women and could better "show them just what is wanted." As Hoffmann put it: "I think I get better results than most men." The "girls try hard to please me, they know I know their tricks, that I have been through just what they are going through, and for this reason they are willing to work." By contrast, she insisted, "a man would only succeed in making them sulk."[142]

While Hoffmann spoke as a woman in sympathy with her trainees, Wayburn portrayed himself as adversary in a pitched military battle of the sexes, deliberately broadcasting his desire to make his female charges sulk. He bragged to a reporter in 1911 that by the time the dress rehearsal was called, he had gained "the deep and undying hatred of every member of the company."[143] He cultivated his personal myth as one of "the most striking disciplinarians in the theatre." Backstage, he told one reporter, he was known to the chorus girls as "the man with the iron hand." Explaining the necessity of patriarchal discipline, Wayburn insisted that "chorus people are much like kindergarten children. I am not opposed to kindness, but it must be tempered by inflexible firmness or the battle is lost before it is begun."[144] In 1924, when Cosmopolitan Pictures restaged a scene from the Ziegfeld *Follies* in a film called *The Great White Way*, Wayburn immortalized this image of himself when he played a dance director who overworked a chorus girl to the point where she collapsed in exhaustion and tumbled down a flight of stairs.[145]

The Problem of Personality

The staging and rhetorical construction of the girls as mathematically engineered performing machines, identical types, and luxurious commodities was among popular theater's most important contributions to modernist concepts of the New Woman. Yet these were not uncontested images. The problem of female individuality and personality posed a thorny dilemma for Wayburn and Ziegfeld. Much of what they did and said undermined the idea that the members of the chorus possessed the slightest degree of individuality. Yet the idea of personality was so firmly implanted in the public's perception of the popular stage and was such an important issue in modern social thought that it eventually came to influence the critical reception of the girls.

Initially, most theater critics had praised the pure aesthetic spectacle of *Follies* chorus numbers.[146] Toward the end of WWI, however, some writers expressed dismay about Ziegfeld's tendency to obliterate the individuality and even the sensuality of his girls. Theater was a site where the distinct personalities of both sexes had reigned supreme, and some observers protested that Ziegfeld's girl spectacles had moved too far in the other direction.[147] A review of chorus numbers in the *Follies of 1920,* for example, praised the "winsome faces and graceful persons" associated with "Mr. Ziegfeld's chorus," but complained that they disappeared into an indistinguishable scenic mass on stage:

> One could not see the girls for their numbers, their faces for their positions, their grace for their gowns. It was only a case of . . . heaping gold upon gold, pounds of flowers upon other pounds, and then stamping the precious masses down until one was blinded by the glare . . . My point is not that Mr. Ziegfeld does not provide quality. He clutters it with quantity . . . and you would love to go up and pull the thing apart and see what is lovely for yourself.

Only the dancing "feet" of Mary Eaton and the "impudent cleverness of Fannie Brice" gave any signs of "life" to "this particular party."[148]

Louis Hirsh had been even more caustic. In his 1919 essay "The Deadly Dull Chorus Girl," he complained that the Ziegfeld *Follies* and the Shuberts' Winter Garden revues "manipulate[d] the chorus girl as they would a piece of scenery." Not only was "individuality . . . dispensed with," but there was "no seeming purpose or design" to the "swayings, wrigglings, kickings, and squirmings" of their movements. The "same result could be achieved by manipulating a set of wooden mannikins." This he contrasted to the "concerted individualism" of the Isadora Duncan dancers. Although there was "one unified plan for the group, each dancer injects her own personality into the performance." Were the Broadway chorus girls "given personality," Hirsh concluded, they would "gain a new independence" for themselves, becoming "an integral" rather than an "ornamental" part of the show.[149]

Such criticisms made it clear that the issue of personality would not go away. Thus with stunning inconsistency Ziegfeld and Wayburn navigated a course of rhetorical claims that sometimes obliterated the individual and at other times insisted upon the importance of the chorus girl's personality. Asked in a 1912 press interview whether he personally got to know the girls of the chorus, Wayburn had barked: "How can I know them when I don't let them speak a word during rehearsals. How can I know them when I have a hundred and fifty of them lined up . . . and am trying to make each one step the same, bend her head the same, wave her arms the same."[150]

Conversely, to reinforce the perception that the stage offered at least some women an opportunity to rise above the common herd, Ziegfeld and Wayburn emphasized personality as a crucial precondition of the chorus girl's ability to climb out of the ranks to attain the status of the star.[151] A headliner like Evelyn Law or Marilyn Miller had to have personality, Ziegfeld claimed. The chorus girl needed only a pretty face, a "good figure," and the ability to dance "or at least carry herself gracefully" in fashionable gowns and elaborate costumes. A "pretty face is the first essential" for a musical show, but "a girl must have something besides beauty, if she is to create more than a passing impression." To be more than a chorus girl, to become "a really big success," to be "pushed to the front" like dancer Marilyn Miller, the principal star of the 1919 *Follies*, one had to have "beauty—*plus personality.*"[152]

By the early 1920s, when Wayburn was presiding over a training studio for Broadway stage dancers, even he invoked the concept of personality as a recruiting tool. Thus the inventor of the chorus girl as an "automaton designed to please" assured prospective pupils for his dancing school that individuality and personality accounted for the difference between the solo dancer who became a "performance star" and the chorus girls who remained in the ranks. The 1925 edition of his *The Art of Stage Dancing* contained an entire chapter on "Personality in the Dance." Here he explained that "the newest of sciences, psychoanalysis," had discovered that the "inferiority complex" interfered with the self-confidence needed to develop personality. Wayburn urged ambitious young dancers to hone personality, or what he called "the characteristics of their individuality."[153] This had become such a critical axiom of stage lore that another training school in Philadelphia even promised to develop the pupil's personality along with her footwork: "TECHNIQUE is the foundation for dancing—But it is the PERSONALITY that reaches out over the footlights and clutches the heartstrings of an audience that creates SUCCESS." The studio announced that "Cowanova Training Develops Personality."[154]

Ziegfeld and Wayburn had worked hard to produce the image of the beautiful, charming, obedient, and pliant girl whose job was to please, in part by synchronizing her movements with others. She was sexy, but never threatening, energetic, but thoroughly rationalized. However, chorus girls were also figures of feminine excess and hedonism. The expensive clothing and costumes they wore, the opulent scenery that surrounded them, the consumer objects they portrayed, and the racy songs and dances they performed symbolized the longings of modern women and men in search of personal freedom and self-gratification. Ziegfeld's special touch, his genius, resided in his capacity to explore and exploit the simultaneous wish for individual pleasure and the assurance of social control. On stage the chorus girl would come to stand for both. Off stage she took on a life of her own.

"Like All the Rest of Womankind Only More So"

THE CHORUS GIRL PROBLEM AND AMERICAN CULTURE

7 Broadway's creation of chorus girls as mechanized, standardized products of the stage barely concealed the anxiety that lurked beneath this fantasy of male control. On stage, chorus girls appeared as obedient machines or erotic objects. Off stage, however, people imagined them as very independent young women—individual personalities with particular needs, desires, and ambitions. In the first two decades of the twentieth century, the chorus girl came to be viewed as a social problem, one that seemed to threaten, along with woman suffrage, the very foundation of traditional gender relations.

The dissonance between the on- and off-stage image of the chorus girl was considerable. Yet these two conceptions were less contradictory than they seem. Both reflected the growing perception that young urban women were now freer than ever to express themselves. Thus the chorus girl became a kind of stand-in or synecdoche for the increasing number of young women who refused to play by the traditional rules of society. "The chorus girl," complained one performer in 1917, "is the particular species of animal" that is held accountable for the "troubles and worries" of "all of mankind" and womankind. "If a woman is mixed up in a divorce scandal, by choice of the press, she is a chorus girl; if a shoplifter is arrested . . . immediately it is chronicled she was a chorus girl." No matter what the source of the trouble, she observed, "the chorus girl" becomes the scapegoat for "the abuse of the world." Although World War I had not yet been blamed on the chorus girl, she figured it was only a matter of time. "I wouldn't be surprised if some future historian should discover that a chorus girl stepped on the kaiser's gout-ridden big toe way back in that fateful August of 1914, and that made the ruler of all the Germans so mad that he took up arms against the world."[1]

A central obsession of American popular culture at the time, the chorus girl embodied modern society's buoyant optimism for change and novelty and its deepest fears about loss of control and tradition. Cultural commentators debated whether chorus girls were a special and particularly dangerous "species" of New Woman or whether, as one theatrical press release suggested, they were "like all the rest of womankind, only more so."[2] The notorious Evelyn Nesbit put this later claim somewhat differently, when she wrote in her autobiography of 1914 that chorus girls "merely put into words what their sisters of the other world think."[3]

These projections are hardly surprising, given the crucial role of the theater in charting the modern sexual terrain. The primary institution of commercial leisure, theater was a powerful agent of cultural experimentation and transformation, and the chorus girl was its most disturbing and absorbing manifestation.

The chorus girl was both a cultural fantasy and a member of the theatrical workforce. Chorus performers (singers and dancers) were essential to the successes of the musical comedies and musical revues in the 1910s and 1920s, and they provided the backbone of the Hollywood musical during the Depression decade. Members of the theatrical chorus (singers and dancers) saw themselves as somewhere between an overworked and abused proletariat and the well-paid stars of the contemporary stage. And as a theatrical workforce in need of basic contractual protections, they succeeded in organizing a Chorus Equity Union in 1919.

But the controversies that swirled around the chorus girl in that period went beyond the peculiarities of an occupational type. Rather, they revealed the broader issues raised by women of the theater, particularly how theater contributed to and expressed the tumultuous phase of social reconstruction that heightened female visibility and influence. For in the American cultural imagination the chorus girl served as a screen for all manner of projection about the changing nature of womanhood and about the excitement and perils of urban life. She was not only a body to watch; she was also a body to worry about. In the period from the late 1890s to the 1930s, she inspired endless discussion and speculation on the part of journalists, reformers, cultural critics, playwrights, theatrical producers, and movie makers, to all of whom she symbolized the larger problem of changing gender relations. Prey and predator, exploited and exploiter, disciplined and out of control, the chorus girl emerged as a capacious symbol of modern womanhood. Variously, and sometimes simultaneously, writers pictured her as a domesticated pet, a wild animal, a hardworking Cinderella, and an unscrupulous gold digger.

In the parlance of the early twentieth century, the New Woman was an untamable creature. But the chorus girl took this to an extreme. The metaphor referred to the threatening impulses that defined her personal character, her psychology, and her soul. In a 1902 satire, columnist Dorothy Dix joked that "there has been much dispute among naturalists as to what class this superb creature belongs." Some maintained she was a "bird," while others classified her as a "peach." The "best authorities," Dix claimed, were the men who "have devoted most time and money to investigating the habit and characteristics of the species" and "agree that she should be placed in the class of man-eating animals (genus feminibus fascinatem)." Though many "brave and daring hunters" have attempted to "capture" and "domesticate" a chorus girl, this was the "most dangerous sport known to civilized man." The "species" was largely incapable of becoming a "household pet." Rather, she belonged to "that class [of] wild animals that can never be thoroughly tamed." Underscoring the dissonance between outward appearance and inward nature, Dix made special note of the chorus girl's insatiable appetite. If the chorus girl looked "delicate, not to say fragile," she nevertheless "possesses the most inordinate ability to consume food. Nobody ever saw a Chorus Girl when she was not hungry." And in the "vain attempt" to "feed" these "beautiful creatures" and supply them with "the necessary diamonds," many "intrepid sportsmen" have "perished and gone broke."[4]

A tale about men who went out to capture women and instead got captured by them, Dix's commentary contradicted the vision of the chorus girl as a pleasing machine or automaton. But these were not irreconcilable concepts. The slippage between technological and natural images in this period was quite common. Many early twentieth-century writers moved back and forth between images of animals and trees and those of engines. The "enmeshment of images," as Cecelia Tichi points out, signaled a new cultural perspective in which the "perceptual boundary" between the "natural" or "organic" on the one hand, and the technological on the other, was beginning to disappear.⁵ Thus with little difficulty one could imagine the chorus girl as "creature" whose wildness could be engineered and repackaged to serve the aesthetic and commercial purposes of mass culture. Broadway producers diffused the erotic and social threat posed by the chorus girl's physical allure by presenting her as a controllable object or a machine. Off stage, however, she embodied every fear of emasculation associated with the ambitious and sexually expressive New Woman.

Chickens, Cinderellas, and Gold Diggers

Theater slang as well as ordinary speech associated chorus girls with animals. Two very different kinds of animal imagery predominated. One was the Darwinian notion of a man-eating wild beast. The other image both masked and expressed the fear of female transgressiveness by associating chorus girls with barnyard creatures that could be mastered, domesticated, and consumed.

In ways that seem paradoxical, the idea of the domesticated animal was closely connected to the image of the woman as machine. Machinery, like armies, could—at least in theory—be controlled by masterful men. So could herds and flocks of animals. In the Progressive era, the popular press referred to chorus girls almost generically as "broilers" (meaning chickens), "squabs" (meaning very young and/or very small chorus girls) or "ponies." The 42nd Street studio of Broadway dance director Ned Wayburn was known as his "squab farm"—a place where, as reporter Roy McCardell put it, Mr. Wayburn raised squabs out of the "raw material" of young girls and "made them ready for the footlights."⁶ In a satirical piece about the "Chorus Girl Famine" published in *The World* in 1908, McCardell likened chorus girls to livestock bought and traded on the commodities market. The artificial demand for squabs and broilers fomented by the "theatrical manipulators" of Broadway, he joked, had driven up the price of "Chorus girl preferred," making it a "feverish week" on the "girl market."⁷

So ensconced in the popular slang of the era were Broadway's barnyard metaphors that audiences for Ned Wayburn's backstage musical of 1912, *The Producer,* did not require any special explanation for why the cast of characters listed in the program included (along with "The Producer," "The Star," "The Composer," "The Costume Designer") "The 'Broiler'" and "The 'Squab'."⁸ Nor did a reporter covering the Actors'

Equity Strike of August 1919 for the Philadelphia *Public Ledger* feel compelled to clarify his reference to "a bunch of sorrel 'ponies'," trotting "up and down in front of the Booth Theater" chanting "Equity Association Slogans."[9] Significantly, no corresponding animal terminology applied to male members of the chorus.[10]

The costuming of the Broadway revue also reinforced these associations between women and birds. After the turn of the century, the feathering of female dress expanded from hats (aigrettes, birds of paradise, and cock feathers were fashionable on and off stage) to the use of plumage on the bodies and heads of show dancers.[11] So powerful was the association between birds and women that from the mid-teens onward, the half-clothed body draped with feathers became almost a cliche of female sexual allure on stage and screen.

In time the wider culture absorbed the vocabulary of the stage to characterize a new type of young urban woman. The upscale humor magazine *Judge* (which frequently featured a special theme) called its May 31, 1913, issue "The Poultry Number." The cover featured a color lithograph by illustrator James Montgomery Flagg called "A Spring Chicken"—a bathing beauty on a diving board. Inside, readers were treated to "*Judge's* Revue of Poultry," a montage of caricatures of fashionable women from Manhattan's neighborhoods, bearing the caption: "Squabs, chickens, and broilers. Drawn from life in the world's greatest poultry yard, New York."[12]

Just how this barnyard vocabulary first attached to chorus girls is difficult to establish with any certainty. In Western culture, poultry symbolism is multifaceted. There are fighting cocks and fiercely protective "mother hens" as well as hen-pecked husbands. But in the North American vernacular, to call someone a "chicken" is to stress their essential weakness (cowardice, for men) and to imply their stupidity.[13]

The term "chicken" also had carnal associations bringing to mind the violence and haste with which the cock mounts the unwilling hen, and how, despite her attempts to escape, she adopts an ultimate posture of resignation.[14] Thus to associate women with chickens was to imply a combination of their desirability and defenselessness. The chorus girl "chicken," like the more modern *Playboy* bunny, was conceived as a passive, consumable sexual object. As the extremely popular show tune from the 1912 musical revue *Broadway to Paris* put it: "Ev'rybody loves a chicken, Ev'ry body wants a girl that's cute and neat."[15]

In early twentieth-century slang, the links between chickens and sexuality grew increasingly explicit. Thus a "hot bird and a cold bottle" referred to the menu at after-hours Broadway restaurants, but was also a double entendre for an attractive chorus girl who dined with a wealthy businessman.[16] References to animals, sexuality, and eating also appeared in popular lithographs of the day. Several of the 1913 issues of *Judge* carried an advertisement for a poster by artist T. V. Kelly called "A Chicken Sand-Witch." It showed a svelte young woman in a bathing suit along with copy that read: "Sweet enough to eat. On our menu she is listed at 25c, so send your quarter right away and we'll serve you immediately."[17] And Ned Wayburn's 1924 revue, *Town Topics,* featured the song "Chicken Leg L'Imperiale," about a "dish" where the "meat's so sweet" that "you haven't got the heart to eat it."[18]

But nothing made the fantasy of the edible woman more graphically clear or showed how deeply entrenched in theatrical and popular culture the analogy between chorus girls and consumable fowl really was than two Broadway revues—The Ziegfeld *Follies of 1914* and the 1925 edition of the Shubert revue *Artists and Models.* In the *Follies* one of the comedians sang a song called "I Like to Broil My Chicken" and, as theater critic Acton Davies put it, "by way of ocular demonstration produced a pretty little girl on a real broiler, ready to be applied to the fire." Davies himself considered the number "a refreshing and deserved compliment . . . to the female sex," but noted that "the audience, ever chivalrous, did not see the humor . . . and positively refused to laugh."[19]

By 1925 audiences seemed less chivalrous and more prepared to find amusement in watching chorus girl chickens being roasted on a spit. The "Rotisserie" number in *Artists and Models* was even more graphic than the original *Follies* skit upon which it was based. "The Rotisserie" featured a male singer, Teddy Claire, and a group of chorus girls called "The Winter Garden Broilers."[20] A giant rotisserie, complete with a revolving spit upon which four trussed chorus girl "chickens" could be roasted at one time, formed the centerpiece of the scene. Two men in chef's hats operated the spit, while the head chef stood by showing a menu to two girls dressed as chickens. The chef piled up the "cooked" broilers on both sides of the rotisserie when they were done, and a line of girl chickens sat at the foot of the rotisserie, awaiting their turn on the spit.[21] As one reviewer described it, "several pretty damsels, tied and bound to as many 'spits' in a restaurant window, are revolved above . . . scorching flames . . . for the repast of customers."[22] Meanwhile, Teddy Claire's song invited male customers to:

Take a little broiler home with you
Take a little broiler do.

. . . .

Ev'ry one will fill you with delight
Tickle up your appetite . . .

The patter chorus followed with:

We've fat chicks and tender chicks
And tough chicks and tender chicks
And chicks that are nice enough to eat
We've chicks that cost a lot
And chicks that are rather hot . . .
We've shy chicks and haughty chicks . . .
And chicks that can show you something new
So try a little tender thing
How about a leg or wing
We've ev'ry kind of chick for you.[23]

The 1925 edition of *Artists and Models* opened in New York and later went on the road. The one critical review of the "Rotisserie" number referred to it simply as "bizarre."[24]

It would be easy to view these Broadway broilers of 1925 as symbols of the silenced woman, as creatures so vulnerable and defenseless they could be captured, trussed, cooked, and eaten. Yet something more complicated was going on here. This was not so much a story about male mastery as it was an expression of the crisis of masculinity in the era of the New Woman.

The macabre excessiveness of the "Rotisserie" scene, portraying the chorus girl as a "fowl prepared for sacrifice," covertly suggested that men needed to eat their broilers before they were eaten by them. The scene's brutal objectification of the female evokes what Eric Lott describes as "the sheer overkill" of nineteenth-century blackface minstrel narratives "in which black men are roasted, fished for, smoked like tobacco, peeled like potatoes."[25] Likewise, representations of women as squabs, chickens, and broilers can be read as a psychological wish, a symbolic attempt to assert male prerogatives and to master the perceived threat of dangerous feminine ambitions.[26]

The same message pervaded Broadway and Tin Pan Alley songs of the Progressive era, songs about the diamond-hungry chorus girl who looks like a cute pet but reveals herself to be an untrustworthy, manipulating, opportunistic fortune-seeker and trickster, always "scratching" for more money, always ready to flee the chicken coop when a better rooster comes along. Typical of this genre was George V. Hobart's song for the Ziegfeld *Follies of 1914*, "My Little Pet Chicken," with lyrics that spelled out the male dilemma:

I had a little pet chicken that I tried to raise by hand;
My money she went through it . . . how she blew it
She could scratch to beat the band . . .
I used to keep my chicken, my little pet chicken in a cage
With wires so fine
But something broke the netting and one day I found her sitting
On some eggs that were not mine.

The refrain continues the innuendo:

She had feathers like curls—though I fed her on pearls,
She got tougher all the time.
When she'd hear a rooster crow she would flap her wings and go
That little pet chicken of mine.[27]

Irving Berlin's "The Chicken Walk" (1916), written for a revue called *The Century Girl*, described a Broadway dance performed by "young and pretty girlies with Mary Pickford Curlies." But the song establishes a tension between the chicken's girlish allure and the threatening quality of her mercenary instincts.

Scratch the ground with your feet and then you gaze a-round,
Should you meet a millionaire—don't stare
Just tell him you won't stop; don't stoop, flap your wings,
Start to talk about engagement rings,
And then you fly back to your coop.
When you get there gently perch,
Don't forget to leave him in the lurch . . .[28]

A somewhat different version of the two-faced chicken appeared in songs and parodies that Harold Atteridge (who wrote the libretto for *Artists and Models*) created for the Shubert revue, *The Passing Show of 1918*. The program anticipated the complex nature of the *Passing Show's* chickens by promising "Alluring Vampire Girls," "Nubian Slave Girls and Salome," and a "nest" of fourteen chorus girls called the "Milk-Fed

Squabs."[29] Atteridge's song "Squab Farm" told of the male "sport" of "watching squabs of every sort" and warned that these "cutest chickadees" were far from docile. As the lyrics cautioned each "farmer": "You'll need a lot of chicken feed . . . For the chickens raise the dickens on the Squab Farm called Broadway."[30]

Chicken and squab metaphors constituted one aspect of theater's contribution to understandings of modern womanhood. But they also contributed a series of different, but closely related concepts having to do with female desire and ambition. A key theme was upward mobility, and the individual who breaks out of the ranks to achieve fame and fortune. At one end of the spectrum stood the chorus girl as Cinderella; at the other extreme was the ambitious gold digger. In fact the distance between Cinderella and the gold digger was sometimes negligible.

Theatrical publicists and journalists had actively cultivated the Cinderella myth since the turn of the century. The publicity surrounding the millionaire marriages of Evelyn Nesbit and the other members of the *Florodoro* sextet spawned regular stories of the upward mobility of chorus girls whose careers had followed a similar path.[31] Throughout the 1910s and 1920s press interviews with theatrical "experts" on the much-asked question "what becomes of the chorus girl?" encouraged the public to believe that, as one Shubert press agent put it, "in nine out of ten cases . . . she is the loving wife of some sickeningly rich old codger or the admired helpmeet of some silken son of dalliance, with plenty of cash to buy her automobiles, yachts, and country houses."[32]

The Cinderella myth actually had two versions. In one the chorus girl is released from her daily grind into the arms of a rich Prince Charming, or at least someone capable of satisfying her appetite for the finer things. In the other, her salvation is stardom. Sometimes the two were combined: girl gets rich husband after girl moves from obscurity to center stage.[33] That occurred in Ziegfeld's extremely popular 1920 musical comedy *Sally,* described by one reporter as a "Cinderella-like story of a little dishwasher . . . who, through the medium of her dancing, wins fame in the 'Follies' and later, *of course,* a fortune, as most of those 'Follies' girls do."[34] But it is significant too that, as the vocal scores for the musical tell us, Sally, a good girl who can't be kept down, also is a woman whose indomitable spirit will challenge men to domesticate her. After she has come up in the world, she sings a song that dares "any man" to get and tame her: "I'm just a wild rose, Not a prim and mild rose. Tame me if you can."[35]

But the Broadway myth of Cinderella was never as one-dimensional as the upward mobility stories or the romances of *Sally* or the *Florodoro* girls suggest. These fame-and-fortune tales with roots in theatrical lore were complicated in particular by the long-standing equation between actresses and the demimonde, and the fantasy that stage women could be hired for a whole range of public and private amusements.[36]

Evelyn Nesbit's story displayed some of the ambiguity in the Cinderella myth that she had helped create. When Nesbit's husband, the wealthy heir Harry Thaw, murdered her erstwhile lover, millionaire architect Stanford White, in 1906, the ensuing "trial of the century" focused as much on the body of Evelyn Nesbit as it did on the murder victim. In his trial the following year, Thaw claimed to have murdered his victim because White had ruthlessly destroyed Nesbit's innocence and turned a hapless teenager into a sexual concubine. The lurid material led journalists in a number of different directions. On the one hand, it reinforced nineteenth-century associations between female performers and prostitution. Yet a number of women journalists covering the trial, including Dorothy Dix, were inclined to present Evelyn Nesbit as a victim of the excesses of two rich, powerful, self-serving men.[37] Whether the cause or the victim of men's irrational actions and appetites, there was no question that Evelyn Nesbit had gotten rich and well-known in the process. The unanswered question was, by what means and under what circumstances had she attained these goals?

If in Nesbit's case the question could never be answered with certainty (she herself spent the rest of her life attempting to redeem her reputation and recover part of Thaw's fortune), any number of cultural commentators were certain they knew the truth about other chorus girl Cinderellas: that the soul of the conniving gold digger lurked within.

No image was as central to the decades-long fascination with theater women as the gold digger. The fabulous salaries paid to egotistical female stars like Sarah Bernhardt and the stories of their endless pursuit of money and celebrity were one confirmation of the gold digger image. A less flattering but more pervasive version in the popular culture of stage and screen was based on the horrific exploits of female vamps (like Theda Bara's characters) whose lust for money, goods, and status knew no bounds.

Chorus girls occupied a ground all their own. By the turn of the century the young and sexy chorus girl emerged as a gold digger par excellence. A young woman who made her living from the stage, her true vocation, it was said, was the ruthless pursuit of the fortunes of wealthy admirers.[38] Indeed, aside from chorus girls no other group of working women in or outside the theater was represented in the popular culture as a species of female hard-wired for gold digging.

Thus well before Avery Hopwood's play of 1919 inscribed the term "gold digger" in the popular lexicon, the chorus girl had emerged as its cultural prototype. Not all gold diggers of Progressive era social reportage and literary production were chorus girls, but almost by definition, all chorus girls were gold diggers. The gold digger myth had cultural power not necessarily because it corresponded to actual behavior, but because it was a peg on which to hang women's economic ambitions and their sexual assertiveness. Like that of the vamp, the image of the gold digger expressed both a growing fascination with and hostility toward public displays of female sexuality. Most importantly, as historian Joanne Meyerowitz has written, it was an image that symbolized the perils in store for men who "indulged naively in urban pleasures."[39] A modern version of Salome, the gold digger was also a greedy consumer of male resources. But unlike Salome, she was not interested in destroying her victim, only in exploiting his economic potential.

The publication of Owen Johnson's novel *The Salamander* in 1914 (it was also turned into a Broadway play that year) registered concern about this new kind of economic predator. A sort of updated *Sister Carrie,* Johnson's protagonist Dore ("Dodo") Baxter is a self-seeking small-town girl who finds the big city as much a place of personal opportunity as of danger. But while Dreiser's Carrie was also a victim of external circumstances, Johnson's Dore—the "Salamander"—is pure agency.

The Salamander character is also pure irony. She plays the male game, selecting and manipulating her admirers as if *they* were objects that could be moved about at will. "Each Salamander of good standing counts from three to a dozen props." In the lexicon of Salamanders, "prop," derived from the theatrical term "property," was the term for a rich young man "not too long out of the nest to be rebellious," and who possessed the "sine qua non"—meaning an automobile. These young props were "kept in a state of expectant gratitude" for the privilege of serving a Salamander's every beck and call: "waiting a summons to fetch and carry, purchase tickets of all descriptions, lead the way to the theater or opera, and, above all, to fill in those blank dates, or deferred engagements, which otherwise might become items of personal expense."[40]

The real significance of Salamanders like Dore Baxter was their rebellion against the gender norms of the time—a rebellion that Johnson attributed by degrees to most urban women between the ages of eighteen and twenty-five. The Salamander claimed the same right as a man to experiment with the opposite sex, to expose herself to evil and danger, to defy "etiquette," to go forth eager and unafraid while holding onto her "innocence." Like the mythical lizard, this human Salamander wanted to "flit miraculously through the flames" without being burned. "She spurns the doctrine that it is woman's position to abnegate and to immolate herself." What the Salamander wanted was equality of pleasure with men.

In his Foreword to the novel, Johnson sought with all the earnestness of a Progressive-era social scientist to portray the "Salamander" as social fact. She was, Johnson insisted "a curious new type of modern young woman, product of changing social forces, profoundly significant of present unrest and prophetic of stranger developments to come." Salamanders worked at any number of jobs, though mainly they were connected to the theater. But as Johnson insisted, "all this is beside the mark." What made a girl a Salamander was not any specific occupation but her love of exploration and excitement. Johnson observed that "the young girl of today . . . whatever her station or opportunity, has in her undisciplined and roving imagination a little touch of the Salamander."[41] Within a year of the book's publication, the term "Salamander" was already enjoying popular usage. An investigator of illicit sexual behavior in New York City dance halls and restaurants noted that in one "dance restaurant" he visited in 1915, the "girls" were all "salamanders" because "they will go all the way up to the limit" with the opposite sex, "but they do not overstep that mark."[42]

Johnson made his Dore Baxter an erstwhile actress whose real work is luring men with her youthful beauty and living off the money she can get from pawning their gifts. If she has a regular occupation or career, Johnson tells us, it must never "interfere with her liberty of pleasure." Yet the Broadway chorus girl haunts the novel as its disembodied subject. She stands as the female type or standard against which Dore must insist, "I am not like other girls." Dore asserts her steadfast claim to individuality and respectability against the rich and powerful men who would assume she is a "commonplace" chorus girl.[43]

This reference to "commonplace" chorus girls was also a convenient euphemism for characterizing young urban women's sexual behavior as a whole. For in the first decade of the twentieth century the terms "salamander," "chicken," and "prostitute" shaded into one another to name the questionable mores of women who, like Dore, traded their company for gifts, money, or an evening's entertainment. Some of these urban adventurers engaged in occasional prostitution, but mainly these "charity" girls, as young pleasure-seeking working women were also called, simply craved a good time.[44]

In the popular imagination of the times, no group of young women was more likely to be singled out as sexual suspects than chorus girls. Many people assumed that women whose occupations placed them on the lower rungs of the theatrical wage scale, and whose roles tended toward impersonality, were especially prone to gratify their desires by using their beauty and charm to seduce and exploit men for financial gain.[45]

Whether or not there was any truth to this claim—and statistical evidence is lacking—is perhaps less important than the fact that many people thought there was.[46] Public outcry against the spread of commercialized prostitution, stirred in part by the mass media, provided one source for this belief. Another was that prostitutes, some of whom claimed to be unemployed chorus girls, traditionally plied their trade on the streets around the theater district.[47] But the charge of the chorus girl's tendency toward immorality also had its roots in the theater as an institution and the new forms of sexual expression it promoted. Broadway producers and performers stimulated fantasies about the sexual desirability and perhaps even the accessibility of theater women. Actresses of all kinds were implicated in the fantasy, but none more so than chorus girls. In Johnson's novel, however, Dore the Salamander claims her rights to play her game without being treated like a common chorus girl. For despite men's assumptions of her sexual availability, the Salamander would not be bought and paid for; she refused to be "caught and mastered" by a wealthy man. She would trade her youth and beauty for a good time and gifts she could pawn for rent money. She would play with fire without being consumed.[48]

If the chorus girl was the disavowed subject of *The Salamander,* she held center stage in the play that critics viewed as its updated offspring: Avery Hopwood's *The Gold Diggers* (1919).[49] As one reviewer put it, Johnson had given a certain "vogue" to "a type of acquisitive woman of easy virtue," and Hopwood "brings her forward again."[50] The play centers on the lives of three chorus girls: Mabel Monroe, who thinks that alimony is a better deal than a husband; Violet Dayne, the wide-eyed romantic of the classic Cinderella tale, and Jerry Lamar, the gold digger with a heart of gold. Like Johnson's Salamander, Hopwood's Jerry Lamar was "virtuous" but didn't "look it." This "chaste cheater" made "promises" with "her eyes" that "are not fulfilled by her body." What all three girls had in common, theater critic Ashton Stevens observed, was their idea of "man" as a "meal ticket." When they took a "John" to "Tiffany's," they left no stone unturned.[51]

Like *The Salamander,* Hopwood's *Gold Diggers* established a tension between the chorus girl stereotype and the individual. Though Hopwood attempted to create the chorus girl/gold digger as flesh-and-blood human, at the outset the young women of the chorus are "predatory through force of circumstances," as one reviewer wrote (read: they don't make enough money to support the life style to which they aspire). But "when afforded the opportunity," they behaved like "genuine human entities who react to the same emotional excitements as their sisters in other walks of life."[52] Hopwood himself seems to have had a somewhat more cynical view of the subject. As his Jerry Lamar put it, "We don't rob anybody!. . . . We take from them who have, and give them value received."[53] Her motto is to get what you can from men while you are still young and beautiful enough to interest them. "They don't want to marry us! They're just out for a good time." As far as Jerry is concerned there are only two choices: "either you work the men, or the men work you."[54] Prey and predator.

Hopwood's play, with its convoluted plot and mistaken identity themes, belongs to a pre-World War I genre of New Woman stories. In the first act, Wally, the young heir to five million dollars, has declared his intention to marry Violet, a chorus girl. His guardian, Uncle Stephen, bitterly objects. Such a person—described as one who performs for the public "partly undressed"—is by definition morally and socially unfit for a Boston blue blood like Wally. In Wally's account, "the minute I mentioned the *chorus,* he flew up and hit the ceiling." To which chorus girl Jerry Lamar responds indignantly: "Oh—the very idea! To object to Vi just because she's in a show—without ever having *seen* her!" "That's what I told him," replies Wally, "but he wouldn't listen to me. 'I don't care *who* she is!' Stephen had said. 'I know *what* she is! A chorus girl! Bah! They're all alike!'"[55]

The various twists and turns of the plot involve a contest of wits between rich and powerful men and wily chorus girls. Stephen thinks he can undercut Wally's marriage plans by getting to know Violet and then gathering ammunition to prove to Wally he is making a terrible mistake. But the guardian himself has mistaken Jerry for Violet, a mistake Jerry doesn't bother to correct, and in fact exploits to teach him a lesson. Meanwhile Jerry plans both to seduce Stephen and to represent herself as the most vulgar chorus girl imaginable in order to create a favorable contrast between the sweetness and innocence of the real Violet and the parodic wildness of Jerry's pretend-Violet. Her goal to derail Stephen (and his lawyer Blake) is designed to make these two representatives of class privilege see that hardworking chorus girls are just as good as the rich men who play with them—worthy of love and respect, possessed of individual personalities. This exercise in don't-judge-a-book-by-its-cover worked simultaneously to reinforce, even as it undermined, stereotypes of the predatory chorus girl. It mattered greatly that the objects of her desire were rich men.

As Stephen discovers, his scheme will put him at a greater personal risk than he imagined. "What *is* she really?" Stephen asks his lawyer. "Can't you see what she is?" Blake replies. "She's a gold digger!"

Stephen: "A gold digger? What's that?"
Blake: "A gold digger is a woman, generally young, who extracts money and other valuables from the gentlemen of her acquaintance, usually without making them any adequate return."

However, Hopwood's gold digger is more than just a woman of the theater; she is first and foremost a woman of the modern world. For when Stephen asks, "how do you know that *this* girl is a gold digger?" Blake replies: "Well, in the first place, *every* woman is! It's a feminine prerogative! They start in as daughters and gold-dig their fathers. . . . The average married woman doesn't leave her husband anything but the gold in his teeth—and that's only safe if it's in the back of his mouth!"[56]

But for Stephen it is already too late. "Damned little gold digger!" Stephen says to Jerry, as he realizes he has fallen for one.[57]

David Belasco's production of the play and the surrounding publicity helped to popularize the title phrase, giving the notion of the predatory chorus girl an even larger presence in the public imagination. *The Gold Diggers* opened on Broadway in September of 1919, ran for 90 successive weeks, toured nationwide with over 500 performances between 1921 and 1923, and led to a spate of takeoffs.[58]

"The Chorus Girls' Rebellion"

Chorus girls themselves rarely had an opportunity to respond to or refute the stories that circulated about them. Apart from the occasional statements by women like Evelyn Nesbit, whose headline-making scandal became another opportunity to further her faltering stage career, the mainly anonymous girls of stage found it difficult to develop alternative self-representations. But they were not entirely silent either. In 1919 a new opportunity came along, and for a brief moment chorus girls and their supporters were able to challenge the tales of ambitious gold diggers and Cinderellas. What they substituted was an image of themselves as exploited working girls who demanded dignified treatment and were ready to fight for it.

On August 7, 1919, barely three months after *Gold Diggers* had opened on Broadway and in the midst of a series of highly disruptive postwar strikes across the nation, many chorus girls performing in the Broadway musical shows found themselves temporarily out of work when the Actors' Equity Association (AEA) called a strike of all Broadway productions in an effort to obtain a standard contract for theatrical performers. Organized in 1913, AEA was in 1919 still a fledgling union under a charter given by the Associated Actors and Artistes of America (an AFL affiliate) when the strike began. Initially, no provision had been made for including chorus girls in the Equity union, which was open only to the principal performers who comprised the elite of the acting profession.

But Equity organizers quickly recognized that the strike, which eventually spread to Philadelphia, Boston, Chicago, Washington, D.C., Providence, Atlanta, and St. Louis, could never succeed without the inclusion of the lower and more numerous theatrical workers. In the middle of August organizers created a separate branch of AEA called Chorus Equity. By opening membership to the chorus and other branches of the theatrical profession, AEA, now with more than 14,000 members (up from about 4,200 when the strike began), won its demands after thirty days out on strike.[59] As a result, chorus performers working for managers that honored Equity standards would be entitled to a contract guaranteeing a minimum weekly salary of $30 in Broadway productions and $35 a week on the road (up from the $18 to $25 that was then the going rate). In addition, managers would be required to pay for shoes and stockings worn in all productions. Finally, chorus girls were to be paid for rehearsal time that extended beyond four weeks—not an insignificant demand considering that when the strike began chorus girls in many productions were required to rehearse without pay for as long as 9 or 10 weeks and, on occasion, as in the Shubert's *Passing Show of 1919,* for twenty-two weeks.[60]

Some, like unemployed chorus girl Frances Gilfoil, could not even afford the $3.00 initiation fee required of new Equity members. "I would love to join as I think it's great the way you are fighting for the rights of the chorus people," she wrote. "I am a good dancer, [and] have been with the best shows for the past seven years," but "small as the [dues] amt. is I am not in a position to lay it out right now—as I have been *idle* all summer."[61]

The participation of chorus girls lent credence to AEA's claims that the strike was not just a dispute between managers and temperamental and well-paid theater artists, but represented the grievances of the entire theatrical profession.[62] And while the press did not make the chorus girls the center of the strike, tending to focus mainly on the rancorous dispute between AEA and the Producing Managers Association (PMA), it did draw attention to the particular vulnerability of this easily replaceable portion of the theatrical workforce.

Economic issues aside, the publicity surrounding what one newspaper labeled "The Chorus Girls' Rebellion" contributed in important ways to the public dialogue about them.[63] While not undercutting the chorus girl stereotype, the strike did complicate the image. It was one thing to see chorus girls as predatory gold diggers, quite another to associate them with the rising mass of organized labor and the women's rights movement. And in the course of the Equity strike, these varied New Woman typologies began to merge in new ways.

By the time the strike began, New Yorkers had already grown accustomed to the spectacle of female activism on streets (and in the theaters) of the Great White Way. In the summer of 1919 some of the same reformers who had marched in the suffrage parades of 1910–1917 again spoke at mass meetings and joined picket lines on behalf of the chorus girls of Broadway. Feminist actresses Ethel Barrymore, Lillian Russell, and Mary Shaw supported their struggles. So did Women's Trade Union League activists Rose Schneiderman, Frieda Miller, Maud Swartz, and reform-minded members of the Federated Women's Clubs.[64]

The moral authority of these female reformers helped bring a fleeting degree of respectability to the image and cause of "the girls." In contrast to the idea of the chorus girl as an immoral, money-hungry predator, Equity supporters painted a picture of her as a vulnerable and exploited proletarian whose struggles for survival were little different from those of the typical New York City working woman. "It is not for Florine Arnold I am kicking [protesting]," a well-known actress and Equity supporter told the press, but for "young people in the rank and file . . . who have just as hard a time as the shop girl."[65] This was not a completely new image of chorus girls. Periodically the press had run articles attempting to prove that the conditions of work at some theaters (such as the New York Hippodrome, where all performers were forced to punch an automatic time clock when entering and leaving), were no different than those at large factories. Similarly, the private correspondence of the Shubert organization discloses punitive measures sometimes used to discipline chorus girls, such as fines levied against any dancer whose clothing and person did not appear "clean and tidy looking" on stage.[66] But it was not until the 1919 Equity strike that the idea of the chorus girl as a proletarian gained some currency as a counterweight to the more popular concept of her as the well-pampered mistress or alimony-collecting ex-wife of the Tired Business Man, or the weekend playmate of the College Boy with a Trust Fund, or what one observer labeled the "champagne-in-a-slipper myth."[67]

Ironically, the leading spokesperson for Chorus Equity and its first president was not a pretty young thing from the *Follies,* but the popular "fat" comic, Marie Dressler. Yet to many people Dressler seemed the perfect choice for this job. The *New York Times* reported that when Dressler headed up a parade of striking Chorus Equity members on August 24th, her "pose" was suggestive of her hit song, "Heaven Will Protect the Working Girl," from her famous role in *Tillie's Nightmare.*[68] A seasoned fundraiser for the New York woman suffrage movement and a performer known for her ability to stand up to theater managers, Dressler now put her off-stage energies into spearheading a campaign to better the lot of her younger and less fortunate sisters in the chorus. Explaining why a well-paid performer would take up the cause of the anonymous mass of chorus girls, Dressler pleaded social conscience when she insisted: "I am doing it for the little ones in the business, it means nothing to me personally; it means nothing to the stars . . . but we are determined that justice shall be done the poor chorus girls."[69] In one public relations statement, Chorus Equity even referred to her as "'the Mother Jones' of the chorus."[70] One newspaper article sarcastically referred to her as "General" Dressler leading "an army of tinsel and tights" and substituting "war paint" for "grease" paint.[71] *Variety,* never a friend of the woman's movement, simply labeled her the "biggest figger from the skirt angle in the current squabble."[72]

In public speeches and in press interviews Dressler described the typical chorus girl as so woefully underpaid that she was "obliged" to "sell herself in sex slavery" in order to make ends meet. The stage should be "a safe and self-respecting" profession, she urged, "a place where any mother can safely send her daughter." Toward that end she called for the establishment of "homelike places" where chorus girls could take their meals, entertain men friends, and, for young mothers, bring their babies.[73] In mid-September Dressler announced at a meeting of the Women's Trade Union League that Mrs. John D. Rockefeller Jr. had agreed to provide a building for a chorus girls' clubhouse.[74] This was not the first clubhouse for women of the stage—the Charlotte Cushman Club for the "comfort and protection" of chorus girls and actresses in road shows had been established in Philadelphia in 1911.

Nevertheless journalists treated it as a novelty, complaining that female do-gooders were about to put the chorus girl off limits to male pleasure seekers. A sarcastic editorial in *The Nation* remarked that, like alcoholic beverages, "the chorus" girl was about to become the latest victim of the "age of reform." This "rollicking, laughing, careless child of a day and night," the girl who is "not a person but a tradition," was now in danger of being "abolished simultaneously with the cocktail." Before she was "uplifted" and "welfared," the "feelings of the TBM" (tired business man) and the "college undergraduate" should be considered, urged the writer.[75]

Despite such laments, the strike did as much to reinforce images of the chorus girl as a creature of pleasure as to turn her into a symbol of women's rights and labor militancy. In part this was because the campaign to change the popular view of the chorus girl's hedonistic off-stage existence relied on that image in order to counter it. Dressler, for example, warned of the need to "rescue" the theater from becoming "the happy hunting ground of the kind of girl I call a luscious and expensive prop" by filling it with "really hard working and earnest" chorus girls.[76]

Moreover, even as Dressler and the other female stars and activists who spoke on behalf of the rank and file of Chorus Equity worked to sanitize the image of the chorus girl, the parent union, AEA, moved in a different direction. To generate public support for the strike, the performers in AEA determined they had to do more than educate and convert; they also had to entertain. Thus the union attempted to replace the shut-down Broadway productions with evening and matinee fundraising performances in the theaters, as well as free and lively outdoor street parades, speeches, and political spectacles featuring a cast of striking Broadway stars, musicians, stagehands, and chorus girls.[77]

Chorus girls played a key role in this public relations campaign. Tellingly, the union never used them as street speakers, because, as AEA organizer Pearl Sindelar later recalled, Equity feared that "they would create a spirit of ridicule in the crowd," which, she insisted, "would listen to a man" but not to a woman.[78] Chorus girls, she might have added, were supposed to be seen but not heard. Instead, Sindelar and other Equity organizers relied upon chorus girls to appeal to more conventional male expectations. While men gave street-corner speeches each evening at 6:30, each day at noon Sindelar sent as many as fifty carloads of chorus girls—described as "the prettiest strikers in history"—down to Wall Street to distribute leaflets to the TBMs working at brokerage houses and banks. As Sindelar put it, the official purpose was to convince members of the New York Stock Exchange to keep their "wives or servants" from patronizing Broadway theaters until the "fight" was won.[79] But as one history of the strike has noted, the girls themselves served as a form of entertainment for the men on Wall Street. More deliberate in that regard was an Equity fundraiser in Chicago, where "bald first-nighters" were permitted to live out their erotic fantasies by dancing with chorus "beauties" dressed as "Parisienne mam'selles," "Broadway flappers," "Spanish señoritas," or in styles only appropriate for a "torrid climate."[80] This clever bit of public relations had its analogy in the suffrage movement's strategy of using pretty girls to legitimate the cause of votes for women.

During and after the strike, Broadway producers like Ziegfeld and the Shubert brothers also worked to reshape the public's understanding of what kind of New Woman the chorus girl was. With the strike in full swing, producers countered the claims of Chorus Equity by pointing to the chorus girl's relatively high wages and arguing that she occupied a privileged status among the ranks of young female wage earners.[81] In the aftermath of the strike, the same producers worked the press to create audience identification with the chorus girl by projecting a stage image of the chorine as a sexy type of the proverbial "girl next door." Simultaneously milking the public's fascination with the chorus girl's dubious reputation while defending her respectability, producers ended up by underscoring the image of her moral ambiguity. Like Henry James's 1878 portrait of the "inscrutable" flirt *Daisy Miller,* they left the public wondering whether she was naughty or nice, audacious or innocent.[82]

Well-seasoned experts in the art of image-making, theatrical producers and their press agents made the reputations of chorus girls into a commodity with a selling power all its own. Their disclaimers were often designed to reinforce the concepts they claimed to attack. "There can be no doubt that the chorus girl is misunderstood," wrote one Shubert press agent; she is not a "desperately immoral," "desperately frivolous" creature who "when not engaged upon the stage" is "occupied in consuming lobsters and champagne."[83] While "there is no denying the fact that some chorus girls have a penchant for night life and others have figured in unpleasant court scandals, the great majority live quiet and sensibly, many of them supporting or helping to support, mothers and sisters, or brothers."[84]

These fiercely competitive Broadway producers were not above using the chorus girl's unsavory reputation as a pretext for clubbing their rivals. The wily head of the Shuberts' publicity department, an eccentric Dane called A. Toxin Worm, devised publicity stunts that were almost as unbelievable as his name. In the fall of 1920, for example, Worm wrote to J. J. Shubert from Boston suggesting that "a good combination of anti-Ziegfeld and [anti] Equity story" might be made of "facts" he had dug up on several "*Follies* girls." The story he concocted would spotlight the unseemly behavior of members of the *Follies* chorus who "had been in the habit of going out to the Fraternity Houses in Harvard in the early hours of the morning [and] with the aid of victrolas and whisky in the possession of the students, carried on their orgies . . . right inside the sacred portals of the staid old Harvard University." Two of the girls who had a "mania for swimming" had got drunk, stripped off their clothing, and went for a swim in the local reservoir. The policeman who arrived to arrest them "got drunk, too, and he joined the swimming party."[85]

Thus if the Equity strike had added a new dimension to the image of the chorus girl, it had not uprooted her reputation as a heedless pleasure seeker and an immoral gold digger. Long after the strike, writers and producers continued to exploit the gold digger idea. As one newspaper reporter put it in 1925, it was no wonder girls wanted to get into the "*Follies*," what with wealthy admirers providing "Riverside Drive apartments furnished like a palace, charge accounts in New York's most exclusive shops, furs and frocks, jewels and Rolls Royce limousines. . . . And the chance for gold-digging. It's like owning the Klondike with a fence around it."[86] Anita Loos's popular novella of 1925, *Gentlemen Prefer Blondes,* only furthered this decades-old stereotype by serving up a Menckenesque satire about a not-so-dumb-blonde, an aspiring movie star turned fortune-hunting mistress, Miss Lorelei Lee from Little Rock.[87]

Hollywood had a field day with the gold digger concept, aggressively mining the commercial potential of this New Woman stereotype. Beginning in 1923 with a silent film version titled *Gold Diggers,* Warner Brothers would adapt Hopwood's play to produce a series of films that focused on manipulating chorus girls who were out to catch wealthy men. These included *Gold Diggers of Broadway* (1929), *Gold Diggers of 1933, Gold Diggers of 1935, Gold Diggers of 1937,* and *Gold Diggers in Paris* (1938).[88]

So profitable was the gold digger theme that the terminology itself became "a property worth fighting for." A court battle ensued in 1934, when Warner Brothers, which had purchased sole rights to the Hopwood play, won an injunction to stop Majestic Pictures Corporation and Capital Film Exchange, Inc. from distributing, exhibiting, or advertising films that contained the words "gold diggers" in the title. In response to a threatened lawsuit, Majestic Pictures retitled its 1933 film (*Gold Diggers in Paris*), *Gigolettes of Paris.*[89]

The Chorus Girl and the Fate of the Nation

These 1930s films, especially the so-called backstage musicals, provide some of our most familiar images of chorus girls. Best remembered are Busby Berkeley's extravagant production numbers and geometric chorus girl designs. But chorus girls also played a new kind of role in these Depression-era tales. By that time, the more than three-decades-old conversation about womanhood and theater was beginning to change. The "chorus girl problem" of the 1910s and 1920s had resided in social anxiety about young women breaking into the world on new terms, and had reflected the confusions of an age of tense and dramatic gender transformations. Chickens, gold diggers, Cinderellas were all cultural projections that revealed the way theater and the larger society manifested those transformations. However, during the Depression, when the chorus girl resurfaced in Hollywood musicals, this new medium of sound films had her serving a different imaginary function—one that was less about women qua women, and more about the nation itself. Backstage movie musicals turned the chorus girl into a gutsy heroine whose energy and determination helped solve the unemployment problem.

In the 1930s the Hollywood film industry replaced the theater as the national medium of entertainment. Yet even in its period of decline, Broadway served as Hollywood's cultural reference point. As the filmmakers of the Depression decade set out to represent the dilemmas of a nation in crisis, the ailing Broadway show served as a metaphor for the ailing national economy, and the combined force of the chorus girl's dancing body and manipulative soul provided the symbolic means by which economic recovery could be achieved. In this context, especially in Warner Brothers backstage movie musicals of the 1930s, images of the chorus girl as gold digger and as exploited proletarian (seen as oppositions at the time of the 1919 strike) melded together to create a new story—this one about her relationship to the national crisis.

What is especially remarkable about the backstage musicals of the 1930s is their capacity to recast the history of the chorus girl problem. Exploiting nearly every stereotype of theatrical and extra-theatrical representations of the chorus girl from the turn of the century on, Hollywood's backstage musicals then refracted them through the lens of the Depression.

That the chorus girl legend played such a prominent part in these movies is hardly surprising. One characteristic of this film genre was its reflexivity. As Jane Feuer puts it, these Hollywood musicals were "an entertainment" which "glorified entertainment." Their subject is "putting on shows."[90] But this leaves aside some crucial issues. Reflexivity, especially self-reflexivity, was not the special property of Hollywood musicals but had been central to American popular theater, particularly the Broadway musical revues of the Progressive era and the 1920s. This is not a trivial point. Only institutions that are supremely self-confident about their centrality to the wider culture could thrive on self-referencing. The presumption was that everyone cared, everyone wanted to know about the show and its performers, everyone had an interest in the chorus girl.

In the 1930s the question of what becomes of the chorus girl was rephrased as what becomes of America's working people. Already a familiar of American popular culture, this flighty figure served new ideological purposes. In these Hollywood backstage musicals the ever capacious symbol of the chorus girl stands for both the beginning and the end of a national crisis. Here as in her earlier incarnations, she embodies a host of contradictions. As a gold digger, she symbolizes pre-Depression national prosperity and the self-indulgent era of the gaudy spree. The story of her life is also the story of a nation; both had been traveling in the fast lane and were suddenly brought to their knees by the crash. In the opening scene of *Gold Diggers of 1933,* some unemployed chorus girls, reduced to stealing a neighbor's milk for their breakfast, sit around reminiscing about the good old days when they were "in the money." "I can remember not so long ago, a penthouse on Park Avenue . . . and a French maid, and a warm bath . . . and a snappy roadster . . ." says Carol. "Even love is not what it used to be," complains Trixie. "When show business was slow, I used to live on my alimony. Now I can't collect a cent of it."[91]

Symbol of the fast and wasteful ways of the nation of the 1920s, the chorus girl is also, paradoxically, the engine of national recovery. On her shoulders the fate of the Broadway musical and by extension the fate of the economy must rest. If the show went on, the national economy would too, and the show could not go on without the committed energy of chorus girls. Warner Brothers backstage musical *Gold Diggers of 1933* builds on stereotypes of chorus girls as "chiselers" and "parasites." But in the environment of economic and social crisis, it sets out to show how their legendary appetites and energies could be turned to new, socially responsible ends. It tells the story of a show that struggles to open, promising jobs and hope to these desperate chorus girls, who then take on the heroic task of rescuing it when the producers cannot pay their bills.

A transparent reference to the failure of the economic system and the struggles of the common people and the New Deal government, *Gold Diggers of 1933* has two famous production numbers. In "My Forgotten Man" we see chorus girl/gold digger Carol leaning against a lamppost in the foreground. In the background panorama are the men of the dispossessed Bonus Army, first marching, then limping and bloody, then standing in a civilian breadline. Almost a reversal of traditional Broadway gender images, the chorus girl appears as an individual pleading the cause of nameless masses of marching men.[92] A paean to the armies of unemployed, it uses the conventions of torch singing—seduction, pathos, melancholy—to weave together private and public pain. In this shrewd bit of social commentary, urging social responsibility for the unemployed men who had fought America's wars and cultivated the land, the chorus girl is no longer a heedless glutton but a compassionate citizen.[93] But Carol herself is also a casualty of the Depression. Out of a man, out of a job, she has been reduced to streetwalker—another member of the forgotten army.[94]

More central to the plot, the ironically titled production number "We're in the Money" works as a double entendre. The health of the show is the health of the economy. The body of the chorus girl is the medium of exchange—coin and woman become one and the same. Staged against a backdrop of five twenty-eight-foot silver dollars bearing the date 1933 and the insignia "In God We Trust," plus dozens of ten-foot-wide gold coins, fifty-four chorus girls wearing maillots festooned with silver coins and carrying other huge coins in each hand framed the lead chorus singer (Ginger Rogers).[95]

> We're in the Money
> The skies are sunny
> Old man depression, you are thru,
> you done us wrong.[96]

But the sheriff and his gruff assistants interrupt the rehearsal of this number to serve the producer with an eviction notice for failure to pay his bills. The lawmen close down the production and attempt to take as capital securities all of the shows properties: sets, costumes, and, of course, the chorus girls themselves. "Legal attachment to pay creditors," explains the sheriff, "Corpus delicti—or seize the body."[97] The show needs the chorus girl as a performer, but it also requires her energies as a gold digger. She attracts the attentions of a rich man who backs the show and keeps the cast employed.[98]

Though they imply that all chorus girls are by definition gold diggers, in a moment of public crisis the Hollywood backstage musicals need them to be individual human beings capable of friendship, compassion, and public-spirited commitment. It was a direction mirrored in other forms of public culture, most notably in New Deal-sponsored murals and plays in which women represented what historian Barbara Melosh describes as the "male ideal of feminism"—that of the "dependable [female] comrade" who repudiated the private consumerist ethos associated with the New Woman of the pre-Depression decades and emerged as an "engaged citizen" and "cheerful partner" to her man and her nation.[99]

Nowhere was the Hollywood version of the dependable female comrade as visible as in Warner Brothers 1933 drama of national salvation, the backstage musical *42nd Street*. Advertised as "Inaugurating a NEW DEAL in ENTERTAINMENT," *42nd Street* depicts the struggles to put on a Broadway revue called "Pretty Lady" during the dog days of the Depression. When the dancing star of the show, Dorothy Brock, breaks her ankle, a "raw kid out of the Chorus," Peggy Sawyer, is suddenly and unexpectedly drafted to replace the injured star and save the production. Sawyer is no self-serving Cinderella; she is "Pretty Lady's" New Deal. As the nervous and initially reluctant heroine is about to make her entrance, musical director Julian Marsh grabs her by the arm and lectures her on the gravity of her responsibilities:

> Sawyer, you listen to me—and listen hard . . . Two hundred people—two hundred jobs—two hundred thousand dollars—five weeks of grind—and blood and sweat—depend upon you. It's the life of all these people who have worked with you. You've got to go on—and you've got to give—and give and give—they've GOT to like you—GOT to—do you understand. You can't fall down, you can't—Your future, my future, and everything all of us have is staked on you.[100]

Chorus girls' heroic deeds also save the day in Warner Brothers' 1933 backstage musical *Footlight Parade,* in which the desperate director brings his cast together as if they were part of a large army preparing for a state of siege. "Nobody leaves this place till Saturday night," he tells the chorus. "You'll eat here . . . sleep here . . . for three days you'll live right in the studio . . . It's war . . . a blockade. You're gonna work your heads off . . . day and night."[101]

But these odes to national recovery also contain a second theme. For if chorus girl heroines save the system that will once again put them and the nation "in the money," their struggles also serve to critique the dehumanizing nature of economic relations. Industrial and military metaphors that had once signaled the optimistic modernism of the age and stage of Ned Wayburn and Florenz Ziegfeld, Jr. now apply to the ironic and paradoxical relationship of machinery to Depression-era society. This was not the liberating pleasure of the "perfection" that Gilbert Seldes had found in the Ziegfeld *Follies* and other musical revues of the 1920s, a perfection that in his mind "corresponds to those *de luxe* railway trains which are always on time, to the millions of spare parts that always fit, to the ease of commerce when there is a fixed price."[102] The critical voice of the 1930s used the exploited figure of the chorus girl to attack the moral and economic cruelties of capitalist enterprise. She represents both the selfless savior and the weary victim of the American Dream. As screenwriter Whitney Bolton described it, Warner Brothers *42nd Street* was the story of the Broadway musical as a ruthless machine that dominates "the creatures in it." It is a machine capable of "glorifying" one person while "maiming" another. This machine provides work and hope to the unemployed at the same time that it "subordinates" them to its will.[103]

In *42nd Street* the chorus girl stands for the working men and women driven by the gears of the capitalist machine. As film critic J. Hoberman puts it, this was the "Times Square of the assembly line."[104] Just after the opening scene of *42nd Street,* as musical director Julian Marsh is about to embark upon five weeks of rehearsal for "Pretty Lady," he assembles the newly picked chorus and dictates to them the harsh terms of their employment:

All right—now—you people . . . Tomorrow morning—we're going to start a show. . . . You're going to work and sweat and work some more. . . . and you're going to work nights—and you're going to work between times . . . when I think you need it—-you're going to dance until your feet fall off—and you aren't able to stand up . . . but six weeks from now—-we're going to have a SHOW.[105]

But the film actually presents a somewhat toned-down version of Bradford Ropes's 1932 novel *42nd Street.* The novel uses the chorus girl and the show to make an even more extensive indictment of the impersonality and brutality of industrial culture: "In the chorus you are part of a machine, except for the fact that instead of coils and wires you possess joints and muscles which ache when you exert them too much. No matter how high your standard you're still only a cog in the works; there's no chance to be a definite personality; you must kick in time, bend in time, exit in time." "No good complaining," another girl replies. "We have to take what's offered . . . If you drop out there are a thousand others eager to replace you."[106]

Ropes extends the metaphor of the ruthless machine beyond the chorus to the whole of the Broadway production and the entire American society. "The machine could not pause to brood over the destinies of the human beings that were caught up in its motion. Machines are impersonal things not given to introspect and retrospect." Relaying back and forth between the larger economic context and the musical show he continues: "All that driving force was pounding relentlessly toward one goal—a successful premiere on Forty-Second Street." Personal feelings, ambitions, even those of the show's stars, could not be considered. "The machine which they had built with infinite care was now their master." Only the musical director could claim the privileges of individuality. He "presided"; he possessed the "vision" and the "mind." The others, "from the lowest chorus girl to the resplendent new star," were "the ground-lings," each a cog which "had to function in its proper place."[107]

For more than three decades, the chorus girl encompassed the cultural fantasies and social anxieties of many Americans as they sought to come to terms with women's newfound freedom and self-assertiveness. Like the female comic and the suffragette, the chorus girl was a figure of excess who defied the rules of society and refused to stay in her place. But she prompted a much wider range of public commentary on women's changing behavior and ambitions. Sexy and fun-loving urban adventurers, worldly wise and scheming gold diggers, selfless comrades, exploited proletarians, and Cinderellas who break out of the mass to save themselves and the show, chorus girls symbolized the moral and psychological dilemmas of an era when women were achieving greater social and political visibility, and when both sexes were experimenting with new forms of urban leisure and social life. To be sure, the chorus girl of the movies, musical revues, plays, journalistic accounts, and social commentaries did not resolve cultural and social tensions so much as she embodied them. First as a reflection of gender upheavals provoked by the New Woman in modern machine age society and consumer culture, and later as a screen for projecting the dilemmas of historical crisis, the chorus girl occupied a central place in America's cultural imagination. Sarah Bernhardt was theater's Superwoman. But the chorus girl was its Everywoman.

Conclusion

THE LEGACY OF FEMALE SPECTACLE

From the great self-advertised dramatic heroine Sarah Bernhardt to the "virile" and "cyclonic" funny women, the attractive and racy singing comediennes, the vaudeville mimics and their creative "camera" work, the knowing band of Salome dancers, and the legions of pretty Broadway chorus girls, the spectrum of female performers on the late nineteenth- and early twentieth-century stage exhibited and encouraged an enlarged sphere for women in what remained male-dominated public spaces. Variously they magnified and pushed to the point of caricature the range of modernized female images: strong and independent personalities, aggressive vamps and sexy sirens, suffragettes and working women, consumers and self-serving gold diggers, and committed foot soldiers in the battle for national economic recovery.

These performers came to the stage at a time when women were already beginning to stretch the limits of middle-class gender roles. The period from the 1880s to the early 1920s was an era of unprecedented cultural visibility and voice for women. "Like all the rest of womankind only more so," these highly individualistic and often eccentric stage personalities symbolized and expressed a much broader female rebellion against tradition. It was the very novelty of stage spectacle that made it so provocative and so relevant to other women. Female performers explored, exaggerated, and exploited modern fears and fantasies about women's roles and identities. In doing so they inspired other women to dream and experiment.

The immediacy and spontaneity that characterized live entertainment and the newness of its forms helped transform public culture and female images. Vaudeville, which attracted the broadest cross-section of the American public, encouraged players to create a feeling of "intimate exchange" between themselves and the spectators, and performers con-

216

stantly altered their material to suit the mood of the moment.[1] The emphasis upon individuality, experimentation, and risk-taking on stage was especially novel for women.

By 1900 American theater had become a player-centered institution where the strong personality and physical vitality of the performer was as important to audiences (sometimes more so) than the play. Bernhardt took this to an extreme by turning every play she performed into a showcase for her eccentric and egotistical self. But she was hardly alone. In the popular theater of late nineteenth- and early twentieth-century America, magnetic and adventurous women of all kinds were willing to make their own strengths and shortcomings the topics of their songs, dances, and skits. Their performances resonated with and articulated the frustrations, fears, and desires of the larger female population.

The shock value of theater women who defied conventional notions of feminine comportment made of them a vital and infectious source of iconoclastic energy. Within the context of the new century's spirited social, political, and intellectual ferment, female stage spectacle and its explorations became all the more meaningful for popular perceptions of woman's nature and role. The result was an extraordinary synergy between the rule-breaking spectacle of New Women on both sides of the footlights. Theater licensed women to say not only "look at me" because I am bizarre, funny, critical, graceful, melodic, or beautiful, but "listen to me" because I have something to say about what it means to be a woman.

Yet self-dramatizing female spectacle stood in uneasy relationship to the fantasy of the stage-managed woman, a fantasy that grew increasingly prominent in the years between the First World War and the early 1920s. By the end of the 1920s the balance between women as active producers and passive reflectors of popular culture had already begun to shift. Elaborate chorus girl shows like the *Follies* cast a longer shadow across the variety stage, and revue comedy was increasingly subsumed under the spectacle of ever more scantily clad female bodies and ever more opulent scenery. And from the end of the 1920s on, as theater had to compete with the new and powerful seductions of sound film, women found fewer opportunities to engage in self-styled theatrical irreverence and creative autonomy.

By the early 1930s live theater was in decline, never to regain its former influence in public life. The Great Depression had a devastating financial impact on the stage, while it increased the profits and the cultural capital of the movies.[2] As film production steadily outpaced theatrical production and talking pictures provided an affordable alternative to live entertainment, the "unreal reality" of cinema replaced the spontaneity and "palpable" intimacy of the stage.[3]

The transition from live theater to sound film was not just a technological transformation; for women it was a social and political one as well. As the backstage musicals reveal, women heroines made their way into the movies. But the Hollywood studio system gave women as performers far less room to maneuver, experiment, innovate, and take risks in front of audiences than popular theater had done. If vaudeville had not lacked managerial control and censorship, the space it provided to daring performers like Eva Tanguay, Gertrude Hoffmann, and Irene Franklin allowed these and other New Women of the stage to explore their talents and expose their audacity in front of audiences in ways that the camera-framed picture never could. For all of his emphasis on turning chorus girls into packaged products and barnyard pets, even Ziegfeld understood the commercial value of women's spontaneous play on stage, which is why he continued to feature innovative performers like Fanny Brice.

True, moviegoers could still find that irreverent female spirit in the films of Mae West and other former vaudevillians who made the transition from live theater to sound comedy in the 1930s.[4] Indeed, it took an uninhibited vaudevillian turned screen writer and actress like Mae West to turn the chicken question on its head, as she did in 1940, when she played con-woman to W. C. Fields's con-man in *My Little Chickadee*. The film's script, written jointly by West and Fields (they wrote their own parts), closes with a clever reversal of their signature repartees.

Fields: "You must come out and see me sometime."
West: "I'll do that, my little chickadee."[5]

In a sense West was merely articulating in humorous terms the fear of gender inversion that had been building since the end of the nineteenth century. West's vampish and campy stage and film characters were so sure of their sexual power that they could announce with confidence to the most puritanical male do-gooder: "You can be had." The 1933 film *She Done Him Wrong* was vintage Mae West. In it she played Lady Lou, "an insouciant, insinuating, sashaying, tough-talking, sultry-voiced, golden-wigged, diamond-encrusted, bone-corseted, wasp-waisted, flaring-hipped, and balloon-bosomed 1890s Bowery saloon hostess and singer," a prototype for her later film roles.[6]

But Mae West was a unique vestige, even a caricature of an earlier era of eccentric, bawdy, and self-magnifying female entertainers. Her most successful films and plays were set in the Gay 1890s of her childhood, and, as film critic Pamela Robertson points out, in them West turned herself into a "deliberate anachronism."[7] As a throwback, she could playfully thumb her nose at the movie censors in the Hays Office who tried to interfere with her ability to control her scripts.[8] And she could celebrate a period when stage women like Bernhardt and Tanguay had refused to behave themselves in public.

West, born in Brooklyn in 1893 and sent on a national vaudeville tour in 1907 at the age of fourteen, had taken her first dancing lessons and received instruction in stage makeup and costumes at Ned Wayburn's Times Square studio, and in 1919 became a featured comic in one of Wayburn's Broadway revues. But she found her real inspiration in the stage routines of vaudeville headliner Eva Tanguay, becoming first an ardent fan and later a friend of the eccentric and self-mocking singing comedienne.[9] In time West went way beyond Tanguay, and indeed way beyond most popular performers, in moving toward a new level of sexual shock value. In the late 1920s West challenged the censors (and lost) by writing and producing plays that were both sexually explicit and deliberately crude in their no-holds-barred exploration of themes like prostitution and homosexuality.[10] Depression-era fans and critics savored her as a nostalgic symbol of all that seemed lost or under attack. "Her cynical swagger," wrote a critic in the *New York Times* in 1934, "casts acid ridicule upon the sulphurous sexdramas of the Dietrichs and Garbos."[11] Likewise, French novelist and former music hall entertainer Colette contrasted West's feisty take-no-prisoners sexuality with the more compliant female goddesses of the cinema, asserting that Mae West "alone" out of "an enormous and dull catalogue of heroines does not get married at the end of the film, does not die, does not take the road to exile." Though in fact the censors in the Hays Office made sure that she was joined in a marital union by the end of the film, West's characters made it clear that this coupling was "only a last resort."[12]

A brazen hold-out of an earlier cultural moment that was already fading by the mid-1920s, Mae West provides a point of high contrast to the trajectory of American popular entertainment. Hollywood was quickly trading much of the free-spirited vaudeville idioms of early sound comedy for a more formal, tightly plotted, and thematically conservative style.[13] Nothing symbolized the newly cautious Hollywood mood more than the so-called screwball comedies made by directors Frank Capra,

Leo McCarey, Howard Hawks, George Cukor, and Preston Sturges in the late 1930s and early 1940s. In these films, the wisecracking, headstrong, and even worldly career women (played by stars such as Katharine Hepburn and Jean Arthur) existed only to be tamed. For the New Woman of screwball comedy was a romantic mate for whom marriage was not a last resort but a predestined fate. Films like *Bringing Up Baby* and *Philadelphia Story,* Stanley Cavell has argued, were comedies of "remarriage" in which the plot revolved around the task of getting the estranged or embattled couple back together again. In the process of battling it out and getting it right, the couple learns to value and recognize each other's humanity, and the domestic world ends up looking like a happier place for both sexes. Yet for all of their utopian resolutions, these romantic comedies usually engaged the couple's "private stuff" rather than women's ambitions or their sexual volatility.[14] Even my personal favorite, Howard Hawks's 1940 *His Girl Friday,* is a comedy of remarriage in which the spitfire newspaper reporter Hildy Johnson (Rosalind Russell) dumps her doting fiance and a chance for a quiet domestic life to return to her old job at the newspaper *and* to take up once again with her cynical ex-husband and fellow reporter Walter Burns (Cary Grant). Admittedly, as Cavell writes, the film makes Hildy's job at the newspaper more exciting than domestic life. But as he also points out, its larger message is "to turn marriage itself into romance, into adventure."[15]

By the time the United States went to war with Japan and Germany, even the Mae West "mania" had come and gone.[16] At the height of her popularity in the 1930s, West was already a dying breed, the last of the old vaudeville-style comics. Here and there one could find echoes of the "I Don't Care" bravado of Tanguay and West. But in mainstream popular culture and films of the post-WWII era, there were no real counterparts to the nothing-sacred style of female irreverence that had been characteristic of the popular stage when Mae West was growing up in turn-of-the-century New York.

When the next important generation of female provocateurs came of age in the 1960s, "daring to be bad," their chosen venue was not theater or film but politics. Yet as was the case with the suffragists of the pre-WWI era, this second wave of feminists also relied heavily upon the concept of theatricality and media-driven self-spectacle.[17] In the age of television, the newest practitioners of female spectacle could claim, along with the anti-war and the civil rights demonstrators and marchers that "the whole world" was "watching." Carrying forward and amplifying some of the feminist demands of the early twentieth century, including the insistence upon ending the double standard of sexual expression, the right to jobs and careers, and the claim to individual selfhood, 1960s feminist activists also practiced the tactics of excess in advancing their political agenda. Some of their most effective media ploys aimed at challenging the very images that Ziegfeld and Ned Wayburn helped create and which popular culture perpetuated. Of all these media spectacles, none received as much attention as the now-legendary September 7, 1968, Miss America protest in Atlantic City. Carrying signs that read "Welcome to the Cattle Auction," and a poster of a naked woman whose body parts were labeled "rump" and "loin," radical feminists crowned a live sheep Miss America.[18] The point of the protest, one participant claimed, was that in the annual Miss America competition "Pageant *contestants* epitomize the roles we are all forced to play as women. The parade down the runway blares the metaphors of the 4-H county fair, where nervous animals are judged for teeth, fleece, etc . . . So are women in our society forced to compete for male approval."[19] Protest organizer Robin Morgan put it somewhat differently when she emphasized that the demonstration meant to take aim at "the degrading mindless-boob-girlie symbol" and the "ludicrous 'beauty' standards" to which all women were expected to conform.[20]

Unlike the suffragists who tried to convince the public that the typical activist was as pretty and charming as an actress, many (though clearly not all) 1960s feminists made a spectacle of abandoning the trappings of middle-class white feminine beauty (high heels, makeup, coiffed hair, girdles, bras, and high fashion) and flaunting a range of counter-cultural looks and images. Thus in contrast to the Progressive era, when theater and popular culture proved to be something of a midwife to feminist street spectacle and new concepts of selfhood, in the 1960s popular culture was viewed by many feminists as a problematic symptom of corporate image manipulation. The "sexist trash" of American popular culture, media historian Susan Douglas has argued, had simultaneously turned feminism into a "dirty word" and created feminine images against which a movement called "women's liberation" would rebel.[21] All through the late 1960s and early 1970s radical women played out their own feminist dramas in the streets of America. But compared to the pre-1920s period, when the New Women of the stage and streets fed off each other's energy and provocations, female entertainers in the 1960s offered relatively little that could inspire or intensify the impact of feminist political protest and street spectacle.

Nor did network television shows and movies provide much space for women to defy gender norms. In 1974, feminist film critic Molly Haskell surveyed the landscape of movies looking for evidence that the previous decade had finally produced some positive models for women, but concluded that rather than providing inspiration for social change, the "treatment of women" in the movies had actually devolved from "reverence" to "rape." In the movies the "ideal woman of the sixties and seventies was not a woman at all," complained Haskell, "but a girl, an ingenue, a mail-order cover girl . . . whose 'real person' credentials were proved by her inability to convey any emotion beyond shock or embarrassment."[22]

The historical trajectory of women's relationship to theater and other forms of popular culture had reversed itself. Instead of theater aiding and abetting the birth of modern feminism by offering women radical new ways of seeing themselves, as it had in the period before 1920, to the eyes of feminists in the 1960s and 1970s popular entertainment had turned into a force for their oppression, an enemy to target rather than a vehicle for liberation.

In the late twentieth century, the one new popular venue of outrageous and irreverent female stage spectacle was music—not the tame girl groups of the late 1950s, but the sometimes raunchy and always forceful voices of a new generation of singers which included Aretha Franklin, Janis Joplin, Laura Nyro, Grace Slick, and the "Divine" Bette Midler. Reaching a wide audience, they helped turn up the decibel of female assertion in the world of live entertainment and turned up the jet of feminine defiance in an industry where men had long held center stage.[23] In the 1980s growing numbers of forceful and independent female singers (among them Madonna) signaled a turn toward greater female authority on stage. The powerful presence of these singers along with the revival of stand-up comedy and more recently the proliferation of urban avant-garde performance artists has reinforced the spirit of second-wave feminist assertiveness, drawing on, and extending its capacity to question, to shock, and to disturb.

As we turn the corner into a new century, we may wonder whether the entertainment industry will produce a cultural and social effect anything like that of the last turn of the century, or even whether it will continue to provide the kinds of expressive outlets that permit women to challenge the cultural and social status quo. Many, though certainly not all, of the issues that made female spectacle such a highly charged affair during the last turn of the century (and even during the 1960s) no longer seem so urgent or so controversial as we head into the twenty-first century. But if Sandra Bernhard's 1998 comeback is any indication, live female performers may be once more pushing the boundaries and helping to change perceptions of women. This "post-modern vaudevillian" and "pop culture arsonist," as she has been called, takes hilarious pot-shots at the shallowness and sexism of the entertainment business in which she makes her living, while at the same time delivering what one reviewer called "equal parts stand-up, performance art, cabaret, world-weariness, and dish." But Sandra Bernhard, whatever her post-modern provocations or aspirations, is no Sarah Bernhardt. Of course, we should not expect her to become one. For Bernhardt's nine American tours between 1880 and 1918 occurred in a historical moment in which art and politics fused to create powerful and dynamic images of New Women. At the threshold of the twenty-first century, it is still too early to know what precise combination of issues might spark yet another era of energetic social activism off stage, and whether theater, an ever-changing institution of cultural expression, will promote a new and perhaps even more far-reaching explosion of politically efficacious female spectacle.

Abbreviations

AEA: Papers of the Actors' Equity Association, Robert Wagner Labor Archives, Bobst Library, New York University

BRTC: Billy Rose Theatre Collection, New York Public Library for the Performing Arts, Lincoln Center

CC: Chorus Clipping Files, Billy Rose Theatre Collection

HRC: Theater Arts Collection, Harry Ransom Humanities Research Center, University of Texas at Austin

HTC: Harvard Theatre Collection

JU: Joseph Urban Papers, Rare Books and Manuscripts, Columbia University

MCNY: Theatre Collection, Museum of the City of New York

NW: Ned Wayburn Scrapbooks, Billy Rose Theatre Collection

RLC: Robinson Locke Collection of Theatrical Scrapbooks, New York Public Library for the Performing Arts, Lincoln Center. This is a multivolume collection of scrapbooks containing newspaper and magazine clippings and other materials on the careers of late nineteenth- and early twentieth-century performers. Some volumes hold scrapbooks on more than one performer, others cover one individual. Notes give the name of the performer, the number of the bound volume containing the scrapbook, and the source and date of the clippings. When the clippings do not contain the name of the publication, I use the notation "np" along with the title and date of the article.

SA: Shubert Archive, New York City

USC: Cinema-Television Library, University of Southern California

Notes

Introduction

1. Carolanne Samuel provided this richly revealing piece of family history.

2. Cornelia Otis Skinner was "stunned" to hear one university drama student ask "Who was Sarah Bernhardt?" See her *Madame Sarah* (Boston, 1967), p. xi.

3. Ann Pellegrini called her a "latter-day Sarah Bernhardt." See her *Performance Anxieties: Staging Psychoanalysis, Staging Race* (New York, 1997), p. 54.

4. Nancy Franklin, "Master of Her Domain," *The New Yorker,* Nov. 16, 1998, pp. 112–113.

5. Important works on gender and turn-of-the-century American theater include: Lewis A. Erenberg, *Steppin' Out: New York Nightlife and the Transformation of American Culture, 1880–1930* (Chicago, 1981); Robert C. Allen, *Horrible Prettiness: Burlesque and American Culture* (Chapel Hill, 1991); Faye E. Dudden, *Women in the American Theatre: Actresses and Audiences, 1790–1870* (New Haven, 1994); M. Alison Kibler, *Rank Ladies: Gender and Cultural Hierarchy in American Vaudeville* (Chapel Hill, 1999). The one study that looks closely at the relationship between turn-of-the-century American theater and the rise of feminism is Albert Auster, *Actresses and Suffragists: Women in the American Theater, 1890–1920* (New York, 1984), which traces the theatrical careers and political consciousness of Mary Shaw, Ethel Barrymore, and Lillian Russell. Several works explore aspects of the British case. See for example Lisa Tickner, *Spectacle of Women* (London, 1987); Viv Gardner and Susan Rutherford, eds., *The New Woman and Her Sisters: Feminism and Theatre, 1850–1914* (Hemel Hempstead, UK, 1992); Julie Holledge, *Innocent Flowers: Women in the Edwardian Theatre* (London, 1981).

6. Nancy F. Cott, *The Grounding of Modern Feminism* (New Haven, 1987).

7. Ibid., pp. 3–9, 39.

8. Ibid., p. 42; Mari Jo Buhle, *Feminism and Its Discontents: A Century of Struggle with Psychoanalysis* (Cambridge, MA, 1998), pp. 35–41.

9. Cott, *The Grounding of Modern Feminism,* pp. 36–39; Buhle, *Feminism and Its Discontents,* pp. 15, 42–48. Parsons quoted in Rosalind Rosenberg, *Beyond Separate Spheres: Intellectual Roots of Modern Feminism* (New Haven, 1982), p. 172.

10. William Leach, *True Love and Perfect Union: The Feminist Reform of Sex and Society* (New York, 1980), pp. 159, 160–162, 180, 362; Barbara Goldsmith, *Other*

Powers: The Age of Suffrage Spiritualism, and the Scandalous Victoria Woodhull (New York, 1999).

11. Caroline Caffin, *Vaudeville* (New York, 1914), pp. 10, 25–26.

12. Henry James, *The Tragic Muse* (1890; rpt. London, 1995), pp. 110–111; 352.

13. On Cather and Austin see Elizabeth Ammons, "The New Woman as Cultural Symbol and Social Reality: Six Women Writers' Perspectives," in Adele Heller and Lois Rudnick, eds., *1915: The Cultural Moment* (New Brunswick, 1991); Susan Rutherford, "The Voice of Freedom: Images of the Prima Donna," in Gardner and Rutherford, eds., *The New Woman and Her Sisters*.

1 The Bernhardt Effect

1. Quoted in Louis Verneuil, *The Fabulous Life of Sarah Bernhardt*, trans. Ernest Boyd (New York, 1942), p. 112.

2. Henry James, "The Comédie Française in London," *The Nation*, July 31, 1879, reprinted in Alan Wade, ed., Henry James, *The Scenic Art: Notes on Acting & The Drama, 1872–1901* (New Brunswick, 1948), p. 128.

3. James, "The Comédie Française in London," p. 128–129. See also "Paris Revisited" in *The Scenic Art*, p. 91.

4. James, "The Comédie Française in London," p. 129.

5. *Spirit of the Times*, Nov. 8, 1880, Bernhardt (hereafter abbreviated as SB), vol. 59, RLC.

6. Ibid.

7. George C. D. Odell, *Annals of the New York Stage* (New York, 1939), vol. 11, pp. 320, 363.

8. Richard Gordon Smith, "Sarah Bernhardt in America," Ph.D. diss., University of Illinois, Urbana, 1971, p. 48.

9. Sarah Bernhardt, *My Double Life: Memoirs of Sarah Bernhardt* (London, 1907), pp. 323–324; Smith, "Sarah Bernhardt in America," Leigh Woods, "Sarah Bernhardt and the Refining of American Vaudeville," *Theatre Research International*, 18 (Spring 1993), pp. 16–24; Woods, "Two-a-Day Redemptions and Truncated Camilles: The Vaudeville Repertoire of Sarah Bernhardt," *New Theatre Quarterly*, 10 (Feb. 1994), pp. 11–23.

10. Daniel Joseph Singal, "Towards a Definition of American Modernism," in Singal, ed., *Modernist Culture in America* (Belmont, CA, 1991), pp. 9–12.

11. Bernhardt and mid-nineteenth-century actress Rachel Felix were associated with many of the same images. On the parallels see Rachel Brownstein, *The Tragic Muse: Rachel of the Comédie Française* (New York, 1993), pp. 237–248.

12. Amy Leslie [pseud. Lilie Brown Buck], *Some Players: Personal Sketches* (New York, 1906), p. 154.

13. Quoted in Maureen E. Montgomery, *Displaying Women: Spectacles of Leisure in Edith Wharton's New York* (New York, 1998), p. 124.

14. John F. Kasson, *Amusing the Million: Coney Island at the Turn of the Century*

(New York, 1978), p. 9; Richard Wightman Fox, "The Discipline of Amusement," in William R. Taylor, ed., *Inventing Times Square* (New York, 1991).

15. Benjamin McArthur, *Actors and American Culture, 1880–1920* (Philadelphia, 1984), p. 88.

16. McArthur, *Actors and American Culture,* pp. 1–26; "The Facts of Vaudeville," *Equity,* 8 (Sept. 1923, Oct. 1923, Nov. 1923, Dec. 1923, and Jan. 1924); Robert C. Toll, *On With the Show: The First Century of Show Business in America* (New York, 1976); Robert W. Snyder, *Voice of the City: Vaudeville and Popular Culture in New York* (New York, 1989).

17. McArthur, *Actors and American Culture,* pp. 30 and 241, n.1.

18. Albert Auster, *Actresses and Suffragists: Women in the American Theater, 1890–1920* (New York, 1984), p. 31.

19. Hartley Davis, "The Business Side of Vaudeville," *Everybody's Magazine,* 17 (Oct. 1907); Auster, *Actresses and Suffragists,* p. 53; Robert Grau, "Sarah Bernhardt," *American Magazine* (Feb. 1913), p. 91; Woods, "Two-a-Day Redemptions," p. 14.

20. Arthur Gold and Robert Fizdale, *The Divine Sarah* (New York, 1991), pp. 279–280.

21. Auster, *Actresses and Suffragists,* pp. 38–42; Richard Butsch, "Bowery B'Boys and Matinee Ladies: The Re-Gendering of Nineteenth Century American Theater Audiences," *American Quarterly,* 46 (Sept. 1994), pp. 374–405; Faye Dudden, *Women in the American Theatre: Actresses and Audiences, 1790–1870* (New Haven, 1994), pp. 6–7; Caroline Caffin, *Vaudeville* (New York, 1914), pp. 16–17; Robert C. Allen, *Horrible Prettiness: Burlesque and American Culture* (Chapel Hill, 1991), pp. 65–66; Kathy Peiss, *Cheap Amusements: Working Women and Leisure in Turn-of-the-Century New York* (Philadelphia, 1986), p. 143; M. Alison Kibler, *Rank Ladies: Gender and Cultural Hierarchy in American Vaudeville* (Chapel Hill, N.C., 1999).

22. Auster, *Actresses and Suffragists,* pp. 41, 39–43.

23. Edmund Milton Royle, "The Vaudeville Theatre," *Scribner's Magazine,* 26 (Oct. 1899), pp. 485–495. Compare Kibler, *Rank Ladies.*

24. Dudden, *Women in the American Theatre,* p. 3; Erenberg, *Steppin' Out,* p. 124.

25. Quoted in Montgomery, *Displaying Women,* p. 122.

26. See Peiss, *Cheap Amusements,* chap. 3.

27. Kathy Peiss, *Hope in a Jar: The Making of America's Beauty Culture* (New York, 1998), pp. 48–50, 54–55, 141–146; Lois Banner, *American Beauty* (Chicago, 1983), pp. 40–44, 216–217.

28. Gold and Fizdale, *The Divine Sarah,* pp. 10–11, 24, 33–34, 129, 141–142; Ruth Brandon, *Being Divine: A Biography of Sarah Bernhardt* (London, 1991), chap. 1; Cornelia Otis Skinner, *Madame Sarah* (Boston, 1967); Joanna Richardson, *Sarah Bernhardt and Her World* (New York, 1977), pp. 20–48; Smith, "Sarah Bernhardt in America," pp. 5–8; Henry Knepler, *The Gilded Stage* (New York, 1968).

29. Gold and Fizdale, *The Divine Sarah,* pp. 140, 133–134.

30. Ibid., pp. 143–144, 165; Smith, "Sarah Bernhardt in America," pp. 5–8, 177–181; J. Brander Matthews, *The Theatres of Paris* (New York, 1880), pp. 81–82.

31. *Dallas Herald,* March 26, 1906; *Los Angeles Examiner,* May 9, 1905; *Bohe-*

mian, Nov. 1908, SB, vol. 63, RLC. See also Stephen M. Archer, "E Pluribus Unum: Bernhardt's 1905–1906 Farewell Tour," in Ron Engle and Tice L. Miller, eds., *The American Stage: Social and Economic Views from the Colonial Period to the Present* (Cambridge, 1993).

32. *Bohemian,* Nov. 1908; Archer, "Bernhardt's 1905–1906 Farewell Tour."

33. *New York World,* Dec. 17, 1905, SB, vol. 62, RLC.

34. *Bohemian,* Nov. 1908.

35. 1913, np, SB, vol. 66, RLC.

36. Program for the Palace Theater (New York City), May 5, 1913, SB, vol. 66, RLC; Woods, "Sarah Bernhardt and the Refining of American Vaudeville."

37. *Vogue,* June 15, 1913, SB, vol. 67; *Chicago Record Herald,* March 13 and 14, 1913; *Colliers Weekly,* March 22, 1913, SB, vol. 66, RLC.

38. Knepler, *The Gilded Stage,* p. 297.

39. "Season of 1917–1918: Last Visit to America," SB, vol. 68, RLC; Richardson, *Sarah Bernhardt and Her World,* p. 203; Smith, "Sarah Bernhardt in America," p. 89; Gold and Fizdale, *The Divine Sarah,* p. 320.

40. *World,* May 6, 1913, SB, vol. 66, RLC. See also Smith, "Sarah Bernhardt in America," pp. 88–90.

41. Bernhardt, *My Double Life,* p. 398.

42. Ibid., p. 375.

43. John Stokes, "Sarah Bernhardt," in Stokes, Michael R. Booth and Susan Bassnett, *Bernhardt, Terry, Duse: The Actress in Her Time* (Cambridge, 1988) pp. 36, 37–44; Marvin Carlson, *The French Stage in the Nineteenth Century* (Metuchen, NJ, 1972), pp. 191–192.

44. On American "Camilles" and Heron's earthy washerwoman sexuality, see Bonnie Jean Eckard, "Camille in America," Ph.D. diss., University of Denver, 1982, pp. 56–60, 122, 152–155. See also Dudden, *Women in the American Theatre,* pp. 132–134. On Bernhardt's erotic physicality see Gerda Taranow, *Sarah Bernhardt: The Art Within the Legend* (Princeton, 1972), pp. 105–107; Elaine Aston, *Sarah Bernhardt: A French Actress on the English Stage* (Oxford, UK, 1989), pp. 50, 81, 159; Brandon, *Being Divine,* pp. 329–330.

45. *New York Dramatic Mirror,* April 16, 1892, SB, vol. 59, RLC.

46. Taranow, *Sarah Bernhardt,* pp. 195–204; Woods, "Two-a-Day Redemptions and Truncated Camilles," p. 22.

47. Verneuil, *The Fabulous Life of Sarah Bernhardt,* pp. 130–131. Brandon, *Being Divine,* p. 328, also notes the duality but stresses a different view of its other aspect.

48. *Atlantic Magazine,* Jan. 1881, pp. 95–108, SB, vol. 59, RLC.

49. Ibid., p. 97.

50. Ibid., p. 102. See also *New York Times,* Nov. 9, 1880.

51. Anne Vincent-Buffault, *The History of Tears: Sensibility and Sentimentality in France,* trans. Teresa Bridgeman (New York, 1991), pp. 110–115, 152, 167, 236, 245, 247; Fred Kaplan, *Sacred Tears: Sentimentality in Victorian Literature* (Princeton, 1987), pp. 3–10.

52. Vincent-Buffault, *A History of Tears,* pp. 158, 164–165, 237–239.

53. Ibid., pp. 117–120, 175, 192–202, 246; Carroll Smith-Rosenberg, "The Hysterical Woman: Sex Roles and Role Conflict in Nineteenth Century America," in Smith-Rosenberg, *Disorderly Conduct: Visions of Gender in Victorian America* (New York, 1985).

54. Gold and Fizdale, *The Divine Sarah,* p. 4; Nina Auerbach, *Woman and the Demon: The Life of a Victorian Myth* (Cambridge, 1982), p. 26.

55. Linton quoted in Elaine Showalter, *Sexual Anarchy* (London, 1990), p. 24; Margaret Deland, "The New Woman Who Would Do Things," *Ladies' Home Journal,* Sept. 1907, p. 17. See also Smith-Rosenberg, "The Hysterical Woman"; Auerbach, *Woman and the Demon,* pp. 186–187.

56. Alan Dale, "Sarah's Amazing Rejuvenation" np, July 16, 1904, SB, vol. 61, RLC.

57. Richard Findlater, "Bernhardt and the British Player Queens," in Eric Salmon, ed., *Bernhardt and the Theatre of Her Time* (Westport, CT, 1984), pp. 95–96; Garff B. Wilson, *A History of American Acting* (Bloomington, 1966), pp. 124–138; Mary C. Henderson, *Theater in America,* rev. ed. (New York, 1996), pp. 153–154; Cady Whaley, *Billboard,* June 14, 1906; Constance Skinner, *Los Angeles Examiner,* May 20, 1906, SB, vol. 63, RLC.

58. T. Allston Brown, *A History of the New York Stage* (New York, 1903), vol. 3, pp. 530–531; Taranow, *Sarah Bernhardt,* pp. 219–221.

59. Kibler, *Rank Ladies,* pp. 89, 95; Marjorie Garber, *Vested Interests: Cross-Dressing and Cultural Anxiety* (New York, 1992), p. 37; Jill Edmonds, "Princess Hamlet," in Viv Gardner and Susan Rutherford, eds., *The New Woman and Her Sisters* (Hemel Hempstead, UK, 1992).

60. Gold and Fizdale, *The Divine Sarah,* p. 176; Martha Vicinus, "Fin-de-Siecle Theatrics: Male Impersonation and Lesbian Desire," in Billie Melman, ed., *Borderlines: Genders and Identities in War and Peace, 1870–1930* (New York, 1998).

61. Quoted in Taranow, *Sarah Bernhardt,* pp. 212–213.

62. Max Beerbohm, "Hamlet, Princess of Denmark," in Beerbohm, *Around Theatres* (London, 1953); *Vanity Fair,* Sept. 1, 1899, SB, vol. 60, RLC.

63. Clipping, np, Sept. 1, 1899; and *Vanity Fair,* Sept. 1, 1899, SB, vol. 60, RLC.

64. *Baltimore Evening Herald,* June 6, 1906, SB, vol. 63, RLC.

65. James, "The Comédie Française in London," p. 130.

66. Quoted in Laurence Senelick, "Chekhov's Response to Bernhardt," in Salmon, ed., *Bernhardt and the Theatre of Her Time,* p. 173.

67. Quoted in Taranow, *Sarah Bernhardt,* p. 243. Italics in original.

68. Quoted in Gail Marshall, *Actresses on the Victorian Stage: Feminine Performance and the Galatea Myth* (Cambridge, 1998), p. 149.

69. Bernhardt, *My Double Life,* pp. 329–330.

70. McArthur, *Actors and American Culture,* pp. 169–175; Senelick, "Chekhov's Response to Bernhardt," p. 179; Marshall, *Actresses on the Victorian Stage,* pp. 148–149.

71. Quoted in Marshall, *Actresses on the Victorian Stage,* p. 149.

72. Hutchins Hapgood, *A Victorian in the Modern World* (New York, 1939), p. 155.

73. Nina Auerbach, *Private Theatricals: The Lives of the Victorians* (Cambridge, 1990), pp. 87–95.

74. Taranow, *Sarah Bernhardt*, p. 92.

75. *Spirit of the Times*, Nov. 27, 1880, SB, vol. 51, RLC. On spectacle and gesture in her visual style, see Taranow, *Sarah Bernhardt*, chap. 3 and pp. 240–241.

76. Quoted in Smith, "Sarah Bernhardt in America," p. 205.

77. Frank Lloyd, "Sarah Bernhardt's Latest Folly," *Broadway Magazine*, 8 (March 1902), p. 381.

78. *Cleveland Leader*, April 27, 1913, SB, vol. 66. See also *Chicago Tribune*, Jan. 30, 1910, SB, vol. 63, RLC.

79. Dudden, *Women in the American Theater*, pp. 78, 160–161; Marvin Carlson, "Ristori in America," in Salmon, ed., *Bernhardt and the Theatre of Her Time*, pp. 207–208, 220; Wolf Mankowitz, *Mazeppa: The Lives, Loves, and Legends of Adah Isaacs Menken* (London, 1982); Allen, *Horrible Prettiness*, pp. 99–100.

80. Marie Colombier, *The Life and Memoirs of Sarah Barnum*, trans. Bernard Herbert (New York, 1884), pp. 27, 40–41, 65, 72–72, 75–79, 85, 106.

81. Quoted in Verneuil, *The Fabulous Life of Sarah Bernhardt*, p. 125.

82. Neil Harris, *Humbug: The Art of P. T. Barnum* (Chicago, 1973), pp. 62–63, 77, 82–83, 247–248.

83. Ibid., pp. 25, 51, 62; Toll, *On With the Show*, p. 31–44.

84. Smith, "Sarah Bernhardt in America," p. 221.

85. Carlson, "Ristori in America," pp. 220–221.

86. Quoted in Smith, "Sarah Bernhardt in America," p. 245.

87. *New York Telegraph*, Dec. 26, 1914, NW, vol. 21, 060.

88. Harris, *Humbug*, pp. 119–121 (quote), 122–141. Italics in original.

89. *The Spirit of the Times*, May 1, 1880, SB, vol. 59, RLC.

90. Henry James, *The Bostonians* (1886) (London, 1994), pp. 240, 348; James, *The Tragic Muse* (1890) (Harmondsworth, UK, 1995) pp. 431–432. See also Richard Salmon, *Henry James and the Culture of Publicity* (Cambridge, 1997).

91. James, *The Tragic Muse*, pp. 126, 354.

92. Ibid., p. 352.

93. Edna Kenton, "Feminism Will Give," *The Delineator*, July 1914, p. 17.

94. George Burman Foster, "The Philosophy of Feminism," *The Forum*, 52 (July 1914), p. 22, italics in original.

95. On Wilde's philosophy see Mary Warner Blanchard, *Oscar Wilde's America: Counterculture in the Gilded Age* (New Haven, 1998), pp. xi, 3, 140–141, 152, 166–174, 237, 243.

96. *The Life of Sarah Bernhardt* (New York, 1880), pp. 3–5, 8–12, 14–15, 24, in SB, vol. 59, RLC.

97. *Gallery of Players*, 1895, SB, vol. 59, RLC.

98. *New York World*, March 22, 1896, SB, vol. 59, RLC. See also Knepler, *The Gilded Stage*, p. 291.

99. Fanny Fair, "Bernhardt," np, Dec. 1905, SB, vol. 62, RLC.

100. Janis Bergman-Carton, "Negotiating the Categories: Sarah Bernhardt and the Possibilities of Jewishness," *Art Journal,* 55 (Summer 1996); Harley Erdman, *Staging the Jew* (New Brunswick, NJ, 1997), pp. 48–49; Bernhardt, *My Double Life,* p. 14.

101. Quoted in Jules Huret, *Sarah Bernhardt,* trans. G. A. Raper (London, 1899), pp. 37–38. See also Erdman, *Staging the Jew,* pp. 48–49.

102. "Bernhardt Not a Jewess," np, [1898], SB, vol.59; "Bernhardt Says: 'The Mob Cried, 'Kill the Jewess!' and I am a Devout Catholic'," np [1905], SB, vol. 61, RLC; Smith, "Sarah Bernhardt in America," pp. 205–209.

103. Carol Ockman, "When Is a Jewish Star Just a Star? Interpreting Images of Sarah Bernhardt" and Sander Gilman, "Salome, Syphilis, Sarah Bernhardt, and the Modern Jewess," both in Linda Nochlin and Tamar Garb, eds., *The Jew in the Text: Modernity and the Construction of Identity* (London, 1995); Bergman-Carton, "Negotiating the Categories, pp. 55–64.

104. "Having Fun With Sarah," [1896], np, SB, vol. 59 RLC; Smith, "Sarah Bernhardt in America," pp. 105–116.

105. Quoted in Bergman-Carton, "Negotiating the Categories," p. 59.

106. Frank Lloyd, "Sarah Bernhardt's Latest Folly," *Broadway Magazine,* March 1902.

107. A. Rosenthal, "Was Sara Bernhardt Jewish?" *The Modern View,* Women's Supplement, March 30, 1923. My thanks to Riv-Ellen Prell for supplying this article.

108. See Bergman-Carton, "Negotiating the Categories"; Erdman, *Staging the Jew,* pp. 42–49.

109. Bernhardt, *My Double Life,* pp. 80–81.

110. Sander Gilman, *The Jew's Body* (New York, 1991); Gold and Fizdale, *The Divine Sarah,* p. 13. Neither mentions the passage in her autobiography, however.

111. *Chicago Record Herald,* April 16, 1913, SB, vol. 66, RLC.

112. Tice L. Miller, *Bohemians and Critics: American Theatre Criticism in the Nineteenth Century* (Metuchen, NJ, 1981), pp. 159–182; Dudden, *Women in the American Theatre,* pp. 59–61.

113. Michael Schudson, *Discovering the News: A Social History of American Newspapers* (New York, 1978), pp. 91–105; Brooke Kroeger, *Nelly Bly: Daredevil, Reporter, Feminist* (New York, 1994), pp. xiii, 86–88.

114. Schudson, *Discovering the News,* p. 69; Hapgood, *A Victorian in the Modern World,* pp. 138–141.

115. Kroeger, *Nelly Bly,* pp. 148, 85–88, 127–128, 136, 140, 146, 162–163, 172.

116. Schudson, *Discovering the News,* pp. 95–96; Gunther Barth, *City People* (New York, 1980), ch. 3.

117. McArthur, *Actors and American Culture,* pp. 146–147.

118. Channing Pollock, *The Footlights: Fore and Aft* (Boston, 1911), pp. 36, 48–71.

119. Walter Prichard Eaton, "Footlight Fiction," *American Magazine,* 65 (Dec.

1907), pp. 164, 165–166, 167, 169. See also Pollock, *The Footlights: Fore and Aft,* p. 36, 49–66; McArthur, *Actors and American Culture,* p. 145.

120. George St. Clair, "The Canned Interview," *The Green Book Album,* Feb. 1912, pp. 409–413; *Bookman,* Dec. 1907, SB, vol. 63, RLC.

121. Bernhardt, *My Double Life,* pp. 323–324.

122. For other "Bernhardtiana" see Smith, "Sarah Bernhardt in America."

123. *Cosmopolitan,* March 1906, SB, vol. 62, RLC.

124. *New York Globe,* May 25, 1912, SB, vol. 66, RLC.

125. *New York World,* Feb. 22, 1898; *Vanity Fair,* Sept. 7, 1899, SB, vol. 59, RLC.

126. *New York Telegraph,* Dec. 1905–Jan. 1906, SB, vol. 62, RLC.

127. *Current Literature,* Jan. 1908, italics in original, SB, vol. 63, RLC.

128. *Current Literature,* Dec. 1910, pp. 664–665. See also Ada Patterson, "Sarah Bernhardt—Superwoman," *The Theatre,* Dec. 1916, p. 342.

129. *Smart Set,* Feb. 1911, SB, vol. 65, RLC.

130. Bernhardt, *My Double Life,* pp. 288, 326.

2 Mirth and Girth

1. Constant Coquelin, "Have Women a Sense of Humor," *Harper's Bazar,* 34 (Jan. 12, 1901), pp. 67–69. (*Bazar* was the spelling at that time.)

2. Robert J. Burdette, "Have Women a Sense of Humor," *Harper's Bazar,* 36 (July 1902), pp. 597–598.

3. Nancy Walker, *"A Very Serious Thing": Women's Humor and American Culture* (Minneapolis, 1988) and Walker, "Nineteenth-Century Women's Humor," in June Sochen, ed., *Women's Comic Visions* (Detroit, 1991).

4. Henry Jenkins, *What Made Pistachio Nuts? Early Sound Comedy and the Vaudeville Aesthetic* (New York, 1992), pp. 26–38; Albert F. McLean Jr., *American Vaudeville as Ritual* (Lexington, KY, 1965), chap. 6; Brett Page, *Writing for Vaudeville* (Springfield, Mass., 1915), pp. 99–108, 147.

5. Quoted in Page, *Writing for Vaudeville,* pp. 103, 107.

6. Jenkins, *What Made Pistachio Nuts?,* pp. 37–38. See also T. G. A. Nelson, *Comedy: The Theory of Comedy in Literature, Drama, and Cinema* (New York, 1990); Eric Lott, *Love and Theft: Blackface Minstrelsy and the American Working Class* (New York, 1995). See also Constance Rourke, *American Humor: A Study of National Character* (New York, 1931).

7. Page, *Writing for Vaudeville,* p. 82.

8. Jean Havez and Leo Donnelly, "The Fun Factory," *The Green Book Album,* Jan. 1912, pp. 129–136, quote p. 135.

9. Jenkins, *What Made Pistachio Nuts?,* pp. 37–39, 46–48.

10. Ibid. pp. 28–39, 41–43; McLean, *American Vaudeville as Ritual,* pp. 107,134–137.

11. *Boston Traveler,* Jan. 2, 1909, Nora Bayes, vol. 46, RLC.

12. Walker, *A Very Serious Thing,* pp. 9–10, 25, 76–79, 80–83.

13. Quoted in ibid., p. 23.

14. Helen Rowland, "The Emancipation of 'The Rib'," *The Delineator,* 77 (March 1911), pp. 176, 231–232. See also Martha Bensley Bruere and Mary Ritter Beard, eds., *Laughing Their Way: Women's Humor in America* (New York, 1934).

15. May Irwin, "My Views on That Ever-Interesting Topic—WOMAN," *Green Book Magazine,* Dec. 1912, pp. 1057–58, 1062.

16. Rowland, "The Emancipation of 'The Rib'," pp. 231–232.

17. "'Comedian' Girls Jump to the Front," np, June 8, 1902, Tanguay, vol. 450, RLC.

18. "The Day of the Lady Comedian," [1902], np, in ibid.

19. See Shirley Staples, *Male-Female Comedy Teams in American Vaudeville: 1865–1932* (Ann Arbor, 1984); M. Alison Kibler, *Rank Ladies: Gender and Cultural Hierarchy in American Vaudeville* (Chapel Hill, 1999). On the soubrette role see Lois W. Banner, *American Beauty* (Chicago, 1983), pp. 125–126.

20. "'Comedian' Girls Jump to the Front."

21. Quoted in Roberta Ann Raider, "A Descriptive Study of the Acting of Marie Dressler," Ph.D. diss., University of Michigan, 1970, p. 117.

22. "Nellie Wallace," *Variety,* Jan. 4, 1908.

23. See Kathleen Rowe, *The Unruly Woman: Gender and the Genres of Laughter* (Austin, 1995), pp. 19, 17, 37; Robert C. Allen, *Horrible Prettiness: Burlesque and American Culture* (Chapel Hill, 1991), pp. 174–175; Mary Russo, "Female Grotesques: Carnival and Theory," in Teresa de Lauretis, ed., *Feminist Studies/Critical Studies* (Bloomington, 1986).

24. Benjamin McArthur, *Actors and American Culture, 1880–1920* (Philadelphia, 1984), p. 41.

25. Quoted in McArthur, *Actors and American Culture,* p. 42. See also Faye Dudden, *Women in the American Theatre* (New Haven, 1994), pp. 64–65, 143–144, 175–180.

26. Dudden, *Women in the American Theatre,* pp. 175, 176–177.

27. "New York's Newest Camera Celebrity," *Broadway Magazine,* Dec. 1902, p. 306.

28. McArthur, *Actors and American Culture,* pp. 41–43; Martha Banta, *Imaging the American Woman* (New York, 1987).

29. *Cleveland News,* June 14, 1907, Louise Dresser, vol. 162, RLC.

30. Quoted in Barbara Grossman, *Funny Woman: The Life and Times of Fanny Brice* (Bloomington, 1991), p. 42.

31. *New York Times,* June 6, 1922, NW, vol. 21,069. See also Geraldine Mascio, "The *Ziegfeld Follies,*" Ph.D. diss., University of Wisconsin, 1981, p. 144.

32. "'Comedian' Girls Jump to the Front."

33. *Toledo Blade,* May 20, 1902, May Robson, vol. 403, RLC.

34. Paul Distler, "The Rise and Fall of the Racial Comics in Vaudeville," Ph.D. diss., Tulane University, 1963; Joseph Boskin, *Sambo: The Rise and Fall of an American Jester* (New York, 1986); Isaac Goldberg, *Tin Pan Alley: A Chronicle of the American Popular Music Racket* (New York, 1930).

35. "Coon Songs Must Go," *Indianapolis Freeman,* Jan. 2, 1909, in Henry T.

Sampson, *The Ghost Walks: A Chronological History of Blacks in Show Business, 1865–1910* (Metuchen, NJ, 1988), p. 446–447.

36. Tom Fletcher, *100 Years of the Negro in Show Business* (1954; reprint, New York, 1984), p. 157.

37. Sampson, *The Ghost Walks*, pp. 140–141, 283; John E. DiMeglio, *Vaudeville U.S.A.* (Bowling Green, Ohio, 1973), pp. 109–118; Kibler, *Rank Ladies*, pp. 116–117.

38. Quoted in Thomas L. Riis, *Just Before Jazz: Black Musical Theater in New York, 1890–1915* (Washington, D.C., 1989), p. 168.

39. Ibid., pp. 77–78, 166–167.

40. Quoted in William C. Young, ed., *Actors and Actresses on the American Stage: Documents of the American Theater* (New York, 1975), vol. 1, pp. 564–565.

41. Riis, *Just Before Jazz*, p. 69.

42. "Even in Coon Songs the Fashions Change," np, March 7, 1904; "Songs May Irwin Thinks Most Of," np (1892), Irwin, vol. 297, RLC.

43. On her complex image see Kibler, *Rank Ladies*, p. 128.

44. Staples, *Male-Female Comedy Teams*, p. 57.

45. Sophie Tucker, *Some of These Days* (New York, 1945), pp. 35, 40, 50, 60, 63.

46. Allen, *Horrible Prettiness*, p. 176.

47. Tucker, *Some of These Days*, pp. 63, 41. See also June Sochen, "Fanny Brice and Sophie Tucker," in Sarah Blacher Cohen, ed., *From Hester Street to Hollywood* (Bloomington, 1983); Lewis Erenberg, *Steppin' Out: New York Nightlife and the Transformation of American Culture* (Chicago, 1981); Robert Dawidoff, "Some of Those Days," *Western Humanities Review* (Autumn 1987), pp. 263–286.

48. Pamela Brown makes a similar observation in "'Coon Shouting' and the Americanization of the Jewish Ziegfeld Girl," paper given at Performance Studies Conference, Northwestern University, March 1996. See also Linda Mizejewski, *The Ziegfeld Girl* (Durham, 1999), p. 59.

49. Lott, *Love and Theft*, p. 122.

50. Clippings, Lillian Russell, vol. 410, RLC; see also Albert Auster, *Actresses and Suffragists: Women in the American Theater, 1890–1920* (New York, 1984), pp. 101–105. Parker Morrell, *Lillian Russell, The Era of Plush* (New York, 1940).

51. Armond Fields and L. Marc Fields, *From the Bowery to Broadway: Lew Fields and the Roots of American Popular Entertainment* (New York, 1993), pp. 154–155; Auster, *Actresses and Suffragists*, p. 104.

52. Fields and Fields, *From the Bowery to Broadway*, pp. 26, 66, 120–128, 145–155, 171–174; Felix Isman, *Weber and Fields* (New York, 1924), p. 247.

53. Hillary Bell, "Funniest Things Said at Weber & Fields New Show," np, Sept. 1899; Alan Dale, "Big Happy Crowd at the Weber and Fields Opening," np [Sept. 1899], both in Russell, vol. 410, RLC.

54. Fields and Fields, *From the Bowery to Broadway*, p. 154.

55. Nora Donley, "Lillian Russell Sings Coon Songs in Burlesque," np, Oct. 4, 1899, Russell, vol. 411, RLC.

56. "Anna Held's New Pictures, Showing Her New Costumes in 'La Poupee',"
np, 1896, Held, vol. 264, RLC.

57. *Vogue,* Oct. 1, 1896, in ibid.

58. *New York World* [1897], in ibid.

59. *Detroit News,* Feb. 7, 1899; New York *Telegraph,* Dec. 5, 1897, in ibid.

60. *New York Telegraph,* Dec. 5, 1897 (with photo), in ibid.

61. Riis, *Just Before Jazz,* p. 84.

62. "This Is Called 'The Charcoal Seller'," captioned photo, np, Sept. 1904,
Held, vol. 265, RLC. On the race/sex nexus see Brown, "Coon Shouting";
Mizejewski, *Ziegfeld Girl,* pp. 58–59, suggests Held first performed the skit some
years earlier.

63. Banner, *American Beauty.*

64. Bios in Anthony Slide, *The Encyclopedia of Vaudeville* (Westport, CT, 1994).

65. *Chicago Post,* April 1902, Trixie Friganza, vol. 220, RLC.

66. Raider, "Marie Dressler," p. 21.

67. Marie Dressler as told to Mildred Harrington, *My Own Story* (Boston, 1934),
p. 3.

68. *Leslie's Weekly,* June 23, 1910, Dressler, vol. 164, RLC.

69. "Dressler Let Loose at Herald Square," [1910]; *Dramatic News,* May 14,
1910, Dressler, vol. 164, RLC. See also Matthew Kennedy, *Marie Dressler: A Biography* (Jefferson, N.C., 1999), pp. 59–75, 233–234.

70. Quoted in Raider, "Marie Dressler," p. 115.

71. *Chicago Tribune,* Jan. 2, 1910; *St. Louis Star,* Jan. 24, 1910; "Marie Dressler at
the Auditorium," np, Feb. 17, 1910; *Chicago Record,* Jan. 4, 1910; *Cincinnati Commercial,* Jan. 31, 1910 in Dressler, vols. 163–164, RLC. See also Raider, "Marie
Dressler," pp. 113, 118.

72. Quoted in Raider, "Marie Dressler," p. 62.

73. *Toledo Blade,* April 27, 1905, Dressler, vol. 163, RLC.

74. Dressler, *My Own Story,* pp. 122–123; *The World,* Oct. 30, 1904, Dressler,
vol. 163, RLC; *The Morning Telegraph,* Oct. 10, 1904, "A More or Less Confidential
Chat About the Weberhelds," np, Nov. 5, 1904, Held, vol. 265, RLC.

75. *The World,* Oct. 21, 1904; *Evening World,* March 16, 1905, Dressler, vol. 163,
RLC.

76. Raider, "Marie Dressler," pp. 80, 82.

77. *Theatre Magazine,* June 1910, Dressler, vol. 164, RLC.

78. *Chicago News,* April 1905, Dressler, vol. 163, RLC.

79. *Theater Magazine,* Feb. 1906, ibid.

80. Quoted in Raider, "Marie Dressler," p. 109.

81. *Brooklyn Eagle,* March 16, 1915, Dressler, vol. 164, RLC.

82. "Passing Show of 1912," press release, Friganza, vol. 220, RLC.

83. Walker, "Nineteenth-Century Women's Humor"; Zita Z. Dresner, "Domestic
Comic Writers," in Sochen, ed., *Women's Comic Visions.*

84. The precedent is mentioned in Walker, *A Very Serious Thing,* p. 153; June
Sochen, "Jewish Women Entertainers as Reformers," in Joyce Antler, ed., *Talking*

Back: Images of Jewish Women in American Popular Culture (Hanover, NH, 1997), p. 71.

85. *The Sunday Telegraph* (New York), March 26, 1905, Friganza, vol. 220, RLC. On *Pearl of Pekin* see Slide, *Encyclopedia of Vaudeville*, p. 198.

86. "Lively Bill at Twenty-Third St.," np, Feb. 12, 1907, Friganza, vol. 220, RLC.

87. Press release, Oct. 19, 1913, Friganza, vol. 220, RLC; Grossman, *Funny Woman*, pp. 22–26; Phyllis Rose, *Jazz Cleopatra: Josephine Baker in Her Time* (New York: 1989), pp. 50–57.

88. On Friganza's costume routine see Anthony Slide, *The Vaudevillians* (Westport, CT., 1981), p. 60. See also Trixie Friganza, "Six Trixie Friganza Tricks Which Make Women Laugh," *Chicago Tribune*, May 16, 1909, Friganza, vol. 220, RLC.

89. *New York Telegraph*, March 24, 1908, in ibid.

90. *Minneapolis Journal*, Sept. 2, 1913; *Variety*, July 26, 1912; *New York Evening Mail*, July 23, 1912, in ibid.

91. "How to Reduce Is an Actresses Problem," np, Feb. 23, 1909; "Too Fat? Drink Buttermilk," np, Aug. 1909, in ibid.

92. *Cleveland News*, Sept. 25, 1907, in ibid.

93. Trixie Friganza, "Comediennes Chosen by Weight," np, April 1907, in ibid.

94. Joan Jacobs Brumberg, *Fasting Girls: The Emergence of Anorexia Nervosa and the Modern Disease* (Cambridge, MA, 1988), pp. 174–188.

95. "Why Fat Women Succeed on Stage," np, May 27, 1907, Friganza, vol. 220, RLC.

96. "May Irwin Afraid of Getting Thin," np [1899], Irwin, vol. 297, RLC.

97. "Six Trixie Friganza Tricks."

98. Nancy Walker "Toward Solidarity: Women's Humor and Group Identity," in Sochen, ed., *Women's Comic Visions*.

99. "Six Trixie Friganza Tricks."

100. Slide, *Encyclopedia of Vaudeville*, p. 198.

101. On self-mockery and female community see Walker, *A Very Serious Thing*, pp. 9–10, and "Towards Solidarity."

102. Rennold Wolf, "The Highest-Salaried Actress in America," *Green Book Magazine*, Nov. 1912, p. 776.

103. Ibid, p. 776. See also Caroline Caffin, *Vaudeville* (New York, 1914), pp. 35–36.

104. For women's responses see *Springfield* [MA] *Republican*, Feb. 23, 1913; *Cleveland Plain Dealer*, Oct. 7, 1907; "Eva Tanguay Vaudeville Company," np, [1913]; *New York Telegraph*, May 26, 1908; *Morning Telegraph*, July 26, 1908; *New York Telegraph*, Oct. 22, 1908, Tanguay, vol. 450 and Tanguay series 2, RLC.

105. Quoted in Robert Snyder, *Voice of the City: Vaudeville and Popular Culture in New York* (New York, 1989), p. 150.

106. *New York Tribune*, Dec. 9, 1913, Tanguay file, HTC.

107. Caffin, *Vaudeville*, pp. 37–40.

108. *Rochester Times,* May 7, 1907; "Eva Tanguay's Acrobatic Leap," np [1902], Tanguay, vol. 450, RLC.

109. Miriam Michaelson, "The Chaperones, A Nondescript Affair," np, Nov. 28, 1901, in ibid.

110. *Cleveland Plain Dealer,* Oct. 7, 1907, in ibid.

111. Lyrics in *Theatre Magazine,* May 1913, in ibid.

112. *Theatre Magazine,* May 1913. See also Wolf, "Highest Salaried Actress."

113. Quoted in Charles and Louise Samuels, *Once Upon a Stage: The Merry World of Vaudeville* (New York, 1974), p. 54.

114. "[Tanguay] Quit the 'Sun Dodgers,'" np, Oct. 24, 1912, Tanguay file, HTC.

115. Caffin, *Vaudeville,* p. 37.

116. Sime [Silverman], "Hammerstein's," *Variety,* May 30, 1908.

117. Quoted in Anthony Slide, *Selected Vaudeville Criticism* (Metuchen, NJ, 1988), p. 181.

118. "The Vulgarization of Salome," *Current Literature,* Oct. 1908.

119. Wolf, "Highest Salaried Actress," p. 780.

120. Samuels and Samuels, *Once Upon a Stage,* pp. 56–7; Noreen Barnes, "Eva Tanguay," in Alice M. Robinson et al., ed., *Notable Women in American Theatre* (New York, 1989).

121. Quote from June 13, 1901, np, Tanguay, vol. 450. See also *Pittsburgh Gazette,* April 5, 1908; *New York Telegraph,* May 26, 1908; *New York Telegraph,* May 13, 1908, Tanguay, vol. 450, RLC; Samuels and Samuels, *Once Upon a Stage,* p. 57

122. *Pittsburgh Gazette,* April 5, 1908, Tanguay, vol. 450, RLC.

123. *New York Telegraph,* Nov. 15, 1906, Bayes, vol. 46, RLC.

124. *Chicago Tribune,* Jan. [9], 1913, in ibid. On her "fragile" curves see Caffin, *Vaudeville,* pp. 27–28.

125. *Toledo Blade,* Jan. 13, 1908, Franklin, vol. 217, RLC.

126. *Chicago News,* Nov. 18, 1907, Bayes, vol. 46, RLC.

127. Nov. 17, 1907, np, in ibid.

128. *Chicago News,* Feb. 8, 1909, in ibid.

129. Caffin, *Vaudeville,* p. 29.

130. *Boston Traveler,* Jan. 2, 1909, Bayes, vol. 46, RLC.

131. Ibid.

132. *Morning Telegraph,* Aug. 12, 1904. See also *Cincinnati Commercial,* Sept. 10, 1911, in ibid.

133. *Cincinnati Commercial,* Sept. 10, 1911; *Baltimore American,* [August] 30, 1910, in ibid.

134. *Cincinnati Commercial,* Sept. 10, 1911.

135. "Singer and Pianist," np, Sept. 14, 1907; *Variety,* Oct. 23, 1907, Franklin, vol. 217, RLC; *New York Dramatic Mirror,* Oct. 17, 1908.

136. *Variety,* Oct. 17, 1908, Franklin, vol. 217, RLC.

137. Sime [Silverman], "Twenty-Third Street," *Variety,* Oct. 19, 1907, in ibid.

138. *Variety,* Oct. 10, 1908, Oct. 19, 1909, in ibid.

139. *Variety,* Oct. 19, 1907, in ibid.

18. "The Parisian Model Ought to Be Spanked and Sent Home," np, Nov. 29, 1906, Hoffmann, vol. 273, RLC.

19. *Variety,* March 7, 1908, March 14, 1908; *New York Dramatic Mirror,* March 21, 1908.

20. Quoted in Linda Martin and Kerry Segrave, *Women in Comedy* (Secaucus, NJ, 1986), p. 62.

21. Juliet, "How We Imitate the Actors You Like," *Green Book Magazine,* Dec. 1912, p. 1064.

22. Quoted in Morrow, "Elsie Janis," p. 61.

23. Max Beerbohm, *Letters to Reggie Turner,* ed. Rupert Hart-Davis (London, 1964), pp. 71, 44–70.

24. Bios in Anthony Slide, *The Encyclopedia of Vaudeville* (Westport, CT, 1994); T. Allston Brown, *A History of the New York Stage* (New York, 1903), vol. 3, p. 575.

25. Morrow, "Elsie Janis," p. 57; *Variety,* April 27, 1907; "Inimitable Child," *Theater Magazine,* August 1905, Janis, vol. 300, RLC.

26. Oct. 1907, np, Loftus, vol. 313, RLC; *Buffalo News,* Nov. 2, 1916, Locke Envelope no. 1210, BRTC.

27. Caffin, *Vaudeville,* p. 26; Henry Jenkins, *What Made Pistachio Nuts?* (New York, 1992), pp. 59–73.

28. Cohen, "Borrowed Art," p. 4; Armond Fields and L. Marc Fields, *From the Bowery to Broadway* (New York, 1993), p. xiii.

29. Morrow, "Elsie Janis," pp. 136–138; *New York Telegraph,* March 21, 1908, Loftus, vol. 313, RLC; "Elsie Janis and the New York Roof," np, July 1, 1905, Janis, vol. 300, RLC.

30. *Variety,* July 25, 1908, March 14, 1908, Sept. 14, 1910.

31. "Give an Imitation of Me." Words and Music by Blanche Merrill. Copyright 1910 by Charles K. Harris, *Delaney Song Book,* no. 59, p. 7, Music Division, NYPL, Lincoln Center.

32. *New York Telegraph,* Feb. 25, 1908, Hoffmann, vol. 273, RLC; *Variety,* March 14, 1908.

33. *Morning Telegraph,* Feb. 26, 1908, Hoffmann, vol. 273, RLC.

34. Quoted in Cohen, "Borrowed Art", p. 4. On Tanguay and Vesta Victoria see *Variety,* Jan. 25, 1908; *Dramatic Mirror,* March 21, 1908.

35. Cohen, "Borrowed Art," p. 4; Stone, "Gertrude Hoffmann," p. 14.

36. Susan K. Cahn, *Coming on Strong: Gender and Sexuality in Twentieth Century Women's Sports* (New York, 1994); Allen Guttman, *Women's Sports: A History* (New York, 1991).

37. *Dramatic Mirror,* April 4, 1908.

38. Miles Orvell, *The Real Thing: Imitation and Authenticity in American Culture* (Chapel Hill, 1989) pp. xv–xvi, 34, 36–37, 142–44; Lawrence W. Levine, *Highbrow/Lowbrow: The Emergence of Cultural Hierarchy in America* (Cambridge, 1986); Hillel Schwartz, *The Culture of the Copy* (New York, 1996).

39. Andreas Huyssen, "Mass Culture as Woman: Modernism's Other," in *After the Great Divide: Modernism, Mass Culture, Postmodernism* (Bloomington, 1986).

40. Theodore Dreiser, *Sister Carrie* (1900), (New York, 1967), pp. 70, 49, 67, 85, 89, 127. See also "Why Women Are Greater Actors Than Men," *Current Literature,* Oct. 1906, pp. 423–424.

41. Benjamin McArthur, *Actors and American Culture, 1880–1920* (Philadelphia, 1984) pp. 171, 175–176, 185–187; Martha Banta, *Imaging the American Woman* (New York, 1987).

42. McArthur, *Actors and American Culture,* pp. 178–83; Garff B. Wilson, *A History of American Acting* (Bloomington, 1966), pp. 140–142; Alan Dale, "Nazimova and Some Others," *Cosmopolitan,* April 1907, pp. 674–683.

43. Oct. 1907, np, Loftus, vol. 313, RLC.

44. "Imitators and Imitations: Elsie Janis and 'Cissie' Loftus Tell What They Think of Each Other," Vaudeville files, HTC.

45. J. Arthur Bleackley, *The Art of Mimicry* (New York, 1911), pp. 9, 80.

46. Quoted in Morrow, "Elsie Janis," p. 123.

47. Juliet, "How We Imitate." See also "Why an Imitation?" np, Sept. 5, 1905, Janis, vol. 300, RLC.

48. Cissie Loftus, "The Art of Imitation, or Imitation as Art," *Broadway Magazine,* May 1899, vol. 312, RLC. See also Constance Ray, "The Art of Imitation: A Talk With Cecilia Loftus," np, Aug. 19, 1911, Vaudeville files, HTC.

49. Bleackley, *The Art of Mimicry,* pp. 9, 80.

50. Robert Howard Russell, *Cissie Loftus, an Appreciation* (New York, 1899), in Loftus clippings, BRTC.

51. Huyssen, "Mass Culture as Woman"; Orvell, *The Real Thing.*

52. Henri Bergson, *Le Rire* (Laughter) (1900), English trans. in Wylie Sypher, ed., *Comedy* (Baltimore, 1994), pp. 80–81, 97.

53. Bergson, *Laughter,* pp. 156–57.

54. Sigmund Freud, "Wit and Its Relation to the Unconscious," in A. A. Brill, trans. and ed., *The Basic Writings of Sigmund Freud* (New York, 1938), pp. 776, 782–783.

55. "Cissie Loftus Is Not a Phonograph," np, Jan. 7, 1899, Loftus, vol. 312, RLC.

56. Dale, "Two Lovely Imitators."

57. "Cissie Will 'Gie Us The Giftie' of Seeing 'How Ithers See Us'" (1899), np, Loftus, vol. 312, RLC.

58. *Dramatic Mirror,* April 4, 1908.

59. Ads for the Victor Talking Machine, *The Theater Magazine,* Oct. 1908, May 1908.

60. Juliet, "How We Imitate," p. 1064.

61. Quoted in Morrow, "Elsie Janis," p. 84. See also "Cissie Loftus Is Not a Phonograph."

62. See Michael Taussig, *Mimesis and Alterity: A Particular History of the Senses* (New York, 1993), pp. xvii–xix, 198–220. See also Walter Benjamin, "The Work of Art in the Age of Mechanical Reproduction" (1936), trans. Harry Zohn, in Benjamin, *Illuminations* (New York, 1969).

63. Benjamin, "The Work of Art in the Age of Mechanical Reproduction," p. 121.

64. Bergson, *Laughter,* p. 82.

65. Beaumont Newhall, *The History of Photography* (New York, 1994), pp. 64–66; Vicki Goldberg, *The Power of Photography* (New York, 1991), pp. 13–14, 107–112; Faye Dudden, *Women in the American Theatre* (New Haven, 1994), pp. 63–64, 157.

66. Allan Sekula, "The Traffic in Photographs, in Benjamin H. D. Buchloh et al., eds. *Modernism and Modernity: The Vancouver Conference Papers* (Halifax, 1983), pp. 124–125; Goldberg, *The Power of Photography,* pp. 19–28, 39–44, 61–62.

67. Orvell, *The Real Thing,* pp. 77, 73–81.

68. Charles Caffin, "Photography as a Fine Art" (1901), in Vicki Goldberg, ed., *Photography in Print: Writings from 1816 to the Present* (New York, 1981), p. 221. See also Orvell, *The Real Thing,* pp. 198–203.

69. Oct. 1907, np, Loftus, vol. 313, RLC.

70. Sandra Lee Underwood, *Charles H. Caffin: A Voice for Modernism, 1897–1918* (Ann Arbor, 1983), pp. 10–11.

71. Caroline Caffin, *Vaudeville,* p. 136.

72. Juliet, "How We Imitate," p. 1068.

73. Quoted in Judith Fryer Davidov, *Women's Camera Work* (Durham, 1998), p. 87. See also Naomi Rosenblum, *A History of Women Photographers* (New York, 1994).

74. Catherine A. Lutz and Jane L. Collins, *Reading National Geographic* (Chicago, 1993), pp. 189–91, 211; Donna Haraway, *Primate Visions: Gender, Race, and Nature in the World of Modern Science* (New York, 1989), pp. 44–46.

75. Sept. 2, 1907, np, Hoffmann, vol. 273, RLC.

76. *Chicago News,* Oct. 30, 1909, Loftus, vol. 313, RLC.

77. Judith Fryer, "Women's Camera Work: Seven Propositions in Search of a Theory," *Prospects,* 16 (1991), p. 73; Lutz and Collins, *Reading National Geographic,* pp. 207–208; Haraway, *Primate Visions,* pp. 45–46.

78. Judith Wechsler, *A Human Comedy: Physiognomy and Caricature in 19th Century Paris* (Chicago, 1982), pp. 174–175. See also Ross Posnock, *The Trial of Curiosity: Henry James, William James, and the Challenge of Modernity* (New York, 1991), pp. 100, 141, 151, 179; Janet Wolff, "The Invisible *Flâneuse:* Women and the Literature of Modernity," in *Feminine Sentences* (Cambridge, 1990); Anke Gleber, "Female Flânerie and the Symphony of the City," in Katharina Von Ankum, ed., *Women in the Metropolis: Gender and Modernity in Weimar Culture* (Berkeley, 1997).

79. Ronald Bogue and Mihai I. Spariosu, "Introduction," *The Play of the Self* (Albany, NY, 1994), p. vii.

80. Warren I. Susman, "'Personality' and the Making of Twentieth Century Culture," in *Culture as History: The Transformation of American Society in the Twentieth Century* (New York, 1973); Richard Sennett, *The Fall of Public Man* (New York, 1974).

81. Elizabeth Lunbeck, *The Psychiatric Persuasion: Knowledge, Gender, and Power in Modern America* (Princeton, 1994), pp. 69, 355, n.95.

82. James Mark Baldwin, *Mental Development: The Child and the Race* (1894) (New York, 1900), pp. 404–406.

83. Morton Prince, M.D., *The Dissociation of a Personality: A Biographical Study in Abnormal Psychology* (1905) (New York, 1930), pp. 116–117, 22–23. See also James H. Hyslop, "Some Amazing Cases of Multiple Personality," *Woman's Home Companion,* Nov. 1905; "Four Different Women in One Body," *Current Literature,* April 1906; J. Corbin, "How One Girl Lived Four Lives," *Ladies' Home Journal,* Nov. 1908. On the dramatic and cinematic versions see Schwartz, *The Culture of the Copy,* p. 84. On Prince's theoretical twists and turns see Ruth Leys, "The Real Miss Beauchamp: Gender and the Subject of Imitation," in Judith Butler and Joan W. Scott, eds., *Feminists Theorize the Political* (New York, 1992).

84. Leys, "The Real Miss Beauchamp," p. 193. See also Elaine Showalter, *Sexual Anarchy* (New York, 1990), pp. 121–123; Nina Auerbach, *Woman and the Demon* (Cambridge, 1982), pp. 26–27.

85. Baldwin, *Mental Development,* p. 349. Baldwin disagreed with this characterization made popular by Janet and Charcot.

86. Taussig, *Mimesis and Alterity,* pp. 207–13.

87. Donna Haraway, *Simians, Cyborgs, and Women: The Reinvention of Nature* (New York, 1991), p. 253, n.8.

88. Taussig, *Mimesis and Alterity,* p. 220.

89. Ruth Leys, "Mead's Voices: Imitation as Foundation, or the Struggle against Mimesis," *Critical Inquiry,* 19 (Winter 1993), pp. 277–303.

90. Rosalind Rosenberg, *Beyond Separate Spheres: Intellectual Roots of Modern Feminism* (New Haven, 1982), pp. 114–147, 160–161.

91. Gabriel Tarde, *The Laws of Imitation,* 2d ed. 1895, trans. Elsie Clews Parsons (New York, 1903), p. xiv.

92. Leys, "Mead's Voices," pp. 279–282.

93. Auerbach, *Woman and the Demon,* pp. 18–21, Henri F. Ellenberger, *The Discovery of the Unconscious* (New York, 1970), p. 165; I. Edward Purcell, "Trilby and Trilby Mania," *Journal of Popular Culture,* 11 (Summer 1977), pp. 62–76.

94. Purcell, "Trilby and Trilbymania"; Ellenberger, *Discovery of the Unconscious,* p. 165.

95. Ellenberger, *Discovery of the Unconscious,* p. 528.

96. Tarde, *Laws of Imitation,* pp. 213–39, 388.

97. Baldwin, *Mental Development,* pp. 278, 353–354, 330, n.1, 487–488; "The Mysteries of Personality," *The Independent,* June 22, 1905, pp. 1419–1420. See also Robert J. Richards, *Darwin and the Emergence of Evolutionary Theories of Mind and Behavior* (Chicago, 1987), pp. 451–475; Dorothy Ross, *Origins of American Social Science* (Cambridge, 1991), pp. 155, 238–239.

98. Charles A. Ellwood, *Sociology in Its Psychological Aspects* (New York, 1912). On William James see David Leary, "William James on the Self and Personality," in Michael G. Johnson and Tracy B. Henley, eds., *Reflections on the Principles of Psy-*

chology: William James after a Century (Hillsdale, NJ, 1990). See also Leys, "Mead's Voices," Rosenberg, *Beyond Separate Spheres;* Desley Deacon, *Elsie Clews Parsons: Inventing Modern Life* (Chicago, 1997).

99. Posnock, *Trial of Curiosity,* pp. 58, 165–166, 172–173, 182, 185–186; Leys, "Mead's Voices," pp. 281–283; Jonas Barish, *The Antitheatrical Prejudice* (Berkeley, 1981), pp. 362, 381–388.

100. George Herbert Mead, "1914 Class Lectures in Social Psychology," in David L. Miller, ed., *The Individual and the Self: Unpublished Work of George Herbert Mead* (Chicago, 1982), p. 67.

101. Ibid., p. 70.

102. Posnock, *Trial of Curiosity,* p. 173.

103. Mead, "1914 Lectures in Social Psychology," p. 71.

104. Tarde, *Laws of Imitation,* preface to 2nd ed., pp. xxii–xxiv; Mead, "1914 Lectures in Social Psychology," pp. 69–70.

105. Charles N. Young, "Real Impersonation Merely Self Hypnotism, Declares Miss Loftus," np [1907], italics added; *Boston Transcript,* Oct. 16, 1909, Loftus, vol. 313, RLC.

106. *Boston Transcript,* Oct. 16, 1909, Loftus, vol. 313, RLC.

107. Loftus, "The Art of Imitation."

108. Russell, *Cissie Loftus, An Appreciation.*

109. *New York Telegraph,* Jan. 1907, Loftus, vol. 313, RLC.

110. Charles Horton Cooley, *Human Nature and the Social Order* (1902) (New York, 1922), p. 302.

111. Mary Whiton Calkins, *An Introduction to Psychology* (New York, 1902), pp. 343–344, 332–333, 341.

112. Rosenberg, *Beyond Separate Spheres,* pp. 67–74, 114–128, 133–134; Deacon, *Elsie Clews Parsons,* pp. 35–38, 53, 113.

113. Rosenberg, *Beyond Separate Spheres,* pp. 139–141, quote on p. 141.

114. Leys, "Mead's Voices," pp. 281, 285–287, 200, 296 ff; Leys, "The Real Miss Beauchamp."

115. Caroline Caffin, *Vaudeville,* pp. 134–135.

116. Caffin, an active participant in the New York woman suffrage movement, had ties to the radical feminist group known as "Heterodoxy." See ch. 5.

117. Bruce Wilshire, *Role Playing and Identity: The Limits of the Theater as a Metaphor* (Bloomington, 1982), p. xiv.

4 The Americanization of Salome

1. *Morning Telegraph,* July 26, 1908, Hoffmann, vol. 274, RLC.

2. "All Sorts and Kinds of Salomes," *The Theatre Magazine,* April 1909, p. 130.

3. "The Vulgarization of Salome," *Current Literature,* Oct. 1908, p. 440.

4. Oscar Wilde, *Salome, A Tragedy in One Act,* trans. Lord Alfred Douglas, illus. by Aubrey Beardsley (London, 1894) (rept. New York, 1967). An English edition was also published in Boston in 1894 by Copeland & Day.

5. Bram Dijkstra, *Idols of Perversity: Fantasies of Feminine Evil in Fin-de-Siecle Culture* (New York, 1986), p. 386 and ch. 11. See also Sander Gilman, "Strauss and the Pervert," in Arthur Groos and Roger Parker, eds., *Reading Opera* (Princeton, 1988) and "Salome, Syphilis, Sarah Bernhardt, and the Modern Jewess," in Linda Nochlin and Tamar Garb, eds., *The Jew in the Text* (London, 1995); Elliott L. Gilbert, "Tumult of Images: Wilde, Beardsley, and *Salome,*" *Victorian Studies*, 26 (Winter 1983).

6. Regenia Gagnier, *Idylls of the Marketplace: Oscar Wilde and the Victorian Public* (Stanford, 1986); Elaine Showalter, *Sexual Anarchy* (New York, 1990); Marjorie Garber, *Vested Interests: Cross-Dressing and Cultural Anxiety* (New York, 1992).

7. Jane Marcus, "Salome: The Jewish Princess Was a New Woman," *Bulletin of the New York Public Library*, 78 (Autumn 1974), pp. 95–117.

8. The exceptions are Elizabeth Kendall, *Where She Danced: The Birth of American Art Dance* (Berkeley: University of California Press, 1979), pp. 74–81; Richard Bizot, "The Turn-of-the-Century Salome Era: High- and Pop-Culture Variations on the Dance of the Seven Veils," *Choreography and Dance*, 2, pt. 3 (1992), pp. 71–87; Barbara Naomi Cohen, "Gertrude Hoffmann: Salome Treads the Boards," *Dance Research Annual*, 9, Essays in Dance Research, Diane L. Woodruff, ed. (New York, 1978), pp. 23–32.

9. Quoted in Gerda Taranow, *Sarah Bernhardt: The Art Within the Legend* (Princeton, 1972), p. 201. Compare Arthur Gold and Robert Fizdale, *The Divine Sarah* (New York, 1991), pp. 246–247.

10. Taranow, *Sarah Bernhardt*, pp. 201–202.

11. Gilman, "Salome, Syphilis, Sarah Bernhardt," p. 113.

12. Deborah Jowitt, *Time and the Dancing Image* (New York, 1988), pp. 123, 111; Felix Cherniavsky, *The Salome Dancer: The Life and Times of Maud Allan* (Toronto, 1991); Emily Apter, "Acting Out Orientalism: Sapphic Theatricality in Turn-of-the-Century Paris," in Elin Diamond, ed., *Performance and Cultural Politics* (New York, 1996); Amy Koritz, *Gendering Bodies/Performing Art: Dance and Literature in Early Twentieth Century British Culture* (Ann Arbor, 1995), pp. 37–40.

13. Jackson Lears, *No Place of Grace: Antimodernism and the Transformation of American Culture, 1880–1920* (New York, 1981), pp. 143, 175–177, 225–241; William Leach, *Land of Desire: Merchants, Power and the Rise of a New American Culture* (New York, 1994), pp. 104–111; Kendall, *Where She Danced*, pp. 13, 27–29, 47–56, 78, 86–87, 136–139.

14. Jane Desmond, "Dancing Out the Difference," *Signs* (Autumn 1991), pp. 28–49; Sandra Gilbert and Susan Gubar, *No Man's Land: The Place of the Woman Writer in the Twentieth Century* (New Haven, 1989), vol. 2, ch. 1.

15. Judith Lynne Hanna, *Dance, Sex, and Gender* (Chicago, 1988), pp. 56–69.

16. Ann Daly, *Done Into Dance: Isadora Duncan in America* (Bloomington, 1995), pp. 174–175; Amy Koritz, "Dancing the Orient for England: Maud Allan's The Vision of Salome," in Jane Desmond, ed., *Meaning in Motion* (Durham, 1997); Lynn Garafola, *Diaghilev's Ballets Russes* (New York, 1989), pp. 43, 54, 277. See also Bizot, "The Turn-of-the-Century Salome Era."

17. Nancy F. Cott, *The Grounding of Modern Feminism* (New Haven, 1987), pp. 42–43; Ellen Kay Trimberger, "The New Woman and the New Sexuality," in Adele Heller and Lois Rudnick, eds., *1915, The Cultural Moment* (New Brunswick, 1991); Sally Banes, *Dancing Women: Female Bodies on Stage* (New York, 1998), pp. 80–89.

18. "Lid Shut Down on Salome," np, Jan. 30, 1907, Olive Fremstad, vol. 219, RLC; Kendall, *Where She Danced*, p. 74.

19. Edward Ziegler, "'Salome' at the Metropolitan Opera House," *The Theatre Magazine,* March 1907, pp. 70–71, ix. See also Kendall, *Where She Danced*, pp. 74–75; Barbara Naomi Cohen, "The Borrowed Art of Gertrude Hoffmann," *Dance Data,* 2 (1977), pp. 2–11; Irving Kolodin, *The Metropolitan Opera, 1883–1939* (New York, 1940), pp. 116–119.

20. "The Vulgarization of Salome."

21. "Mlle. Bianca Froelich, Salome," *Variety,* Sept. 12, 1908; Kendall, *Where She Danced,* p. 74; Kolodin, *Metropolitan Opera,* p. 545.

22. "Salome Stirs," *New York American* [1907], Fremstad, vol. 219, RLC.

23. *New York Evening World,* Jan. 23, 1907, in ibid.

24. "The Vulgarization of Salome." See also "The Salome Costume," np, Aug. 25, 1908; *Variety,* July 4, 1908, Hoffmann, vol. 273, RLC. On Little Egypt see Irving Zeidman, *The American Burlesque Show* (New York, 1967) pp. 61–63.

25. *Morning Telegraph,* June 1, 1905; "The Girl in the Red Domino," np, July 1905; *The Standard & Variety,* Jan. 12, 1906; *New York Telegraph,* March 12, 1906, May 1, 1906; "Le Domino Rouge Unmasks," np, May 1906; *New York Evening World,* Jan. 12, 1907, Dazie, vol. 147, RLC.

26. "*Follies of 1907,*" np, July 20, 1907, Aug. 4, 1907, in ibid.

27. Kendall, *Where She Danced*, pp. 74–75; Stephen Burge Johnson, *The Roof Gardens of Broadway Theaters, 1883–1942* (Ann Arbor, 1985), p. 122.

28. "Salome on 14th Street," ·*Variety,* Aug. 8, 1908.

29. "The Vulgarization of Salome."

30. Advertisement, *The Theatre Magazine,* Nov. 1909, p. xix.

31. *New York Telegraph,* June 3, 1908, Oscar Hammerstein, vol. 259, RLC. On the London parodists see Cherniavsky, *The Salome Dancer,* p. 187, n.21.

32. *Musical America,* Feb. 24, 1906; *New York American,* Feb. 23, 1906, Hammerstein, vol. 259, RLC; Cohen, "Gertrude Hoffmann," p. 26.

33. Cherniavsky, *The Salome Dancer,* pp. 176, 161–167; Koritz, "Dancing the Orient for England."

34. *New York Telegraph,* June 3, 1908; "Oscar Relents and William May Present Maud Allan's Dances," np [1908], Hammerstein, vol. 259, RLC; Cohen, "The Borrowed Art of Gertrude Hoffmann"; Cohen, "Gertrude Hoffmann," pp. 23–32; Kendall, *Where She Danced,* p. 76.

35. *Variety,* July 4, 1908.

36. *New York Telegraph,* July 14, 1908, Hoffmann, vol. 274, RLC. On publicity for Allan see Cherniavsky, *The Salome Dancer,* pp. 162–163; Koritz, "Dancing the Orient."

37. *New York Telegraph,* July 14, 1908, Hoffmann, vol. 274, RLC.

38. *Chicago News,* July 19, 1908, Hoffmann, vol. 273, RLC.

39. "The Vulgarization of Salome."

40. *New York World,* Aug. 23, 1908.

41. *The Morning Telegraph,* July 19, 1908, Hoffmann, vol. 273, RLC.

42. *New York Evening Journal,* July 14, 1908, Hoffmann, vol. 274, RLC.

43. *Morning Telegraph,* July 19, 1908.

44. Cherniavsky, *The Salome Dancer,* pp. 178–79; Koritz, *Gendering Bodies/Performing Art,* pp. 37–38, 42–44.

45. "Salome Is Naughty, or Else Very Silly," [Cleveland], March 3, 1909, np, Hoffmann, vol. 273, RLC.

46. "The Salome Costumes," np, Aug. 25, 1908, in ibid; Claudia B. Stone, "Gertrude Hoffmann: Artist or Charlatan?" M.A. thesis, New York University, 1987, p. 26.

47. "Lotta Faust 'Salome' Dance," *Variety,* Aug. 8, 1908.

48. *Columbus Dispatch,* Aug. 25, 1908, Hoffmann, vol. 273, RLC; Cohen, "Borrowed Art."

49. "Modern Viciousness and Western Audiences," np [1909]; "Gertrude Hoffman's Salome Is Too Much for Kansas City," np, March 4, 1909, *Boston Traveler,* March 5, 1909; "Senators from Des Moines and Council Bluffs Introduce Bill on High Kicking and Gauzy Raiment," np, March 17, 1909; "Miss Hoffmann Answers Her Critics," np, March 17, 1909; *New York Telegraph,* Aug. 30, 1908, July 24, 1909; "Crowds Flock to 'A Vision of Salome'," np, July 27, 1909, all in Hoffmann, vol. 273, RLC.

50. *New York Telegraph,* July 3, 1909, July 24, 1909; *Variety,* July 31, 1908, in ibid.; Cohen, "Borrowed Art."

51. "Crowds Flock to 'A Vision of Salome'"; *New York Telegraph,* July 25, 1908, Hoffmann, vol. 273, RLC.

52. *Chicago Examiner,* December 27, 1908; "About Plays," *Cleveland Plain Dealer,* March 26, 1909, in ibid.

53. Cohen, "Gertrude Hoffmann, Salome Treads the Boards," and "Borrowed Art."

54. On the concept of "parodic overload" see Jane Gaines "Fabricating the Female Body," in Gaines and Charlotte Herzog, eds., *Fabrications: Costume and the Female Body* (New York, 1990).

55. Garber, *Vested Interests,* p. 280.

56. "Eva Tanguay Has the Salome Bee," np, July 18, 1908. See also *New York Telegraph,* Aug. 4, 1908, in Tanguay, vol. 450, RLC.

57. On the "feud," see ch. 3. On the concept of "creative hysteria" see Judy Little, "Humoring the Sentence: Women's Dialogic Comedy," in June Sochen, *Women's Comic Visions* (Detroit, 1991), p. 21.

58. "The Real Salome," np, Aug. 2, 1908, Tanguay, vol. 450, RLC.

59. "Eva Tanguay," *Variety,* Aug. 8, 1909.

60. *New York Telegraph,* Aug. 4, 1908, Tanguay, vol. 450, RLC.

61. "Salome in Harlem," *New York Globe,* Aug. 4, 1908, in ibid.

62. *St. Louis Star,* Aug. 7, 1908, in ibid.

63. *The World,* Aug. 4, 1908, in ibid.

64. *New York Telegraph,* Aug. 17, 1908, in ibid.

65. *Variety,* Oct. 3, 1908.

66. Ibid.

67. *Variety,* Aug. 8, 1908.

68. Quoted in Cherniavsky, *The Salome Dancer,* n.21, pp. 187–188.

69. "All About Salome," *Variety,* Aug. 7, 1908. See also Stone, "Gertrude Hoffmann," p. 30.

70. *New York Telegraph,* Aug. 4, 1908, Tanguay, vol. 450, RLC.

71. "Salome in Harlem," *Variety,* Aug. 8, 1908.

72. *New York Telegraph,* Aug. 17, 1908, Tanguay, vol. 450, RLC.

73. Quoted in Charles and Louise Samuels, *Once Upon a Stage* (New York, 1974), p. 64. See also *New York Telegraph,* Aug. 17, 1908.

74. *New York Telegraph,* Aug. 17, 1908.

75. On female humor as "subversive protest" see Nancy Walker, *A Very Serious Thing* (Minneapolis, 1990), pp. 10–12; Regina Barreca, "Making Trouble: An Introduction," in Barreca, ed. *New Perspectives on Women and Comedy* (Philadelphia, 1992), p. 6; Kathleen Rowe, *The Unruly Woman,* p. 19. My own views are closer to Robert C. Allen, *Horrible Prettiness* (Chapel Hill, 1991), pp. 33–36.

76. Reviews of "The Chaperones," Nov. 28, 1901; Dec. 31, 1901, June 8, 1902, Tanguay, vol. 450, RLC.

77. "The Plot of the Sambo Girl" *[Dramatic] Mirror,* Oct. 16, 1905; "Sambo Girl," *Pittsburgh Gazette,* April 5, 1908, in ibid.

78. Ann Charters, *Nobody: The Story of Bert Williams* (New York, 1970), p. 89.

79. *Variety,* Aug. 15 and 22, 1908. See also "The Keith and Proctor Theaters—125th Street," *New York Dramatic Mirror,* July 25, 1908.

80. *Variety,* July 25, 1908, Aug. 1 and 5, 1908; *New York Dramatic Mirror,* Aug. 1, 1908. On "La Sylphe" see Stone, "Gertrude Hoffmann," p. 30.

81. John B. Hymer, "De Sloamey Dance," *Variety,* Aug. 1, 1908.

82. Eddie Cantor as told to David Freedman, *My Life Is in Your Hands* (New York, 1928), pp. 121–123.

83. Robert C. Toll, *Blacking Up: The Minstrel Show in Nineteenth Century America* (New York, 1974), pp. 139–140; Laurence Senelick, "Boys and Girls Together: Subcultural Origins of Glamour Drag and Male Impersonation on the Nineteenth Century Stage," in Lesley Ferris, ed., *Crossing the Stage* (London, 1993), pp. 84–85.

84. Allen, *Horrible Prettiness,* pp. 168–169; Robert C. Toll, *On With the Show* (New York, 1974), pp. 242–243.

85. See Toll, *Blacking Up;* Garber, *Vested Interests,* p. 277.

86. Joan Vale, "Tin Type Ambitions: Three Vaudevillians in Search of Hollywood Fame," M.A. Thesis, University of San Diego, 1985, pp. 23–24; Toll, *On With the Show,* p. 251.

87. "Minstrels Immense Hit," *Variety,* Aug. 1, 1908.

88. *Variety,* Aug. 8, 1908; *New York Globe,* Aug. 7, 1908, Julian Eltinge, vol. 182, RLC.

89. Clipping, np [1908], in ibid.

90. *Variety,* Aug. 8, 1908; Aug. 1, 1908.

91. Vale, "Tintype Ambitions," p. 24. On his off-stage manliness see Sharon Ullman, *Sex Seen: The Emergence of Modern Sexuality in America* (Berkeley, 1997), pp. 55–57.

92. Laurence Senelick, "Lady and the Tramp: Drag Differentials in the Progressive Era," in Senelick, ed., *Gender in Performance* (Hanover, NH, 1992); Ullman, *Sex Seen,* pp. 59–60. On "Salome" as a gay nickname, see George Chauncey, *Gay New York* (New York, 1994), p. 50.

93. Kendall, *Where She Danced,* p. 78.

94. "Cakewalk in Society," np, March 29, 1903, Williams and Walker clippings, Locke Envelope, #2461, BRTC.

95. Richard Newman, "'The Brightest Star': Aida Overton Walker in the Age of Ragtime and Cakewalk," *Prospects: An Annual of American Cultural Studies,* 18 (1993), pp. 465–481; Jo A. Tanner, *Dusky Maidens: The Odyssey of the Early Black Dramatic Actress* (Westport, CT, 1992).

96. Aida Overton Walker, "Color Line in Musical," [1906], *Chicago Herald,* Locke Envelope #2461, BRTC.

97. Ibid.

98. David Krasner, *Resistance, Parody, and Double Consciousness: African American Theatre, 1895–1910* (New York: St. Martin's Press, 1997), pp. 82–93; Paula Giddings, *When and Where I Enter: The Impact of Black Women on Race and Sex in America* (New York, 1984); Hazel Carby, "'It Jus Be's Dat Way Sometime': The Sexual Politics of Black Women's Blues," in Ellen Carol DuBois and Vicki L. Ruiz, eds. *Unequal Sisters* (New York, 1990).

99. See Krasner, *Resistance,* pp. 84–88, 91–92 and "Black Salome," in Harry J. Elam, Jr. and David Krasner, eds., *Performing Blackness* (forthcoming).

100. *Brooklyn Eagle,* Oct. 20, 1908, in Locke Envelope #2461, BRTC. See also Eric Leddell Smith, *Bert Williams: A Biography of a Pioneer Comedian* (Jefferson, NC, 1992), p. 109; Newman, "'The Brightest Star'."

101. "Boston to Have Dance of Salome," np [Sept. 1908], Locke Envelope #2461.

102. "Two Dusky Salomes," np [Chicago], Jan. 1909, in ibid.

103. "Two Dusky Salomes."

104. "Boston to Have Dance of Salome."

105. "Two Dusky Salomes." See also Smith, *Bert Williams,* p. 109 and Newman, "The Brightest Star," p. 472.

106. *The Theatre Magazine,* March, 1909, p. 76.

107. "Salome Was a Dark Secret" [Hammerstein press release, 1912], Locke Envelope #2461. See also Newman, "The Brightest Star," p. 473.

108. "Salome Was a Dark Secret."

109. "A Salome of Color," *Stage Pictorial,* Sept. 1912, Locke Envelope #2461.

110. "Victoria Show Pleases Crowd," *New York Telegraph,* Aug. 6, 1912, in ibid.

111. For another view see Newman, "Brightest Star," pp. 273–274.

112. "Ada Overton Walker 'Salome'," *Variety,* Aug. 9, 1912.

113. Marshall and Jean Stearns, *Jazz Dance: The Story of African American Vernacular Dance* (1968) (New York, 1994), pp. 127–129; Lewis A. Erenberg, *Steppin' Out* (Chicago, 1981), p. 151.

114. Barbara Grossman, *Funny Woman: The Life and Times of Fanny Brice* (Bloomington, 1991), p. 24.

115. Grossman, *Funny Woman,* pp. 7–11, 26–29; June Sochen, "Fanny Brice and Sophie Tucker," in Sarah Blacher Cohen, ed., *From Hester Street to Hollywood* (Bloomington, 1983).

116. Harley Erdman, *Staging the Jew* (New Brunswick, 1997), pp. 41–60.

117. Dijkstra, *Idols of Perversity,* pp. 385–401; Gilman, "Strauss and the Pervert," and "Salome, Syphilis, Sarah Bernhardt."

118. Erdman, *Staging the Jew,* pp. 105, 110, 155–157.

119. Grossman, *Funny Woman,* pp. 35–45, 95, 101–106; Erdman, *Staging the Jew,* p. 158; Herbert G. Goldman, *Fanny Brice: The Original Funny Girl* (New York, 1992), p. 36.

120. Grossman, *Funny Woman,* pp. 28–29, 32–33, 98, 101; Goldman, *Fanny Brice,* pp. 36–37; Stanley Green, *The Great Clowns of Broadway* (New York, 1984), pp. 3–9. On Irving Berlin see Laurence Bergreen, *As Thousands Cheer, The Life of Irving Berlin* (New York, 1990), p. 53.

121. "Sadie Salome Go Home!" Words and Music by Edgar Leslie and Irving Berlin (New York, 1909).

122. Grossman, *Funny Woman,* p. 32ff.

123. Ibid., p. 226; Erdman, *Staging the Jew,* p. 158.

124. Bergreen, *As Thousands Cheer,* p. 35.

125. Grossman, *Funny Woman,* pp. 86, 96–98.

126. Frederic La Delle, *How to Enter Vaudeville: A Complete Illustrated Course of Instruction* (Jackson, MI, 1913), n.p., Lester Sweyd Collection, BRTC.

127. Program for the *Passing Show of 1918,* SA.

128. Lyrics and scripts for the *Passing Show of 1918,* by Harold Atteridge, SA. See also Channing Pollock's review in *New York Dramatic Mirror,* Aug. 10, 1918, in Anthony Slide, ed., *Selected Vaudeville Criticism: Volume I, 1900–1919* (Metuchen, NJ, 1985), pp. 205–206.

129. On the cinematic incarnations see William Tydeman and Steven Price, *Wilde, Salome* (Cambridge, 1996), pp. 152–156.

130. In 1917 the entire Goodman family changed their names to "Bara." See "Theda Bara Legalized," np, Nov. 17, 1917, Bara clippings, HTC.

131. "'To Bara' Means to Vamp," np, Cleveland, Aug. 4, 1918, Bara, vol. 32, RLC.

132. "The Wickedest Face in the World," press release, May 1915; *Fort Wayne Journal,* March 16, 1916; *Cleveland Plain Dealer,* March 16, 1916; "Why Do the People Hate and Detest Me So?," np, April 6, 1916. On Bara's references to Bernhardt

see "How I Became a Film Vampire," *The Forum,* June 1919; "Theda Bara—the Vampire Woman," *Theatre Magazine,* Nov. 1915, all in Bara, vols. 31–32, RLC.

133. *The Forum,* June 1919, p. 92.

134. Ibid., p. 88.

135. Quoted in Lary May, *Screening Out the Past* (New York, 1980), p. 106. See also "'Woman Must Chose to Love or Be Loved' Says Vampire," *Peoria Journal,* May 6, 1915, Bara, vol. 31, RLC.

136. *New York Telegraph,* Feb. 3, 1918, Bara, vol. 32, RLC.

137. "Theda Issues a Challenge to Critics of her Salome," np [1919], in ibid.

138. Quoted in Michael Morris, *Madam Valentino: The Many Lives of Natacha Rambova* (New York, 1991), p. 90; on the film see pp. 85–92; Tydeman and Price, *Wilde, Salome,* pp. 161–165.

139. Gay Wilentz, "Introduction," Anzia Yezierska, *Salome of the Tenements* (1923) (Urbana, 1995). On the 1925 film see Kevin Brownlow, *Behind the Mask of Innocence* (Berkeley, 1990), pp. 404–405. Brownlow neglects to mention that the film revised the plot and stripped it of its Jewish feminist message.

140. Yezierska, *Salome of the Tenements,* pp. 24, 58, 66, 161, 163, 181.

5 "The Eyes of the Enemy"

1. Emma Goldman to Ben L. Reitman, Feb. 22, 1914, Emma Goldman Correspondence files, The Emma Goldman Papers, Berkeley, CA. See also Emma Goldman, *Living My Life* (1931) (rpt. New York, 1970), vol. 2, p. 526.

2. Emma Goldman to Ben L. Reitman, Feb. 22, Feb. 26, and March 2, 1914, Goldman Papers; Goldman, *Living My Life,* vol. 2, p. 526.

3. Candace Falk, *Love, Anarchy, and Emma Goldman: A Biography* (New Brunswick, 1990), pp. 9, 48, 53, 94.

4. Quoted in Alice Wexler, *Emma Goldman, An Intimate Life* (New York, 1984), p. xv.

5. Richard Drinnon, *Rebel in Paradise* (Chicago, 1961), p. 155, n. 1. See also Wexler, *Emma Goldman,* pp. 173, 183.

6. Wexler, *Emma Goldman,* pp. xv–xvi, 79, 95, 151, 165–166, 169–170, 175–177.

7. Quoted in ibid., p. 198.

8. Ibid., pp. 173–174, 198.

9. Elizabeth Gurley Flynn, *The Rebel Girl: An Autobiography* (New York, 1973), pp. 63–65.

10. Susan G. Davis, *Parades and Power* (Philadelphia, 1986), pp. 5–6ff; Michael E. McGerr, *The Decline of Popular Politics: The American North, 1865–1928* (New York, 1986) pp. 3–41; McGerr, "Political Style and Women's Power, 1830–1930," *Journal of American History,* 77 (Dec. 1990), pp. 864–885.

11. Davis, *Parades and Power,* pp. 47, 149, 157, 194 n.2; David Glassberg, *American Historical Pageantry* (Chapel Hill, 1990), pp. 39, 135, 152; Mari Jo Buhle,

Women and American Socialism (Urbana, 1981), p. 112; Mary P. Ryan, *Women in Public* (Baltimore, 1990).

12. Glassberg, *American Historical Pageantry;* McGerr, "Political Style and Women's Power."

13. McGerr, *The Decline of Popular Politics,* pp. 106, 146–147, 148–151; Margaret Finnegan, *Selling Suffrage: Consumer Culture and Votes for Women* (New York, 1999).

14. Bertha Damaris Knobe, "Spectacular Woman Suffrage in America," *The Independent,* 71, Oct. 12, 1911.

15. Knobe, "Spectacular Woman Suffrage in America." Carrie Chapman Catt and Nettie Rogers Shuler, *Woman Suffrage and Politics: The Inner Story of the Suffrage Movement* (1923) (rpt. Seattle, 1970), p. 289; Harriot Stanton Blatch and Alma Lutz, *Challenging Years: The Memoirs of Harriot Stanton Blatch* (New York, 1940); Ellen Carol DuBois, "Working Class Women, Class Relations and Suffrage Militance," in DuBois and Vicki Ruiz, eds., *Unequal Sisters* (New York, 1990); Sharon Hartman Strom, "Leadership and Tactics in the American Woman Suffrage Movement: A New Perspective from Massachusetts," in Jean E. Friedman, William G. Shade, and Mary Jane Capozzoli, eds., *Our American Sisters,* 4th ed. (Lexington, MA, 1987); Finnegan, *Selling Suffrage.*

16. Linda G. Ford, *Iron-Jawed Angels* (Lanham, MD, 1991); Andrew Rosen, *Rise Up Women* (London, 1974).

17. Ford, *Iron-Jawed Angels,* chap. 1; Ellen Carol DuBois, *Harriot Stanton Blatch and the Winning of Woman Suffrage* (New Haven, 1997).

18. Nancy Shrom Dye, *As Equals and As Sisters* (Columbia, MO, 1980); DuBois, "Working Women and Suffrage Militance."

19. Nancy F. Cott, *The Grounding of Modern Feminism* (New Haven, 1987), pp. 26–28; DuBois, "Working Women"; Buhle, *Women and American Socialism,* pp. 109–110, 248; Rosalyn Fraad Baxandall, *Words on Fire: The Life and Writing of Elizabeth Gurley Flynn* (New Brunswick, 1987), pp. 8–11; Elizabeth Gurley Flynn, *Rebel Girl,* pp. 88–89. Most were Socialists. Goldman and de Cleyre were anarchists.

20. Albert Auster, *Actresses and Suffragists* (New York, 1984). On the British case see Susan Terry Barstow, "Acting Like a Feminist," Ph.D. diss., University of Virginia, 1994, ch. 4.

21. Sarah Hunter Graham, *Woman Suffrage and the New Democracy* (New Haven, 1996), pp. 40–42, 51–52, 54–55, 56–74; Ronald Schaffer, "The New York City Woman Suffrage Party," *New York History,* 43 (July 1962), pp. 269–287.

22. Graham, *Woman Suffrage and the New Democracy,* pp. 81–84.

23. Ibid., pp. 73–74; Finnegan, *Selling Suffrage,* p. 57; Harriot Stanton Blatch, "Why Suffragists Will Parade on Saturday," *New York Tribune,* May 3, 1912.

24. Blatch and Lutz, *Challenging Years,* p. 93.

25. Quoted in DuBois, "Working Women, Class Relations." See also Finnegan, *Selling Suffrage,* pp. 71–75, 79–81.

26. Gertrude Foster Brown, "Suffrage and Music—My First Eighty Years,"

p. 145, Gertrude Foster Brown Papers, Women's Studies Manuscript Collections from the Schlesinger Library, Woman Suffrage (New York), Microfilm, reel 1. See also DuBois, *Harriot Stanton Blatch,* p. 106.

27. Blatch and Lutz, *Challenging Years,* pp. 191–192; Graham, *Woman Suffrage and the New Democracy,* pp. 66–68; Finnegan, *Selling Suffrage,* pp. 61–63.

28. Alice Sheppard, *Cartooning for Suffrage* (Albuquerque, 1994); Lisa Tickner, *The Spectacle of Women: Imagery of the Suffrage Campaign, 1907–1914* (Chicago, 1988); Finnegan, *Selling Suffrage.*

29. Tickner, *The Spectacle of Women,* pp. 167, 213–226; Joel H. Kaplan and Sheila Stowell, *Theater and Fashion: Oscar Wilde to the Suffragettes* (Cambridge, 1994), ch. 5; Gina Adrianne Grossfeld, "Constructing Cultures of Resistance: The American and British Women's Suffrage Movements," Ph.D. diss., State University of New York at Stony Brook, 1993, pp. 96–101; Martha Banta, *Imaging American Women* (New York, 1987), pp. 9, 64–65, 83–84, 138–139. See also Carol Smith-Rosenberg, *Disorderly Conduct* (New York, 1985), pp. 280–289.

30. Tickner, *Spectacle of Women,* pp. 222–223; Paula Baker, "The Domestication of Women's Politics," in DuBois and Ruiz, eds., *Unequal Sisters;* Finnegan, *Selling Suffrage,* pp. 27–31.

31. Tickner, *Spectacle of Women,* pp. 205–219.

32. Mary Holland Kinkaid, "The Feminine Charms of the Woman Militant," *Good Housekeeping,* 54 (Feb. 1912), pp. 146–155.

33. Ford, *Iron-Jawed Angels,* pp. 236, 249 n.33; Tickner, *Spectacle of Women,* pp. 205–219.

34. Tickner, *Spectacle of Women,* pp. 174–182; DuBois, "Working Women."

35. Banta, *Imaging the American Woman,* pp. 62–69, 71–74, 78–82; Tickner, *Spectacle of Women,* pp. 167–223; Sheppard, *Cartooning for Suffrage,* pp. 187, 138; Grossfeld, "Constructing Cultures," pp. 99–100; Kaplan and Stowell, *Theatre and Fashion,* pp. 152–153, 159, 178–179.

36. Quoted in DuBois, "Working Women," p. 189. See also "Suffragettes are 'Slab-sided Frumpy Old Maids,' Says Beautiful Anti," *Philadelphia Telegraph,* Feb. 9, 1909, Blanche Ring, vol. 397, RLC; "Fashion and Suffrage," *Harper's Monthly Magazine,* vol. 121, Oct. 1910, pp. 795–798.

37. Auster, *Actresses and Suffragists;* Finnegan, *Selling Suffrage,* pp. 87–88.

38. Benjamin McArthur, *Actors and American Culture* (Philadelphia, 1984), pp. 164–166.

39. Israel Zangwill, "Actress Versus Suffraget," *The Independent,* 67 (Dec. 2, 1909), pp. 1248–1250.

40. "Pledge Actresses to Suffrage Parade," *New York Times,* April 22, 1912.

41. "Welcome to Bernhardt," *New York Times,* Oct. 30, 1910; "Sarah Bernhardt and the Young Actor," *New York Times,* Dec. 3, 1911, pt.3.

42. "To Greet Sarah Bernhardt," *New York Times,* Oct. 29, 1910; "Sarah Bernhardt Sails," *New York Times,* Oct. 22, 1910.

43. "To Greet Sarah Bernhardt," *New York Times,* Oct. 29, 1910; "Bernhardt

Joins Suffrage League," *New York Times,* April 8, 1910; "Hail Bernhardt as Suffragette," *New York Sun,* Oct. 29, 1910, SB, vol. 64, RLC.

44. *Evening World,* May 10, 1913, SB, vol. 66, RLC.

45. Knobe, "Spectacular Woman Suffrage in America."

46. "Suffragists Are Active," *New York Times,* March 3, 1909; "'Votes for Women' Wins Applause," *New York Times,* Jan. 10, 1909; *New York Telegram,* Oct. 8, 1910.

47. "Pledge Actresses to Suffrage Parade," *New York Times,* April 22, 1912; "Dress Rehearsal of Suffrage Parade," *New York Times,* April 21, 1912; "Suffragette Hats, 39 Cents Trimmed," *New York Times,* April 9, 1912; Blatch and Lutz, *Challenging Years,* p. 138.

48. Gertrude Foster Brown, "Suffrage and Music," pp. 147–148.

49. "Suffraget Stock Players Preach Cause From Stage," *Toledo News,* Feb. 29, 1912; "Parrot Play Latest Whim of New York Suffragists," *Cleveland Leader,* Feb. 1913, in Mary Shaw, vol. 431, RLC.

50. Julie Holledge, *Innocent Flowers: Women in the Edwardian Theater* (London, 1981), pp. 50–62, 73–101.

51. "Suffraget Stock Players Preach Cause from Stage," *Toledo News,* Feb. 29, 1912, Shaw, vol. 431, RLC. The NAWSA branch in New York City marketed Shaw's plays. See *Catalogue and Price List or Woman Suffrage Literature, Entertainment, and Supplies,* May 1916, NAWSA Papers, Microfilm reel 14 (New York). See also Judith Schwarz, *The Radical Feminists of Heterodoxy,* rev. ed. (Norwich, VT, 1986), pp. 14, 26–37.

52. "Women of the Stage All Desire to Vote," *The Billboard,* Nov. 6, 1909. See also Auster, *Actresses and Suffragists,* p. 85; McArthur, *Actors and American Culture,* p. 155.

53. Marian Strohman, "Actresses and Woman Suffrage," *The Green Book Album,* April 1909; "Melba a Suffragist," *New York Times,* Jan. 2, 1909; "'Votes for Women' Wins Applause"; "Mary Garden a Suffragette," *New York Times,* Dec. 13, 1908, pt.3.; Blatch and Lutz, *Challenging Years,* p. 138.

54. John D. Irving, "Mary Shaw, Actress, Suffragist, Activist," Ph.D. diss., Columbia University, 1978.

55. *Minneapolis Journal,* Feb. 27, 1916, *Philadelphia Press,* April 19, 1916, Shaw, vol. 431, RLC. See also Irving, "Mary Shaw," pp. 75. 134–135; Auster, *Actresses and Suffragists,* pp. 75–86.

56. Program for *Votes for Women,* March 15, 1909, MCNY; *New York World,* March 13, 1909; *New York Star,* March 20, 1909, Shaw, vol. 431, RLC. See also Bettina Friedl, ed., *On to Victory: Propaganda Plays of the Woman Suffrage Movement* (Boston, 1987), p. 33.

57. *New Orleans States,* Nov. 7, 1915; *New York World,* Feb. 9, 1912, Shaw, vol. 431, RLC. In 1914 she spoke at the Second Feminist Mass Meeting in New York. See Cott, *The Grounding of Modern Feminism,* pp. 12, 38.

58. "Mary Shaw's Hit," np, March 20, 1909, Shaw, vol. 431, RLC.

59. *New York Telegram,* March 13, 1909, in ibid.

60. Auster, *Actresses and Suffragists*, pp. 93, 109–110; Parker Morell, *Lillian Russell: The Era of Plush* (New York, 1940), pp. 280, 262–263.

61. *New York Telegraph*, Oct. 27, 1908, Friganza, vol. 220, RLC.

62. October [27] 1908, np, in ibid.

63. "Fair Actress Works Hard for Woman Suffrage Cause," np, Jan.3, 1909, in ibid.

64. "Buxom Marie Deprecates Militancy of Womankind," np, Dressler, vol. 164, RLC.

65. *Philadelphia Record,* Oct. 5, 1913, Dressler, vol. 164, RLC.

66. Ibid.

67. *Musical America*, Jan. 22, 1916; *Minneapolis Journal*, Feb. 19, 1916, *New York Review,* Feb. 19, 1916, Dressler, vol. 164, RLC. The operetta was written by Alva Belmont and composer Elsa Maxwell; see Friedl, ed., *On to Victory*, pp. 36–38.

68. Graham, *Woman Suffrage and the New Democracy,* pp. 59–60.

69. George Burman Foster, "The Philosophy of Feminism," *The Forum,* 52, July 1914, pp. 10–22. See also Finnegan, *Selling Suffrage,* pp. 79–80, 87–90, 107.

70. "Rules for Open-Air Meetings," *Woman's Journal,* April 30, 1910, p. 70; Mary Ware Dennett, "Headquarters Letter," *Woman's Journal,* April 29, 1911.

71. Quoted in Grossfeld, "Constructing Cultures," p. 142.

72. Ford, *Iron-Jawed Angels,* p. 102.

73. Barbara Goldsmith, *Other Powers: The Age of Suffrage, Spiritualism, and the Scandalous Victoria Woodhull* (New York, 1998), pp. 117, 146, 173; William Leach, *True Love and Perfect Union* (New York, 1980), pp. 254–255.

74. "State Correspondence. Massachusetts," *Woman's Journal,* April 16, 1910, p. 62; Finnegan, *Selling Suffrage,* pp. 81–82, 96. Fola La Follette was married to pro-suffrage playwright George Middleton and had ties to the Actresses Franchise League in England. See "Fola La Follette," in *Woman's Who's Who of America* (New York, 1914), p. 469; Schwarz, *Radical Feminists of Heterodoxy,* pp. 31–32.

75. "The Spokesman for Suffrage in America," *McClure's Magazine,* 39, July 1912, pp. 335 337; Ford, *Iron-Jawed Angels,* pp. 49, 75–77.

76. Brett Page, *Writing for Vaudeville* (Springfield, MA, 1915), p. 82; Shirley Staples, *Male-Female Comedy Teams in American Vaudeville* (Ann Arbor, 1984), pp. 153, 241, 243.

77. "'Woman's Suffrage Week' Flivs at Hammerstein's," *Variety,* Sept. 13, 1912; "'The Suffrage Week' Drawing Down No Salary," *Variety,* Aug. 3, 1912.

78. "Women to Vote Here," *New York Times,* Oct. 28, 1908.

79. Charles and Louise Samuels, *Once Upon a Stage* (New York, 1974), p. 239; Andrew Sinclair, *Era of Excess: A Social History of the Prohibition Movement* (New York, 1964), pp. 56–57.

80. Auster, *Actresses and Suffragists,* p. 86; "Suffrage Party to Move," *New York Times,* March 11, 1913.

81. "Big Suffrage Week at Hammerstein's," *Woman's Journal,* Sept. 7, 1912; "Party Plans Big Bill at Vaudeville," *Woman's Journal,* Aug. 31, 1912.

82. "New York Has Big Suffrage Week"; "Suffragists Do Turn," *Woman's Journal,* Sept. 7, 1912.

83. "Suffragists Start Week in Vaudeville," *New York Times,* Sept. 10, 1912; "Suffragists on the Stage," *New York Times,* Sept. 12, 1912.

84. "'Woman's Suffrage Week' Flivs at Hammerstein's"; Big Suffrage Week," "Suffragists Do Turn."

85. "Suffragists Start Week in Vaudeville," "New York Has Big Suffrage Week."

86. Quoted in Staples, *Male-Female Comedy Teams,* p. 152.

87. "New York Has Big Suffrage Week."

88. Ibid.

89. "Theaters to Aid Suffrage Fight," *New York Tribune,* Oct. 25, 1915.

90. "*Help!!* We Need It" (flyer, Jan. 31, 1913), NAWSA Papers Microfilm, reel 6.

91. Finnegan, *Selling Suffrage,* pp. 69, 111.

92. Blatch and Lutz, *Challenging Years,* pp. 130–131.

93. Ibid. pp. 129, 194; Blatch, "Why Suffragists Will Parade on Saturday," *New York Tribune,* May 3, 1912.

94. Blatch and Lutz, *Challenging Years,* pp. 130–131.

95. Ibid., pp. 130–132, 180.

96. Glassberg, *American Historical Pageantry,* pp. 26–31, 33–34, 58, 118–120, 214; Karen Blair, *The Torchbearers: Women and Their Amateur Arts Associations* (Bloomington, 1994), pp. 122, 128, 136.

97. Ann Daly, *Done Into Dance: Isadora Duncan in America* (Bloomington, 1995), p. 130; Genevieve Stebbins, *The Delsarte System of Expression* (New York, 1902), pp. 74–75, 135–202, 440; Barbara Stratyner, *Ned Wayburn and the Dance Routine,* Studies in Dance History, 13 (1996), pp. 4–5; Nancy Chalfa Ruyter, *Reformers and Visionaries: The Americanization of the Art of Dance* (New York, 1979).

98. "Vast Suffrage Host Is On Parade," *New York Times,* May 4, 1912.

99. "Suffrage Parade Orders," *New York Times,* April 28, 1912; "Suffragette Rush for 37-Cent Hats," *New York Times,* April 30, 1912.

100. "A Demonstration That Made an Impression," *New York Times,* May 9, 1911.

101. "20,000 Women in Suffrage March," *New York Tribune,* May 5, 1912.

102. "Vast Suffrage Host Is On Parade." See also "Suffrage Army Out on Parade"; "The Line of March," *New York Times,* May 5, 1912.

103. "Suffrage Army Out on Parade."

104. "The Parade of Woman Suffragists," *Current Literature,* 52 (June 1912), p. 627.

105. Blatch and Lutz, *Challenging Years,* pp. 183, 182.

106. Tickner, *The Spectacle of Women,* p. 81. For different views see Kaplan and Stowell, *Theatre and Fashion,* pp. 153–156; Finnegan, *Selling Suffrage,* pp. 118, 129–138.

107. Israel Zangwill, "Actress Versus Suffraget."

108. "Parade of the Women," *New York Times,* May 6, 1911.

109. On the *Black Crook* see Robert Toll, *On With the Show* (New York, 1976), pp. 173–175; Robert Allen, *Horrible Prettiness* (Chapel Hill, 1991), pp. 108–117.

110. "Parade of the Women."

111. Quoted in Fairfax Downey, *Portrait of an Era as Drawn by C. D. Gibson* (New York, 1936), p. 318.

112. Grossfeld, "Constructing Cultures," p. 137.

113. "Big Demand for Tall Girls," *New York Times*, Oct. 22, 1915.

114. "The Suffrage Parade" (editorial), *New York Times*, Oct. 24, 1915. See also "25,340 March in Suffrage Parade to the Applause of 250,000 Admirers," *New York Times*, Oct. 24, 1915; "Big Finish to Parade," *New York Times*, Oct. 19, 1915; "30,000 Await Marching Call of Suffrage," *New York Tribune*, Oct. 23, 1915.

115. Script for Ziegfeld *Follies of 1912*, by Harry B. Smith, p. 29, MCNY.

116. Geraldine Maschio, "The *Ziegfeld Follies*," Ph.D. diss., Univ. of Wisconsin, 1981, p. 63.

117. Ibid., pp. 32–33, 63.

118. "The Never Homes," *Theater Magazine*, Nov. 1911; Armond Fields and L. Marc Fields, *From the Bowery to Broadway* (New York, 1993), pp. 293–294. On Monroe see Barbara Naomi Cohen, "The Dance Direction of Ned Wayburn," Ph.D. diss., NYU, 1980, p. 98, n.15.

119. Fields and Fields, *From the Bowery to Broadway*, pp. 293–294.

120. Jason Rubin, "Lew Fields and the Development of the Broadway Musical," Ph.D. diss., NYU, 1991, p. 265; Fields and Fields, *From the Bowery to Broadway*, pp. 293–294.

121. Program and Script for the *Passing Show of 1913* by Harold Atteridge, SA; Scripts for Act I and Act II of *The Passing Show of 1913* and Layout for Winter Garden Company's Production of *The Passing Show of 1913*, Ned Wayburn Collection, Ole Olsen Papers, Box 3, USC.

122. "That Ragtime Suffragette" (1913), words by Harry Williams, music by Nat D. Ayer, Sheet music, Ziegfeld Files, HRC.

123. Quoted in Blair, *The Torchbearers*, p. 138.

124. Ibid., p. 137; Finnegan, *Selling Suffrage*, p. 78.

125. "Stars for Suffrage Parade," *New York Times*, Jan. 19, 1913.

126. "5,000 Women March, Beset By Crowds," *New York Times*, March 4, 1913; "Parade Protest Arouses Senate," *New York Times*, March 5, 1913; "Police Idly Watched Abuse of Women," *New York Times*, March 7, 1913; Ford, *Iron-Jawed Angels*, pp. 50–51.

127. "Says Police Sided with Mob," *New York Times*, March 11, 1913; "Police Idly Watched Abuse of Women."

6 "Nationally Advertised Legs"

1. George Jean Nathan, *The Theatre, the Drama, the Girls* (New York, 1921) pp. 292–294. Italics in original.

2. Faye Dudden traced this tension back to the mid-nineteenth century. See

Women in the American Theatre: Actresses and Audiences, 1790–1870 (New Haven, 1994).

3. Nathan, *The Theatre, The Drama, The Girls,* pp. 145–146. See also Eddie Cantor and David Freedman, "Ziegfeld and His *Follies,*" *Collier's,* Jan. 13, 1934, pp. 7–9, 50; Richard and Paulette Ziegfeld, *The Ziegfeld Touch: The Life and Times of Florenz Ziegfeld Jr.* (New York, 1993), pp. 12, 44–45.

4. Nathan, *The Theatre, The Drama, the Girls,* pp. 276–277.

5. J. J. Shubert to Charles B. Dillingham, August 2, 1920, General Correspondence File no. 800, SA.

6. Robert Baral, *Revue* (New York, 1962); Gerald Bordman, *American Musical Revue from the Passing Show to Sugar Babies* (New York, 1985); Brooks McNamara, *The Shuberts of Broadway* (New York, 1990); Jerry Stagg, *The Brothers Shubert* (New York, 1968).

7. Marshall and Jean Stearns, *Jazz Dance* (1968; rpt. New York, 1994), pp. 132–143; Allen Woll, *Black Musical Theatre* (New York, 1991), pp. 74–77.

8. J. E. Hirsch, "Glorifying the American Showgirl: A History of Revue Costume in the United States," Ph.D. diss., NYU, 1988, part 2, Appendix B; Hirsch, "The American Revue Costume," in Glenn Loney, ed., *Musical Theatre in America* (Westport, CT., 1984).

9. J. P. McEvoy, "He Knew What They Wanted," *The Saturday Evening Post,* Sept. 10, 1932, p. 51.

10. "Nothing Dull About the *Follies,*" *Evening Journal* [1919], vol. 2, JU.

11. Baral, *Revue,* p. 33; "'Follies' 1915 Model," np, vol. 1, JU.

12. Charles Higham, *Ziegfeld* (Chicago, 1972), pp. 1–12; Ziegfeld and Ziegfeld, *The Ziegfeld Touch.*

13. Geraldine Mascio, "The *Ziegfeld Follies,*" Ph.D. diss., Univ. of Wisconsin, 1981, pp. 1–2.

14. Programs for *The Passing Show* (1913–1918), SA. Programs for the Ziegfeld *Follies* (1910–1916), MCNY. See also Rosaline Biason Stone, "The Ziegfeld *Follies,*" Ph.D. diss., University of Denver, 1985, pp. 59–60; Mascio, "The *Ziegfeld Follies,*" p. 2.

15. "The Show Girl," *Broadway Magazine,* 10, Oct. 1902. Typically the programs for Broadway revues listed "Show Girls" and "Chorus Girls" separately. On featured show girls see Marjorie Farnsworth, *The Ziegfeld Follies* (New York, 1956); Baral, *Revue,* pp. 59–74. On the size of the typical chorus see Mascio, "The *Ziegfeld Follies,*" pp. 1–2.

16. Higham, *Ziegfeld,* pp. 123–124; Ziegfeld and Ziegfeld, *The Ziegfeld Touch,* p. 245; Stone, "The Ziegfeld *Follies,*" pp. 200–202.

17. Stone, "The Ziegfeld *Follies,*" pp. 245–247; Baral, *Revue,* p. 82.

18. Rennold Wolf, "'Hello Broadway,'" *New York Telegraph,* Dec. 26, 1914, vol. 21,060, NW. See also Barbara Naomi Cohen, "Ballet Satire in the Early Broadway Revue," *Dance Scope,* 13 (Winter/Spring 1979), pp. 44–50.

19. Louis Sherwin, "News of the Theatres," *New York Globe,* July 23, 1912, vol. 21,052, NW.

20. Editorial, *Vanity Fair* (1914) attributed to editor Frank Crowninshield, quoted in George H. Douglas, *The Smart Magazines* (New York, 1991), p. 96. See also Carl R. Dolmetsch, *The Smart Set: A History and Anthology* (New York, 1966).

21. William R. Taylor, *In Pursuit of Gotham: Culture and Commerce in New York* (New York, 1992), pp. 142–144, and ch. 9.

22. Mascio, "The *Ziegfeld Follies*," p. 159.

23. Information on ticket prices from correspondence files, SA; Alfred L. Bernheim, *The Business of the Theatre* (New York, 1933); Bordman, *American Musical Revue,* p. 35.

24. "'*Follies* of 1915'," np, vol. 1, JU. See also "Enthusiastic Over the New 'Follies," *New York Tribune,* June 23, 1920.

25. Stone, "The Ziegfeld *Follies*," Mascio, "The *Ziegfeld Follies.*"

26. Edmund Wilson, "The *Follies* as an Institution" (April, 1923), *The American Earthquake* (1958; rpt. New York, 1996), p. 52.

27. Quoted in Shelley Armitage, *John Held, Jr.: Illustrator of the Jazz Age* (Syracuse, 1987), p. 72.

28. "Specialties Are Loudly Applauded by Audience," np, Ziegfeld *Follies of 1914,* folder, MCNY.

29. Thomas Richards, *Commodity Culture of Victorian England* (Stanford, 1990), p. 241; Peter Bailey, "'Naughty but Nice': Musical Comedy and the Rhetoric of the Girl, 1892–1914," in Michael R. Booth and Joel H. Kaplan, eds., *The Edwardian Theatre* (Cambridge, 1996); Charles Rearick, *Pleasures of the Belle Epoque: Entertainment and Festivity in Turn-of-the-Century France* (New Haven, 1985) pp. 94–95.

30. These have been central themes in literary modernism. See Rita Felski, *The Gender of Modernity* (Cambridge, 1995).

31. H. E. Cooper, "Glorifying the American Leg," *The Dance,* March 1927, p. 26.

32. Stone, "The Ziegfeld *Follies*," pp. 46, 15; Hirsch, "Glorifying the American Showgirl," pt. 1, pp. 140–141; Angela J. Latham "The Right to Bare: Containing and Encoding American Women in Popular Entertainments," *Theatre Journal,* 49 (Dec. 1997), pp. 455 474.

33. "The New Play," *Commercial Advertizer* [1915]; Frederick Johns, "1915 *Follies,*" np, vol. 1, JU.

34. "Censor Orders Tights," np [Chicago], Jan. 30, 1913, JU; Henry Lehmann to J. J. Shubert, Oct. 27, 1914, General Correspondence File, no. 1020, SA.

35. Stephen M. Vallillo, "Broadway Revues in the Teens and Twenties: Smut and Slime?" *The Drama Review,* 25 (March 1981), pp. 25–34. See also Derek and Julia Parker, *The Natural History of the Chorus Girl* (Indianapolis, 1975).

36. Rennold Wolf, "'Midnight Frolic,'" *New York Telegraph,* Jan. 7, 1915; Stella Flores, "Midnight Frolic," *New York Evening Journal* [n.d. 1915], vol. 21,060, NW.

37. Stella Flores, "Midnight Frolic." See also Lewis Erenberg, *Steppin' Out: New York Nightlife and the Transformation of American Culture* (Chicago, 1981), p. 217.

38. Hirsch, "Glorifying," and "The American Revue Costume."

39. Lady [Lucile] Duff Gordon, *Discretions and Indiscretions* (New York, 1932), pp. 243–251; Ziegfeld and Ziegfeld, *The Ziegfeld Touch,* p. 304.

40. Duff Gordon, *Discretions and Indiscretions,* pp. 69, 74–75, 149; Hirsch, "Glorifying," pt.2, pp. 340, 352; Joel H. Kaplan and Sheila Stowell, *Theatre and Fashion: From Oscar Wilde to the Suffragettes* (Cambridge, 1994), pp. 117–120.

41. Duff Gordon, *Discretions and Indiscretions,* p. 149.

42. Mascio, "The *Ziegfeld Follies,*" pp. 138–139.

43. Louis V. De Foe, "The Puritan and the Player," *Theatre Magazine,* vol. 30, August 1919, pp. 74, 76.

44. William R. Leach, "Transformations in a Culture of Consumption: Women and Department Stores, 1890–1925," *The Journal of American History,* 71 (Sept. 1984), pp. 319–342; Leach, *Land of Desire: Merchants, Power, and the Rise of a New American Culture* (New York, 1993), pp. 58–61, 64–70, 83, 106–108; Erika Diane Rappaport, "The West End and Women's Pleasure: Gender and Commercial Culture in London," Ph.D. diss., Rutgers University, 1993, and *Shopping for Pleasure* (Princeton, forthcoming).

45. Bailey, "Musical Comedy and the Rhetoric of the Girl"; Rappaport, "The West End and Women's Pleasure."

46. "The American Woman," *The Living Age,* April 27, 1907, pp. 250–251.

47. Kristin Ross, intro. Emile Zola, *The Ladies' Paradise* (Berkeley, 1992). See also Judith Walkowitz, *City of Dreadful Delight* (Chicago, 1992); Leach, *Land of Desire.*

48. Mascio, "The *Ziegfeld Follies,*" pp. 156–159, 161–167.

49. Lyrics to the "Hat Song," p. 36, Act II, Script for the *Follies of 1908* by Harry B. Smith, MCNY.

50. Jackson Lears, *Fables of Abundance* (New York, 1994), pp. 18–19, 28–30, 38, 103–108, 117; Lois Banner, *American Beauty* (New York, 1983), p. 262; Richards, *Commodity Culture,* pp. 240–244.

51. Charles Goodrum and Helen Dalrymple, *Advertising in America: The First 200 Years* (New York, 1990), pp. 28–29; Lori Anne Loeb, *Consuming Angels: Advertising and Victorian Women* (New York, 1994), pp. 95–99.

52. Roland Marchand, *Advertising the American Dream: Making Way for Modernity* (Berkeley, 1985), pp. 96, 183.

53. Ibid., pp. 180, 167–168, 185–186, 155; Lears, *Fables of Abundance,* pp. 18–19, 28–30, 103–108, 117.

54. Barbara Barker, "Imre Kiralfy's Patriotic Spectacles: *Columbus, and the Discovery of America* (1892–1893) and *America* (1893)," *Dance Chronicle,* 17 (1994), pp. 149–178; Robert Toll, *On With the Show* (New York, 1976), pp. 179–183.

55. Barker, "Imre Kiralfy's Patriotic Spectacles," pp. 171, 153.

56. Martha Banta, *Imaging the American Woman* (New York, 1987), pp. 532–533, 680.

57. Script for "The *Follies of 1908,* A Review in Two Acts" by Harry B. Smith (1908), MCNY; Randolph Carter, *The World of Flo Ziegfeld* (New York, 1974), p. 29; Stone, "The Ziegfeld *Follies,*" p. 162.

58. "*Follies of 1909,*" *Theatre Magazine,* August 1909, p. 37; Carter, *The World of*

Flo Ziegfeld, p. 29; Stone, "Ziegfeld *Follies,*" pp. 165, 168; Toll, *On With the Show,* p. 304.

59. Toll, *On With the Show,* p. 304.

60. Hirsch, "Glorifying the American Showgirl," pt. 1, p. 7.

61. Ibid., pt. 2, pp. 339, 352, 354, 361, 366, 370 and pt. 1, p. 354. See also Banta, *Imaging the American Woman,* p. 680–682.

62. Duff Gordon, *Discretions and Indiscretions,* pp. 289–290; Barbara Naomi Cohen-Stratyner, "Welcome to 'Laceland'," in Glenn Loney, ed., *Musical Theatre in America* (Westport, CT., 1984), pp. 318–319; Hirsch, "Glorifying," part 1, pp. 310–311, 314–15.

63. Hirsch, "Glorifying," pt. 1, p. 291.

64. Marjorie Farnsworth, *The Ziegfeld Follies* (New York, 1956) (photos), pp. 172–173; Hirsch, "Glorifying," p. 292.

65. Hirsch, "Glorifying," pt. 1, p. 98, 246.

66. "They've Got to Have Legs," *Midnight,* Nov. 1922, vol. 21,070, NW.

67. Quoted in Latham, "The Right to Bare," p. 460.

68. "Audience at the New Amsterdam," *New York Herald,* June 6, 1922, vol. 21,069, NW.

69. John Dos Passos, *Manhattan Transfer* (1925; rpt. Boston, 1960) p. 365. Cf. Mascio, "The *Ziegfeld Follies,*" p. 178.

70. Florenz Ziegfeld Jr., "How I Pick Beauties," *Theatre Magazine,* 30 (Sept. 1919), pp. 158, 160. See also Higham, *Ziegfeld;* Latham, "The Right to Bare," p. 460. Linda Mizejewski, whose book appeared just as this one was going to press, calls this product identity, the Ziegfeld "guarantee." See *Ziegfeld Girl* (Durham, 1999), p. 90.

71. Salita Solano, "Zippiest of Long Line" [New York Evening] *Journal,* Sept. 18, 1917, vol. 2, JU.

72. Erenberg, *Steppin' Out,* pp. 214–216.

73. "How I Pick Beauties," pp. 160, 158.

74. Ibid., p. 158

75. "Picking Out Pretty Girls for the Stage," *American Magazine,* Dec. 1914, pp. 35, 125.

76. Ibid., pp. 120, 125. See also Erenberg, *Steppin' Out,* pp. 214–215, 217–219.

77. "Picking Out Pretty Girls," pp. 120–121, 37.

78. Ibid., p. 158.

79. Florenz Ziegfeld Jr., "When Is a Woman's Figure Beautiful," *The Evening Journal,* n.d. [1922] Evelyn Law Scrapbook, BRTC.

80. J. J. Shubert to Henry Lehmann, Jan. 22, 1913, and Jan. 18, 1915. See also letters of Dec. 7, 1917, Feb. 11, 1918, General Correspondence File no. 1020, SA.

81. Florenz Ziegfeld, Jr. "Why I Produce the Kind of Shows I Do," *The Green Book Album,* Jan. 1912, p. 174.

82. Gertrude Lynch, "Racial and Ideal Types of Beauty," *The Cosmopolitan,* 38 (Dec. 1904), pp. 223–224, 230, 233. See also Banner, *American Beauty,* p. 206.

83. "How I Pick Beauties," p. 158.

84. J. Chapman Hilder, "The Darktown Follies," Theatre Magazine, March 1914, p. 135; Woll, Black Musical Theatre, pp. 56–57.

85. Woll, Black Musical Theatre, p. 76; Stearns and Stearns, Jazz Dance, p. 141.

86. Eric Ledell Smith, Bert Williams: A Biography of the Pioneer Broadway Comedian (Jefferson, NC., 1992), p. 133; Jo A. Tanner, Dusky Maidens (Westport, CT., 1992), p. 16; Henry T. Sampson, Blacks in Blackface (Metuchen, N.J., 1980), pp. 20, 86, 110.

87. Edmund Wilson, "The Finale at the Follies," March 25, 1925, The American Earthquake, pp. 45–46.

88. "Picking Out Pretty Girls for the Stage," p. 121.

89. "How I Pick Beauties," p. 158.

90. "Picking Out Pretty Girls for the Stage," p. 121.

91. See Daniel J. Kevles, In the Name of Eugenics: Genetics and the Uses of Human Heredity (Berkeley, 1985); Nancy Leys Stepan, "The Hour of Eugenics": Race, Gender, and Nation in Latin America (Ithaca, 1991); John Higham, Strangers in the Land (New York, 1975). On eugenics and beauty standards see Elizabeth Haiken, Venus Envy: A History of Cosmetic Surgery (Baltimore, 1997), pp. 177–178, 181; Banta, Imaging the American Woman, pp. 136–137; Mizejewski, Ziegfeld Girl, pp. 116, 119.

92. "Fall—and the Follies," Boston Transcript, [1917], vol. 2, JU; "The New Play, Mr. Ziegfeld's 'Follies' of 1919,'" np, vol. 2, JU; "F. Ziegfeld Jr's Annual Production, 14th of the Series of A NATIONAL INSTITUTION," [1920], np, vol. 3, JU.

93. New York World, Feb. 5, 1923; "Most Brilliant 'Follies'" Women's Wear, June 6, 1922, vol. 21,069. NW. See also "American Girl Duly Glorified," Detroit News, Dec. 10, 1923; Leonard Hill, "'The Follies'" Nov. 19, 1924, np, Evelyn Law Scrapbook, BRTC.

94. "Nine O'Clock Revue," New York Dramatic Mirror, March 20, 1920.

95. "The 'Follies,'" New York Tribune, June 6, 1922, vol. 21,069, NW.

96. H. E. Cooper, "Glorifying the American Leg," pp. 26–27. Italics in original.

97. Wilson, "The Follies as an Institution," p. 51.

98. "They've Got to Have Legs."

99. Barbara Stratyner, Ned Wayburn and the Dance Routine: From Vaudeville to the Ziegfeld Follies, Studies in Dance History, 13 (Madison, 1996), p. 1.

100. Mary Morgan, "Handling Humanity in the Mass," Theatre Magazine, May 1913, pp. 146–147. On Wayburn's early career see Stratyner, Ned Wayburn and The Dance Routine, pp. 10–13; Barbara Naomi Cohen, "The Dance Direction of Ned Wayburn," Ph.D diss. NYU, 1980, pp. 8–35.

101. Quoted in Richard Kislan, Hoofing on Broadway (New York, 1987), p. 53. See also Morgan, "Handling Humanity in the Mass," p. vi.

102. Variety, Jan. 23, 1924.

103. For similar observations see Bailey, "Musical Comedy and the Rhetoric of the Girl," pp. 39–40; Mizejewski, The Ziegfeld Girl, p. 66.

104. Stratyner, Ned Wayburn and the Dance Routine, pp. 3–8, 18–19; Kislan, Hoofing on Broadway, pp. 3–52.

105. Martin Rubin, *Showstoppers: Busby Berkeley and the Tradition of Spectacle* (New York, 1993).

106. "'Follies' Opens at New Amsterdam," *New York Telegraph*, June 6, 1922, vol. 21,069, NW.

107. Cecelia Tichi, *Shifting Gears: Technology, Literature, Culture in Modernist America* (Chapel Hill, 1987), pp. 18–25, 35, 99–123.

108. Stratyner, *Ned Wayburn and the Dance Routine*, pp. 52–53, 61. Kislan, *Hoofing on Broadway*, p. 52.

109. Stratyner, *Ned Wayburn and The Dance Routine*, pp. 61, 17.

110. Cohen-Stratyner, "Welcome to Laceland," pp. 319–321; Ziegfeld and Ziegfeld, *The Ziegfeld Touch*, pp. 252–253.

111. Stratyner, *Ned Wayburn and the Dance Routine*, pp. 6–7; Hirsch, "Glorifying the American Showgirl," part 1, pp. 5, 39–41.

112. "Making Faces," *The Star* (London), Sept. 22, 1913, vol. 21,054, NW.

113. Stratyner, *Ned Wayburn and the Dance Routine*, pp. 5–7.

114. Ibid., pp. 2–3, 6–7, 15, 21; Cohen, "Dance Direction of Ned Wayburn," 24. On Berkeley's military background see Tony Thomas and Jim Terry with Busby Berkeley, *The Busby Berkeley Book* (New York, 1973), pp. 18–19.

115. Joseph Mulvaney, "The Tireless Tillers," *The Dance Magazine*, June 1926, pp. 22–23, 61. See also Curtis Mitchell, "Tiller Tells His Dancing Secrets," *Dance Lover's Magazine*, July 1925, pp. 13–14.

116. Morgan, "Handling Humanity in the Mass," pp. 146–147.

117. Glenmore Davis, "The Ladies of the Chorus," *Green Book Magazine*, May 1911.

118. Ned Wayburn, "The Chorus Girl—Old and New," *Theatre*, May 1920, vol. 21,069, NW.

119. Gail Marshall, *Actresses on the Victorian Stage: Feminine Performance and the Galatea Myth* (Cambridge, 1998).

120. John F. Kasson, *Civilizing the Machine: Technology and Republican Values in America, 1776–1900* (New York, 1976), pp. 158, 154–161; Richards, *The Commodity Culture*, pp. 56–57; Tichi, *Shifting Gears*, p. 5.

121. Patricia Mellencamp finds the same impulse in Berkeley's films. See "The Sexual Economics of Gold Diggers of 1933," in Peter Lehman, ed., *Close Viewings: An Anthology of New Film Criticism* (Tallahassee, 1990), pp. 187–189.

122. Andreas Huyssen, *After the Great Divide: Modernism, Mass Culture, Postmodernism* (Bloomington, 1986), pp. 68, 71–72.

123. Dickran Tashjian, *Skyscrapper Primitives: Dada and the American Avant Garde, 1910–1925* (Middletown, 1975), pp. 8, 20, 30. See also Amelia Jones, "Eros, That's Life, or the Baroness' Penis," and Jay Bochner, "dAdAmAgs," both in Francis M. Naumann, ed., *Making Mischief: Dada Invades New York* (New York, 1996).

124. Tashjian, *Skyscrapper Primitives*, p. 35.

125. Quoted in Tashjian, *Skyscrapper Primitives*, pp. 43–44. See also Linda Dalrymple Henderson, "Reflections of and/or on Marcel Duchamp's *Large Glass*," and Jones, "Eros, That's Life or the Baroness' Penis," in Naumann, ed., *Making Mischief*.

126. Tashjian, *Skyscrapper Primitives,* pp. 45–46; Tashjian, "Authentic Spirit of Change: The Poetry of New York Dada," pp. 267–268 and Jones, "Eros, That's Life," pp. 240–241.

127. Henderson, "Reflections," pp. 229–230, 236.

128. Jane Goodall, "Transferred Agencies: Performance and the Fear of Automatism," *Theatre Journal,* 49 (Dec. 1997), pp. 444–446.

129. "Mysteries of the Chorus," *New York Tribune,* May 7, 1916; Ada Patterson, "Broadway's King of the Chorus," *Theatre Magazine,* Dec. 1923, p. 22.

130. "'King' Who Ought to Understand Women," *New York Press,* Dec. 22, 1912, vol. 21,054, NW.

131. George Vaux Bacon, "Chorus Girls in the Making," *Green Book,* Oct. 1913, p. 575, Locke Envelope no. 2509, BRTC; Stratyner, *Ned Wayburn and the Dance Routine,* pp. 53–54, 18–19.

132. Stratyner, *Ned Wayburn and the Dance Routine,* pp. 20, 52–54, 55–57.

133. Morgan, "Handling Humanity in the Mass," p. 146.

134. "They've Got to Have Legs."

135. "The Father of Ragtime," *New York Times,* Sept. 12, 1915, vol. 21,063, NW.

136. "The Stage Producer's Job," *Green Book Albumn,* Oct. 1911, p. 805, Locke Envelope, no. 2509.

137. Morgan, "Handling Humanity in the Mass," p. 146. See also "Mysteries of the Chorus."

138. "Wayburn Despot of the Chorus, or Practical Philanthropist, Which?," np, 1912, vol. 21,052, NW.

139. Frank W. D. Ries, "Albertina Rasch: The Broadway Career," *Dance Chronicle,* 6 (1983), pp. 95–137.

140. Ibid., pp. 99, 103, 125. See also Ries, "Albertina Rasch: The Hollywood Career," *Dance Chronicle,* 6 (1983), pp. 281–362.

141. Barbara Cohen-Stratyner, "Gertrude Hoffmann," *Biographical Dictionary of American Dance* (New York, 1982), pp. 430–432.

142. "Mrs. Gertrude Hoffmann Stage Manager," np, June 15, 1903, Hoffmann, vol. 273, RLC. See also Vera Caspary, "The Secret of Gertrude Hoffmann's Success," *The Dance Magazine,* Nov. 1925, p. 14.

143. "The Stage Producer's Job."

144. "Ned Wayburn Uncorks Wisdom," *The Inter Ocean,* August 4, 1912, vol. 21,052, NW.

145. Stratyner, *Ned Wayburn and The Dance Routine,* pp. 12–13.

146. "Audience at the New Amsterdam," *New York Herald,* June 6, 1922.

147. The most scathing critique came from German writer Siegfried Kracauer. See "The Mass Ornament" (1927), trans. Jack Zipes and Barbara Correll in *New German Critique,* 5 (Spring 1975), pp. 67–76.

148. "At the Play" (1920), np, vol. 3, JU. See also Leonard Hill, "'The *Follies*'," np, Nov. 19, 1924, Evelyn Law Scrapbook, BRTC.

149. Louis Hirsh, "The Deadly Dull Chorus Girl," *Theatre Magazine,* 29 (May 1919), p. 282.

150. "'King' Who Ought to Understand Women," *New York Press,* Dec. 22, 1912, vol. 21,054, NW.

151. "How I Pick Beauties," p. 158. See also George White as told to Byrne MacFadden, "What Is a Good Chorus?" *The Dance Magazine,* Nov. 1925, p. 33.

152. "Picking Out Pretty Girls for the Stage," pp. 34, 119. Italics in original.

153. Ned Wayburn, *The Art of Stage Dancing: A Manual of Stage-Craft* (New York, 1925), pp. 282, 280–282.

154. Advertisement, *Dance Lovers Magazine,* Sept. 1925.

7 "Like All the Rest of Womankind Only More So"

1. "What [the] Chorus Girl Worries About," np, 1917, CC.

2. "Chorus Girls of Yesteryear," press release [1918]. See also "Society Women Have Stolen the 'Stuff' of the Chorus Girl," np, Nov. 12, 1916, both in CC.

3. Evelyn Thaw [Nesbit], *The Story of My Life* (London, [1914]), p. 33, copy in BRTC.

4. Dorothy Dix, "Studies in Natural History—the Chorus Girl," (1902) [*New York Journal*], CC.

5. Cecelia Tichi, *Shifting Gears: Technology, Literature, Culture in Modernist America* (Chapel Hill, 1987), p. 34.

6. Roy L. McCardell "At Ned Wayburn's 'Squab Farm'," *The World,* July 5, 1906, Wayburn, ser. 2, vol. 305, RLC; Mary Morgan, "Handling Humanity in the Mass," *Theatre Magazine,* May 1913; "Ned Wayburn's 'Broilers'," *Variety,* July 25, 1908, p. 14; Barbara Stratyner, *Ned Wayburn and the Dance Routine, Studies in Dance History,* 13 (Madison, 1996), pp. 53–55.

7. "All Theatredom in a Panic Over the Chorus Girl Famine," *The World,* August 18, 1908, CC.

8. Program for *The Producer,* May 12, 1912, vol. 21,059, NW.

9. "Actors Strike Fills Rialto," Philadelphia *Public Ledger,* August 18, 1919, Ethel Barrymore, vol. 39, RLC.

10. "Handling Humanity in the Mass," p. 146; "At Ned Wayburn's Squab Farm"; "The Chorus Man," *The Green Book Album,* March 1912, pp. 547–533; Stratyner, *Ned Wayburn and the Dance Routine,* p. 53; Camille Hardy, "Ballet Girls and Broilers," *Ballet Review,* 8 (1980), p. 113.

11. J. E. Hirsch, "Glorifying the American Showgirl," part I, Ph.D. diss., 1988, NYU, pp. 14–15; 325–333.

12. *Judge,* 64, May 31, 1913.

13. James M. Shultz, M.D., "The Chicken: A Psychological Study," unpub. ms. (Austin, 1991). Copy in author's posssession.

14. Page Smith and Charles Daniels, *The Chicken Book* (Boston, 1975), p. 224.

15. "Everybody Loves a Chicken," Lyrics from *Broadway to Paris,* Wayburn Papers, Ole Olsen Collection, USC. See also *Boston Globe,* Oct. 11, 1912, vol. 21,053, NW.

16. Lewis Erenberg, *Steppin Out'* (Chicago, 1981), p. 52.

17. *Judge*, 65, August 2, 1913, Sept. 13, 1913.

18. Lyrics for "Chicken Leg L'Imperiale," from *Town Topics* (1924), Wayburn Collection, Ole Olsen Papers, USC.

19. Acton Davies, "News of the Theatres," *New York Sun*, June 2, 1914; "The *Follies of 1914*," *New York Sun*, June 2, 1914, Ziegfeld *Follies of 1914* file, MCNY.

20. Program for *Artists and Models* (Paris edition), June 24, 1925, Winter Garden Theater, SA.

21. Program, lyrics, and clipping files for *Artists and Models* 1925–27 editions, SA.

22. *Chicago Evening Post*, n.d. [1925], reprinted in "The Mssrs. Shubert Present 'ARTISTS AND MODELS, Paris Edition'" n.d. [1925]. Publicity pamphlet, *Artists and Models* file, SA.

23. Script for *Artists and Models* (1925). Songs by Clifford Grey, libretto by Harold Atteridge and Harry Wagstaff Gribble, SA.

24. "Artists and Models," *Boston Daily*, Nov. 13, 1926, Phil Baker Scrapbook, BRTC.

25. Eric Lott, "Love and Theft: The Racial Unconscious of Blackface Minstrelsy," *Representations*, 39 (Summer 1992), pp. 23–50 (the quoted passage appears on p. 23). See also his *Love and Theft: Blackface Minstrelsy and the American Working Class* (New York, 1993).

26. James Moy, "Subversion of the Pornographic in Mass Entertainments," in James Redmond, ed., *Themes in Drama* (Cambridge, 1985), pp. 197–199.

27. "My Little Pet Chicken" (1914), lyrics by George V. Hobart, Ziegfeld Collection, HRC.

28. "The Chicken Walk" (1916), by Irving Berlin. Written for Charles Dillingham and Florenz Ziegfeld Jr.'s revue, *The Century Girl*, MCNY.

29. Program for the *Passing Show of 1918*, SA.

30. Lyrics for the "Squab Farm" by Harold Atteridge, in script for the *Passing Show of 1918*, SA.

31. On Cinderella as a white woman's myth see Erenberg, *Steppin' Out*, p. 223.

32. "What Becomes of the Chorus Girl," CC. This was a common theme in the stories of press agents.

33. Clippings on Marilyn Miller in *Sally* (1920), Brown, Chamberlain, and Lyman Collection of Dramatic Scrapbooks, BRTC.

34. *New York Clipper*, Dec. 2, 1920, Miller Clippings, Locke Envelope #1469, BRTC.

35. "Wild Rose" lyrics by Clifford Grey. Vocal score for *Sally*, lyrics by Guy Bolton, Clifford Grey, and P. G. Wodehouse, music by Jerome Kern (New York: T. B. Harms, 1920), UCLA Music Library, Special Collections.

36. Tracy C. Davis, *Actresses as Working Women* (London, 1991), p. 69ff; Erenberg, *Steppin' Out*, pp. 217, 221.

37. Phyllis Leslie Abramson, *Sob Sister Journalism* (Westport, CT., 1990).

38. On turn-of-the-century gold digger prototypes see Robert C. Allen, *Horrible Prettiness* (Chapel Hill, 1991), pp. 201, 206–214. On early twentieth-century im-

ages see Joanne Meyerowitz, *Women Adrift: Independent Wage Earners in Chicago, 1830–1930* (Chicago, 1988), pp. 126–138.

39. Meyerowitz, *Women Adrift,* p. 126.

40. Owen Johnson, *The Salamander* (Indianapolis, 1914), p. 15.

41. Ibid., Foreword.

42. "Report on Strand Roof Garden," May 16, 1915, box 28, Committee of Fourteen Papers, Rare Books and Manuscripts, New York Public Library.

43. Johnson, *The Salamander,* p. 174.

44. See, for example, "The Tokio," Jan. 11, 1919, Committee of Fourteen Papers, box 17. On "charity girls," see Kathy Peiss, *Cheap Amusements* (Philadelphia, 1985), pp. 110–112; Meyerowitz, *Women Adrift,* pp. 101–102.

45. Davis, *Actresses as Working Women,* pp. 77–78.

46. "Resume of Cabaret Situation 1917"; "Restaurant and Cafe," Jan. 28, 1917, Committee of Fourteen Papers, box 31. On the occupational backgrounds of prostitutes see Ruth Rosen, *The Lost Sisterhood* (Baltimore, 1982), p. 155; George Kneeland, *Commercialized Prostitution in New York City* (1913; rpt. Montclair, NJ, 1969), (tables) pp. 257, 241, 222.

47. Unpublished vice reports, 1918–1919, Committee of Fourteen Papers, boxes 31 and 28. On theater districts and prostitution see Davis, *Actresses as Working Women;* Timothy Gilfoyle, *City of Eros* (New York, 1992).

48. Johnson, *The Salamander,* pp. 20–21, 25–33, 63–64.

49. Ashton Stevens, "The Gold Diggers," np, June 24, 1919; "Good Little Gold Diggers," np (1919), "The Gold Diggers," *Cosmopolitan,* Dec. 1919, in Ina Claire, vol. 116, RLC.

50. *New York Telegram,* n.d. [1919, review of *The Gold Diggers*], Claire, vol. 116, RLC.

51. Ashton Stevens, "The Gold Diggers."

52. *Morning Telegraph,* July 13, 1919, Ina Claire Scrapbook, Microfilm Reel 71, BRTC.

53. Avery Hopwood, Script for *The Gold Diggers: A Comedy in Three Acts* (1919), Act 1, p. 30. Warner Bros. Archives, State Historical Society of Wisconsin, Madison.

54. Ibid., pp. 11, 13, 27, 29.

55. Ibid., pp. 34–35. Italics in original.

56. Ibid., pp. 62–63, Italics in original.

57. Ibid., p. 72.

58. For the production history see Arthur Hove, "Introduction: In Search of Happiness," in *Gold Diggers of 1933,* Wisconsin/Warner Brothers Screenplay Series (Madison, 1980), pp. 9–31 (hereafter cited as "screenplay." On 1920s gold digger films see Lea Jacobs, *The Wages of Sin* (Madison, 1991), pp. 66–69.

59. "Collective Bargaining by Actors," *Bulletin of the United States Bureau of Labor Statistics,* no. 402 (Washington, 1926); Vincent Harding, *The Revolt of the Actors* (New York, 1929); Sean Patrick Holmes, "Weavers of Dreams, Unite: Constructing an Occupational Identity in the Actors' Equity Association, 1913–1934," Ph.D. diss., NYU, 1994, pp. 129–137, 164–165.

60. "Collective Bargaining by Actors," pp. 13,50–54; Holmes, "Weavers of Dreams, Unite," p. 137, p. 174, n. 38; Hardy, "Ballet Girls and Broilers," p. 111.

61. Frances Gilfoil to Marie Dressler, Sept. 4, 1919, box MC3, file 4, AEA Papers, Bobst Library, NYU. See also Matthew Kennedy, *Marie Dressler* (Jefferson, NC, 1999), pp. 102–105.

62. Holmes, "Weavers of Dreams, Unite," pp. 126–134.

63. *Cleveland Plain Dealer,* Oct. 19, 1919, Dressler, vol. 164, RLC.

64. "A.E.A.'s Fund Raising Campaign at Packed Meeting Yesterday," *Variety Daily Bulletin,* August 23, 1919. On Chorus Equity and the Women's Trade Union League see Frieda S. Miller (Philadelphia WTUL) to Marie Dressler, Sept. 6, 1919; Maud Swartz, WTUL to Marie Dressler, Sept. 5, 1919, in folder 4, box MC3, Chorus Equity Association Correspondence, AEA Papers. See also "Lauds Chorus Girls to Working Women," *New York Sun,* Sept. 4, 1919, Dressler, vol. 164, RLC. On the participation of Russell and Barrymore see Albert Auster, *Actresses and Suffragists* (New York, 1984), pp. 109, 111, 137; Harding, *Revolt of the Actors,* pp. 115–118.

65. "Florine Arnold's Interview—Why She Joined the Strikers," *Evening World,* August 12 [1919]. Typed transcript of article in box MR1, folder 18, AEA Papers.

66. "How They Pay Off at the Hippodrome," *Theater Magazine,* Dec. 1908, "The Experience of a Chorus Girl," *The Independent,* 61, July 12, 1906; "Chorus Girls I Know," *Variety,* Dec. 12, 1908. On fines for poor grooming and dirty clothing see J. J. Shubert to Henry Lehmann, Jan. 18, 1915, Feb. 11, 1918, General Correspondence File no. 1020, SA.

67. Quoted in Holmes, "Weavers of Dreams, Unite," p. 136. Holmes argues that it was not an image of a proletarian that Equity substituted for the gold digger, but the idea of the chorus girls as young married women with babies. See p. 138.

68. "Heaven Will Protect the Working Girl: Marie Dressler," *New York Times,* Aug. 24, 1919.

69. "Why 'Gen' Dressler put on a War Paint Make Up," np, Aug. 31, 1919, Dressler, vol. 164, RLC. See also Harding, *Revolt of the Actors,* pp. 115–116, 127, 132–134; Holmes, "Weavers of Dreams, Unite," pp. 135–139. On Dressler's reputation among managers see Kennedy, *Marie Dressler,* pp. 35, 101.

70. Typed memo [n.d., August 1919], folder 4, box MC3, Chorus Equity Association Correspondence, AEA Papers.

71. "Why 'Gen' Dressler put on a War Paint Make Up."

72. "Who's Who—and Why," *Variety* (n.d.) [Aug. 1919]; "Along the Rialto in 'Strike Days,'" np [Aug. 1919], Dressler, vol. 164, RLC.

73. Quoted in Holmes, "Weavers of Dreams, Unite," pp. 137–138. In an earlier organizational strike vaudeville players also stressed the need to protect female virtue. See M. Alison Kibler, *Rank Ladies* (Chapel Hill, 1999), pp. 184–185.

74. "Clubhouse for Chorus Girls," *New York Dramatic Mirror,* Sept. 18, 1919.

75. "The Chorus Girl Irredenta," *The Nation,* Sept. 20, 1919. On the Charlotte Cushman Club see Charles Belmont Davis, "Chorus Girls' Club," *Collier's,* 47, May 20, 1911.

76. "The Chorus Girls' Rebellion." Dressler later ran afoul of AEA when she re-

fused to pay wages owed to the cast of "Tillie's Nightmare." See "Marie Dressler in Another Jam with the Actors' Equity," *Variety*, April 21, 1920 and Kennedy, *Marie Dressler*, p. 106.

77. Holmes, "Weavers of Dreams, Unite," pp. 119–20, 141–147; "'Follies' Gives Performance Protected by Injunction," *Variety Daily Bulletin*, Aug. 12, 1919.

78. "Notations on the Strike, by Miss [Pearl] Sindelar," n.d. [Aug. 1919], p. 3, folder 13, box MR1, AEA Papers. See also Holmes, "Weavers of Dreams, Unite," p. 141.

79. "Notations on the Strike," pp. 1–2.

80. Holmes, "Weavers of Dreams, Unite," pp. 143–144.

81. "Interview—Ziegfeld," *Morning Telegraph*, Aug. 13, 1919, folder 18, box MR1, AEA Papers. "Official Statements—Ziegfeld Chorus Girls," *Variety Daily Bulletin*, no. 8, Aug. 18, 1919.

82. Henry James, *Daisy Miller* (1878; rpt. London, 1986), p. 90.

83. "Truthful Information About the Chorus," n.d. [c.1919], Chorus Press Releases, CC.

84. "Chorus Develops Many Real Stars," [Shubert] press release, n.d., Press Releases, 1915–1919, CC. See also Florenz Ziegfeld, Jr., "Era of 'Stage Door Johnnies' Banished," *New York American*, Aug. 28, 1921; "What Becomes of Ziegfeld *Follies* Girls?," *Pictorial Review*, May 1925, CC.

85. A. T. Worm to J. J. [Shubert], Nov. 13, 1920, file no. 76, General Correspondence, SA. On Worm's career see Brooks McNamara, *The Shuberts of Broadway* (New York, 1990), pp. 65–66.

86. "How the Prince of Wales Met Evelyn, *Follies* Beauty," *New Orleans States*, Sept. 6, 1925, Evelyn Law Scrapbook, BRTC.

87. Anita Loos, "The Biography of a Book," Ray Pierre Corsini, ed., *Fate Keeps on Happening: The Adventures of Lorelei Lee and Other Writings* (New York, 1984), p. 55.

88. Hove, "Introduction." On gold digger titles see Kenneth W. Munden, ed., *American Film Institute Catalogue of Motion Picture Production in the United States* (New York, 1971).

89. Hove, "Introduction," p. 22.

90. Jane Feuer, *The Hollywood Musical*, 2nd. ed. (Bloomington, 1993), p. 90ff; Feuer, "The Self-reflective Musical and the Myth of Entertainment," in Rick Altman, ed., *Genre: The Musical* (London, 1981).

91. *Gold Diggers of 1933*, screenplay, p. 55.

92. Scholars debate whether such films were about escapism or political engagement. On escapism see Hove, "Introduction"; Richard Dyer, "Entertainment and Utopia," in Altman, ed., *Genre: The Musical*; Andrew Bergman, *We're in the Money: Depression America and Its Films* (New York, 1971). On political engagement see Mark Roth, "Some Warners Musicals and the Spirit of the New Deal" in Altman, ed., *Genre: The Musical*; Pamela Robertson, *Guilty Pleasures: Feminist Camp from Mae West to Madonna* (Durham, 1996), p. 82. Jason Rubin provides the most detailed treatment of the production numbers. See *Showstoppers* (New York, 1993).

93. *Gold Diggers of 1933,* screenplay, pp. 70–73, and Hove, "Introduction," pp. 28–29; Gerald Mast, *Can't Help Singin': The American Musical on Stage and Screen* (Woodstock, NY, 1987); Hove, "Introduction," p. 28; Robertson, *Guilty Pleasures,* pp. 76–84.

94. *Gold Diggers of 1933,* screenplay, p. 72.

95. This was originally titled "Gold Diggers' Song." See "Notes to the Screenplay," *Gold Diggers of 1933,* p. 185.

96. *Gold Diggers of 1933,* screenplay, p. 47.

97. Ibid., p. 50.

98. Compare Roth, "Some Warners Musicals," p. 54.

99. Barbara Melosh, *Engendering Culture: Manhood and Womanhood in New Deal Public Art and Theater* (Washington, D.C., 1991), pp. 31, 155ff.

100. Warner Bros. *42nd Street,* Rocco Fumento, ed., *42nd Street,* Wisconsin/ Warner Bros. Screenplay Series (Madison, 1980), p. 182. Hereafter cited as "screenplay." See also Roth, "Some Warners Musicals," pp. 47–49, and J. Hoberman, *42nd Street* (London, 1993), p. 28.

101. Quoted in Roth, "Some Warners Musicals," pp. 48–49.

102. Gilbert Seldes, "A Tribute to Florenz Ziegfeld," in Seldes, *The 7 Lively Arts* (1924; rpt. New York, 1957), p. 133.

103. Whitney Bolton condensed Bradford Ropes's 345-page *42nd Street* into a 38-page "treatment." Quoted in Fumento, "Introduction: From Bastards and Bitches to Heroes and Heroines," *42nd Street,* p. 14.

104. J. Hoberman, *42nd Street,* p. 9.

105. *42nd Street,* screenplay, pp. 91–93, 39.

106. Bradford Ropes, *42nd Street* (New York, 1932), p. 147.

107. Ibid., p. 314.

Conclusion

1. Robert W. Snyder, *Voice of the City: Vaudeville and Popular Culture in New York* (New York, 1989), pp. 107–109, 123, 129.

2. Brooks McNamara, "The Entertainment District at the End of the 1930s," and Margaret Knapp, "Introductory Essay," in William R. Taylor, ed., *Inventing Times Square* (New York, 1991); David Nasaw, *Going Out* (New York, 1993), pp. 224–226.

3. Herbert Blau, *Blooded Thought: Occasions of Theatre* (New York, 1982), pp. 120–124; Louis Giannitti, *Understanding Movies,* 7th ed. (Upper Saddle River, NJ: 1996), ch. 7.

4. Gerald Mast, *The Comic Mind: Comedy and the Movies* (Chicago, 1979); Raymond Durgnat, *The Crazy Mirror: Hollywood Comedy and the American Image* (New York, 1970); Walter Kerr, *The Silent Clowns* (New York, 1975); Henry Jenkins, *What Made Pistachio Nuts?* (New York, 1992).

5. Ethan Mordden, *Movie Star: A Look at the Woman Who Made Hollywood* (New York, 1983), pp. 120–121; June Sochen, *Mae West: She Who Laughs, Lasts* (Arlington Heights, IL, 1992), pp. 91–92.

6. Emily Wortis Leider, *Becoming Mae West* (New York, 1997), p. 10.

7. Pamela Robertson, *Guilty Pleasures* (Durham, 1996), pp. 27, 41–43; Leider, *Becoming Mae West*, pp. 187–189.

8. Marybeth Hamilton, *When I'm Bad I'm Better: Mae West, Sex, and American Entertainment* (New York, 1995), p. 180.

9. Leider, *Becoming Mae West*, pp. 38, 41, 71, 109, 187–189, 245–246; Sochen, *Mae West*, pp. 9–34.

10. Lillian Schlissel, ed., *Three Plays by Mae West* (New York: 1997); Leider, *Becoming Mae West*, pp. 143–144.

11. Quoted in Robertson, *Guilty Pleasures*, p. 39.

12. Quoted in ibid., p. 46.

13. Molly Haskell, *From Reverence to Rape: The Treatment of Women in the Movies* (New York, 1974); Lea Jacobs, *The Wages of Sin: Censorship and the Fallen Woman Film, 1928–1942* (Madison, 1991).

14. Stanley Cavell, *Pursuits of Happiness: The Hollywood Comedy of Remarriage* (Cambridge, 1981), pp. 1–2, 16–19.

15. Ibid., p. 186.

16. Hamilton, *When I'm Bad, I'm Better*, pp. 240–242.

17. Alice Echols, *Daring to Be Bad: Radical Feminism in America, 1967–1975* (Minneapolis, 1989).

18. Susan J. Douglas, *Where the Girls Are: Growing Up Female With the Mass Media* (New York, 1994), pp. 140–141.

19. Quoted in Echols, *Daring to Be Bad*, p. 95.

20. Quoted in Douglas, *Where the Girls Are*, p. 157.

21. Ibid., p. 10.

22. Haskell, *From Reverence to Rape*, p. 329.

23. Douglas, *Where the Girls Are*, pp. 97–98, 150, 202, 304–305.

Acknowledgments

This book would not have been possible without the help of scholars and archivists who understood where I was headed and helped me to see more clearly how to get there. I thank Barbara Cohen Stratyner at the New York Public Library for the Performing Arts at Lincoln Center, Maryann Chach and Reagan Fletcher at the Shubert Archive in New York City, and Melissa Miller at the Theater Arts Collection, Harry Ransom Humanities Research Center, University of Texas at Austin. I want to express my appreciation to Candace Falk for providing material on Emma Goldman's invitation to perform in vaudeville and for helping me think about the relationship between acting and activism. Many thanks as well to Liz Fugate at the University of Washington Drama Library, Marty Jacobs at the Theater Collection at the Museum of the City of New York, Heather Ahlstrom at Harvard Theater Collection, Ned Comstock at the Cinema/Television Library, University of Southern California, and the librarians at Rare Books and Manuscripts, Butler Library, Columbia University, and the Robert Wagner Labor Archives at New York University.

I wish to thank several institutions for their generous support. A National Endowment for the Humanities Fellowship for University Teachers and a Fellowship from the University of Washington Royalty Research Fund gave me time for uninterrupted writing. The University of Washington History Department's Keller Fund provided research support, and a visiting fellowship at the University of California at Davis Humanities Center helped me launched this project.

I am tremendously grateful for the intellectual generosity of Elizabeth Blackmar and John Kasson, who read my manuscript with great care and provided invaluable suggestions for improving the final draft of the book. The members of my interdisciplinary writing group at the University of Washington—Priscilla Wald, Caroline Chung Simpson, Shirley

Yee, and Angela Ginorio—critiqued my work and provided the kind of intellectual camaraderie that every scholar hopes for. At various points in the life of this project Reginald Butler, Ross Posnock, Bill Rorabaugh, Karen Shabetai, Richard White, Frank Conlon, Uta Poiger, Laurie Sears, Sandra Joshel, Richard Pells, Faye Dudden, Lynn Dumenil, Jane Desmond, Robert Allen, Lillian Schlissel, Lewis Erenberg, Lizabeth Cohen, Kathy Peiss, and Michael Rogin read work in progress and gave me a number of important suggestions. Many thanks as well to Tom Dublin for many years of support. An earlier version of chapter 3 appeared as "Give an Imitation of Me: Vaudeville Mimics and the Play of the Self," in the March 1998 *American Quarterly,* and I thank the American Studies Association for honoring it with the Constance Rourke Prize.

At a critical juncture Joyce Seltzer, my editor at Harvard University Press, asked me where the idea for this project began in my heart-of-hearts. As I answered that question the underlying vision of the book came more sharply into focus. It is a pleasure to thank her for her expert guidance, her insightful criticisms, and her amazing ability to be both hardhitting and supportive. Many thanks as well to David Lobenstine and Anita Safran.

I also want to express my gratitude to friends and family who sustained me during the long process of researching and writing, especially Karen Shabetai, Renee LeBoeuf, Jack Oram, Sandy Lorentzen, and Rhoda and Norman Glenn.

My deepest debt is to Jim Gregory, who took time away from his own work to give me perceptive readings and crucial advice on this book, and whose moral support and companionship make everything possible. Finally, I thank my daughter, Rachel, whose enthusiasm and laughter lifted my spirits all the while.

Index

Abbey, Henry, 17

Activism, female, 4, 6, 29, 126–127, 128, 130–131, 154, 220–221; militant/radical, 5, 133, 206; political, 6, 8, 29, 126–127, 129, 130–131; street protest, 130; Voiceless Speech concept, 132; popular theater and, 134–148; public anxiety about, 152–153; chorus girl strike of 1919, 203–209, 210; spectacle of, 204. *See also* Suffrage movement: activism and politics

Actors' Equity Association (AEA), 191–192, 203, 204, 205, 208

Actresses: as proto-feminist figures, 6; star phenomenon, 13–14; activism and, 134–148, 149, 153, 204; prostitution and, 197. *See also* Female performers

Actresses Committee, 135, 136

Actresses Franchise League, 137

Addams, Jane, 140

Adrienne Lecouvreur play, 20, 23

Advertising, 12, 91, 130, 134, 156; publicity, 108; use of female images, 165–167

African Americans: performers, 50, 51, 55, 111, 112–114, 115, 116, 117–118; social roles, 111; love stories portrayed by, 113–114; Salome portrayed by, 115, 116–117, 118; suffrage movement and, 147–148; as theatrical producers, 157. *See also* Blackface comedy

Aggression, female, 11, 56–58, 80, 162, 216

Aiglon, L' (Rostand), 22

Alhambra Theater, New York, 69, 107, 110, 143

Allan, Maud, 57, 76, 102–103, 104, 105

"All Coons Look Alike to Me" song, 52

"All Wrong" song, 70

Amazon woman image, 150, 151

Ambition, female, 162, 215

America musical revue, 166–167

American Beauty, An (Kerker), 54

Anderson, John Murray, 157

Androgyny, 97, 112

Animated song sheets, 55

Anthony, Susan B., 5, 129

Anti-Semitism, 31, 32, 33–34, 97, 118

Archer, William, 23

Army and soldier images. *See* Female army image

Arnold, Florine, 205

Arthur, Jean, 220

Artists and Models musical revues, 193, 194, 195

Art of Stage Dancing, The (Wayburn), 186

Assertiveness, female, 3, 98, 99, 125, 135, 148, 198, 215, 222

Associated Actors and Artistes, 203